Humanitarianism and Challenges of Cooperation

T0298689

Humanitarianism as a moral concept and an organised practice has become a major factor in world society. It channels an enormous amount of resources and serves as an argument for different kinds of interference into the "internal affairs" of countries and regions. At the same time, and for these very reasons, it is an ideal testing ground for successful and unsuccessful cooperation across borders.

Humanitarianism and Challenges of Cooperation examines the multiple humanitarianisms of today as a testing ground for new ways of global cooperation. General trends in the contemporary transformation of humanitarianism are studied, and individual cases of how humanitarian actors cooperate with others on the ground are investigated. This book offers a highly innovative, empirically informed account of global humanitarianism from the point of view of cooperation research in which internationally renowned contributors analyse broad trends and present case studies based on meticulous fieldwork.

This book will be of great interest to students and researchers in the areas of political science, international relations and humanitarianism. It is also a valuable resource for humanitarian aid workers.

Volker M. Heins is Permanent Fellow at the Institute for Advanced Study in the Humanities, Essen, Germany as well as Senior Researcher at the Käte Hamburger Kolleg/Centre for Global Cooperation Research, University of Duisburg-Essen, Germany. He is also a member of the social science faculty at Ruhr University Bochum, Germany.

Kai Koddenbrock is a Lecturer at the Institute for Political Science, RWTH Aachen University, Germany and an alumni fellow at the Käte Hamburger Kolleg/Centre for Global Cooperation Research, University of Duisburg-Essen, Germany.

Christine Unrau is a Researcher for the Käte Hamburger Kolleg/Centre for Global Cooperation Research, University of Duisburg Essen, Germany.

Routledge Global Cooperation Series

This series develops innovative approaches to understanding, explaining and answering one of the most pressing questions of our time – how can cooperation in a culturally diverse world of nine billion people succeed?

We are rapidly approaching our planet's limits, with trends such as advancing climate change and the destruction of biological diversity jeopardising our natural life-support systems. Accelerated globalisation processes lead to an ever-growing interconnectedness of markets, states, societies and individuals. Many of today's problems cannot be solved by nation states alone. Intensified cooperation at the local, national, international and global levels is needed to tackle current and looming global crises.

Series Editors:

Tobias Debiel, Claus Leggewie and Dirk Messner are Co-Directors of the Käte Hamburger Kolleg/Centre for Global Cooperation Research, University Duisburg-Essen, Germany. Their research areas are, among others, Global Governance, Climate Change, Peacebuilding and Cultural Diversity of Global Citizenship. The three Co-Directors are, at the same time, based in their home institutions, which participate in the Centre, namely the German Development Institute/Deutsches Institut für Entwicklungspolitik (DIE, Messner) in Bonn, the Institute for Development and Peace (INEF, Debiel) in Duisburg and the Institute for Advanced Study in the Humanities (KWI, Leggewie) in Essen

Titles:

Global Cooperation and the Human Factor in International Relations
Edited by Dirk Messner and Silke Weinlich

Peacebuilding in Crisis
Rethinking paradigms and practices of transnational cooperation
Edited by Tobias Debiel, Thomas Held and Ulrich Schneckener

Humanitarianism and Challenges of Cooperation
Edited by Volker M. Heins, Kai Koddenbrock and Christine Unrau

Humanitarianism and Challenges of Cooperation

Edited by
Volker M. Heins, Kai Koddenbrock
and Christine Unrau

SPONSORED BY THE

Federal Ministry
of Education
and Research

First published 2016
by Routledge

2 Park Square, Milton Park, Abingdon, Oxfordshire OX14 4RN
711 Third Avenue, New York, NY 10017

Routledge is an imprint of the Taylor & Francis Group, an informa business

First issued in paperback 2017

British Library Cataloguing-in-Publication Data
A catalogue record for this book is available from the British Library

Library of Congress Cataloging-in-Publication Data
Names: Heins, Volker M., 1957- editor. | Koddenbrock, Kai, editor. |
Unrau, Christine, editor.Title: Humanitarianism and challenges of
cooperation / edited by Volker Heins, Kai Koddenbrock and Christine
Unrau.Description: New York, NY : Routledge, 2016. | Series: Routledge
global cooperation series | Includes bibliographical references.Identifiers:
LCCN 2015034029| ISBN 9781138963375 (hb) | ISBN 9781315658827
(ebook)Subjects: LCSH: Humanitarian assistance--International
cooperation. | International relief. | Humanitarianism.Classification: LCC
HV553 .H859 2016 | DDC 361.2/6--dc23LC record available at http://
lccn.loc.gov/2015034029

ISBN: 978-1-138-96337-5 (hbk)
ISBN: 978-0-8153-6449-8 (pbk)
DOI: 10.4324/9781315658827

This work and its open access publication has been supported by the Federal
Ministry of Education and Research (BMBF) in the context of its funding of
the Käte Hamburger Kolleg/Centre for Global Cooperation Research at the
University of Duisburg-Essen (grant number 01UK1810).

Contents

Abbreviations

AA	Auswärtiges Amt (German Federal Foreign Office)
ADRA	Adventist Development and Relief Agency
AIDS	Acquired Immune Deficiency Syndrome
AIIB	Asian Infrastructure Investment Bank
ALNAP	Active Learning Network for Accountability and Performance in Humanitarian Action
AMA	African Muslims Agency
ASEAN	Association of Southeast Asian Nations
AU	African Union
AWSD	Aid Worker Security Database
BICE	Bureau International Catholique de l'Enfance (International Catholic Child Bureau)
BMZ	Bundesministerium für Wirtschaftliche Zusammenarbeit und Entwicklung (German Federal Ministry for Economic Cooperation and Development)
BRICS	Brazil, Russia, India, China, South Africa
CAF	Charities Aid Foundation
CAP	Consolidated Appeal Process (United Nations)
CARE	Cooperative for Assistance and Relief Everywhere
CDKN	Climate and Development Knowledge Network
CGT	Confédèration Générale du Travail (General Confederation of Labor)
CIA	Central Intelligence Agency
CIE	Centre International de l'Enfance (International Children's Centre)
CIFRC	China International Famine Relief Commission
CRS	Catholic Relief Services
CSR	Corporate Social Responsibility
DIAC	Dodoma-IAC (IAC sub-group in the region of Dodoma, Tanzania)
DNA	deoxyribonucleic acid (molecule that carries all genetic information of an organism)
DfID	Department for International Development (UK)

DRC	Democratic Republic of the Congo
DSG	Defence Strategic Guidance
ECB	Emergency Capacity Building Project
EISF	European Interagency Security Forum
FBO	faith-based organisation
FCO	Foreign and Commonwealth Office (UK)
FGC	female genital cutting
FGM	female genital mutilation
FIC	Feinstein International Center
GCC	Gulf Cooperation Council
GDP	gross domestic product
GHA	Global Humanitarian Assistance Report
GONGO	government-operated non-governmental organisation
GNI	gross national income
GPPI	Global Public Policy Institute
HIF	Humanitarian Innovation Fund
HIV	Human Immunodeficiency Virus
HPG	Humanitarian Policy Group
IAC	Inter-African Committee on Traditional Practices
ICC	International Criminal Court
ICCB	International Catholic Child Bureau
ICCO	Interchurch Coordination Commission for Development Co-operation
ICISS	International Commission on Intervention and State Sovereignty
ICJ	International Court of Justice
ICRC	International Committee of the Red Cross
IDP	internally displaced person
IEEE	Institute of Electrical and Electronics Engineers
IFRC	International Federation of Red Cross and Red Crescent Societies
IGO	intergovernmental organisation
IHL	International Humanitarian Law
IIRO/IIROSA	International Islamic Relief Organization Saudi Arabia
IMF	International Monetary Fund
IR	international relations
IRA	Irish Republican Army
IRC	International Rescue Committee
IRDR	Integrated Research on Disaster Risk Programme
ISDR	*see* UNISDR
ISOA	International Stability Operations Associations
JOC	Jeunesse Ouvrière Chrétienne (Young Christian Workers)
MIAC	Mara-IAC (IAC sub-group in the region of Mara, Tanzania)
MDGs	Millennium Development Goals
MoD	Ministry of Defence
MPRI	Military Professional Resources Inc.

MSF	Médecins sans Frontières (Doctors without Borders)
NGO	non-governmental organisation
NGDO	non-governmental development organisation
NRC	Norwegian Refugee Council
NSS	National Security Strategy
OCHA	United Nations Office for the Coordination of Humanitarian Affairs
ODSG	OCHA Donor Support Group
OECD	Organisation for Economic Co-operation and Development
OECD-DAC	OECD Development Assistance Committee
OHCHR	Office of the High Commissioner for Human Rights
P5	Permanent Five (Permanent Members of the United Nations Security Council)
PLA	People's Liberation Army
PMSC	private military and security companies
PR	public relations
PRC	People's Republic of China
R2P	Responsibility to Protect
RBM	results-based management
RP	responsible protection
RUF	Revolutionary United Front
RwP	Responsibility while Protecting
SCO	Shanghai Cooperation Organisation
SIPRI	Stockholm International Peace Research Institute
SOP	standard operating principle/procedure
TIAC	Tanga-IAC (IAC sub-group in the region of Tanga, Tanzania)
UJMS	Union de la Jeunesse Musulmane du Sénégal (Senegalese Union of Muslim Youth)
UNDP	United Nations Development Programme
UNFPA	United Nations Population Fund
UNHCR	United Nations High Commissioner for Refugees
UNICEF	United Nations International Children's Emergency Fund
UNIFEM	United Nations Development Fund for Women
UNIPID	Finnish University Partnership for International Development
UNISDR	United Nations Office for Disaster Risk Reduction
UNITA	União Nacional para a Independência Total de Angola (National Union for the Total Independence of Angola)
UNSC	United Nations Security Council
UPC	Union des Populations du Cameroun
USAID	US Agency for International Development
USD	US dollars
WAMY	World Assembly of Muslim Youth
WFP	World Food Programme
WHO	World Health Organization
WMD	weapon of mass destruction

Contributors

David Chandler is Professor of International Relations and Director of the Centre for the Study of Democracy. He was the founding editor of the *Journal of Intervention and Statebuilding* and currently edits the journal *Resilience: International Policies, Practices and Discourses*. He also edits two Routledge book series, *Studies in Intervention and Statebuilding* and *Advances in Democratic Theory*. His research interests focus on analysis of policy interventions in the international arena, including humanitarianism, statebuilding and the promotion of resilience. Recently, he has published *Resilience: The Governance of Complexity* (Routledge 2014) and *Freedom vs Necessity in International Relations: Human-Centred Approaches to Security and Development* (Zed Books 2013).

Mathis Danelzik is a Project Coordinator at the Institute for Advanced Study in the Humanities, Essen, Germany. His research interests include communication for social/cultural change, transcultural communication and organisational communication. He is the winner of the 2013 dissertation award of the Communication and Media Sociology Section of the German Association for Communication Studies. His publications include *Kulturen verändern – Kampagnen gegen weibliche Genitalverstümmelung zwischen ethischen und strategischen Herausforderungen* (Springer VS 2016) and 'Racialized body modifications – framing genital mutilation, cosmetic surgery and gender assignment surgery' (2014, *Networking Knowledge*, 7(3), 21–39).

Dennis Dijkzeul is Professor of Organization and Conflict Research, as well as Research Coordinator of the Institute for International Law of Peace and Armed Conflict, at Ruhr University Bochum, Germany. He was the founding Director of the Humanitarian Affairs Programme at the School of International and Public Affairs of Columbia University in New York, where he still teaches as an adjunct professor. His main areas of interest are humanitarian studies, the management of international and local organisations in crises, and local participation. Recent publications include *Handbuch humanitäre Hilfe* (edited with Jürgen Lieser, Springer 2013) and *The NGO Challenge for International Relations Theory* (edited with William DeMars, Routledge 2015).

Antonio Donini is Research Associate at the Geneva Graduate Institute's Programme for the Study of Global Migration, as well as Visiting Fellow at the Feinstein International Center at Tufts University. He works on issues relating to humanitarianism and the future of humanitarian action. He served as Director of the UN Office for the Coordination of Humanitarian Assistance to Afghanistan (1999–2002) and earlier was Chief of the Lessons Learned Unit at OCHA, where he managed a programme of independent studies on the effectiveness of relief efforts in complex emergencies. He coordinated the Humanitarian Agenda 2015 research project which analysed local perceptions of humanitarian action in 13 crisis countries and authored the final HA 2015 report, *The State of the Humanitarian Enterprise*. He is also the editor of *The Golden Fleece. Manipulation and Independence in Humanitarian Action* (Kumarian Press 2012).

Aidan Hehir is a Reader in International Relations at the University of Westminster. His research interests include humanitarian intervention, statebuilding, and the laws governing the use of force. He is the author of various books, including *Humanitarian intervention: An Introduction* (Palgrave 2010 and 2013) and *The Responsibility to Protect. Rhetoric, Reality and the Future of Humanitarian Intervention* (Palgrave 2012), as well as numerous journal articles, including in *International Security*, *International Relations*, *Third World Quarterly* and *Political Studies Review*. He is also a regular media contributor.

Volker M. Heins is Permanent Fellow at the Institute for Advanced Study in the Humanities, Essen, Germany, and a Senior Researcher at the Käte Hamburger Kolleg/Centre for Global Cooperation Research, University of Duisburg-Essen, Germany. He is also a member of the social science faculty at Ruhr University Bochum, Germany. His research focuses on international political thought, multiculturalism and conflicts over human rights. Recent publications include: 'Recognition, multiculturalism, and the allure of separatism', in Patrick Hayden and Kate Schick (eds), *Recognition and Global Politics: Critical Encounters between State and World* (Manchester University Press 2015) and *Der Skandal der Vielfalt: Geschichte und Konzepte des Multikulturalismus* (Campus 2013).

Dorothea Hilhorst is Professor of Humanitarian Aid and Reconstruction at the International Institute of Social Studies of Erasmus University Rotterdam. Her research concerns the aidnography of humanitarian crises and fragile states. Her publications focus on the everyday practices of humanitarian aid, disaster risk reduction, climate change adaptation, reconstruction and peace building. She coordinates research programmes in Angola, DRC, Afghanistan, Ethiopia, Sudan, Mozambique and Uganda. Her recent publications include 'Power holders and social dynamics of participatory development and reconstruction: cases from the Democratic Republic of Congo' (with P.M. Kyamusugulwa, 2015, *World Development* 70, 249–59) and 'Floods, resettlement and land access and use in the lower Zambezi, Mozambique' (with L. Arthur, 2014, *Land Use Policy* 36, 361–8).

Jutta Joachim is Associate Professor of International Relations at Leibniz University Hannover, Germany. Her research interests include non-state actors in international relations, security governance, the Common Foreign and Security Policy of the EU, human rights and gender and international relations. She is author of *Agenda Setting, The UN, and NGOs: Gender Violence and Reproductive Rights* (Georgetown University Press 2007), and co-editor of *Transnational Activism in the UN and the EU: A Comparative Study* (Routledge 2009) and *International Organizations and Implementation: Enforcers, Managers, Authorities?* (Routledge 2008). She has also published in various journals, including *International Studies Quarterly, Security Dialogue, Millennium* and *Comparative European Politics.*

Mayke Kaag is Senior Researcher at the African Studies Centre, Leiden University, the Netherlands. She is a social anthropologist interested in processes of change and continuity in West and West-Central Africa and has conducted extensive field research in various African countries, including Senegal, Chad and Cameroon. Her current research focuses primarily on African transnational relations, including land issues, transnational Islamic charities and engagements with the diaspora. Recent publications include 'Gulf charities in Africa' (in *Gulf Charities and Islamic Philanthropy in the 'Age of Terror' and Beyond* (Gerlach 2014) and *The Global Land Grab: Beyond the Hype* (with Annelies Zoomers, Zed Books 2014).

Kai Koddenbrock is Lecturer at the Institute of Political Science at the RWTH Aachen University and a fellow at the Global Public Policy Institute, Berlin. He was a visiting scholar at Columbia University, New York, at the Max-Planck Institute for the Study of Societies, Cologne, and a postdoc fellow at the Centre for Global Cooperation Research, University of Duisburg-Essen. His research focuses on capitalism, intervention and postcolonial Africa. In addition to his book on *The Practice of Humanitarian Intervention: Aid workers, Agencies and Institutions in the Democratic Republic of Congo* (Routledge 2015) he has published in *Third World Quarterly* and the *European Journal of International Relations* among others, and is currently working on a book project on money and global capitalism in international relations.

Hanna Bianca Krebs is a Research Officer at the Humanitarian Policy Group, Overseas Development Institute in London. Her research focuses on historical approaches to humanitarianism, regional organisations, humanitarian diplomacy, and the relationship between statecraft and aid. She conducts research in the East and Southeast Asian region in particular. Her recent publications include *Regional Organisations and Humanitarian Action: The Case of ASEAN* (with Lilianne Fan, ODI 2014), and *Responsibility, Legitimacy, Morality: Chinese Humanitarianism in Historical Perspective* (ODI 2014).

Anthony F. Lang, Jr holds a Chair in International Political Theory in the School of International Relations at the University of St Andrews and is Director of the Centre for Global Constitutionalism. His research focuses on the intersection of ethics, politics, and law at the global level. He is currently a co-editor of the journal *Global Constitutionalism*, and serves on the editorial boards of the *Journal of International Political Theory* and *Ethics & International Affairs*. He is also commissioning editor of the new series *Global Ethics* from Routledge. Some of his books include *International Political Theory: An Introduction* (Palgrave 2014) and *Punishment, Justice and International Relations: Ethics and Order after the Cold War* (Routledge 2008).

Kristin Bergtora Sandvik is the Director of the Norwegian Centre for Humanitarian Studies and a senior researcher at the Peace Research Institute Oslo. Her research focuses on international law, humanitarianism and technology, with a particular focus on displacement and humanitarian drones. Recently, she has co-published *Shifting Frames, Vanishing Resources, and Dangerous Political Opportunities: Legal Mobilization among Displaced Women in Colombia* (Law and Society Review 2015), *The Rise of the Humanitarian Drone: Giving Content to an Emerging Concept* (Millennium 2014), and 'Humanitarian technology: a critical research agenda' (*International Review of the Red Cross* 2014). Her new edited volume, *UNHCR and the Struggle for Accountability Technology, Law and Results-based Management* (Routledge, with Katja Lindskov Jacobsen) will be published in 2016.

Andrea Schneiker is Lecturer (*Juniorprofessorin*) of International Relations at the Department of Social Sciences of the University of Siegen, Germany. Her primary research areas are security governance, private military and security companies, theories of international relations, humanitarianism, NGOs, and international organisations. She is author of *Humanitarian NGOs, (In)Security and Identity. Epistemic Communities and Security Governance* (Ashgate 2015). She has also published extensively in journals including *Critical Military Studies*, *Cambridge Review of International Affairs*, *Comparative European Politics*, *Millennium* and *Security Dialogue*.

Christine Unrau is a Researcher at the Käte Hamburger Kolleg/Centre for Global Cooperation Research, University of Duisburg-Essen, Germany. She is currently completing her PhD thesis at the department of Political Science of the University of Cologne. Her research interests include globalisation, religion and politics, political emotions and transcultural political thought. Her publications include 'Cultures of humanitarianism' (with Volker M. Heins in *Global Trends 2015. Prospects for World Society*, Fischer 2015) and 'Imitation, Abgrenzung und Interkulturalität. Zur Frage der Emanzipation vom Westen im politischen Denken Lateinamerikas' (in *Einführung in die transkulturelle Politische Theorie*, Springer VS 2015).

Charlotte Walker-Said is an Assistant Professor of History in the Department of Africana Studies at the John Jay College of Criminal Justice, City University of New York. She is completing a book manuscript on Christianity, human rights, and family law in French colonial Cameroon. Her research focuses on the French Empire in Equatorial Africa, the history of Christianity in Africa, and the relationships between family law, religion, and human rights in Africa and across the Global South. She has taught African history and human rights at Harvard University, the University of Chicago, and Webster University. With John Kelly, she is editor of the anthology *Corporate Social Responsibility? Human Rights in the New Global Economy* (University of Chicago Press 2015).

Thomas G. Weiss is Director Emeritus of the Ralph Bunche Institute for International Studies and Presidential Professor of Political Science at The Graduate Center, CUNY (The City University of New York). He is one of the leading experts on the theory and practice of humanitarian intervention and the responsibility to protect, with special expertise in the politics of the United Nations. At present he serves as an advisory board member for the Global Centre for the Responsibility to Protect, member of the editorial boards of a number of academic journals, and also as an editor of Routledge's Global Institutions Series. Recent publications include *Humanitarian Business* (Polity Press 2013) and *Humanitarian Intervention: Ideas in Action*, 3rd edition (Polity Press 2016).

Acknowledgements

The basis for this book was laid at the international conference entitled "Humanitarianism and Changing Cultures of Cooperation", which took place from 5–7 June 2014 and was jointly organised by the Käte Hamburger Kolleg/ Centre for Global Cooperation Research, Duisburg and the Institute for Advanced Study in the Humanities, Essen. We are grateful for many inspiring conversations with the participants at the conference. We also would like to thank our friends and colleagues at both institutions who supported (and endured) us in the process of putting together this volume. Sibylle Kranwetvogel's and Mark Fries's assistance was of great help for the preparation of the manuscript. We also wish to thank Margaret Farrelly at Routledge for her encouragement and patient advice, and two anonymous reviewers who made us think through (and hopefully improve) the project. Finally, we would like to thank Berghahn Journals and Springer for their permission to include Chapters 7 and 12 in this edited volume.

Introduction

Cultures of humanitarianism, old and new

Volker M. Heins and Christine Unrau

In spite of a long history of crises and contestations, humanitarianism is a permanent, increasingly important and well funded field of ideas, institutions and practices in global society. Its backbone is formed by NGOs such as the Red Cross and Red Crescent Societies, Doctors Without Borders, Islamic Relief and numerous other agencies. As NGOs, all these groups are highly engaging facilitators of global cooperation, well equipped to reach out to a broad range of actors, from businesses and military forces to government officials, warlords and celebrities. They are multifunctional and "multilingual", adept at switching codes and interacting simultaneously with a number of different environments. They are also "third-party interveners in global struggles for recognition" (Heins 2015), who combine the pursuit of moral causes with constant jockeying for funding and turf. What makes them different from interest groups is the motivation of their core members and supporters, who are drawn from amongst a strongly value-oriented pool of true believers in the cause of humanity. This explains why many practitioners keep telling the fairly simple tale of the Good Samaritan to explain the fundamental moral meaning of humanitarian action, even though the reality of humanitarianism has become much more diverse and complex since its emergence in the nineteenth century.

This well known story from the Gospel of Luke is about an ordinary man from Samaria, who on his way to Jericho spotted a badly beaten crime victim on the roadside, then "went to him and bandaged his wounds, pouring on oil and wine" (Luke 10:34), before bringing him to an inn on his donkey and paying the innkeeper to take care of the man. Certainly in the western world, this parable has been an inexhaustible source of inspiration for humanitarian relief organisations. Max Huber, a Swiss lawyer and former president of the International Committee of the Red Cross (ICRC), is not the only one who has drawn attention to some key elements in Luke's narrative: the helper and the victim are mutual strangers, the victim is helped simply because he is a human being, no accusations are levelled against those who were responsible for beating and robbing the man, or against earlier passers-by who failed to offer help. In an emergency, Huber insists, "the duty is to act, not to talk" (cited in Thürer 2007, 51).

While much of this still resonates with us, many would also agree with Michael Barnett, who in his important book *Empire of Humanity* calls modern

DOI: 10.4324/9781315658827-1

humanitarianism a "morally complicated creature" (Barnett 2011, 7). A lot of what has changed since the early days of the Red Cross can be summarised by adding new twists to the story of the Good Samaritan. Today, Samaritans and their beneficiaries are watched by spectators from the surrounding hills. Some of the spectators are paying both the Samaritan and the innkeeper. Some Samaritans are funded by and aligned with the government of Samaria (or other governments). Samaritans no longer stumble upon victims by chance, but are called in by messengers who tell a captivating story about monstrous injustices and disastrous misfortunes, innocent victims and ruthless perpetrators. Sometimes Samaritans are denied access to victims by armed robbers or rogue governments. On other occasions, the robbers, who have left their victim by the wayside, still lurk behind shrubs, waiting to pounce on unsuspecting Samaritans. Anticipating the danger, some Samaritans arm themselves or arrive on the scene with armed guards. Other Samaritans have wine and oil businesses and see charity as a publicity measure. Some victims are exploited and moved by people-smugglers across the sea and international borders, and left at the doorsteps of potential Samaritans in the Global North. And, of course, there have been genocides, which can be defined by the goal of destroying the very possibility of giving aid to victims as well as the possibility of witnessing what is happening.

Red Cross humanitarianism and after

Some of these developments, for example the trend of rendering distant crises and relief operations imaginable for global publics, have already been initiated by the International Red Cross and Red Crescent Movement. Other developments have thrown the organisation into crisis, giving rise to various "new" humanitarianisms. If we ignore for a moment the colonial predecessors of modern humanitarianism, the ICRC is a good starting point for a reflection on the evolving challenges for aid agencies in contemporary international society.

In light of the general idea behind this book, it is useful to translate some of the fundamental principles of the Red Cross and Red Crescent Movement, such as impartiality, neutrality and independence, into a different language. Unlike previous humanitarian activists, the Red Cross aimed at separating aid workers legally, operationally and culturally from soldiers and other officials on the battlefield and in disaster areas. This means that Red Cross organisations *coordinate*, but do not *cooperate*, with states and governments.[1] Coordination is what we do, for example, when we merge into traffic on a busy street, while cooperation means that self-regarding actors are prepared to forgo their immediate interest to help one another or to achieve a common goal. The distinction between coordination and cooperation is crucial for understanding the middle road taken by Red Cross humanitarianism: between a vision of peaceful order in human society as a whole, which was articulated by the founders, and the constraints of a political world composed of nation-states, which the Red Cross also had to accept, thereby relegating more far-reaching ideals to the status of an "unspoken mission" (Berry 1997). Coordinating with states implies preserving the good will of governments without either getting in their way or sharing their particularistic and utilitarian goals.

Since the end of the Second World War, the compromise on which humanitarian action by the Red Cross is based has been challenged from two angles. First, non-Red Cross agencies have in many situations become subservient to state interests. This is especially true for private aid agencies in the United States, which rarely saw a reason to defend or cherish their non-cooperative neutrality in the way Europeans did. US humanitarianism did not start as an independent movement trying to constrain state action. Rather, after the Second World War agencies such as CARE and others believed that the interests of the government and of humanitarians were best served when both sides agreed on a strategy of cooperation. CARE started as an agency closely associated with the strategic interests of the United States, which in the immediate aftermath of the Second World War were often inextricably linked to humanitarian efforts. This link is best epitomised by the Berlin airlift in 1948–49, in which CARE played a substantial role. Similar observations have been made with regard to other agencies such as Catholic Relief Services (CRS) or World Vision, which until around 1967 were supporting the US war effort in Vietnam (Heins 2008, 129–32).

The second attack against the Red Cross tradition came from groups such as Médecins Sans Frontières/Doctors Without Borders (MSF), whose founders worked to radicalise the principle of independence at the expense of the principle of neutrality, which was identified with the ICRC ethics of discretion. The common understanding was that the ethics of remaining silent at all costs, and not reporting what aid workers observe on the ground, contributed to the monumental failure of humanitarianism in the face of the German policy of genocide, of which the ICRC was fully aware in late 1942 (Forsythe 2005, 44–50). While remaining silent or keeping a secret can be highly ethical or even a powerful tool in sending a message, it can also degenerate into a kind of *omertà* to prevent the truth from surfacing. This is precisely what happened when Switzerland discreetly cooperated with Nazi Germany and the ICRC was pressured to fall in line with this policy.

More consistently than the Red Cross, and as part of a much larger trend in the humanitarian world, MSF started out by defending a notion of independence as radical separation of humanitarianism from the state. This modified approach was again one of standing outside the mundane work of states and soldiers, and of not cooperating with them, but the "French doctors" wanted to go further than their predecessors. The moral enthusiasts who founded MSF were inclined to blame the Red Cross for accepting the world of states as it is, and for redefining injustice as misfortune.[2] Rather than simply attempting to safeguard the survival of people in need, the "new" humanitarians committed themselves to legally enforceable universal human rights. To achieve the goal of alleviating unnecessary and unjust, politically induced human suffering, MSF believed that it was necessary to change humanitarianism itself, and specifically the structure of the game between states and aid agencies, in which humanitarians have so far played the part of an always-too-late "after-sales service of politics" (Kouchner 1995, 103). As a consequence, Doctors Without Borders and other organisations supported – even if only occasionally and hesitantly – military interventions and the "right to intervene" in other states in situations of gross human rights violations and similar agendas, which from the late 1980s onwards inspired a number of UN initiatives.

Unfortunately, however, the ambition to politicise humanitarianism while staying aloof from state politics got the new humanitarians entangled in contradictions. MSF never quite solved the dilemma of how to stay politically independent while at the same time appealing to and relying on sovereign decisions taken by both home and host governments, in particular in the field of security. To use Albert Hirschman's terms, in the humanitarian field, the activation of "voice" often entails being forced to "exit" the field altogether (Hirschman 1970). In recent years, MSF has thus returned to a less outspoken, more pragmatic approach closer to the Red Cross tradition, while the ICRC, conversely, has become less reluctant to protest publicly and more inclined to join broad coalitions of like-minded people, for example in favour of the Ottawa treaty banning anti-personnel land mines and other global harm conventions.

Recent trends affecting the humanitarian field

Now, let us take a closer look at various new trends affecting the humanitarian field by unpacking some strands of our amended version of the Samaritan story.

Manipulation

Because injustice is "complex" and "intractable", as American political theorist Judith Shklar has pointed out, we can rarely be quite sure "who the victims really are" (Shklar 1990, 28). While this has always been true, many conflicts today have made things significantly worse. It is often difficult to clearly identify and distinguish victims, perpetrators and rescuers, and to point to quick-fix solutions. The reality of suffering, and of victims and perpetrators, is not simply out there to be discovered and reported; it has to be brought forth and produced. This has complicated, among other things, the Red Cross concept of neutrality. Aid agencies have got into trouble as they wanted to remain neutral even in situations where civilians and combatants can hardly be told apart, where impartiality is perceived as an insult to deeply held beliefs about the status of certain groups, where regimes are seeking humanitarian rents by deliberately inducing and exposing massive civilian suffering, or where aid is granted by democratic states as a placebo substituting for effective political action. In recent crises, we have seen perpetrators pretending to be victims; rebels falsely crying genocide in order to unleash a foreign intervention (Kosovo in 1999, Libya in 2011); or militants guilty of mass killings seeking a safe haven and humanitarian assistance in refugee camps (Rwanda and Congo post-1994). We have also seen humanitarian organisations dexterously playing on the rescue fantasies of a paternalistic western public without really helping anybody.[3]

Other agencies have claimed to help victims while acting as fronts for perpetrators of crimes. Like other governments before, German authorities, too, have recently considered banning organisations such as "Ansaar International" or "Medizin ohne Grenzen" ("Medicine without Borders"), which were suspected of supporting Islamist terrorism. Some of these issues may be easily resolved by revealing the true nature of self-proclaimed humanitarian organisations with the help of police or intelligence. However, in many cases the mixture of humanitarian motivations and political, commercial or military instrumentalisation is harder to disentangle, because the connections are structural or based on an overlap of interest between humanitarian and other actors (see Thomas G. Weiss, Chapter 1; Dennis Dijkzeul and Thea Hilhorst, Chapter 3 in this volume).

Cultural pluralism

The parable of the Good Samaritan epitomises our innate ability to empathise with strangers in need. Contrary to a deep-seated and negative preconception about ourselves, *Homo sapiens* is a cooperative and "ultra-social animal" (Tomasello 2014). However, for this positive attribute to have a broader political effect, it must be organised in accordance with cultural traditions and codes of conduct, such as the Christian ethic of love and its equivalents in other faiths, philosophies and worldviews. It was partly due to the influence of these traditions that standards of international law were established after the Second World War, in the form of the Geneva Conventions, whose purpose is to afford protection to wounded combatants and prisoners of war, civilian persons in time of war, and victims of civil wars. Since then, humanitarianism has diversified into many different forms of activism.

There is ample evidence, of course, that ideals of giving and altruism have deep roots in other cultural formations as well. People all over the world are willing to help others. This is apparent from the World Giving Index, which looks at three aspects of giving behaviour – donating money to charity, volunteering, and helping a stranger – across a range of countries. The US, Canada, Australia and the United Kingdom regularly top the list of most generous countries, but a more complex picture emerges if other forms of generosity are considered or if the analysis is based on the percentage of the national adult population donating money to charity, or the percentage of money donated as percentage of GDP. In Thailand, Indonesia and Myanmar, a much higher percentage of the population responds to charitable appeals than in many western countries, although the sums donated are relatively small (CAF 2013). Following the earthquake in Haiti on 12 January 2010, Guyana, one of the poorest countries in South America, was by far the most generous donor nation, if we look at donations as percentage of GDP. The second most generous country was Ghana (Shilliam 2013). The lesson from these experiences is that the ethical commitment to humanitarianism is alive and well all over the world – in the North and the South, and in rich and poor societies alike.

In the long run, this worldwide commitment may present a powerful challenge to western dominance in humanitarianism and give rise to a new, genuinely global and cooperative humanitarianism. Currently, however, the standards and procedures of humanitarianism continue to be shaped by strong and powerful actors from the northern hemisphere. Since the adoption of their standards and guidelines is often the precondition for access to funding, a truly pluralistic setting for global humanitarianism is still far from being achieved (see Antonio Donini, Chapter 4 in this volume). Still, some emerging countries have contributed to new global norms or reinterpretations of contested norms such as the "Responsibility to Protect" (R2P). Brazil's new concept of a "Responsibility while Protecting" is a case in point (Almeida 2013). At the same time, the rise of powerful non-western countries such as China and India in the humanitarian field has worrisome consequences. Some of the new donor countries have proven to be unmoved by, or even hostile to, the idea of universal human rights (Hopgood 2013). India, for example, objected to the UN Secretary-General's call for relief organisations to be granted better access to disaster-affected populations. For the Indian government, the army is the main legitimate humanitarian actor, with assistance to be provided in accordance with the needs defined by the affected governments, whose sovereignty is regarded as sacrosanct (Meier and Murthy 2011). Another example is Turkey, which has evolved into the world's fourth largest humanitarian donor in recent years, with a clear focus on Somalia and Syria. Besides the Turkish Red Crescent, which has a good reputation, privately funded conservative and faith-based NGOs play a major role. However, they have an "ambiguous reputation" (Binder 2014, 8), not least because their principles are regarded as incompatible with impartiality, which is a fundamental principle in both classic and new humanitarianism.

Attacks on aid workers

Another trend can be gleaned from the Aid Worker Security Database (AWSD), according to which the number of assaults, kidnappings and killings of humanitarian personnel has consistently increased since the turn of the century (Humanitarian Outcomes 2014). This development is exemplified by the murder of five MSF aid workers by the Taliban in a roadside attack in north-west Afghanistan on 2 June 2004, prompting MSF and, later, other organisations to suspend their activities in Afghanistan. Islamist militias, especially in Syria and Iraq, are notorious for their extreme brutality towards aid workers and other civilians, as they demonstrated, for example, with the beheading of British aid volunteer Alan Henning in October 2014.

This catastrophic trend cannot be explained by the fusion of humanitarianism and politics championed by Doctors Without Borders as well as by some western governments.[4] Rather, what has dramatically changed is the nature of the conflicts into which humanitarians are drawn. As Hikaru Yamashita has convincingly argued, the proliferation of non-state actors and "violent mobs", the breakdown of legitimate hierarchies, the rise of the internet and diffusion of power have made it hopeless to structure political conflicts around stable territorial lines of separation, which in turn makes it increasingly difficult to carve out a safe humanitarian space where aid workers and victims can meet (Yamashita 2015). Increasingly chaotic conflicts in some parts of the world are also conducive to the routine involvement of military forces in humanitarian efforts, even though this type of cooperation has proved problematic. Another outcome is the involvement of private security companies, which have begun to use humanitarian rhetoric to neutralise their ambiguous reputation (see Jutta Joachim and Andrea Schneiker, Chapter 11 in this volume).

Although most of the violence against aid workers has occurred in Islamic countries, the crisis facing humanitarianism does not sit easily with "clash of civilisations" theories. At their core, the conflicts are not cultural or religious, but political. Showing a "western" face is dangerous in some parts of the world, but it bears emphasising that most of the aid workers who have fallen victim to Islamist violence were themselves Muslims. The growth and expansion of a new and mainly US-based Christian humanitarianism in the Global South has not led to more conflicts (Barnett and Gross Stein 2012, 5). There have been encouraging examples of direct transcultural cooperation between humanitarian actors. Already back in the 1990s, devout Muslims in Yemen decided to support MSF, recognising that it had mounted a more effective response to a flood disaster than their own charitable organisations. After the Indian Ocean tsunami in 2004, the Christian network World Vision joined with the Indonesian organisation Muhammadiyah to rebuild schools and hospitals. Two years later, a partnership developed between American Methodists, represented by the traditional United Methodist Committee on Relief, and Muslim Aid, resulting in the two organisations' joint work in Sri Lanka.

Moral scepticism

Last, but not least, we may have reasons to be sceptical about some of the assumptions taken for granted in the story of the Good Samaritan. In contemporary society, many people doubt whether the motives and intentions of "Samaritans" in faraway places are really morally good; or, even if they are, whether their action is as beneficial for the victims as is being claimed. The first type of critique is usually directed against the alleged "hypocrisy" of humanitarian organisations or their campaign rhetoric. This is, of course, a theme with a long tradition. Hypocrisy is an accusation levelled at anyone who is taking any sort of moral stand. It is said that hypocrisy invites cynicism, which unmasks and exposes its hollowness. But cynicism is often also the only alternative to hypocrisy, which is why theorists such as Judith Shklar (1984) have rightly considered hypocrisy to be a lesser vice. Humanitarianism is "covered with a thick hypocritical layer" (Shklar 1984, 41), but, on the positive side, it takes up the fight against the biggest vice: cruelty. More recently, the problem of humanitarian hypocrisy has been brought up again by Didier Fassin in his influential *Humanitarian Reason*. The humanitarian enterprise, he writes, "has a salutary power for us because by saving lives, it also relieves the burden of this unequal world order" (Fassin 2012, 252). The attention given to saving of lives creates the illusion of an equal worth of each human life, which, however, is not warranted given the prevailing priorities in domestic and global politics.

A second culturally effective critique targets not the motives of humanitarianism, but its consequences. When giving aid to victims becomes an institution, the danger of paternalism arises. Paternalism entails the perpetuation of the asymmetry between the receivers and givers of aid, which in turn makes it impossible for both sides to see themselves as partners in a common cooperative effort. Beneficiaries of aid may even feel offended or humiliated through the gift of aid. This idea that gifts are sometimes perceived as "injurious patronage" and hence as *poisoning* social relationships was first expressed by the French social anthropologist Marcel Mauss (1990, 83).[5]

These and other problems are compounded once we look at international relations. Internationally, humanitarianism is seen as more critical today because the expansion of humanitarian sensibilities has provided powerful states with additional reasons to intervene in other states and regions. These interventions can take a variety of forms: material assistance through relief aid; coercive but non-military sanctions to end human rights violations; and, finally, the dispatch of military forces. All these forms of intervention are difficult and have often turned philanthropy into its opposite. Scholars such as Alex de Waal (1997) have shown that aid given for the best motives can have counterproductive consequences. For example, generous aid to help refugees can have the effect of enriching human smugglers or elites without promoting stability or long-term economic development. Sanctions and embargoes usually contribute to human suffering, even if they are imposed to punish the rulers. In worst cases, such as the US-led war against Iraq, we have even witnessed a new variety of what Edmund Burke called "homicide philanthropy" (Burke 1801, 204). And yet, none of this allows us to conclude that humanitarian sensibilities are bound to lead us astray, or that relief programmes in wars or other man-made disasters have never been, or cannot be, successful and just.

This book and beyond

All of these developments – manipulation and politicisation, "cultural" friction, aid worker insecurity and the exposure of moral dilemmas – lead to new and often unprecedented challenges of cooperation. They have turned humanitarianism into one of the areas of global governance in which cooperation among different kinds of actors has become more urgent, but at the same time more difficult to achieve: humanitarian NGOs have to cooperate with private military and security companies to provide security for their staff; engineering and financial companies provide "digital humanitarians" with innovative products; western NGOs cooperate more closely with African local activists in humanitarian campaigns to avoid the charge of paternalism; emerging powers such as China have begun to make considerable contributions to global humanitarian efforts, which are no less controversial than older western aspirations.

Against this backdrop, the contributors to this volume explore the challenges of cooperation that are arising from current transformations of the humanitarian landscape. The book is divided into two sections. Section I contains broad-brushed accounts of the developments which are currently affecting and transforming global humanitarianism. Section II presents various case studies of new interactions, alliances and forms of cooperation in humanitarianism.

In Chapter 1, Thomas G. Weiss argues that understanding the ongoing transformations in contemporary humanitarianism requires examining the evolution of humanitarian culture away from an agreed culture of cooperation to a contested culture of competition. The latter reflects a trend towards militarisation, politicisation and marketisation. According to Weiss, what is required if one hopes to attenuate the counter-productive culture of competition is a learning culture for practitioners and a consequentialist ethics oriented towards responsible reflection rather than rapid reaction.

In contrast to Weiss, David Chandler suggests in Chapter 2 that the main shift in recent humanitarian culture is one from intervention designed to address the causes of humanitarian problems (conflict, underdevelopment or a lack of rights) to the regulation of the consequences and fallout of these unresolved problems. In rearticulating the goals of international actors, the means and mechanisms of international humanitarian intervention have also changed, as they are no longer focused on the universal application of western knowledge and resources, but rather on the specific and unique local and organic processes at work in societies afflicted by these problems. The governance of effects casts problems in increasingly naturalised or essentialised ways, suggesting that coping strategies are more effective and sustainable than political strategies of transformation.

In Chapter 3, Dennis Dijkzeul and Dorothea Hilhorst revisit the transformations analysed by Weiss and Chandler and discuss them from the perspective of instrumentalisation of humanitarianism. They contend that instrumentalisation is likely to increase when protracted crises bring humanitarian organisations in contact with a wide variety of other actors, such as warlords, the military, diaspora networks, intelligence agencies, new donors and national government institutions. The chapter offers a first step towards a deeper exploration of these interactions and discusses possible solutions to the ensuing problems, including those recommended by Thomas Weiss.

Chapter 4 is dedicated the basic question of the "universality" or "pluriversality" of humanitarianism. Antonio Donini argues that coloniality and network power combine to shape the humanitarian enterprise and stifle the emergence of more grounded, indigenous or non-westernised approaches. As he points out, understanding these trends is crucial for any discussion on the future of humanitarianism and, more specifically, on the viability of a certain type of universalism. The question is whether organised humanitarianism will morph into something different by encompassing non-western approaches, or splinter into western and non-western segments and rivulets.

In Chapter 5, Kai Koddenbrock explores the disconnect between humanitarian PR campaigns on the one hand and actual humanitarian operations on the other. While humanitarian agencies present themselves as focusing on the "vulnerability" of target populations, their day-to-day interactions are based on a myriad of other incentives and constrained by the necessity to cooperate and negotiate with powerful actors such as local authorities. He suggests that the massive expansion of the professional field of humanitarianism as well as the funds spent in relief operations can be explained in terms of the ability of relief agencies to successfully camouflage the reality of what they actually do.

Another major transformation of humanitarianism is discussed in Chapter 6 by Kristin Bergtora Sandvik. From her perspective, much of what has been argued by Donini and Koddenbrock amounts to what she calls the "discursive self-flagellation inherent to the DNA of contemporary humanitarianism". Taking a different approach, she uses the new concept of "futureproofing" to investigate the ability of an increasingly digitalised humanitarian enterprise to improve the management of crises in disaster zones. She argues that while cooperation between the public and private sector is rhetorically framed as intrinsic to the future of humanitarian action, the quest for cooperation is both filled with ambiguities and riddled with interesting paradoxes. The chapter highlights some of these ambiguities and paradoxes and analyses practices of cooperation through the prism of different logics of humanitarian futureproofing.

Section II, which is dedicated to case studies of humanitarian cooperation, is opened by a chapter on a historical moment of transition, which already anticipates many of the challenges of cooperation that humanitarianism faces today. Charlotte Walker-Said explores in Chapter 7 the interactions within different fractions of the Catholic Church and between the church and local populations at the end of colonial rule in Africa. These interactions were shaped by the competition between two legitimating paradigms for humanitarianism: "science" and "charity". As Walker-Said points out, welfare ideologies reoriented international agendas towards strategies addressing the needs of "innocent" victims, rather than empowering those who had a stake in changing the conditions in which people suffered.

Chapter 8 by Mathis Danelzik contributes to this investigation of the dilemmas and paradoxes of cooperation in humanitarianism by focusing on the case of campaigns to end female genital mutilation in Africa. These campaigns have often been evoked to discuss fundamental issues of liberal humanitarianism in a postcolonial world. Danelzik makes it clear that the African activists involved in those campaigns can be regarded neither as acting simply as implementation tools for dominant global norms nor as guardians protecting the international fetish of "indigenous cultures". The practice of the campaigns is rather characterised by a constant negotiation between collaborative and non-collaborative forms of action and advocacy.

In Chapter 9, Mayke Kaag looks at how Islamic charities from the Arab World are engaged in specific African contexts. Particular attention is paid to these charities' interactions with other humanitarian actors, such as western (Christian as well as secular) NGOs. These encounters can be labelled transcultural in terms both of cultural/religious background and of working approaches. In addition, the chapter explores transcultural encounters with African target groups; even in cases where Islam may seem to form a common denominator at first sight, different views of Islam often require intercultural navigating, competition and sometimes clashes between Arab charities and African populations.

Another important aspect of the growing importance of non-western regions is taken up in Chapter 10 by Hanna Krebs, who explores the role of China in international humanitarianism. The chapter sheds light on the main challenges with regard to cooperative arrangements between China and the international humanitarian community. These arrangements will depend strongly on the degree to which either side is prepared to seek common ground on shared norms and to engage in joint training or regular dialogue.

Chapter 11 by Jutta Joachim and Andrea Schneiker analyses a challenge to cooperation created by militarisation. In addition to business actors and regular armies, private military and security companies (PMSCs) have entered conflict and disaster zones across the world, either because they are hired to guard relief agencies or companies, or because they are themselves involved in the delivery of humanitarian aid. The chapter addresses the relations between humanitarian NGOs and PMSCs, showing that the interactions between the two types of actors are not limited to their cooperation in the field, but also extend to and influence their self-understandings. The authors find evidence of increasing isomorphism among "new" and "old" humanitarians, to the point where it sometimes becomes difficult to distinguish PMSCs and NGOs in the field.

Finally, in Chapter 12, Aidan Hehir and Anthony Lang turn to the level of global humanitarian governance and the global enforcement of human rights by examining the roles of the Security Council and the International Criminal Court (ICC) in implementing R2P. They offer an explanation as to why international cooperation with regard to the protection of human rights and the punishment of human rights violators is currently impeded. Implicitly addressing the famous assertion made by former UNHCR director Ogata that humanitarian problems cannot be solved by humanitarian solutions (alone), they also propose a reform of the current international order that would allow for a better integration of R2P and the ICC into international law and practice.

All the chapters can be read in the light of two basic questions: How can we describe the new modes of cooperation among different actors and under what circumstances are they successful or bound to fail? And, if successful, are these emerging patterns also desirable from a normative point of view?

As the various case studies included in this volume demonstrate, normative desirability and success need not go hand-in-hand. For example, the cooperation between private military and security companies and humanitarian NGOs (Chapter 11) might work rather smoothly, precisely because both groups have come to resemble each other in terms of rhetoric and style. However, the outcomes of such a cooperation may be less than desirable from the point of view of NGO reputation and sensitivity to recipients' needs. As shown in the analysis of campaigns against female genital cutting (Chapter 8), cooperation between western donors and African activists can be both successful in reaching the respective target groups and desirable in terms of cultural sensitivity and postcolonial critique. However, the attempt to cooperate fully with local activists turns out to have negative side effects, such as the fostering of an authoritarian understanding of religion, which raises questions about the overall desirability of this way of humanitarian cooperation. More broadly speaking, cooperation between western and non-western donors, as well as between givers and recipients of humanitarian aid, is desirable insofar as it contributes to the decentring of the global power system and reducing domination; however, it often turns out that these patterns of cooperation are unsuccessful or non-existent because non-western actors are simply sidelined if they do not correspond to western standards (Chapter 4). At the same time, cooperation with actors who do not accept norms such as human rights, women's rights or self-determination at all is not desirable.

At this stage of research, the answers to these questions can only be preliminary, not least because the attempt to answer them is entangled in the epistemological difficulties addressed by some researchers. For example, in order to answer the question whether a certain form of cooperation is normatively desirable, we have to agree on standards of normative desirability. But precisely these standards are by no means self-evident in a world of deep differences.

Given this difficult terrain, the multidisciplinary perspectives united in this volume – including from history, political science, anthropology and sociology – will help us take the first step in exploring the challenges of cooperation posed by current transformations of humanitarianism. We also hope they will pave the way for further research in this area, which will have to extend the range of issues covered but also move towards more far-reaching questions. Some of these questions for future research are suggested here.

1   How are we (or they, or all of us) going to integrate and make use of the growing diversity of humanitarian efforts, and what is a more globally cooperative humanitarianism going to look like?
2   If humanitarian aid can sometimes be likened to unilateral acts of gift-giving (Mauss 1990), under what circumstances are these acts likely to foster robust and reciprocal patterns of cooperation?
3   What are we going to do about the midlife crisis of global humanitarianism and the failure of many humanitarian efforts and doctrines (such as R2P)? How much depends on better cooperation across regions and ideologies if we are serious about closing the "responsibility gap" (Carment et al. 2015) left by failing states in the Global South and failed interventionist approaches in the Global North?

Notes

1 This distinction goes back to David Hume, whose example for coordination is two men rowing a boat by pulling the oars spontaneously in the same way, whereas cooperation is illustrated by the example of two farmers who would increase their wealth if they would help each other in the harvest season, regardless of whether they like each other or not. Both cases are discussed in his book A *Treatise of Human Nature* (Book III, part II, sections 2 and 5).

2 For more on the relationship between misfortune and injustice, which is key to understanding the transformations of humanitarianism, see Shklar (1990, 51–82). For the case that in contemporary society large-scale "misfortunes" are ultimately injustices, see Eyerman (2015).
3 A recent example is the Somaly Mam Foundation, named after its Cambodian-born director, who raised millions by claiming for years to rescue sex workers from brothels in her native country before it turned out that her organisation provided cover for brutal assaults on prostitutes instead of helping them (Grant 2014).
4 It bears recalling that traditional non-political humanitarians have also been systematically targeted in recent conflicts. Consider the case of the bombing of the Red Cross headquarters in Baghdad on 27 October 2003, discussed in Anderson (2004).
5 For an interesting discussion of Mauss in connection with global humanitarianism, see Shilliam (2013).

References

Almeida P.W. (2013) *From Non-indifference to Responsibility while Protecting: Brazil's Diplomacy and the Search for Global Norms*. SAIIA Occasional Paper No. 138, Johannesburg: South African Institute for International Affairs.

Anderson K. (2004) "Humanitarian Inviolability in Crisis: The Meaning of Impartiality and Neutrality for U.N. and NGO Agencies Following the 2003–2004 Afghanistan and Iraq Conflicts", *Harvard Human Rights Journal*, 17, 41–74.

Barnett M.N. (2011) *Empire of Humanity: A History of Humanitarianism*, Cornell University Press, Ithaca, NY.

Barnett M.N. and Gross Stein J. eds (2012) *Sacred Aid: Faith and Humanitarianism*, Oxford University Press, New York.

Berry N.O. (1997) *War and the Red Cross: The Unspoken Mission*, St Martin's Press, New York.

Binder A. (2014) "The Shape and Sustainability of Turkey's Booming Humanitarian Assistance", *International Development Policy/Revue internationale de politique de développement*, 5 (2) (http://poldev.revues.org/1741#toctoln1) accessed 30 May 2015.

Burke E. (1801) "Three Letters Addressed to a Member of the Present Parliament on the Proposals for Peace with the Regicide Directory of France [1796]" in *The Works of the Right Honourable Edmund Burke* Vol. VIII, Rivington, London.

CAF (2013) *World Giving Index 2013. A Global View of Giving Trends*, Charities Aid Foundation (https://www.cafonline.org/about-us/publications/2013-publications/world-giving-index-2013) accessed 30 May 2015.

Carment D., Landry J. and Winchester S. (2015) "On R2P: How NGO and Tech Sectors can Help Protect Communities", *Opencanada.org*, 7 April.

Eyerman R. (2015) *Is This America? Katrina as Cultural Trauma*, University of Texas Press, Austin, TX.

Fassin D. (2012) *Humanitarian Reason: A Moral History of the Present*, translated by Rachel Gomme, University of California Press, Berkeley, CA.

Forsythe D.P. (2005) *The Humanitarians: The International Committee of the Red Cross*, Cambridge University Press, Cambridge, UK.

Grant M.G. (2014) "The Price of a Sex-Slave Rescue Fantasy", *New York Times*, 29 May.

Heins V.M. (2008) *Nongovernmental Organizations in International Society: Struggles over Recognition*, Palgrave Macmillan, New York.

Heins V.M. (2015) "Recognition Going Awry: NGOs and the Rise of the Unelected" in Daase C., Fehl C., Geis A. and Kolliarakis G. eds, *Recognition in International Relations: Rethinking a Political Concept in a Global Context*, Palgrave Macmillan, New York.

Hirschman A.O. (1970) *Exit, Voice, and Loyalty: Responses to Decline in Firms, Organizations, and States*, Harvard University Press, Cambridge, MA.

Hopgood S. (2013) *The Endtimes of Human Rights*, Cornell University Press, Ithaca, NY.

Humanitarian Outcomes (2014) *Unsafe Passage: Road Attacks and their Impact on Humanitarian Operations*, Aid Worker Security Report 2014 (www.humanitarianoutcomes. org/publications) accessed 30 May 2015.

Kouchner B. (1995) *Ce que je crois*, Grasset, Paris.

Mauss M. (1990) *The Gift: Forms and Functions of Exchange in Archaic Societies* [1925], translated by W.D. Halls, Routledge, London.

Meier C. and Murthy C.S.R. (2011) "India's Growing Involvement in Humanitarian Assistance", GPPI Research Paper No. 13, Global Public Policy Institute, Berlin.

Shilliam R. (2013) "The Spirit of Exchange" in Seth S. ed., *Postcolonial Theory and International Relations: A Critical Introduction*, Routledge, London.

Shklar J.N. (1984) *Ordinary Vices*, Belknap Press, Cambridge, MA.

Shklar J.N. (1990) *The Faces of Injustice*, Yale University Press, New Haven, CT.

Thürer D. (2007) "Dunant's Pyramid: Thoughts on the 'Humanitarian Space'", *International Review of the Red Cross*, 89 (865) 47–61.

Tomasello M. (2014) "The Ultra-Social Animal", *European Journal of Social Psychology*, 44 (3) 187–94.

de Waal A. (1997) *Famine Crimes: Politics and the Disaster Relief Industry in Africa*, John Currey, Martlesham, UK.

Yamashita H. (2015) "New Humanitarianism and Changing Logics of the Political in International Relations", *Millennium*, 43 (2) 411–28.

Part I

Transforming the humanitarian enterprise

Principles, politics and professionalism

1 Humanitarianism's contested culture in war zones[1]

Thomas G. Weiss

The dominant culture, the Good Samaritan

The 'H' word is rooted in morality and principle—the parable of the 'Good Samaritan' often comes to mind. The objective is noble, to help vulnerable populations, irrespective of who they are, where they are located, or why they are needy. Aid agencies are interested in the welfare of those in their care and unaffected by political and market factors in the countries that provide or receive assistance. Humanitarian action consists of delivering life-saving emergency relief to, and protecting the fundamental human rights of, endangered people. Both tasks are meant to catch in the global safety net individuals trapped in the vortex of human-made disasters. The two tasks are supposed to be mutually reinforcing, although many humanitarians specialise and try to insulate one from the other lest, by making life-saving succour subservient, emergency relief is held hostage to human rights.

The very word 'humanitarian' retains great resonance, but one searches in vain for an unequivocal definition. Provided an opportunity in the *Nicaragua v. United States* case, the International Court of Justice (ICJ) waffled. It stated that humanitarian action is what the International Committee of the Red Cross (ICRC) does—by inference the independent, neutral, and impartial provision of relief to victims of armed conflicts and natural disasters.

The *Oxford English Dictionary*—whose 1819 edition had the first citation—uses tautologies: humanitarian is 'having regard to the interests of humanity or mankind at large; relating to, or advocating, or practising humanity or human action.' In common discourse, humanitarianism (noun) consists of actions to improve well-being or welfare; a humanitarian (noun) is a person who actively promotes such improvements; and humanitarian (adjective) usually means philanthropic or charitable.

The ICJ's definition requires parsing the ICRC's gold standard. The politics of helping when a natural disaster strikes are relatively simple because every country, no matter how sophisticated, can encounter a disaster resembling the 2011 tsunami and Fukushima nuclear meltdown; and it would be peculiar to decline outside help. Asking for assistance in the midst of wars is another matter, however, far more fraught. Governments in the throes of armed conflict—especially in civil

DOI: 10.4324/9781315658827-3

wars—often view help as an all-too-visible indication of weakness. Moreover, aid and protection represent fungible resources that are part of the calculations of winning a war, and belligerents are not averse to manipulating assistance and civilian lives as part of their arsenals.

The ICRC occupies an unusual position and customarily is treated as *sui generis*. It is the oldest international humanitarian organisation and the largest outside the UN system. A private organisation with a board of governors of prominent Swiss citizens, the ICRC resembles nongovernmental organisations (NGOs) in that it receives both private and public contributions. However, governments provide 90 percent of its annual budget, about $1.2 billion, to cover some 11,000 staff in 80 countries. Nonetheless, it occupies a category by itself as the custodian of the Geneva Conventions—it is a hybrid, neither an intergovernmental organisation (IGO) nor an NGO.

Unlike most humanitarian agencies, the ICRC has elaborated core principles, and its disciplined staff is committed—always on paper, and often in reality—to respecting them. Unlike most NGOs and IGOs that mount a range of activities from relief to reconstruction and development, the ICRC works only in active war zones. The ICRC's ground rules focus on what humanitarianism is supposed to do, and how it is supposed to do it. In his famous desiderata, Jean Pictet (1979) identified seven defining principles: humanity, impartiality, neutrality, independence, voluntary service, unity, and universality.[2]

The first four arguably constitute the core. Humanity (or human dignity) is uncontested and commands attention from all, whereas the other three key principles are debatable and debated. Impartiality requires that assistance be based on need and not discriminate on the basis of nationality, race, religion, gender, or political affiliation. Neutrality demands that humanitarian organisations refrain from taking part in hostilities or any action that either benefits or disadvantages belligerents. Independence necessitates that assistance not be connected to any party with a stake in the outcome of a war; accordingly, there is a general rule to refuse or limit reliance on government funding from those with interests in the outcome.

The ICRC derived these principles based on decades of practical experience with what works best. Although many observers now treat them as sacrosanct— indeed, the essence of humanitarian culture—these principles began as pragmatic judgments. Simply put, traditional principles helped guide humanitarians to reach people under duress in inter-state conflicts and natural disasters. If aid agencies are perceived by combatants as allied with the opposing side, or having a vested interest in the outcome, they have difficulty in getting access; or they may become targets. If principles are religiously respected, so the argument goes, both aid workers and recipients benefit from a sanctuary. Operating according to these principles and being perceived as apolitical has been crucial during wars.

In short, the culture of humanitarianism reflects the desire and ability to provide life-saving assistance while honoring neutrality, impartiality, and independence. But how pertinent is that tradition in today's war-torn societies? Remaining above the fray and respecting principles is virtually impossible in the face of rampant militarisation, politicisation, and marketisation. The questionable relevance of traditional humanitarian culture in many contemporary contexts requires that we revisit their impact on humanitarianism's SOPs (standard operating 'principles' or 'procedures').

Militarisation

The routine involvement by third-party military forces in humanitarian efforts is a remarkable phenomenon of the post-Cold War era—especially for Africa where three-quarters of UN or UN-authorised forces are deployed (Center on International Cooperation 2013; Adebajo 2011). Yet using military forces for such purposes is not new because a quantum expansion took place after World War II, when occupying Germany and Japan as well as reconstructing their economies required new types of personnel within the armed forces: administrators, planners, and logisticians. The military often possess a cornucopia of resources in the shortest supply when disaster strikes: transport, fuel, communications, commodities, building equipment, medicines, and provisions. The military's 'can-do' mentality, self-supporting character, rapid-response capabilities, and hierarchical discipline are assets amidst catastrophic turmoil. Most dramatically, humanitarian benefits can result from the military's direct exercise of its primary war-fighting functions and superior force to overwhelm hostile forces. Such deployments should be distinguished from those after natural disasters or in tandem with traditional peacekeepers. Military humanitarians can gain access to suffering civilians when insecurity makes it impossible or highly dangerous, and they can foster a secure-enough environment to permit succour and protection by others. Such interveners can also change the regime responsible for suffering, admittedly a more contested outcome of their efforts.

Militarisation has proved problematic for humanitarians, and critics have lambasted the security function. They view 'humanitarian intervention' or 'humanitarian war' or especially the 'humanitarian bombing' of Kosovo or Libya as an oxymoron (Roberts 1993; Rieff 2002a; see also Bass 2008). Moreover, the use of the military to do what only military can do—provide security— complicates protection and delivery by civilian organisations because the military dominates priority-setting. 'Humanitarian intervention' is truth-in-packaging that preceded and perhaps more accurately depicts military humanitarianism than the more recent and politically palatable 'responsibility to protect.'[3] Adam Roberts (2002) is clear: 'coercive action by one or more states involving the use of armed force in another state without the consent of its authorities, and with the purpose of preventing widespread suffering or death among the inhabitants.' Military interventions with substantial humanitarian justifications—against the wishes of a government, or without their genuine consent—figure prominently in the post-Cold War era and make action possible in areas where it previously had not been.

Intervention is not involved when an action is based on a freely given request from, or with the unqualified consent of, a state. All foreign policy aims to persuade or cajole other states to change behaviour. The absence of consent is required to merit the label 'intervention' because otherwise any outside involvement or attempt to influence another political authority would constitute intervention. If it covers everything, the term loses salience. In a world of asymmetrical power, what constitutes genuine 'consent' also may be questionable. Nonetheless, consent has a distinct international legal character; and its expression is a conceptual distinction for military measures against a state as well as for political and economic sanctions, arms embargoes, and international criminal prosecution.

Consent is an essential building block in the foundations of traditional humanitarian culture, but militarisation removes it. Humanitarians cannot be independent when they rely on the military and its priorities; and coercion requires taking sides, thereby robbing neutrality and impartiality of meaning.

Politicisation

The use of the military anywhere reflects high politics, of course. However, the last quarter-century has witnessed a witches' brew of intensely politicised decisions that have substantially altered humanitarian culture. There are four ingredients in the recipe.

The first is the switch from inter-state to intra-state armed conflict. Civil wars are transformative for the culture because humanitarians are no longer dealing with authorities of separate governments, but with a host of armed belligerents. Advanced by such scholars as Mary Kaldor (1999) and Mark Duffield (2001) as well as by such journalists as Robert Kaplan (2000), the catchy moniker of 'new wars' can lead to confusion. It is less that totally new elements have appeared, than that elements thought extinct or tangential have come to the fore or been combined in ways that were heretofore unremarkable (Newman 2004; Kalyvas 2001). Hence change often is so quantitatively high, or the elements are combined in such previously unfamiliar ways, that numerous wars effectively merit the shorthand 'new' (see Hoffman and Weiss 2006).

Many countries have central governments whose existence takes the form of UN membership and control of the capital city or the main exports. They scarcely resemble their stable Westphalian counterparts (see Badie 2000). They exercise little or no authoritative control over populations and resources; and they certainly do not have a monopoly of the use of force. Such states suffer from the 'unbundling' of territory from authority—a negation of the exclusive authority as states (Ruggie 1993, 165). Drug-crazed child soldiers who hack off the limbs of terrorised civilians in Sierra Leone capture some of the horror, as does seeking agreement from the forty or so 'main' armed opposition movements in the Democratic Republic of the Congo (DRC). 'Weak' and 'failed' and 'fragile' states—various observers have preferences and problems with all the adjectives, but the reality is clear—are the scene for most contemporary humanitarian action. Traditional humanitarian culture has meant the continued application of tactics that worked well in the past for interstate armed conflicts but are less useful in today's civil wars. Neither organised violence nor humanitarianism is any longer beholden only, or even mainly, to state authorities, and the de-institutionalisation of sovereign central authority means a diminished impact of international humanitarian law.

The second manifestation of politicisation is that government donors have moved away from investing in untied multilateral disbursements through the UN system—especially through the big three of the Office of the UN High Commissioner for Refugees (UNHCR), UNICEF, and the World Food Programme (WFP)—toward tying resources to particular groups or conflicts, particular agencies, or particular priorities. Bilateral or collective European assistance is more vulnerable to politicisation than is UN or NGO assistance. With the end of the Cold War, bilateral aid agencies increasingly provided resources to IGOs and NGOs, but that did not mean the disappearance of political concerns by governments. Donors are not bashful about exercising control over funds channelled through intergovernmental and nongovernmental agencies. Earmarking is clearly manipulation, and the priority of donor agendas is hardly subtler within agencies that depend on voluntary funding because the power of the purse is correlated with enhanced power in decision making.

Instead of setting the agenda as the independence of the traditional culture would dictate, aid agencies often are sub-contractors for donors whose preferences are clear and affect the bottom line, whereas those of recipients are tough to gauge and can be less consequential for the resource base (Hammond 2008). Particular donor countries can apply leverage and dictate to a multilateral organisation either how money should be spent, or how it should be subcontracted to local or international NGOs; they have geopolitical interests to protect and domestic constituencies to satisfy. Providing a Volvo to a recipient of Swedish aid is easier than a Toyota or Ford; channelling resources to favoured locales, belligerents, or target audiences is an easier sell than unrestricted grants. Only the naïve would ignore the tune and the preferences of donors that pay the piper.

The shift away from unrestricted multilateral toward bilateral aid, as well as away from untied (or core) grants to multilateral organisations, toward earmarking or multi-bi grants is unsettling for humanitarians (Barnett and Snyder 2008). In 1988 states provided roughly 45 percent of humanitarian assistance through UN agencies (Randel and German 2002, 21); and over the past five years about 50 percent of such aid was disbursed through multilateral organisations according to the *Global Humanitarian Assistance Report* (Development Initiatives 2013, 6; hereafter GHA 2013). As most aid is earmarked for specific crises, only a small percentage can be used wherever a multilateral agency wishes—the last time such a figure was calculated, it was about 11 percent, or some $913 million of multilateral funds in the total of $8.7 billion in 2007's humanitarian contributions from country members of the Development Assistance Committee (DAC) of the Organisation for Economic Co-operation and Development (OECD) (Development Initiatives 2009, 8).

Whereas multilateral funding once permitted greater flexibility to pursue agency-determined priorities, it is now customarily tied to specific activities or locations identified by funders even when channelled through multilateral and nongovernmental organisations. The shorthand 'bilateralisation' essentially means earmarking or coopting multilateralism as government donors unabashedly pursue more compatibility between their contributions and national priorities. Figures vary by agency, but UNDP's core budget is now around 20 percent and the UN's own development activities about 30 percent, a mirror image of twenty years earlier when untied resources were by far the norm (Weinlich 2014). While some argue that little harm is done by tying aid to such internationally agreed goals as the Millennium Development Goals and the UN's Consolidated Appeal Process (CAP) (Jenks 2014), programming is increasingly linked to donor- rather than agency-determined priorities; and risk-taking and experimentation are virtually excluded under such conditionality.

Accordingly, the needs of affected populations may be secondary in determining allocations and programs. For instance, of the top 50 recipients of bilateral assistance between 1996 and 1999, the states of the former Yugoslavia, Israel/Palestine, and Iraq received half of available resources (Randel and German 2002, 27). By contrast, in 2000 the DRC ranked as the country with the lowest level of needs met—a mere 17.2 percent of its CAP; four years later it was Zimbabwe at 14.2 percent. In 2012 the total shortfall was $3.3 billion with only 63 percent of identified needs met—Zimbabwe the highest at 86 percent of unmet needs and Liberia the lowest at 38 percent (GHA 2013, 5). The impact of 9/11 already was obvious in 2002 as nearly half of all funds given by donor governments to the UN's 25 appeals went to Afghanistan (Smillie and Minear 2004, 145; Oxfam 2003, 2). A decade later, the appeal for Afghanistan remained among the best-funded in proportion to estimated requirements. Unsurprisingly, in the wake of the 2011 intervention that ousted Muammar el-Gaddafi, Libya immediately assumed a position among the better-funded CAPs while Sudan, Sri Lanka, and Haiti rounded out the top five. The most underfunded included the countries of West Africa, Zimbabwe, and Djibouti (OCHA 2011, 13). By 2012, Pakistan, Somalia, and the Occupied Territories headed the list (GHA 2013, 6).

There is virtually no difference between the motivations of Western and non-traditional donors; geopolitics often trumps humanitarian values. For instance, non-DAC humanitarian funds increased dramatically from 2011 to 2012 as Turkey almost doubled its contribution—most going to its neighbour Syria, which accounted for half a million refugees in the host country and disruption of Turkey's economy and domestic politics (GHA 2013, 4, 36).

The third factor in increased politicisation results from the policies of humanitarian agencies, which have decided that band-aids are insufficient, and that they should alleviate the causes of suffering by addressing poverty and human rights. The shift from emergency relief to attacking root causes and post-conflict peace-building is ambitious. No longer satisfied with saving individuals today to place them in jeopardy tomorrow—the infamous 'well fed dead' is a memorable framing about aid in the former Yugoslavia[4]—many humanitarians now aspire to nothing less than improving the structural conditions that endanger vulnerable populations. Their help also should somehow be supportive of negotiations and peace processes. Rather than applying salve, they wish to use assistance and protection to spread development, democracy, and human rights and to create stable, effective, and legitimate states (Donini 2004; Fox 2001).

Neutrality and impartiality can be obstacles to promoting human rights. Reciting the humanitarian mantra is of little avail; traditional principles provide no or even bad guidance. As David Rieff (2011: 254) tells us, 'humanitarian space is a sentimental idea, neutrality a bogus one, and impartiality an abstraction ... The sooner they are given a decent burial, the sooner we can all move on.'

The fourth factor is post-9/11 politics. Since the attacks on the United States in September 2001, many countries have viewed counter-terrorism and humanitarianism as crime-fighting partners—with conflict-prone states as sanctuaries and staging platforms for terrorists. Humanitarian organisations, in this view, are part of wider 'hearts and minds' campaigns, attempting to convince local populations of the goodness of armies invading in the name of stability and freedom. US secretary of state Colin Powell (2001) told a gathering of private aid agencies that 'just as surely as our diplomats and military, American NGOs are out there [in Afghanistan] serving and sacrificing on the frontlines of freedom. NGOs are such a force multiplier for us, such an important part of our combat team.' Whether or not humanitarians are opposed to elements of Western, and especially US, foreign policy, in the field they often are perceived as supporters.

In a related fashion, governments have discovered that humanitarian action could be instrumental in postponing or avoiding more costly political decisions and actions, a 'humanitarian alibi.' UN High Commissioner for Refugees Sadako Ogata (2005, 25), for one, became an outspoken opponent of such contrivances: 'There are no humanitarian solutions to humanitarian problems.' The major powers authorised UNHCR to deliver relief in Bosnia in part because they wanted to relieve the growing pressure for a military intervention. Yet to the extent that aid became a substitute for politics and a sop to hopeful publics, according to Alex de Waal (2001, 221), it led 'Western governments and donating publics to be deluded into believing the fairy tale that their aid can solve profound political problems, when it cannot.'

Marketisation Part 1: Outsiders in the humanitarian business

'Humanitarian' and 'business' are juxtaposed for two reasons: provocation and accuracy (Weiss 2013). Jarring for those who idealise the humanitarian enterprise, the adjective has essentially uncontested positive connotations while the noun usually is associated with wheeling and dealing and at odds with the values and self-image of true believers. If humanitarian action claims the moral high ground, business is customarily seen to occupy less lofty territory. In contrast to humanitarians, those in the market operate where deals are cut, money buys access, the common good is ignored, talk is cheap, and decisions about profit margins ignore human costs.

Of course, outside humanitarians coming to the rescue and, in Nicholas Wheeler's words, 'saving strangers' (Wheeler 2000) are not divorced from but rather are steeped in politics; and they operate in the marketplace. The day-to-day functioning of all aid agencies intersects in myriad ways with home and host governments, with armed forces and armed insurgents as well as military peacekeepers and local populations; and most crucially, it confronts the priorities of funders. As agents engaged in resource acquisition and distribution, where they get their resources, and how and to whom they deliver relief, can have significant consequences for aid personnel in headquarters and in war zones. Staff cannot ignore bottom lines; they are not apolitical.

The Good Samaritan characterises the aspirations and expectations of numerous aid workers. This idealistic embrace is understandable because humanitarian organisations are required to project this image to Western publics as part of a marketing logic: contributions emanate from donors whose heart-strings and purse-strings are tugged in tandem with a story and image of a single suffering child (two reduce the dramatic effect), caught in the crosshairs of war, who can be saved only by generous donations. Contributors want to be assured that their inputs are directly helping to improve lives. Fund-raising brochures depict relief workers wearing T-shirts with a recognisable logo posing beside seemingly happier and better-nourished kids.

Like entrepreneurs, humanitarians are concerned with image and marketing in an expanding and competitive global business in which suppliers vie for market shares. While funding is more abundant than ever, resources are still 'scarce' in light of the magnitude of the needs—as indicated, less than two-thirds of such needs were met in the most recent year for which data are available. For die-hard humanitarians who claim to be apolitical and are offended by the allegation that they are not, the term 'business' will unsettle. True believers will be uneasy about being analysed as part of a marketplace because marketing involves four 'Ps': product, price, place, and promotion. Yet the entire business, as Hugo Slim (2012) writes, begins with 'selling the idea of restraint and compassion in war.' Marketisation in the globalising world of the twenty-first century means that everything has a price—from access, to moral authority, to lives.

Institutional innovations usually occur after wars when conscience-shocking horrors expose the inadequacies of existing response mechanisms. Henri Dunant's revulsion with Solferino's carnage led to creating the ICRC in 1865. The bloody aftermath of World War I and the Russian Revolution led to founding the International Office for Refugees and Save the Children. Similarly, World War II led to a host of agencies—Oxfam, Catholic Relief Services, World Vision, and CARE along with members of the UN family, including UNICEF and UNHCR. The French Doctors Movement—beginning with Médecins sans Frontières (MSF)—emerged when dissident staff revolted against ICRC's dysfunctional orthodoxy during the Nigeria–Biafra War.

The end of the Cold War resulted in no transformation of international law or institutions but rather new conflicts and crises, along with the eruption of long-simmering ones held in check during the era of acute East–West tensions; and it also resulted in the proliferation of humanitarian agencies and opening resource floodgates. The budgets of humanitarian organisations had a five-fold increase from about $800 million in 1989 to some $4.4 billion in 1999, with an additional quadrupling to $16.7 billion in 2009—after peaking at just over $20 billion in 2010, the figures drifted downward to $19.4 billion in 2011 and

$17.9 billion in 2012 (the last year for which data are available) (GHA 2013: 4). Some individual agencies (like the International Rescue Committee) or federations (like Oxfam and Save the Children) are big enterprises while others are smaller, many even artisanal. While the number of UN organisations has not grown, their budgets have (accounting for about two-thirds of total DAC humanitarian disbursements). At least 2,500 international NGOs are in the business, even if only a tenth of them are truly significant. There could be 37,000 international NGOs with some relevance for what Linda Polman (2010) calls 'the crisis caravan.' On average a bevy of some 1,000 international and local NGOs flocks to a contemporary emergency.

Over the past decade, governments have disbursed some $110 billion for humanitarian assistance. In 2010 and 2011, they provided some $14 billion per year and almost $13 billion in 2012; and private voluntary contributions reached a peak of $6.3 billion in 2010 (roughly $5 billion in 2012), up from $3.0 billion in 2007 (GHA 2013, 20, 30). Moreover over the past half-decade UN peace operations have added between $8 and $10 billion annually, with most soldiers deployed in the same target countries. More and more governments are responding to disasters of all sorts, and the numbers have expanded beyond the West to the Rest. Whereas 16 states pledged their support to Bosnia in the mid-1990s, mostly from the West, a diverse group of 73 attended the 2003 pledging conference in Madrid for Iraq, and 92 responded to the December 2004 tsunami. While OECD governments almost doubled their assistance between 2000 and 2010 from $6.7 billion to $11.8 billion, non-OECD governments increased their contributions from $35 million to $623 million—an 18-fold increase, albeit from a much lower base. In 2011 and 2012, DAC donors decreased from $13 to $11.6 billion whereas non-DAC donors increased from $0.8 to $1.4 billion (GHA 2013, 4).

What about the number of aid workers worldwide? Abby Stoddard and colleagues hazard a guess of over 200,000 (Stoddard, Harmer, and Haver 2006). But Peter Walker and Catherine Russ are undoubtedly closer to the mark: 'We have no idea what size this population is.' Estimates include everyone from cleaning personnel and drivers in field offices to CEOs in headquarters. Walker and Russ extrapolate from Oxfam data and estimate some 30,000 humanitarian professionals (both local and expatriate) worldwide (Walker and Russ 2010).

One need not agree with Naomi Klein's (2007) characterisation of the business model for emergency relief as 'disaster capitalism' to appreciate the extent to which the global bottom line of some $18–20 billion in recent years, with personnel spread across the planet helping 75–100 million people, would, on the face of it, strike most observers as a substantial business. The culture of humanitarian cooperation has been replaced by one of humanitarian competition. James Ron and Alexander Cooley point to 'the scramble' for resources, which channels the priorities and programs for humanitarian agencies—public and private, large and small, religious and secular. The result is a 'contract culture' among outsiders that is 'deeply corrosive' of the humanitarian soul (Cooley and Ron 2002, 13).

Marketisation Part 2: Insiders in war economies

The contestation of traditional humanitarian culture also reflects the ugly reality of local economies in war-torn and conflict-prone countries. Two kinds of local market forces influence contemporary humanitarian culture: economic interests that directly profit from armed conflict, and peculiar political economies.

The idiosyncratic economies of contemporary war zones represent alternative ways to make a profit. Carl von Clausewitz's celebrated dictum that war is the continuation of politics was adapted by David Keen (2000, 27): 'war may be the continuation of *economics* by other means.'[5] When states are falling apart or putting themselves back together, peculiar opportunities for profit abound. Balance sheets have always been important in fueling war, and certainly captains of industry from Krupp in the Third Reich to Halliburton in Iraq have been more than willing to help the national cause as well as enrich corporate and personal coffers.

However, the local economy in contemporary wars plays a quantitatively and qualitatively different role than previously (Reno 2000, 44–5; Mehlum, Moene, and Torvik 2002). There is little production, mainly destruction. The economy and society as a whole suffer while isolated individuals benefit. With cash, arms, and power flowing into their hands, warring factions have no incentive to proceed to or remain at the negotiating table; instead, their interests are served by prolonging war and the accompanying economy that is of direct benefit. Local actors can concentrate their energies on controlling and illegally or legally exporting a few key resources such as diamonds or tropical timber. Much spoiler behaviour—before, during, and after wars—can be explained by perverse economic incentives and rewards.

Conventional international relations theory emphasises the control of territory as essential to maintain authority, but contemporary wars compel actors to concentrate their energies on controlling commerce in key commodities. Commercial activity in many wars is premised on the continuation of violent conflict or is used to fuel it, or both. A form of criminal, distorting, and debilitating trade is often the product of the exploitation of natural resources by private interests. Sometimes the formal economy of the state is manipulated for private gain, an 'economy of plunder' (Hibou 1999, 71, 96). At other times, criminals, especially those operating as part of transnational networks, foster the erosion of state power to prevent governmental regulation and taxation (Shelly 1995; Williams 1994). The opportunities to pursue personal gain and to finance war lead many non-state actors to emphasise access to and control over natural resources, frequently resulting in heightened violence and humanitarian needs. In short, contemporary wars present opportunities for personal enrichment (protection and plunder) in addition to the prospects of an infusion of resources from outsiders.

The latter constitutes the second local economic distortion in today's wars. The provision of external resources designed to help the helpless drives local 'aid economies.' More violence means more suffering and more aid, with more opportunities for local profit for the lucky few.

Unpacking the politics of war-torn societies reveals three problems for aid workers within that local marketplace. First, it is virtually impossible not to work with 'spoilers' (Stedman, Rothchild, and Cousens 2002), but humanitarians have to pay particular attention to minimise the chances that they may inadvertently enhance the legitimacy of illegitimate actors. Formal relations with spoilers implicitly acknowledge their authority; and improving their ability to provide relief can bolster claims to legitimacy.

Second, humanitarian aid is fungible and can relieve belligerents of some burdens of waging war, effectively increasing their capacity to continue fighting by diminishing the demands of governing and cutting the costs of sustaining casualties. Perhaps the most significant manifestation of what would usually be called 'corruption,' but is now labelled the 'cost of doing humanitarian business,' consists of purchasing access through payments to those who control territory. Central government authorities and warlords try to siphon off as large a portion of aid supplies as they can. Estimates range from 15 to 80 percent. A 25–30 percent 'tax' seems to be a working average, which was actually the documented figure for the share claimed by Indonesian soldiers from the tsunami relief in Aceh, where a guerrilla group had been operating; and the figure was comparable throughout the former Yugoslavia where the UNHCR regularly surrendered comparable portions to Serbian soldiers (Polman 2010, 96–9).

Third, outside agencies may constitute virtually the entire formal monetised sector. International salaries paid regularly in foreign exchange are attractive not only to skilled workers, technicians, and those with language skills, but also to drivers, guards, gardeners, and maids. With remuneration that is 10 to 30 times as high as the equivalent position in the local economy, hundreds of applicants appear for any vacancy posted by aid agencies. Moreover, hyper-inflation often afflicts the economy along with the accompanying costs of prostitution, drugs, contraband, and social mores. Moving from the 'economics of war' to the 'economics of peace' in conflicts like those in Afghanistan and Liberia is, according to Graciana del Castillo (2009), perhaps the toughest challenge in post-conflict peacebuilding.

Toward an evidence-based culture

Usually soldiers and humanitarians are seen as different species; in particular, their respective cultures emphasise distinct values toward and perspectives on violence and the use of force. Although approaching war from differing philosophical positions, their respective organisations share at least one characteristic: thriving ones learn and adapt. Yet the dominant humanitarian culture discounts, if not disparages, in-depth research. Many aid officials are impatient with the culture of inquiry, which they see as the antithesis of their own.[6] Analysis is a luxury, an investment in problem-finding not problem-solving. For the most part, humanitarians and their fiduciary boards have neglected, or at least relegated to a tertiary or even symbolic status within their organisations, the tasks of formally identifying problems, gathering data, drawing conclusions, and translating lessons into new policies and actions—a cumulative process known as 'learning.'

Much experience since the 1990s demonstrates that reactions to crises are routine, but serious reflections are too infrequently part of job descriptions. For example, in his detailed look into UNHCR, Gil Loescher (2001) points to the institution's conservative culture, which is resistant to change and inhospitable to the infusion of new ideas and outside criticism. This organisational pathology is not a UNHCR monopoly but a widespread malady.

The value of learning is not necessarily apparent to practitioners if links to policies and programs are absent. 'Adaptation' occurs when an organisation identifies short-term modifications to solve problems. But 'change' takes place after substantial reflections about the premises of particular modalities for humanitarian action and the most desirable ways to alter policies, to adapt principles, and ultimately to redesign and conduct a subsequent generation of operations. 'Transformation' refers to profound change.

While the international humanitarian system certainly has adapted over the years, the challenges of new wars and new humanitarianisms are momentous enough to necessitate bold changes, even transformations, in strategic thinking and acting. However, aid agencies are far more likely to tinker modestly than to change substantially let alone to transform dramatically.

A comparison of military institutions and humanitarian agencies—and their respective cultures—is instructive. Critics customarily castigate a hierarchical and over-funded military, but the soldierly pursuit of order and discipline is the expected result. SOPs reflect an approach to managing and executing tasks under centralised authority. One might expect such a culture to be rigid and unreceptive to learning. But success and promotion are contingent on flexibility and openness to change in strategy and tactics, as well as discipline in carrying out new procedures that result from analysing past successes and failures. And new technologies and investments in them are routine.

Recognising a need to innovate is not cheap, and significant budgetary resources are normally dedicated to evaluation and analysis. National defence occupies a privileged position in governmental battles for resources. The potential costs of falling behind—defeat—are high enough to ensure allocations for research, training, and investment. The material incentives for the military to succeed on the battlefield typically guarantee parliamentary largesse toward budgetary requests. There is no question of going out of business, or being second-best.

The contrast with the culture and expenditures of the vast majority of humanitarian organisations could hardly be greater. They normally beg for what may be inadequate resources to react and provide relief and protection in war's wake; budgets are not guaranteed but reflect perpetual fund-raising. Aid agencies almost always work with other actors. In mobilising resources, agencies rely on donors. In providing relief and protection, their work hinges on access facilitated by a host of other agencies, including soldiers. In short, the challenges of fundraising and securing access often make humanitarian action contingent on an alignment of donor wishes and the whims of interlocutors. Individual aid agencies are essential cogs in a much larger international machine. This case is especially evident in the non-permissive operational environments of today's armed conflicts.

Despite the ever-changing institutional environment and character of different war zones, humanitarians have no boot camps or laboratories for experiments to help overcome bureaucratic inertia and operational difficulties. Other than an occasional master's program, there are no specialised academies. And virtually no resources, at least as a percentage of overall budgets, are allocated to understanding current and previous operations with a view toward changing tactics and strategies. Indeed, a virtue has often been made from what in other organisations would be seen as a grave shortcoming—namely, moving as quickly as possible to the next crisis without having gathered data and digested the evidence from the last catastrophe, evaluated it, and attempted to formulate alternative policies and approaches. Bragging rights and the highest ratings go to those spending the least on training and evaluation and other overhead expenses that supposedly indicate waste.

Why is it so difficult, as the annual report from the International Federation of Red Cross and Red Crescent Societies asked over a decade ago, to exercise 'humanitarian judgment to analyse context' (IFRC 2003, 36)? David Kennedy provides the answer: 'When data are uncertain, humanitarians are guided by hunches, inferences, and conceptions of best practice.' In the rush to respond, humanitarians repeat 'pat answers' that may have once made sense. But instead of mindless repetitions and reactions, hard-headed reflections should guide agencies: 'A pragmatism of consequences runs into difficulty when expertise of this type substitutes for careful analysis of long- and short-term consequences.' And the humanitarian culture should change because humanitarians 'tend to be uncomfortable thinking of themselves making the kind of distributional choices among winners and losers which seem required by a pragmatism of consequences' (Kennedy 2005, xxiii–xxiv). Based on her searing experiences with Médecins sans Frontières, Fiona Terry (2002, 44) uses her book's title to ask an obvious rhetorical question: *Condemned to Repeat?* She and others detail missed opportunities for learning since the 1990s, which led Ian Smillie and Larry Minear (2004, 224) to recommend 'a more holistic approach … that puts learning at center stage.'

Unfortunately, slowing down to reflect is doubly problematic. Not only are too few resources devoted to reflection, but the incentive structure rewards those at the head of the response queue. Comparing the military's approach to learning with that of humanitarians results in a gross disparity, the low priority accorded by the latter to understanding and adapting to the dynamics impairing effective action in war zones.

The lack of a learning orientation is structural. Randolph Kent (2004, 9) noted a decade ago that 'Strategy formulation requires at a minimum the involvement of all the main components within the organisation—in other words, an unusual degree of intra-organisational cooperation among those responsible for emergencies, policies, development and budgeting.' Thus strategising involves two steps: first, learning and adapting behaviour; and second, disseminating such knowledge and ensuring coherent implementation. For humanitarian strategic thinking to become strategic doing, agencies desperately require a program to develop and strengthen in-house and system-wide analytical capacities.

Improvements are necessary throughout the system, but individual agencies should begin to develop and nurture three analytical capabilities as part of a different humanitarian culture. Better intelligence is the first. A severe obstacle for agencies operating in the field or planning future efforts is an absence of timely and accurate information (see Stanley Foundation 2003; Weiss and Hoffman 2005). Without it, humanitarians can blunder into aiding manipulative parties and participating in other counterproductive endeavours. Information about the intentions and conduct of actors in a theatre can help in selecting tactics, negotiating access, and sequencing other aspects of operations that ultimately contribute to success.

Aid agencies often enter theatres without even the most basic knowledge about belligerents and the history and dynamics of the area in which violence is raging. Not only is such knowledge inadequate, rarer still are personnel devoted to monitoring local politics once an operation is underway in order to inform policy- and decision-makers. Knowledge of local societies and languages are obvious lacunae, and many practitioners have lamented their absence long before the standard bill-of-fare became Islamic countries, for which Western expertise is in especially short supply. But there are less-obvious shortcomings, namely, how several sources of humanitarian intelligence—data and analyses of belligerents, local conditions, indigenous humanitarian resources, and the impacts of assistance—can be developed and utilised.

The second capacity is not unrelated: namely, the need to improve institutional memory, to document activities and the resulting repercussions. George Santayana's warning that 'those who do not know the lessons of history are doomed to repeat them' has too little resonance among humanitarians. What business analysts would call a 'flat learning curve' characterises the humanitarian enterprise, in which participants compare notes mainly with those who reside in the same echo chamber. Understanding the scope and nature of problems and critically evaluating options are keys to avoiding previous mistakes and grappling with alternatives. Agencies should establish formal documentation and research units. Institutional memory could draw on graduate students in history and the social sciences for technical support in fact-finding and analysis, a process that could also help future recruitment and nourish the next generation of practitioners.

The third capacity is communications and networking, which should accompany improved intelligence and institutional memories to collect and process data for those about to enter new positions or theatres. The discussion of the marketplace suggested the structural and cultural difficulties in promoting coordination and coherence within the international humanitarian system. Completely eliminating these tensions is unrealistic, but certainly better communications are more feasible and essential for better coordination or even modest coherence. An important step in the right direction would be long-term relationships between key research institutions—both universities and think-tanks—and operational agencies.

Consequentialist ethics

At bottom, the change in culture requires recognising a single first-order principle—the sanctity of life or human dignity, but relegating the three operational ones that form the core of traditional humanitarian culture—independence, neutrality, and impartiality—to second-order status. They are means not ends; they may be helpful but are not moral absolutes. They necessarily take a backseat to more consequentialist calculations about specific inputs based on better knowledge about specific armed conflicts and their likely operational outcomes and impacts.

The age of innocence, if there ever was one, is over (see Weiss 1999; Wood, Apthorpe, and Borton 2001). Instead of rushing, humanitarians urgently need to slow down and move beyond the dominant cultural trait of 'we need immediate action' (Levine and Chastre 2004, 19). Wars are not tsunamis or earthquakes, and humanitarians should approach them differently. The required cultural change is dramatic: to navigate the shoals of the troubled waters in contemporary war zones, humanitarians must reflect before acting. 'The remedy is a more thoroughgoing pragmatism,' David Kennedy (2005) suggests. 'By rooting out bias, disenchanting the doctrines and institutional tools which substitute for analysis, insisting on a rigorous pragmatic analysis of costs and benefits, we might achieve a humanitarianism which could throw light on its own dark sides.'

Thoughtful and informed strategic humanitarianism is more appropriate than the rigid application of traditional, second-order principles, for at least four reasons. Goals often conflict. Good intentions can have catastrophic consequences. Ends can be achieved in multiple ways. And choices are necessary even if the options are less than ideal.

Humanitarians should thus set aside ideology, weigh alternatives, and consider longer-term outcomes. In short, judgments should not be derived a priori from second-order principles. Empirical assessments are essential because the darker sides of virtue can overwhelm the benefits of humanitarianism; the availability of resources is an insufficient argument for action. There are always winners and losers, virtuous outcomes and horrendous costs. Humanitarianism provides an idealistic vocabulary and institutional machinery; but it should be judged by consequences and not intentions, by the quality of results and impacts and not merely inputs and outputs.

It would be unfair and inaccurate to imply that nothing has changed in the post-Cold War era. Efforts over the past two decades point to a gradually increased appetite among practitioners for social science research. Oxfam-UK has long led the way with paid staff for research and evaluation. Seasoned observers are familiar with the ICRC's *Avenir* efforts, the International Federation of Red Cross and Red Crescent Societies' Sphere Project, and the Active Learning for Accountability and Performance in Humanitarian Action (ALNAP). Research from the Humanitarianism & War Project (first at Brown and later Tufts University), the Overseas Development Institute, Global Humanitarian Assistance, and the Centre for Humanitarian Dialogue, along with university researchers in many other places, have helped generate data and metrics.

A significant indication of the need for changing the dominant culture was the Emergency Capacity Building Project (ECB), a decade-long effort financed mainly by the Bill & Melinda Gates Foundation.[7] In 2004 the emergency directors from seven of the largest NGOs—CARE International, Catholic Relief Services,

International Rescue Committee, Mercy Corps, Oxfam GB, Save the Children and World Vision International—focused on persistent challenges. An initial ECB report on capacity identified key gaps constraining the ability to provide timely, effective, and quality responses. Between 2005 and 2013, 20 publications (both research and guides) resulted.

Better information and baselines certainly are a step in the right direction, but successful learning requires not only diagnoses and prescriptions (by outsiders and insiders), but implementation. Yet the dominant culture of humanitarian agencies resists cures for what ails the system. Three well placed analysts note that since the trauma of Rwanda, 'the humanitarian sector has witnessed an (incomplete) trend toward professionalisation' (Dijkzeul, Hilhorst, and Walker 2013, s4).[8]

'Incomplete' is indeed a generous depiction. As a result of their frenzied fervour to react to crises and strong commitment to saving strangers, humanitarian organisations devote far too little energy and far too few of their own discretionary resources to understanding the nature of a particular disaster and tailoring their responses accordingly. Doing something or doing nothing may be acceptable options. What Larry Minear and I wrote two decades ago retains salience: 'Don't just do something, stand there' (Minear and Weiss 1993). Reflection is required as a prerequisite for action and will amortise investments better than hasty reactions, however heartfelt and well intentioned.

Whereas 'humanitarian' has the tone of selfless caring, 'strategic' has the ring of cold-hearted calculation, at least in too many humanitarian ears. Strategic thinking is not merely for specialists in foreign policy or international security, but for humanitarians as well. Strategic thinking would be amortised by strategic doing. Saving lives is not only a question of the heart but also of the mind. Tempering idealism with improved analytical capacities will enhance the tensile strength of the international humanitarian system, an approach that the late Myron Wiener (1998) long ago dubbed 'instrumental humanitarianism.'

Evidence-based humanitarian action must also be context-driven. Social science can be helpful in tailoring activities to local sensitivities and in monitoring ongoing operations. Alternative sources should be drawn on, including journalists who may have access to political leaders and politically marginal and neglected areas, or truck and taxi drivers who have insights into local logistics. The participation by users and target groups is part of an essential partnership in research (Hammond 2008).

Practitioners should be more receptive toward social science whose strength is its ability to gather, organise, interpret, and disseminate evidence-based and context-driven findings, policy recommendations, and tailored guidelines. This recommendation is not a self-serving justification by a researcher, but a conviction that more reflection and less reaction would not only help improve the efficiency of the humanitarian enterprise but also better assist vulnerable populations.

Over a decade ago, Larry Minear (2002, 7) argued that 'humanitarian organisations' adaptation to the new realities has been for the most part lethargic and phlegmatic.' Humanitarians still are learning-disabled—they possess neither the capabilities nor cultural inclinations to process information, correct errors, and devise alternative strategies and tactics. Delivery and protection, not analysis, properly preoccupy them, but aid officials should recognise the value-added of social scientists. A partnership would be beneficial for aid agencies and academics as well as the denizens of war-torn societies.

Part of changing the dominant humanitarian culture will involve the humanitarian equivalent of military science. For too long, aid workers have talked about becoming more professional but have been unwilling to accept the discipline and costs that necessarily would follow.[9] While data and research are more prevalent than in the early post-Cold War period, too much relief and protection is driven by anecdote and angst, by intuition and instinct rather than by evidence, strategy, and outcomes. Seed money from the Gates Foundation and other donors is welcome and helpful, to be sure, but agencies themselves should devote more core resources to improving their knowledge base and training staff.

While humanitarians will undoubtedly bristle at the comparison, professional militaries—unlike professional humanitarians—have a culture that values learning and invests substantial human and financial resources in the institutional infrastructure to assemble and act on lessons. Military academies epitomise how this works; previous and ongoing operations are dissected, new procedures are tried and tested, and student-soldiers are educated about best practices and adapting tactics to field specifics. Career development requires time off for study and reflection before new assignments. Ongoing operations have historians. While critics could ridicule these orientations as a result of institutional 'fat' and overly generous allocations from parliaments, they are better viewed as an essential cultural difference that humanitarians should emulate. It is overly simplistic summarily to dismiss the military for fighting the last war. They devote substantial professional energies to learning lessons; humanitarians virtually never do, but sprint to the next emergency.

Humanitarian culture should switch from reaction to reflection-and-action, from being not simply strong and sincere but also smart. The trademark of humanitarians is responding from the heart. However, an equal dose of well informed tough-mindedness is required. Why? Humanitarian personnel are specific targets of warring parties; insignia no longer afford protection; and emergency responses are but one element of complicated processes of conflict resolution and peacebuilding. With humanitarians competing on two fronts—for resources from donors and for access from belligerents—they also should devote more energy to thinking about goals and roles, ends and means, results and impacts; and to pursuing new strategies, tactics, and tools for contemporary wars.

Reconsidering independence, impartiality, and neutrality has led to a collective identity crisis. In an increasingly competitive marketplace, the proposition here is straightforward: those who are clear about the costs of deviating from guiding principles will be more successful in helping affected populations than those with no principles (opportunists) or with inflexible ones (ideologues).

Modesty is a virtue for aid workers *and* social scientists. Yet many of the most committed humanitarians would have us believe in the humanitarian 'imperative' (see Weiss 2015), the moral obligation to treat affected populations similarly and react to every crisis consistently. No two crises are the same, however, and this notion flies in the face of politics, which consists of drawing lines as well as weighing options and limited resources to make tough decisions about doing the greatest good or the least harm because there invariably will be more humanitarian demand than supply.

A more accurate description of coming to the rescue in today's wars would be the humanitarian 'impulse'—sometimes we should and can act, and sometimes we can but should not. Humanitarian action is desirable, not obligatory. The humanitarian impulse is permissive; the humanitarian imperative is peremptory. Altering the slope of the curves for demand and supply necessitates hard-headed analysis and not the rigid application of moral absolutes. Although fashionable, one humanitarian size, particularly as it was tailored from the cloth of a different epoch, no longer fits.

Frequently, the word 'dilemma' is employed to describe painful decision-making, but the word 'quandary' is more apt. A dilemma involves two or more alternative courses of action with unintended, unavoidable, and *equally* undesirable consequences. If consequences are equally unpalatable, remaining on the sidelines is a viable and moral option. Humanitarians find themselves perplexed, or in a quandary, but they are not and should not be immobilised by contemporary wars. The key lies in making a good-faith effort to analyse the advantages and disadvantages of any military or civilian course of action and opt for what may be the least worst option.

The calculations are agonising but inescapable for those working in today's humanitarian business. The cost of spurning lessons is more than the expense of learning them. Consequentialist ethics are essential.

Conclusion

Approaching contemporary humanitarian action as a deeply militarised and politicised activity that is also commercial will be scandalous to those who see a healing profession based exclusively on values and principles. Most people become humanitarians or donate to aid agencies because they care about alleviating suffering, not because they want to be involved in military and political manipulation or make a profit. But it is myopic to ignore the military and political overlay of contemporary efforts in war zones and the market dynamics of the multibillion dollar business—supply, demand, competition, market distortions, monopolies, cost, price, efficiencies, and investor bias influence how money flows in emergencies, and how aid agencies respond.

Militarisation, politicisation, and marketisation are not the whole truth of the humanitarian project, but they are essential components. It is crucial to understand how the international humanitarian system functions if one hopes to improve its operations and attenuate, if not eliminate, the culture of competition and counter-productivity. Evidence-based and context-driven social science can ameliorate the performance of the humanitarian enterprise. The culture should move away from input- and output-based decisions towards outcomes and impacts. The transformation of war and the marketplace requires the transformation of humanitarianism as well.

Politicisation no less than militarisation calls into question the independence, neutrality, and impartiality that previously were the solid foundations for humanitarian culture and action. These two factors alone would have undermined the dominant, traditional humanitarian culture. But the third and less obvious influence, the humanitarian marketplace, combines with the other two so that today's war zones are distinctly different from earlier ones. Humanitarianism ain't what it used to be, but it could approach its lofty ideals if strategic-thinking were routinely a prelude to strategic-doing.

Notes

1 This chapter was first published as: Thomas G. Weiss, *Humanitarianism's Contested Culture in War Zones* (Global Cooperation Research Papers 8), Duisburg, 2014, doi: 10.14282/2198-0411-GCRP-8.
2 See Weiss (1999, 1–22).
3 International Commission on Intervention and State Sovereignty 2001. Interpretations by commissioners are Evans (2008) and Thakur (2006); see also Bellamy (2009); Orford (2011); Hehir (2012). The author's interpretation is *Humanitarian Intervention: Ideas in Action*, 2nd edn, 2012.
4 Fred Cuny's phrase was popularised by Cohen and Deng (1998a, 10; 1998b, 15).
5 Emphasis in original.
6 This section draws on Hoffman and Weiss (2008).
7 See www.ecbproject.org
8 The authors are guest editors for a special issue devoted to this topic.
9 For a discussion of internal clashes, including among founding and subsequent generations, see Vallaeys (2004); Hopgood (2005).

References

Adebajo A. (2011) *UN Peacekeeping in Africa: From the Suez Crisis to the Sudan Conflicts*, Lynne Rienner, Boulder, CO.

Badie B. (2000) *The Imported State: The Westernization of the Political Order*, Stanford University Press, Stanford, CA.

Barnett M. (2011) *Empire of Humanity: A History of Humanitarianism*, Cornell University Press, Ithaca, NY.

—— and Snyder J. (2008) "The Grand Strategies of Humanitarianism", in M. Barnett and T.G. Weiss, eds, *Humanitarianism in Question: Politics, Power, Ethics*, Cornell University Press, Ithaca, NY, 143–71.

Bass G. (2008) *Freedom's Battle: The Origins of Humanitarian Intervention*, Random House, New York.

Bellamy A.J. (2009) *Responsibility to Protect: The Global Effort to End Mass Atrocities*, Polity Press, Cambridge.

del Castillo G. (2009) *Rebuilding War-Torn States: The Challenge of Post-Conflict Economic Reconstruction*, Oxford University Press, Oxford.

Center on International Cooperation (2013) *Global Peace Operations 2013*, Lynne Rienner, Boulder, CO.

Cohen R. and Deng, F.M. (1998a) *Masses in Flight: The Global Crisis of Internal Displacement*, Brookings Institution, Washington, DC.

—— (1998b) "Exodus within Borders: The Uprooted Who Never Left Home", *Foreign Affairs*, 77 (4), 12–16.

Cooley A. and Ron J. (2002) "The NGO Scramble: Organizational Insecurity and the Political Economy of Transnational Action", *International Security*, 27 (1), 5–39.

Development Initiatives (2009) *Global Humanitarian Assistance Report 2009*, Development Initiatives, Wells, UK (www.globalhumanitarianassistance.org/wp-content/uploads/2009/07/GHA-Report-2009.pdf)

—— (2013) *Global Humanitarian Assistance Report 2013*, Development Initiatives, Wells, UK, (www.globalhumanitarianassistance.org/wp-content/uploads/2013/07/GHA-Report-20131.pdf) accessed 15 April 2015.

Dijkzeul D., Hilhorst D. and Walker P. (2013) "Introduction: Evidence-based Action in Humanitarian Crises", *Disasters*, 37 (S1) (July), s1–s19.

Donini A. (2004) *The Future of Humanitarian Action: Implications of Iraq and Other Recent Crises*, Tufts University, Medford, MA.

Duffield M. (2001) *Global Governance and the New Wars: The Merging of Development and Security*, Zed Books, London.

Evans G. (2008) *The Responsibility to Protect: Ending Mass Atrocity Crimes Once and For All*, Brookings, Washington, DC.

Forsythe D.P. (2005) *The Humanitarians: The International Committee of the Red Cross*, Cambridge University Press, Cambridge.

Fox F. (2001) "New Humanitarianism: Does It Provide a Moral Banner for the 21st Century?", *Disasters*, 25 (4), 275–89.

Hammond L. (2008) "The Power of Holding Humanitarianism Hostage and the Myth of Protective Principles", in M. Barnett and T.G. Weiss, eds, *Humanitarianism in Question: Politics, Power, Ethics*, Cornell University Press, Ithaca, NY, 172–95.

Hehir A. (2012) *The Responsibility to Protect: Rhetoric, Reality and the Future of Humanitarian Intervention*, Palgrave Macmillan, Basingstoke.

Hibou B. (1999) "The 'Social Capital' of the State as an Agent of Deception", in J.-F. Bayart, S. Ellis and B. Hibou, eds, *The Criminalization of the State in Africa*, Indiana University Press, Bloomington, 69–113.

Hoffman P.J. and Weiss T.G. (2006) *Sword and Salve: Confronting New Wars and Humanitarian Crises*, Rowman & Littlefield, Lanham, MD.

—— (2008) "Humanitarianism and Practitioners: Social Science Matters", in M. Barnett and T.G. Weiss, eds, *Humanitarianism in Question: Politics, Power, Ethics*, Cornell University Press, Ithaca, NY, 264–85.

Hopgood S. (2005) *Keepers of the Flame: Amnesty International and the Politics of Authority*, Cornell University Press, Ithaca, NY.

IFRC (2003) *World Disasters Report 2003: Focus on Ethics in War*, Kumarian, West Bloomfield, CT.

International Commission on Intervention and State Sovereignty (2001) *The Responsibility to Protect*, International Development Research Centre, Ottawa.

Jenks B. (2014) "Financing of the UN Development System and the Future of Multilateralism", in T.G. Weiss and A. Erthal Abdenur, eds, special issue of *Third World Quarterly*, 35(10), 1809–28.

Kaldor M. (1999) *New & Old Wars: Organized Violence in a Global Era*, Stanford University Press, Stanford, CA.

Kaplan R. (2000) *The Coming Anarchy: Shattering the Dreams of the Post-Cold War*, Random House, New York.

Keen D. (2000) "Incentives and Disincentives for Violence", in M. Berdal and D. Malone, eds, *Greed and Grievance: Economic Agendas in Civil War*, Lynne Rienner, Boulder, CO, 19–41.

Kennedy D. (2005) *The Dark Sides of Virtue: Reassessing International Humanitarianism*, Princeton University Press, Princeton, NJ.

Kent R. (2004) *Humanitarian Futures: Practical Policy Perspectives*, HPN Paper 46, Humanitarian Practice Network, Overseas Development Institute, London.

Klein N. (2007) *The Shock Doctrine: The Rise of Disaster Capitalism*, Metropolitan Books, New York.

Levine S. and Chastre C. (2004) *Missing the Point: An Analysis of Food Security Interventions in the Great Lakes*, HPN Paper 47, Humanitarian Practice Network, Overseas Development Institute, London.

Loescher G. (2001) *The UNHCR and World Politics: A Perilous Path*, Oxford University Press, Oxford.

Mehlum H., Moene K.O. and Torvik R. (2002) "Plunder & Protection, Inc.", *Journal of Peace Research*, 39 (4), 447–59.

Minear L. (2002) *The Humanitarian Enterprise: Dilemmas and Discoveries*, Kumarian, West Bloomfield, CT.

—— and Weiss T.G. (1993) *Humanitarian Action in Times of War: A Handbook for Practitioners*, Lynne Rienner, Boulder, CO.

Newman E. (2004) "The 'New Wars' Debate: A Historical Perspective Is Needed", *Security Dialogue*, 35 (2), 173–89.

Kalyvas S.N. (2001) "'New' and 'Old' Civil Wars: A Valid Distinction?", *World Politics*, 54 (October), 99–118.

OCHA (2011) *Chapeau of the Mid-Year Review of the Humanitarian Appeal for 2011*, United Nations, Geneva.

Ogata S. (2005) *The Turbulent Decade: Confronting the Refugee Crises of the 1990s*, Norton, New York.

Orford A. (2011) *International Authority and the Responsibility to Protect*, Cambridge University Press, Cambridge.

Oxfam (2003) *Beyond the Headlines: An Agenda for Action to Protect Civilians in Neglected Countries*, Oxfam International, Oxford.

Pictet J. (1979) *The Fundamental Principles of the Red Cross*, ICRC, Geneva.

Pinker, S. (2011). *The Better Angels of Our Nature*, Viking, New York.

Polman L. (2010) *The Crisis Caravan: What's Wrong with Humanitarian Aid?* Henry Holt, New York.

Powell C. (2001) *Remarks to the National Foreign Policy Conference for Leaders of Nongovernmental Organizations*, October 26, http://2001-2009.state.gov/secretary/former/powell/remarks/2001/5762.htm accessed 15 July 2014.

Randel J. and German T. (2002) "Trends in Financing of Humanitarian Assistance", in Joanna Macrae (ed.), *The New Humanitarianisms: A Review of Trends in Global Humanitarian Action*, Overseas Development Institute, London, 19–28.

Reno W. (2000) "Shadow States and the Political Economy of Civil War", in M. Berdal and D. Malone, eds, *Greed and Grievance: Economic Agendas in Civil Wars*, Lynne Rienner, Boulder, CO, 43–68.

Rieff D. (2002a) *A Bed for the Night: Humanitarianism in Crisis*, Simon & Schuster, New York.

—— (2002b) "Humanitarianism in Crisis", *Foreign Affairs*, 81 (6) (November/December), 111–21.

—— (2011) "Afterword", in C. Magone, M. Neuman and F. Weissman, eds, *Humanitarian Negotiations Revealed: The MSF Experience*, Hurst, London, 251–8.

Roberts A. (1993) "Humanitarian War: Military Intervention and Human Rights", *International Affairs*, 69 (3), 429–49.

—— (2002) "The So-Called 'Right of Humanitarian Intervention'", *Yearbook of International Humanitarian Law*, (3), T.M.C. Asser Press, The Hague, 3–51.

Ruggie J.G. (1993) "Territoriality and Beyond: Problematizing Modernity in International Relations", *International Organization*, 47 (1), 139–74.

Shelly L. (1995) "Transnational Organized Crime: An Imminent Threat to the Nation-State", *Journal of International Affairs*, 48 (2), 463–89.

Slim H. (2012) "Marketing Humanitarian Space: Argument and Method in Humanitarian Persuasion", in *Essays In Humanitarian Action*, Oxford Institute for Ethics, Law, and Armed Conflict, University of Oxford, Oxford.

Smillie I. and Minear L. (2004) *The Charity of Nations: Humanitarian Action in a Calculating World*, Kumarian, West Bloomfield, CT.

Stanley Foundation (2003) *UN on the Ground*, Stanley Foundation, Muscatine, IA.

Stedman S.J., Rothchild D. and Cousens E.M., eds (2002) *Ending Civil Wars: The Implementation of Peace Agreements*, Lynne Rienner, Boulder, CO.

Stoddard A., Harmer A. and Haver K. (2006) *Providing Aid in Insecure Environments: Trends in Policy and Operations*, HPG Report 23, Humanitarian Policy Group, Overseas Development Institute, London.

Terry F. (2002) *Condemned to Repeat? The Paradox of Humanitarian Action*, Cornell University Press, Ithaca, NY.

Thakur R. (2006) *The United Nations, Peace and Security: From Collective Security to the Responsibility to Protect*, Cambridge University Press, Cambridge.

Vallaeys A. (2004) *Médécins Sans Frontières: La Biographie*, Fayard, Paris.

de Waal A. (2001) *Famine Crimes*, Indiana University Press, Bloomington, IN.

Walker P. and Russ C. (2010) *Professionalizing the Humanitarian Sector: A Scoping Study*, Report Commissioned by the Enhancing Learning and Research for Humanitarian Assistance, April.

Weinlich S. (2014) "Funding the UN System", in S. Browne and T.G. Weiss, eds, *Post-2015 UN Development: Making Change Happen*, Routledge, London, 75–94.

Weiss T.G. (1999) "Principles, Politics, and Humanitarian Action", *Ethics and International Affairs*, 13, 1–22.

—— (2012) *Humanitarian Intervention: Ideas in Action*, 2nd edn, Polity Press, Cambridge.

—— (2013) *Humanitarian Business*, Polity Press, Cambridge.

—— (2015) "Humanitarian Action and Intervention", in S. von Einsedel, D. Malone and B. Stagno, eds, *The UN Security Council in the 21st Century*, Lynne Rienner, Boulder, CO, 217–34.

—— and Hoffman P.J. (2005) "Making Humanitarianism Work", in S. Chesterman, M. Ignatieff and R. Thakur, eds, *Making States Work: State Failure and the Crisis of Governance*, UN University Press, Tokyo, 296–317.

Wheeler N.J. (2000) *Saving Strangers: Humanitarian Intervention in International Society*, Oxford University Press, Oxford.

Wiener M. (1998) "The Clash of Norms: Dilemmas in Refugee Politics", *Journal of Refugee Studies*, 11 (4), 1–21.

Williams P. (1994) "Transnational Criminal Organizations and International Security", *Survival*, 36 (1), 96–113.

Wood A., Apthorpe R. and Borton J., eds (2001) *Evaluating International Humanitarian Action: Reflections from Practitioners*, Zed Books, London.

2 Humanitarianism reborn

The shift from governing causes to governing effects

David Chandler

Introduction

This chapter seeks to conceptualise a fundamental shift in the understanding of humanitarian intervention, which will be analysed in relation to the decline of traditional disciplinary understandings of sovereignty and increasing scepticism towards Western, liberal or modernist forms of knowledge. Over the past two decades, debates over humanitarian intervention have seen a shift from political concerns of sovereign rights under international law to concerns of knowledge claims of cause and effect highlighted through the problematisation of interventions' unintended consequences. This can be illustrated through contrasting the difference between the confidence – today, critics would say 'hubris' (Mayall and Soares de Oliveira 2011) – of 1990s understandings of the transformative nature of humanitarian intervention with current, much more pessimistic approaches.

In the 1990s, leading advocates understood humanitarian intervention as a clear exercise of Western power in terms of a 'solutionist' approach to problems which could otherwise have increasingly problematic knock-on effects in a global and interconnected world (see, for example, Blair 1999). Today, analysts are much more likely to highlight that the complexity of global interactions and processes mitigates against ambitious schemas for humanitarian intervention – aspiring to address problems at the level of either universalisable or generalisable solutions exported from the West ('top-down' interventions), or through ambitious projects of social and political engineering (attempting to transform society from the 'bottom-up') (see, for example, Ramalingam et al. 2008; Ramalingam 2013).

The governance of effects can therefore be seen as a retreat from the commitments of earlier humanitarian interventionist approaches of the 1990s, in terms of both resources and policy goals. However, the shift from causation to effects involves a shifting conceptualisation of humanitarian intervention itself; it is this conceptual connection which is the central concern of this chapter. Humanitarian intervention conceptualised as the governance of effects relocates the subject position of the intervener in relation to both the problem under consideration – which is no longer amenable to external policy solutions – and the society or community being intervened upon – which is no longer constructed as lacking knowledge or resources,

DOI: 10.4324/9781315658827-4

but as being the key agency of transformation. Transformation comes not through external cause-and-effect policy interventions but through the facilitation or empowerment of local agential capacities. The regulation of effects shifts the focus away from the formal public, legal and political sphere to the more organic and generative sphere of everyday life. The management of effects involves ongoing facilitative engagement in social processes and evades the question of government as political decision-making (see further, Chandler 2014a).

In analysing the radical shifts in the framing of humanitarian intervention from the 1990s to the 2010s, three frameworks or models can be illustrated heuristically. These frameworks can be demarcated both in their conceptualisation of the formal political categories of sovereignty and humanitarian intervention and in their approach to causal knowledge claims. It is these discursive linkages that enable evolving forms of humanitarian intervention, which tend no longer to engage at the level of formal political authority and thus no longer require legitimisation on the basis of hierarchical claims of power or knowledge superiority.

The hierarchy model of humanitarian intervention

The 'solutionist' cause-and-effect model – the archetypal model of intervention in the policy debates of the 1990s and early 2000s (particularly around the legal and political concerns of the right of humanitarian intervention and regime change under the auspices of the War on Terror) – operated on the basis of crisis or the exception. In this framing, the policy-response tended to be one of centralised direction, under United Nations or United States and NATO command, based upon military power or bureaucratic organisation, which often assumed that policy-interveners operated in a vacuum, where social and political norms had broken down, and little attention needed to be given to the particular policy-context.

This hierarchical model was articulated in universalist terms. Intervening states and international institutions were understood to have the power, resources and objective scientific knowledge necessary to solve the problems of conflict and human rights abuses. This framework of intervention reached its apogee in international statebuilding in the Balkans, with long-term protectorates established over Bosnia and Kosovo, and was reflected in the RAND Corporation's reduction of such interventions to simple cost and policy formulae that could be universally applied (Dobbins et al. 2007).

Debates in the early and mid-1990s assumed that Western states had the knowledge and power to act and therefore focused on the question of the political will of Western states (see, for example, Held 1995; Wheeler 2000). Of particular concern was the fear that the United States might pursue national interests rather than global moral and ethical concerns (Kaldor 2007, 150). In this framework, problems were seen in terms of a universalist and linear understanding. For 'solutionists', humanitarian and human rights interventions, even including regime change and post-conflict management, could be successful on the basis that a specific set of policy solutions could solve a specific set of policy problems. This set up a universalist understanding of good policy making – the idea that certain solutions were timeless and could be exported or imposed – like the rule of law, democracy and markets.

This policy framework was highly mechanistic. The problems of non-Western states were understood in simple terms of the need to restore the equilibrium of the status quo – which was understood as being disrupted by new forces or events. Illustrated, for example, in the popular 'New Wars' thesis, which argued that stability was disrupted by exploitative elites seeking to destabilise society in order to cling to resources and power (Kaldor 1999), or that the lack of human rights could be resolved through constitutional reforms (Brandt et al. 2011). The assumption was that society was fundamentally healthy and that the problematic individuals or groups could be removed or replaced through external policy-intervention which would enable equilibrium to be restored. This was a mechanistic view of how societies operated – as if they were machines and a single part had broken down and needed to be fixed. There was no holistic engagement with society as a collective set of processes, interactions and inter-relations. The assumption was that external policy interveners could come up with a 'quick fix' – perhaps sending troops to quell conflict, or legal experts to write constitutions – followed by an exit strategy.

The universalist framework legitimising humanitarian intervention thereby established a hierarchical and paternalist framework of understanding. Western liberal democratic states were understood to have the knowledge and power necessary to solve the problems that other 'failed' and 'failing' states were alleged to lack. It was therefore little surprise that these interventions challenged the sovereign rights to self-government, which had long been upheld after decolonisation in the 1950s and 1960s. Many commentators have raised problems with the idealisation of liberal Western societies and the holding up of abstract and unrealistic goals which tended to exaggerate the incapacity or lack of legitimacy of non-Western regimes (see, for example, Heathershaw and Lambach 2008; Lemay-Hébert 2009). Beneath the universalist humanitarian claims of promoting the interest of human rights, human security or human development, critical theorists suggested new forms of international domination were emerging, institutionalising market inequalities or restoring traditional hierarchies of power reminiscent of the colonial era (see, for example, Chandler 1999; 2006; Bain 2003; Bickerton et al. 2007; Hehir and Robinson 2007; Douzinas 2007; Duffield 2007; Pugh et al. 2008; Dillon and Reid 2009; Barnett 2010).

However, the problems with humanitarian intervention went much deeper than problems of the challenge to the hierarchy of power. The critique of humanitarianism extended to the knowledge assumptions at play in Western discourses. The knowledge critique, in fact, was more devastating than the critique of power inequalities, and combined they appeared fatal to morally or ethically motivated forms of international humanitarian intervention. As Tom Weiss succinctly puts it, it appears that humanitarians no longer are necessarily on the side of the angels. Something seems to have gone wrong with the humanitarian intervention paradigm, so that 'their motivations and mastery, their principles and products are questioned from within and from without' (ibid.). The issue at stake is the analysis of this sea-change in understanding. Whilst Weiss argues that the problems can be addressed through an increased professionalisation of humanitarian actors, this chapter seeks to draw out the broader shifts in both policy practices and conceptual discourses, which reflect much deeper ontological concerns over the traditional hierarchical models of power and linear epistemes of knowledge presupposed by the humanitarian paradigm, and which often go entirely unchallenged in the discussion of it.

The pluralist model of humanitarian intervention

The 'solutionist' perspective, with its clear hierarchies of power and knowledge, began to be transformed with less linear and universal and more plural and endogenous views of causation. This shift began to be articulated in ways which understood sovereignty and intervention to be compatible, becoming increasingly predominant in the 2000s. This second model took local context much more into account, understanding problems as results of complex processes of social and historical path dependencies that needed to be careful intervened in and adjusted. Thus the relation between external intervening actors (as agents or causes of policy changes) and the subsequent policy outcomes becomes understood to be much more socially, politically and historically mediated and contingent. This model is exemplified by the work of Roland Paris in the early 2000s on the need for 'institutionalisation before liberalisation', in which it was argued that external interventions needed to work 'bottom-up' on the social and historical preconditions for statebuilding, rather than 'top-down' with the wholesale export of Western models and assumptions (Paris 2004).

This model was popularised in the discipline of International Relations by Stephen Krasner, who argued that the concept of sovereignty could be 'unbundled' into three types of sovereignty: international legal sovereignty, the right to formal legal recognition; domestic sovereignty, the capacity to maintain human rights and good governance; and 'Westphalian sovereignty', the medieval concept of autonomy and self government, where whatever the Prince declared right was accepted as law (2004, 2005). Krasner argued that fragile states, which lacked the full capacities of domestic sovereignty, required international intervention, but that this intervention should not be viewed as undermining sovereignty. Instead, international legal sovereignty should be used to sign international agreements allowing external governing intervention in order to build sovereignty, understood as a set of functional capacities. In this way, the Westphalian sovereignty of political autonomy was weakened, but in exchange for the strengthening of domestic sovereignty.

This position gained further traction as international statebuilding and the extension of peacekeeping interventions led international interveners to expand the remits of their humanitarian policy interventions well beyond the initial problem-solving policy-interventions with their short time-spans and exit strategies. The response to the shock terrorist attacks of 9/11 appeared to intensify the trend towards extended international policy-interventionism. The 2002 US

National Security Strategy expanded and securitised the interventionist remit, arguing that: 'America is now threatened less by conquering states than we are by failing ones' (NSS 2002, 1). The recognition that we lived in a globalised and interconnected world seemed to bind the needs of national security with those of human rights, democracy and development, creating a powerful interventionist consensus around humanitarian-driven conceptions of intervention as building rather than undermining sovereignty (see Mazarr 2014).

Pluralist framings of humanitarian intervention shifted the focus away from addressing causes in universal and linear ways and towards a focus on endogenous processes and new institutionalist framings; easing a transition to the governance of effects. Rather than going for quick problem-solving fixes, policy advocates increasingly argued that policy needed to be concerned more holistically with social processes and analysis of state–society relations in order to overcome the 'sovereignty gap' (Ghani et al. 2005; Ghani and Lockhart 2008). However, this perspective can still be understood as having some legacies of universalist cause-and-effect understandings in that it aimed at establishing viable market-based democracies and still presupposed that external policy-interveners had the necessary superior knowledge and resources to shape policy outcomes (see, for example, Bliesemann de Guevara 2012; Kühn 2011; Tadjbakhsh 2011).

Humanitarian intervention without hierarchies of power and knowledge?

The third form of intervention, that of governing effects without a concern for causation, increasingly prevalent today, is a framing that entirely evades any discussion of the relationship between intervention and sovereignty. Western policy-interveners increasingly claim not to be taking over decision-making processes, to be setting external goals, or to be measuring progress using external yardsticks. Rather than the external provision of policy solutions or the use of 'conditionality' to guide states in specific directions, international actors are more likely to understand intervention in terms of enabling organic systems and existing knowledges, practices and capacities. This model forwards more homeopathic forms of policy-intervention designed to enhance autonomous processes rather than undermine or socially engineer them (see, for example, Drabek and McEntire 2003; Kaufmann 2013, on emergent responses to disasters). These forms of intervention cannot be grasped within the paradigm of claims for political authority central to the discipline of International Relations.

The shift from humanitarian intervention at the level of causation to intervention at the level of effects has been discussed predominantly in relation to the need to take into account the 'law of unintended consequences'. The problem of 'unintended consequences' has become a policy trope regularly used as a shorthand expression for the profound shift in the understanding of intervention addressed in this article, and can be understood as a generalised extension of Ulrich Beck's view of 'risk society' with the determinate causal role of 'side effects', or of Bruno Latour's similar analysis of today's world as modernity 'plus all its externalities' (see further, Beck 1992; Latour 2003). It seems that there is no way to consider intervention in terms of intended outcomes without considering the possibility that the unintended outcomes will outweigh these.

While, in 2002, the US State Department was focusing on extensive statebuilding operations to address the crucial question of state failure, in 2012, a decade later, the US Defence Strategic Guidance policy is illustrative of a different set of assumptions: that US forces would pursue their objectives through 'innovative, low-cost, and small-footprint approaches' rather than the conduct of 'large-scale, prolonged stability operations' (DSG 2012, 3, 6). In 2013, discussion over potential coercive intervention in Syria was dominated by fears that the unintended outcomes would outweigh the good intentions of external actors (Ackerman 2013). General Martin Dempsey, chairman of the US Joint Chiefs of Staff, warned that policy caution was necessary as: 'We must anticipate and be prepared for the unintended consequences of our action' (Ackerman 2013; see also Phillips 2013).

As Michael Mazarr argued in the influential US foreign policy journal *Foreign Affairs* in 2014, securing US goals of peace, democracy and development in failing and conflict-ridden states could not, in fact, be done by instrumental cause-and-effect external policy-interventions: 'It is an organic, grass-roots process that must respect the unique social, cultural, economic, political, and religious contexts of each country ... and cannot be imposed' (Mazarr 2014). For Mazarr, policy would now follow a more 'resilient mindset, one that treats perturbations as inevitable rather than calamitous and resists the urge to overreact', understanding that policy-intervention must work with rather than against local institutions and 'proceed more organically and authentically' (Mazarr 2014). This shift is also reflected by high-level policy experts in the US State Department; according to Charles T. Call, senior adviser at the Bureau of Conflict and Stabilization Operations, current US approaches seek not to impose unrealistic external goals but instead to facilitate local transformative agency through engaging with local 'organic processes and plussing them up' (cited in Chandler 2014b).

Humanitarian intervention, today, is increasingly understood to be problematic if it is based upon the grand narratives of liberal internationalism, which informed and drove the debate on international intervention in the 1990s, when issues of intervention and non-intervention in Africa and the Balkans were at the centre of international political contestation. International humanitarian intervention is not opposed per se or on principle, but on the basis of the universalist and hierarchical knowledge assumptions which informed policy-interventions and produced the hubristic and reductionist promises of transformative outcomes (see, for example, Owen 2012; Stewart and Knaus 2012; Mayall and Soares de Oliveira 2011; Mazarr 2014).

'Organic' versus 'political' understandings of humanitarian intervention

The critique of cause-and-effect understandings of humanitarian intervention has a long scientific heritage in similar critiques of modern medical interventions based upon antibiotics and other artificial chemical and technical remedies (see, for example, Thacker and Artlett 2012; Krans 2014; O'Neal et al. 2014, 877–8). The reductionist understanding of intervention in the biomedical sciences has often been problematised for its lack of attention to unintended consequences, which can easily mean that the cure can be worse for individual and societal healthcare than the initial affliction. These critiques have operated as a readily available template for the rapid development of a critical conceptualisation of intervention in the discipline of International Relations; one that bears little relation to traditional concerns of international stability, international law, sovereign rights of independence or post-colonial sensibilities.

These critiques of linear and reductionist cause-and-effect approaches have tended to focus upon the value of organic, natural, or endogenous powers of resistance and resilience which have been understood to be unintentionally undermined through the mechanistic assumptions of modern Western science (see, for example, Capra 1983, 118–165). In the parallel arguments in discourses of humanitarian intervention and statebuilding, the organic processes of endogenous development tend to be prioritised over universalising, mechanistic or reductionist approaches to policy-intervention which seek to introduce policy-solutions from the outside. For example, while markets, development, democracy, security and the rule of law might be good when they develop organically, it is often argued that when they are extracted from their context and applied in a 'pure' form they can be dangerous as they lack the other ingredients connected to institutions and culture.

This perspective first began to be argued in relation to humanitarian intervention in the Balkans in the late 1990s, when interventionist policy-making began to shift attention to the endogenous or internal capacities and capabilities of the local society rather than seeking externally managed 'military solutions, quick fixes [and] easy, early exits', associated with simple cause-and-effect understandings (Bildt 2003). However, the critique of cause-and-effect assumptions, which focused on the knowledge and expertise of external policy-interveners, rapidly extended beyond the critique of coercive or military interventions to cover a broad range of policy-interventions, including 'bottom-up' attempts at socio-political engineering, associated with liberal internationalist goals of promoting markets, democracy and the rule of law.

The governance of effects, increasingly taken up by international policy-interveners, thereby insists that humanitarian problems cannot be dealt with merely at the level of causation, by identifying and categorising a problem as if it could be understood in the reductionist terms of cause-and-effect. Intervention based on the governance of effects therefore has no need for ready-made international policy solutions that can simply be applied or implemented, and therefore implies little possibility of learning generic lessons from intervention that could be applied to all other cases of conflict or of underdevelopment on the basis that if the symptoms appeared similar the cause must be the same. Crucially, this framing takes intervention out of the context of policy-making and policy-understanding and out of the political sphere of democratic debate and decision-making.

The focus therefore shifts away from international policies (supply-driven policy-making) and towards engaging with the internal capacities and capabilities that are already held to exist. In other words, there is a shift from the agency, knowledge and practices of humanitarian policy-interveners to that of the society which is the object of policy-concerns. As the 2013 updated UK Department for International Development (DfID) Growth and Resilience Operational Plan states: 'We will produce less "supply-driven" development of product, guidelines and policy papers, and foster peer-to-peer, horizontal learning and knowledge exchange, exploiting new technologies such as wiki/huddles to promote the widest interaction between stakeholders' (DfID 2013, 8).

'Supply-driven' policies – the stuff of politics and of democratic decision-making – are understood to operate in an artificial or non-organic way, and to lack an authentic connection to the effects which need to be addressed. The imposition of (accountable) external institutional and policy-frameworks has increasingly become seen as artificial and thereby as having counterproductive or unintended outcomes. Effects-based approaches thereby seek to move away from the 'liberal peace' policy-interventions – seeking to export constitutional frameworks, to train and equip military and police forces, to impose external conditionalities on the running of state budgets, to export managerial frameworks for civil servants and political representatives, or to impose regulations to ensure administrative transparency and codes of conduct – which were at the heart of international policy prescriptions in the 1990s and early 2000s (World Bank 2007; Eurodad 2006; ActionAid 2006).

It is argued that the 'supply-driven' approach of external experts exporting or developing liberal institutions does not grasp the complex processes generative of instability or insecurity. Instead, the cause-and-effect model of intervention is seen to create problematic 'hybrid' political systems and fragile states with little connection to their societies (Roberts 2008; Mac Ginty 2010; Richmond and Mitchell 2012; Millar 2014). The imposition of institutional frameworks, which have little connection to society, is understood as failing, not only in not addressing causal processes, but in making matters worse through undermining local capacities to manage the effects of problems, shifting problems elsewhere and leaving states and societies even more fragile or vulnerable.

This approach is alleged to fail to hear the 'message' of problematic manifestations or to enable societies' own organic and homeostatic processes to generate corrective mechanisms. Triggering external humanitarian interventions is said to shortcut the ability of societies to reflect upon and take responsibility for their own affairs, and is increasingly seen as a counterproductive 'over-reaction' by external powers (see further, Desch 2008; Maor 2012). There is an increasingly prevalent view that, contrary to earlier assumptions, policy solutions can be developed only through practice by actors on the ground.

As noted above, the conceptualisation of humanitarian interventions in terms of the governance of effects evades the traditional disciplinary understanding of intervention as an exercise of external political power and authority. It does this through denying intervention as an act of external decision-making and policy-direction as understood in the political paradigm of liberal modernist discourse.

This can be illustrated through highlighting some examples of policy shifts in key areas of international concern: security and the rule of law; development; and democracy and rights.

Security and the rule of law

Humanitarian interventions are increasingly shifting in relation to the understanding of conflict. There is much less talk of conflict prevention or conflict resolution and more of conflict management. As the UK government argues, in a 2011 combined DfID, Foreign and Commonwealth Office and Ministry of Defence document, conflict per se is not the problem: 'Conflict is a normal part of human interaction, the natural result when individuals and groups have incompatible needs, interests or beliefs' (DfID et al. 2011, 5). The problem which needs to be tackled is the state or society's ability to manage conflict: 'In stable, resilient societies conflict is managed through numerous formal and informal institutions' (DfID et al. 2011, 5). Conflict management, as the UK government policy indicates, is increasingly understood as an organic set of societal processes and practices, which international policy-intervention can influence, but solutions to which cannot be imported from outside or imposed. This understanding very much follows the approach long advocated by influential peace theorist Jean Paul Lederach, who argued that: 'The greatest resource for sustaining peace in the long term is always rooted in the local people and their culture' (1997, 94). For Lederach, managing conflict meant moving away from cause-and-effect forms of instrumental external intervention which see people as 'recipients' of policy, and instead seeing people as 'resources', integral to peace processes. Therefore it was essential that:

> we in the international community adopt a new mind-set – that we move beyond a simple prescription of answers and modalities for dealing with conflict that come from outside the setting and focus at least as much attention on discovering and empowering the resources, modalities, and mechanisms for building peace that exist within the context.
>
> (Lederach 1997, 95)

One of the central shifts in understanding conflict as something that needs to be 'coped with' and 'managed' rather than something that can be 'solved' or 'prevented' is the view that state-level interventions are of limited use. Peace treaties can be signed by state parties, but unless peace is seen as an ongoing and transformative inclusive societal process, these agreements will be merely superficial and non-sustainable (ibid., 135).

Just as peace and security are less understood as able to be secured through cause-and-effect forms of intervention, reliant on policy-interveners imposing solutions in mechanical and reductive ways, there has also been a shift in understanding the counterproductive effects of attempts to export the rule of law (Cesarini and Hite 2004; Zimmermann 2007; Chandler 2014b). The governance-of-effects approach is driven by a realisation of the gap between the formal sphere of law and constitutionalism and the social 'reality' of informal power relations and informal rules. This perspective has also been endorsed by Douglass North, the policy guru of new institutionalist economics, who has highlighted the difficulties of understanding how exported institutions will interact with 'culturally derived norms of behavior' (1990, 140). The social reality of countries undergoing post-conflict 'transition' is thereby less capable of being understood merely by an analysis of laws and statutes. In fact, there increasingly appears to be an unbridgeable gap between the artificial constructions of legal and constitutional frameworks and the realities of everyday life, revealed in dealings between individual members of the public and state authorities.

Development

A key policy area where the shift from addressing causes to the governance of effects has had an impact has been in the sphere of development – the policy sphere previously most concerned with transformative policy interventions. Coping with poverty and with disasters is clearly a very different problematic from seeking to use development policy to reduce, or to end, extreme poverty. However, discourses of disaster risk reduction have increasingly displaced those of sustainable forms of development because of the unintended side effects of undermining the organic coping mechanisms of communities and therefore increasing vulnerabilities and weakening resilience (see, for example, IRDR 2014; UNDP 2014). Claudia Aradau has highlighted the importance of the UK DfID's shift in priorities from poverty reduction strategies to developing community resilience, which assumes the existence of poverty as the basis of policy-making (Aradau 2014). As she states: 'resilience responses entail a change in how poverty, development and security more broadly are envisaged'; this is clearly highlighted in DfID's 2011 report outlining the UK government's humanitarian policy:

> Humanitarian assistance should be delivered in a way that does not undermine existing coping mechanisms and helps a community build its own resilience for the future. National governments in at-risk countries can ensure that disaster risk management policies and strategies are linked to community-level action.
>
> (DfID 2011, 10, cited in Aradau 2014)

As George Nicholson, Director of Transport and Disaster Risk Reduction for the Association of Caribbean States, argues explicitly: 'improving a person's ability to respond to and cope with a disaster event must be placed on equal footing with the process to encourage economic development', highlighting the importance of disaster risk as a strategy for managing effects versus the cause-and-effect approach associated with development policy interventions (Nicholson 2014). Whereas development approaches put the emphasis on external policy assistance and expert knowledge, disaster risk reduction clearly counterposes an alternative framework of intervention, where it is local knowledge and local agency that counts the most. Disaster risk reduction strategies stress the empowerment of the vulnerable and marginalised in order for them to cope and to manage the effects of the risks and contingencies that are concomitant with the maintenance of their precarious existence.

Democracy and rights

As emphasised above, the management-of-effects approach does not seek to assert sovereign power or Western hierarchies of power and knowledge; in fact, the governance of effects operates as both an epistemological and ontological challenge to the cause-and-effect understandings of intervention, dominant until the previous decade. These points are highlighted, to take a recent example, in Bruno Latour's critical engagement with modernist modes of understanding: arguing that Western societies have forgotten the lengthy processes which enabled them to build liberal institutions dependent on the establishment of a political culture, which has to be steadily maintained, renewed and extended and cannot be exported or imposed (Latour 2013, 343).

This shift away from formal universalist understandings of democracy and human rights is increasingly evidenced in the shifting understanding of human rights-based approaches to empowerment. Understanding empowerment in instrumental cause-and-effect terms based upon the external provision of legal and political mechanisms for claims is increasingly seen to be ineffective. Rights-based NGOs now seek not to empower people to access formal institutional mechanisms, but to enable them to empower themselves. The governance-of-effects approach places the emphasis on the agency and self-empowerment of local actors, not on the introduction of formal frameworks of law, supported by international human rights norms (Moe and Simojoki 2013, 404).

The approach of 'finding organic processes and plussing them up' (as articulated by the US State Department policy advisor, cited above) is not limited to government policy-interventions but has increasingly been taken up as a generic approach to overcome the limits of cause-and-effect understandings. A study of Finnish development NGOs highlights that rather than instrumentally selecting groups or civil society elites, new forms of intervention appear as anti-intervention, denying any external role in this process and stressing that there is no process of external management or selection as policy-interveners work with whatever groups or associations already exist and 'have just come together … it is not our NGO that brought them together but we just found them that way' (Kontinen 2014).

A similar study, in south-eastern Senegal, notes that humanitarian interveners are concerned to avoid the 'moral imperialism' of imposing Western human rights norms, but also to avoid a moral relativism which merely accepts local traditional practices (Gillespie and Melching 2010, 481). The solution forwarded is that of being non-prescriptive and avoiding and 'unlearning' views of Western teachers as 'authorities' and students as passive recipients (ibid., 481). Humanitarian intervention is articulated as the facilitation of local people's attempts to uncover traditional practices and in 'awakening' and 'engaging' their already existing capacities: 'By detecting their own inherent skills, they can more easily transfer them to personal and community problem solving' (ibid., 490). These processes can perhaps be encouraged or assisted by external policy-interveners but they cannot be transplanted from one society to another; still less can they be imposed by policy-actors.

Conclusion

The shift in understanding humanitarian intervention from addressing causes to the governance of effects, focusing on the problem society's own capacities and needs and internal and organic processes, has been paralleled by a growing scepticism of attempts to export or impose Western models. The governance of effects thereby evades the political problematic of sovereign power and is often understood as non-interventionist because of its organicist conceptualisation. Interventions of this sort require no specialist knowledge and, in fact, tend to problematise such knowledge claims, and instead could be understood to require more therapeutic capacities and sensitivities, more attuned to open and unscripted forms of engagement, mutual processes of learning and unpredictable and spontaneous forms of knowledge exchange (see for example Duffield 2007, 233–4; Jabri 2007, 177; Brigg and Muller 2009, 130).

   In the illustrative examples of the governance of effects, given above, it is clear that problems are no longer conceived as amenable to political solutions in terms of instrumental humanitarian interventions on the basis of cause-and-effect understandings. Those subject to new forms of empowerment and capacity-building are not understood as citizens of states – capable of negotiating, debating, deciding and implementing policy agendas – but instead are caught up in never-ending processes of governing effects at the local or community level. Politics disappears from the equation, and with it the clash of the co-constitutive concepts of sovereignty and intervention and the legitimating claims of power and knowledge through which these claims were contested.

References

Ackerman S. (2013) "US Military Intervention in Syria would Create 'Unintended Consequences'", *The Guardian*, 22 July (www.theguardian.com/world/2013/jul/22/us-military-intervention-syria), accessed 5 May 2015.

ActionAid (2006) *What Progress? A Shadow Review of World Bank Conditionality*, Action Aid, Johannesburg (www.actionaid.org.uk/sites/default/files/what_progress.pdf), accessed 5 May 2015.

Aradau C. (2014) "The Promise of Security: Resilience, Surprise and Epistemic Politics", *Resilience: International Practices, Policies and Discourses*, 2(2), 73–87.

Bain W. (2003) *Between Anarchy and Society: Trusteeship and the Obligations of Power*, Oxford University Press, Oxford.

Barnett M.N. (2010) *The International Humanitarian Order*, Routledge, Abingdon.

Beck U. (1992) *Risk Society: Towards a New Modernity*, Sage, London.

Bickerton C.J., Cunliffe P. and Gourevitch A. eds (2007) *Politics without Sovereignty: A Critique of Contemporary International Relations*, University College London Press, Abingdon.

Bildt C. (2003) "Europe's Future in the Mirror of the Balkans", *openDemocracy*, 3 April (www.opendemocracy.net/democracy-open_politics/article_1123.jsp), accessed 27 April 2015.

Blair T. (1999) "Doctrine of the International Community", 24 April (http://webarchive.nationalarchives.gov.uk/+/www.number10.gov.uk/Page1297), accessed 30 April 2015.

Bliesemann de Guevara B. ed. (2012) *Statebuilding and State-Formation: The Political Sociology of Intervention*, Routledge, London.

Brandt M., Cottrell J., Ghai Y. and Regan A. (2011) *Constitution-making and Reform: Options for the Process*, Interpeace, Geneva (www.constitutionmakingforpeace.org/sites/default/files/Constitution-Making-Handbook.pdf), accessed 4 May 2015.

Brigg M. and Muller K. (2009) "Conceptualising Culture in Conflict Resolution", *Journal of Intercultural Studies*, 3(2), 121–140.

Capra F. (1983) *The Turning Point: Science, Society and the Rising Culture*, Flamingo, London.

Cesarini P. and Hite K. (2004) "Introducing the Concept of Authoritarian Legacies", in Hite K. and Cesarini P. eds, *Authoritarian Legacies and Democracy in Latin America and Southern Europe*, University of Notre Dame Press, Notre Dame, IN.

Chandler D. (1999) *Bosnia: Faking Democracy after Dayton*, Pluto, London.

Chandler D. (2006) *Empire in Denial: The Politics of State-Building*, Pluto, London.

Chandler D. (2014a) "Democracy Unbound? Non-Linear Politics and the Politicisation of Everyday Life", *European Journal of Social Theory*, 17(1), 42–59.

Chandler D. (2014b) "Resilience and the 'Everyday': Beyond the Paradox of 'Liberal Peace'", *Review of International Studies*, 40(1), 27–48.

Collier P. (2010) *War, Guns and Votes: Democracy in Dangerous Places*, Vintage, London.

Desch M.C. (2008) "America's Liberal Illiberalism: The Ideological Origins of Overreaction in US Foreign Policy", *International Security*, 32(3), 7–43.

DfID (2011) *Saving Lives, Preventing Suffering and Building Resilience: The UK Government's Humanitarian Policy*, Department for International Development, London.

DfID (2013) *Operational Plan 2011–2015 DFID Growth and Resilience Department*, Department for International Development, London.

DfID et al. (2011) *Building Stability Overseas Strategy*, Department for International Development, Foreign and Commonwealth Office and Ministry of Defence, London.

Dillon M. and Reid J. (2009) *The Liberal Way of War: Killing to Make Life Live*, Routledge, London.

Dobbins J., Jones S.G., Crane K. and DeGrasse B.C. (2007) *The Beginner's Guide to Nation-Building*, RAND, Santa Monica, CA.

Douzinas C. (2007) *Human Rights and Empire: The Political Philosophy of Cosmopolitanism*, Routledge-Cavendish, Abingdon.

Drabek T.E. and McEntire D.A. (2003) "Emergent Phenomena and the Sociology of Disaster: Lessons, Trends and Opportunities from the Research Literature", *Disaster, Prevention and Management*, 12(2), 97–112.

DSG (2012) *Sustaining US Global Leadership: Priorities for 21st Century Defense*, White House, Washington, DC.

Duffield M. (2007) *Development, Security and Unending War: Governing the World of Peoples*, Polity, Cambridge.

Eurodad (2006) *World Bank and IMF Conditionality: A Development Injustice*, European Network on Debt and Development, Brussels (www.eurodad.org/uploadedfiles/whats_new/reports/eurodad_world_bank_and_imf_conditionality_report.pdf), accessed 4 May 2015.

Ghani A., Lockhart C. (2008) *Fixing Failed States: A Framework for Rebuilding a Fractured World*, Oxford University Press, Oxford.

Ghani A., Lockhart C. and Carnahan M. (2005) "Closing the Sovereignty Gap: an Approach to State-Building", Working Paper, No. 253, Overseas Development Institute, London.

Gillespie D. and Melching M. (2010) "The Transformative Power of Democracy and Human Rights in Nonformal Education: The Case of Tostan", *Adult Education Quarterly*, 60(5), 477–98.

Held D. (1995) *Democracy and the Global Order: From the Modern State to Cosmopolitan Governance*, Polity, Cambridge.

Heathershaw J. and Lambach D. (2008) "Introduction: Post-Conflict Spaces and Approaches to Statebuilding", *Journal of Intervention and Statebuilding*, 2(3), 269–89.

Hehir A. and Robinson N. eds (2007) *State-Building: Theory and Practice*, Routledge, Abingdon.

IRDR (2014) *Integrated Research on Disaster Risk programme*, Issue Brief: Disaster Risk Reduction and Sustainable Development, Institute for Risk and Disaster Reduction (IRDR), University College London (www.preventionweb.net/english/professional/publications/v.php?id=35831), accessed 30 April 2015.

Jabri V. (2007) *War and the Transformation of Global Politics*, Palgrave, Basingstoke.

Kaldor M. (1999) *New and Old Wars: Organized Violence in a Global Era*, Polity, Cambridge.

Kaldor M. (2007) *Human Security: Reflections on Globalization and Intervention*, Polity, Cambridge.

Kaufmann M. (2013) 'Emergent Self-Organisation in Emergencies: Resilience Rationales in Interconnected Societies', *Resilience: International Policies, Practices and Discourses*, 1(1), 53–68.

Kontinen T. (2014) "Rights-based approach in practice? Dilemmas of empowerment in a development NGO" unpublished paper, presented at 'After Human Rights' workshop, University of Helsinki, 13–14 March.

Krans B. (2014) "5 Frightening Consequences of Overusing Antibiotics", *HealthlineNews*, 11 March (www.healthline.com/health-news/five-unintended-consequences-antibiotic-overuse-031114), accessed 2 May 2015.

Krasner S.D. (2004) "Sharing Sovereignty: New Institutions for Collapsed and Failing States", *International Security*, 29(2), 85–120.

Krasner S.D. (2005) "The Case for Shared Sovereignty", *Journal of Democracy*, 16(1), 69–83.

Kühn F.P. (2011) "Less is More: International Intervention and the Limits of External Stabilization", *Canadian Foreign Policy Journal*, 17(1), 62–74.

Latour B. (2003) "Is Re-modernization Occurring – And If So, How to Prove It? A Commentary on Ulrich Beck", *Theory, Culture & Society*, 20(2), 35–48.

Latour B. (2013) *An Inquiry into Modes of Existence: An Anthropology of the Moderns*, Harvard University Press, Cambridge, MA.

Lederach J.P. (1997) *Building Peace: Sustainable Reconciliation in Divided Societies*, United States Institute of Peace, Washington, DC.

Lemay-Hébert N. (2009) "Statebuilding without Nation-building? Legitimacy, State Failure and the Limits of the Institutionalist Approach", *Journal of Intervention and Statebuilding*, 3(1), 21–45.

Mac Ginty R. (2010) "Hybrid Peace: The Interaction between Top-Down and Bottom-Up Peace", *Security Dialogue*, 41(4), 391–412.

Maor M. (2012) "Policy Overreaction", working paper, Hebrew University of Jerusalem (http://portal.idc.ac.il/he/schools/government/research/documents/maor.pdf), accessed 2 May 2015.

Mayall J. and Soares de Oliviera R. eds (2011) *The New Protectorates: International Tutelage and the Making of Liberal States*, Hurst & Co., London.

Mazarr M.J. (2014) "The Rise and Fall of the Failed-State Paradigm: Requiem for a Decade of Distraction", *Foreign Affairs*, Jan/Feb (www.foreignaffairs.com/articles/140347/michael-j-mazarr/the-rise-and-fall-of-the-failed-state-paradigm), accessed 30 April 2015.

Millar G. (2014) "Disaggregating Hybridity: Why Hybrid Institutions do not Produce Predictable Experiences of Peace", *Journal of Peace Research*, 51(4), 501–14.

Moe L.W. and Simojoki M.V. (2013) "Custom, Contestation and Cooperation: Peace and Justice in Somaliland", *Conflict, Security & Development*, 13(4), 393–416.

Nicholson G. (2014) "Inequality and its Impact on the Resilience Of Societies", Association of Caribbean States, 22 July (www.eturbonews.com/48253/inequality-and-its-impact-resilience-societies), accessed 5 May 2015.

North D.C. (1990) *Institutions, Institutional Change and Economic Performance*, Cambridge University Press, Cambridge.

NSS (2002) *The National Security Strategy of the United States of America*, White House, Washington, DC. (www.state.gov/documents/organization/63562.pdf), accessed 6 May 2015.

O'Neal H., Thomas C.B. and Karam G. (2014) "Principles Governing Antimicrobial Therapy in the Intensive Care Unit", in J.E. Parrillo and R.P. Dellinger eds, *Critical Care Medicine: Principles of Diagnosis and Management in the Adult*, Elsevier, Philadelphia, PA.

Owen D. (2012) *The Hubris Syndrome: Bush, Blair and the Intoxication of Power*, revised edn, Methuen, York.

Paris R. (2004) *At War's End: Building Peace after Civil Conflict*, Cambridge University Press, Cambridge.

Phillips D.L. (2013) "Unintended Consequences of Striking Syria", *World Post*, 11 September (www.huffingtonpost.com/david-l-phillips/unintended-consequneces-o_b_3902414.html), accessed 2 May 2015.

Pugh M., Cooper N. and Turner M. eds (2008) *Whose Peace? Critical Perspectives on the Political Economy of Peacebuilding*, Palgrave Macmillan, London.

Ramalingam B. (2013) *Aid on the Edge of Chaos: Rethinking International Cooperation in a Complex World*, Oxford University Press, Oxford.

Ramalingam B., Jones H., Reba T. and Young J. (2008) *Exploring the Science of Complexity: Ideas and Implications for Development and Humanitarian Efforts*, ODI Working Paper 285, Overseas Development Institute, London.

Richmond O.P. and Mitchel, A. eds (2012) *Hybrid Forms of Peace: From Everyday Agency to Post-Liberalism*, Palgrave, Basingstoke.

Roberts D. (2008) "Hybrid Polities and Indigenous Pluralities: Advanced Lessons in Statebuilding from Cambodia", *Journal of Intervention and Statebuilding*, 2(1), 63–86.

Stewart R. and Knaus G. (2012) *Can Intervention Work?* W. W. Norton & Co, London.

Tadjbakhsh S. ed. (2011) *Rethinking the Liberal Peace: External Models and Local Alternatives*, Routledge, London.

Thacker J.D. and Artlett C.M. (2012) "The Law of Unintended Consequences and Antibiotics", *Open Journal of Immunology*, 2(2), 59–64.

UNDP (2014) *Disaster Risk Reduction Makes Development Sustainable*, United Nations Development Programme, New York (www.undp.org/content/dam/undp/library/crisis%20prevention/UNDP_CPR_CTA_20140901.pdf), accessed 28 April 2015.

Wheeler N.J. (2000) *Saving Strangers: Humanitarian Intervention in International Society*, Oxford University Press, Oxford.

World Bank (2007) *Conditionality in Development Policy Lending*, World Bank, Washington, DC (http://siteresources.worldbank.org/PROJECTS/Resources/40940-1114615847489/Conditionalityfinalreport120407.pdf), accessed 2 May 2015.

Zimmermann A. (2007) "The Rule of Law as a Culture of Legality: Legal and Extra-legal Elements for the Realisation of the Rule of Law in Society", *ELaw –Murdoch University Electronic Journal of Law*, 14(1), 10–31.

3 Instrumentalisation of aid in humanitarian crises

Obstacle or precondition for cooperation?

Dennis Dijkzeul and Dorothea Hilhorst

Introduction

In Chapter 1 of this volume, Tom Weiss challenges current humanitarian approaches and discusses them in relation to their instrumentalisation: politicisation, militarisation, and marketisation, and then proposes alternative courses of action. He advocates, in particular, establishing better evidence for humanitarian action and working with a consequentialist ethic. Although we concur with the need for evidence-based humanitarian action (Dijkzeul et al. 2013), we argue that these recommendations can only partially address the problem of the ongoing instrumentalisation of humanitarian action, because they in turn can also be instrumentalised.

Hence a central theme of this chapter is that instrumentalisation is bound to happen when crises bring humanitarian organisations into active contact with a wide variety of other actors (see Donini 2012; DeMars and Dijkzeul 2015). These may vary, for instance, from regional organisations to warlords, the military, diaspora networks, intelligence agencies, new donors, and national government institutions. For many of them humanitarian action is a renewable resource, and all of these groupings may see their goals, principles, and mandates differently, and may not be naturally inclined to cooperate with humanitarian organisations. At the very least, they will attempt to realise their own interests. Hence they will carefully observe a humanitarian organisation to determine whether they or their adversaries will benefit from its work. They will then see the humanitarian organisation as either a prize to capture or a threat to neutralise (DeMars 2005). Working in a multi-actor environment is often frustrating and always challenging. To complicate these challenges further, humanitarian organisations themselves are frequently not above instrumentalising their own work for organisational growth, survival, status, or job security for their employees.

In all social endeavours, the reactions by others to our activities regularly lead to our goals being thwarted and frequently lead to unintended outcomes. In this respect, the dynamics of human interaction are always—but never in exactly the same way—impossible to fully control. They unravel the best designed plans, frustrate (presumed) ideological purity, and undo principled approaches.

DOI: 10.4324/9781315658827-5

This chapter first provides a critique of the recommendations that Weiss makes. In particular, it discusses the interaction of humanitarians with other actors within and outside the aid system. Next, it takes up two alternative angles to the discussion. First, we look at the diversity—coupled with occasional overlap—of different types of crisis. Understanding the various types of crisis is a precondition for understanding options for different forms of humanitarian action. The actual type of crisis sets the parameters for both humanitarian action and its instrumentalisation. Second, we need to establish which alternative, non-humanitarian approaches exist to address crises. The chapter also assesses to what extent these alternatives offer feasible solutions.

Culture or political economy?

Weiss's title focuses on the culture of humanitarians in war zones, but his analysis is much broader and includes the political economy of humanitarian crises and humanitarian action. A central aspect of the political economy approach is the analysis of how various actors pursue their own—often hidden—economic and political agendas. They can use humanitarian action as an instrument to further their own aims. A good political economist is able to describe the ensuing dynamics by which a diverse set of actors cause unintended, often suboptimal consequences, how and why worthwhile goals are not met, and why such actors cannot live by their principles alone.

Noting that humanitarian action becomes a fungible resource that is "part of the calculations of winning a war, and belligerents are not averse to manipulating assistance and civilian lives as part of their arsenals" (Chapter 1 in this volume),[1] Weiss masterfully describes three forms of instrumentalisation—politicisation, militarisation, and marketisation—which increasingly complicate humanitarian action and call into question traditional humanitarian principles. He does not succumb to easy cynicism; he attempts to understand crises better and to improve how these three forms of instrumentalisation are addressed. He prefers a humanitarian culture that is more modest in its claims that it can help significantly, and details two admittedly imperfect solutions.

First, looking at the example of the military, he defines what an *evidence-based culture* should look like. Second, he wants a much stronger *consequentialist ethic* to be followed. Elsewhere, he also writes about accreditation of humanitarian organisations and the need for consolidation of the humanitarian system (Weiss 2013). While Weiss's prescriptions help deal with some of the shortcomings of humanitarian action, they cannot do so fully, because they cannot overcome the root causes of politicisation, militarisation, and marketisation. Hence his solutions only partially address the problem, as they also run into the problems of instrumentalisation he describes.

On evidence-based action as an antidote to instrumentalisation

Let's start with a rhetorical question: did the evidence-based culture of the military matter for the decisions to intervene in Iraq in 2003?[2] Obviously not, as evidence alone did not inform the decision to intervene. A political process overtook the decision-making authority of the military. Political leaders and other decision-makers often use evidence that fits a direction usually decided on other grounds. Even if they choose to, it is only on occasion that evidence is specific enough to be actionable. Some of the evidence to justify the military intervention in Iraq—the presence of weapons of mass destruction (WMDs)—was actually made up. It is not entirely clear how much then US Secretary of State, Colin Powell, knew or wanted to know about the quality of the evidence. Which other actors in the Bush Administration had specific interests or convictions to justify the intervention? How much did Dick Cheney, Donald Rumsfeld, and President Bush, or the CIA, actually know that Colin Powell did not know? Which other goals did they feel they could realise through the intervention? Ending the unfinished work of the former Bush presidency, raising the Administration's popularity, promoting Halliburton, winning elections, projecting an image of strong US power, or restoring justice after 9/11? The point is that it is not easy to come up with a clear answer. On the one hand, political scientists and management scholars rarely or never have direct access to such decision-making. On the other hand, those involved are rarely open about all their intentions; they may have a hidden agenda next to their open one.

We are not in any way negative about the potential advantages of the use of evidence,[3] but we are sceptical about the extent to which it will shape political or humanitarian decision-making. Instrumentalisation of action, be it politicisation, militarisation, or commercialisation, is an everyday political phenomenon. Even the solutions to this instrumentalisation are likely to be used by actors to further their own purposes. It is here that humanitarian (and human) interactions become hard to track for scholars and practitioners alike.

To give another example, a former head of an agency charged with supporting disaster response expressed that he did not want to know everything his trusted staff or tested and responsible NGOs did on all occasions, because then they could implement their own solutions, within understood parameters and without unproductive interference. He also did not tell his superiors everything he knew when it would only produce a round of less-than-useful discussion. At the same time, he tried to attend as many general meetings as possible: "to be present", so as to share in understanding the overall direction of his organisation. He worked hard on gaining information, understanding the dynamics of political action, which varied in every situation, including the levers of power and how these influenced humanitarian action. In the process, he was sometimes able to create an organisational space complementary with humanitarian space, but not entirely based on the traditional humanitarian principles—so that humanitarian action could proceed, responding to local circumstances instead of primarily political directives.

In sum, evidence is important. It should be used more in humanitarian circles. But at best it is just one aspect of political decision-making and humanitarian leadership. The main epistemological limitation is not establishing evidence, but applying evidence.

On ethics as an antidote to instrumentalisation

Weiss advocates a consequentialist ethic. In other words, he favours an ethic that focuses more on the outcomes of action than on the purity of its intentions. He doubts the humanitarian imperative—a deontological or duty-based ethic centred on intentions in which humanitarian organisations always have to assist people in need. Instead, he wants it replaced by the "humanitarian impulse", meaning that humanitarian actors can sometimes decide not to provide aid. He is even more scathing about the principles of impartiality, neutrality, and independence.

Yet it is important to note that the two different ethical approaches have always been used in the humanitarian field, but differently by different organisations. International Committee of the Red Cross (ICRC) and Médecins sans Frontières (MSF) as single-mandate organisations operate in the Dunantist vein; they follow a deontological ethic. They thus consider themselves duty-bound to alleviate suffering and save lives. This ethic constitutes an attempt to prevent politicisation, militarisation, and marketisation by carving out a limited humanitarian role, with ideally no influence on the other parties involved in the conflict—it aims only to assist victims. ICRC and MSF are a minority of two that consciously respect and promote the humanitarian principles. Most other humanitarian organisations— and this is a large majority—are multi-mandated organisations, combining humanitarian with development, human rights, or conflict-resolution work. These kinds of work automatically imply political and societal change to a preferred end-state (e.g. peace). Hence multi-mandate organisations operate with a consequentialist approach. Among these organisations, the degree of respect for the principles differs pragmatically (Hilhorst and Pereboom 2015). They may respect them to an extent, but more as a tactical move than a universal duty.[4]

Moreover, in practice both ethics interact regularly, for example within each organisation or with its local contacts. In the eastern Democratic Republic of the Congo (DRC) in the late 1990s, there were a few organisations, such as Agro Action Allemande (Welthungerhilfe) and the Life and Peace Institute, that built large networks of contacts on all sides of the conflict, in particular with traders who worked across battle lines, traditional chiefs and family members, and local officials. They then communicated and used the humanitarian principles in their daily activities to build trust on all sides. In other words, they used a deontological ethic to facilitate the impact of their work, implementing it in a consequentialist manner. This is not easy, but some organisations manage it. MSF, to give another example, is an organisation that consciously bases itself on Dunantist principles. Yet, once it decides to become active somewhere, it follows a rigorous decision-making approach, in which it focuses on its (potential) health and medical impacts. In this way, it also combines both ethics (Heyse 2006). In a recent volume, MSF further explains how, in many situations, access is negotiated whereby adherence to principles may be sacrificed to more effective relief of suffering (Magone et al. 2012). In sum, the two ethics are not mutually exclusive (see below).[5]

In all crises, the degree of success of both ethics depends on the interaction with a wide cast of other actors—local and international—that follows its own interests.

These actors calculate whether they see a specific humanitarian organisation or activity as an opportunity to grasp or a threat to suppress (DeMars 2005). And the humanitarian organisation's staff is rarely fully aware of these actors' specific interests and tactics.

The basic image behind the consequentialist ethic is a *Homo economicus*, who knows his interests (a.k.a. utilities or preferences), and is able to calculate strategically (all) possible consequences and select his desired option. The deontological ethic works with the *Homo sociologicus*, who follows societal norms, because that is the right, good, or appropriate thing to do. Yet norms and interests are not separate entities. They mutually influence each other, as societal norms and individual interest constitute each other. Yet we rarely know how exactly they form and shape each other. Hence norms and interests are basic concepts of the social sciences that are nevertheless ill suited to fully understand the dynamics of social interaction, including its instrumentalisation. The difficulty in understanding the diversity of actors and the resulting social dynamics has long been known, before the modernist liberal interventions of the post-Cold War era (compare Chandler's Chapter 2 in this volume).[6]

For humanitarian action, focusing more strongly on the dynamics of working in a multi-actor environment is crucial. Its degree of success cannot be determined beforehand, because one cannot control the behaviour of all the other actors. Other actors will hijack or simply attempt to influence humanitarian action for their own benefit. Yet humanitarians are rarely completely powerless in their reactions to these actors and their efforts at instrumentalisation. Weiss's text helps the humanitarians to come up with at least partial approaches.

However, understanding the three forms of instrumentalisation can be taken one step further. One can ask to which extent such instrumentalisation is necessary for humanitarian organisations to receive at the least a modicum of *cooperation*. If those other actors would not see some of their interests realised by—working with—the humanitarians, they would only obstruct or neglect. Usually, their interests may be very different from those of humanitarian actors. For instance, warlords may negotiate with humanitarian organisations to gain legitimacy towards the population under their control or to appropriate food aid to feed their rebels. As a result of such influence, humanitarian action can have a completely different impact on aid than would be expected if one follows the normative claims of the humanitarian organisations and their principles. Fiona Terry (2002) studied these unintended consequences of humanitarian action when she formulated the humanitarian paradox: humanitarian action can worsen or lengthen the suffering it is supposed to address. She focuses on the effects, the study of instrumentalisation on their causes. Paradoxically, instrumentalisation can be simultaneously a *precondition for cooperation* in, and the main *obstacle* for, humanitarian action (Barnett 2012, 1171–1172).

The two ethics suggest different ways to deal with instrumentalisation. The deontological ethic focuses on the importance of good or pure intentions, so that the humanitarians are not seen as a threat in the hope of safeguarding access to and security of recipients (and staff). The consequentialist ethic centres on outcomes. Both are needed in humanitarian crises, but none works perfectly.

Consequently, both multi-mandate and Dunantist organisations are necessary. Yet the difficult question of when and how to combine them cannot be answered *a priori*. It is always a tough judgment call.

In sum, there is room for the humanitarian principles and the deontological ethic, but it is limited room that requires continuous care (Slim 1997), as other actors will attempt to realise their own interests. We do not know beforehand whether and when the humanitarians or other actors will succeed.[7]

Partial global alternatives

How, then, to deal with instrumentalisation and foster cooperation? Ms Ogata, a former UN High Commissioner for Refugees, famously quipped: "There are no humanitarian solutions to humanitarian problems" (Rieff 2002, 22). We need to understand not only how and to what extent the humanitarian system can function better, but also the various actors in different crises[8] and the broader global context in which these crises take place (Sezgin and Dijkzeul 2016). Briefly, we need to broaden our focus from the humanitarian aid system to crises and global politics. Hence we will look first at the different types of crisis and what they imply for both ethics and evidence-based action. Second, we will discuss several policy options that (partly) need to be realised outside the humanitarian crisis areas, in particular in the Global North.

Understanding crisis-scenarios

Weiss focuses explicitly on armed conflict, and most multi-mandated organisations would agree that the utility of their work "depends on what crisis we are talking about."[9] After all, humanitarian budgets are being used to achieve several ends. These vary from responding to acute crises to supporting victims of those continuing for years or even decades. Addressing crises requires support in many forms, such as care and maintenance of refugees, building institutions in fragile states, and disaster prevention, risk reduction, and preparedness. General discussions of humanitarianism(s) and the ethics behind the humanitarian principles are often hindered by the fact that proponents have different humanitarian scenarios in mind. This section introduces a number of these scenarios.

Open armed conflicts

Historical commentary on modern humanitarian action usually begins with a reference to the battlefield of Solferino in 1859, where Henry Dunant witnessed heavy and bloody fighting inspiring him to organise medical care, and leading to the formation of the ICRC and the development of International Humanitarian Law. Ironically, humanitarian action is least effective in accessing and assisting affected people in these iconic situations of open, violent conflict. Conflict areas are often inaccessible. When it is too dangerous for aid workers, aid will be withdrawn. Needs in these situations are always vastly larger than aid can cover.

The problem of instrumentalisation in these kinds of situations is nothing new. There are, however, some recent developments. Since 9/11 and the proclaimed 'war on terror', we are faced with international conflicts in which the so-called international community acts as a 'neutral outsider' or as a 'warring party' depending on the point of view of the observer. In some conflicts, politicisation and militarisation have indeed led to distrust of humanitarian organisations and the United Nations, as they are frequently associated with Western domination of the international response. The independence of humanitarian aid, and hence its credibility, have been severely affected in some countries.

Although every type of organisation faces problems of access in areas of open, high-intensity conflict, single-mandate organisations are better suited to addressing this concern than consequentialist, multi-mandate organisations. The ICRC will typically play a large role, and MSF is usually also at the forefront of aid delivery, though an increasing number of agencies with broader mandates are becoming more active in this regard. Scenarios of open, violent conflicts are often local and periodic. That means that parts of the country are for certain periods subjected to heavy fighting, while in other parts of the country aid is being delivered for reconstruction or development. Proportionality may be an issue. In a recent report, MSF attempts to raise awareness of these situations. Titled *Where Is Everyone? Responding to Emergencies in the Most Difficult Places* (MSF 2014), the report states that in the worst conflicts few organisations are able to provide aid well. While this is ascribed partly to contextual issues, the report raises questions about the efficiency and independence of aid delivery. One of the examples is the situation in Goma in the eastern DRC in 2012, where an intensification of violence of rebel group M-23 led to the evacuation of aid organisations just when people needed aid more than ever.

Fragile settings—chronic crises

Although a number of countries have an official peace agreement and/or an internationally accepted government, conflict continues at a low level or flares up intermittently. Governments in these countries are often not willing or able to provide basic services. These fragile settings often end up developing into a long-standing humanitarian crisis, challenging long-term development objectives. These are settings where, with variations, the government does not function well, civil society is weak, poverty indicators are in the red, fertility is high, the rate of urbanisation is increasing, *and* criminality is abundant. Progress with the Millennium Development Goals bypasses these countries, and the risk of relapsing into open, armed conflict in the absence of fundamental change is always present (Milante 2015).

Fragile settings demand multiple types of aid, varying from emergency aid, to development cooperation, to support for institution building. One will find agencies with different mandates, programmes, and ethics in these situations. Multi-mandated organisations may alternate between direct support of the most vulnerable groups and institution building. They often deal with 'wicked problems':

vicious problems that are practically unsolvable and where specific solutions often evoke new problems (ibid.). In these crises, aid stands little chance of success in meeting needs or bringing about sustainable change. This can feed into the increasing critique on aid. Arguments in favour of maintaining a high level of aid in fragile settings (where 'do no harm and try doing good' is often the *leitmotif*) include the high level of vulnerability leading to immediate humanitarian needs, and the risks of renewed conflict, which can have all kinds of spill-over effects regionally and internationally.

The complex nature of these problems does not mean that aid cannot do better than it does. There are some recurring aid 'traps' in these situations. For example, aid organisations tend to underestimate the capacity of local actors to offer solutions and function efficiently. Some organisations also tend to focus on implementing specific projects without taking a holistic view and operating in cooperation with other groups, including local entities. This often leads to duplication of work and waste of resources, as well as local resistance. For instance, when humanitarian medical organisations entered the South-Kivu province in the eastern DRC after the Rwandan genocide, they often failed to contact the provincial health inspection. Only over time did cooperation improve (Dijkzeul and Lynch 2006). We also may see an inability to switch modes between the provision of direct relief and other types of support. Lessons learned as a result of monitoring and evaluations are not always followed up. Accountability to the local population and local institutions can be vastly improved.[10]

Some of these critiques on aid recur over decades. We see, however, some positive developments concerning aid in fragile settings. Compared with the 1990s, aid is more often directed towards existing institutions and the resilience of the population (Hilhorst et al. 2011), so the likelihood of sustainable change is slowly garnering more strength. Coordination systems are being improved, and a growing number of governments have more space to take and maintain initiative and define their own development agenda.[11] Yet, all in all, in this type of crisis tensions between deontological and consequentialist actors are bound to arise.

Refugees and displaced persons

Care for refugees and displaced persons is part of humanitarian budgets and is considered as humanitarian aid.[12] Humanitarian aid in conflict areas—as described above—is highly difficult and, in practice, aid is often provided to people who flee from the open conflict. Problems of internally displaced persons (IDPs) are often more difficult when there are multiple displacements, where people fleeing from violence arrive in insecure areas and have to flee again.

Humanitarian aid has been criticised for many years because it did not take into account the resilience of refugees and IDPs and hence did not build on their initiatives (Harrel-Bond 1986). Even where aid agencies want to break through this situation, they are often constrained by national laws that forbid refugees from undertaking (economic) activities. Currently, however, we see many developments for dealing with refugees more effectively, partly triggered by technical progress.

Instead of distributing goods, for example, agencies often provide cash or vouchers so that refugees can decide what they need. Where refugee movements become massive, aid is confronted with huge logistical, organisational, and financial problems. Because camps are often the only place where aid can be provided, there can still be an oversupply of aid organisations locally.

Issues of IDPs are complex, because IDPs establish camps in some countries but also often stay in the periphery of cities. Some will wait to return home at the end of the conflict, while others decide to stay in the city. As a result, displacement intertwines with rapid urbanisation in fragile settings. It is not always clear what roles humanitarian action can play in addressing these complex problems, and in what ways governments can realise the basic rights of these people, together with the international community. As IDPs in urban environments usually blend with the urban poor, the issue on how to provide adequate aid is equally intertwined with issues of development, making the concern of IDPs by nature apt for multi-mandate organisations, following a consequentialist ethic.

Disasters triggered by natural hazards

Recognising that vulnerability to natural hazards is largely human-made, the world community has vastly improved prevention, preparedness, and response to small- and medium-scale disasters. The Hyogo Framework for Action of 2004 (ISDR 2005) has played an important role in reinforcing national governments to make disaster prevention and preparedness a policy priority and to improve responses. In more and more countries, small- and medium-scale and recurrent disasters are being addressed by government and non-governmental institutions, sometimes with the cooperation of international development organisations residing in the country, sometimes as the result of local action, as happens for example in the many recurring floods in the Philippines and Bangladesh.

Increasingly occurring large-scale disasters are a different story. These disasters cannot be dealt with at the national level alone. They require massive efforts from outside. The international humanitarian system has made enormous progress in the past 20 years on first care and emergency aid in these kinds of disasters. These changes have supported life-saving aid in slow-onset disasters that slowly reach crisis proportions, such as the drought in the Horn of Africa in 2011. Despite the momentous logistical challenges of large-scale aid interventions in circumstances where roads are blocked, aid workers are themselves affected, and communication lines are broken down, the aid community has managed to significantly bring down mortality figures in these situations.

After the first crisis period, usually lasting several weeks, the situation becomes more complicated. The acute needs are not over, but the response falls into a certain routine. Reconstruction also starts. Reconstruction after large-scale disasters is an extraordinarily complex operation which is always politicised. Most efforts occur outside the framework of humanitarian aid, like the (corruption-sensitive) rebuilding of infrastructure, or political measures to strengthen the position of vulnerable groups such as the poor or ethnic minorities. Humanitarian organisations focus mainly on the local level where communities try to resume daily life together and rebuild their habitats. Reconstruction is often characterised by politicisation and bureaucracy. In this process, aid organisations often make mistakes because their aid supply does not complement activities people undertake themselves, and a lack of accountability to affected populations may prevail.

Natural disasters are dealt with mainly by multi-mandate organisations. MSF does not reckon natural disaster its core competency, while the International Federation of Red Cross and Red Crescent Societies (IFRC) and several national societies are the more prominent players in the Red Cross family. This is, of course, different in the large number of cases where disasters take place in conflict areas. Natural hazards do not stop at the border or wait for peace. The Hyogo Framework for Action ascribes the primary role in disaster response to the national government. However, disasters often occur in situations where the government does not function well or where more or less intensive conflicts take place. In these situations, natural hazards may lead to catastrophes because the response capacity is lacking and people in conflict circumstances become more and more vulnerable and poor. While natural disaster response is mainly a multi-mandate, consequentialist affair, there continue to be issues concerning the balance between immediate relief and recovery efforts.

Biological, chemical, and nuclear disasters

While biological, chemical, or nuclear disasters can and will occur in the future and will no doubt raise humanitarian needs, this is not a subject for discussion within humanitarian organisations, and there is almost no preparation for these types of disaster.

Although weapons of mass destruction have not been found in Iraq and have not been used between the superpowers, that does not mean that such weapons will never be used. Within US military policy-making circles, the use of small nuclear weapons has been advocated, and terrorist organisations are known to develop or try to get their hands on WMDs. Unstable states such as North Korea, Pakistan, and India with regard to Kashmir, the Arab–Israeli conflict, and Iran still create risks of nuclear or other WMD attacks. The traditional principles of humanitarian aid are not applicable on the ground after the use of these weapons, because the humanitarian organisations lack the knowledge and capacity to address the horrific consequences of such attacks. They will probably need to cooperate with the military because the military possess some of the technological and healthcare capacities that humanitarian organisations do not have. At the moment, such cooperation, which will need to include a division of labour, training, and planning, is woefully underdeveloped (see Prescott et al. 2002; Dijkzeul 2004).

In addition, summer 2014 brought the spread of the Ebola virus, a disaster caused by a biological vector. While the Ebola virus caused a horrible epidemic, it became clear that the humanitarian world—starting with the agencies of the United Nations—had no adequate answer.[13] On 2 September 2014, the international Chair of MSF called upon the UN to deploy military troops to deal with this crisis (MSF 2014). The Ebola crisis and the use of WMDs, be they atomic, biological, or chemical, thus raise several questions that are missing in the humanitarian agenda up to now. How can the international community respond to biological, chemical, and nuclear disasters? Is this the exclusive domain of military actors and governments? What mandate do humanitarian organisations need to be able to play a role in this scenario? What ethical approach should they follow? Are they equipped and prepared for it?

Concluding the scenarios

This overview of different scenarios brings out that single-mandate humanitarian agencies are particularly prominent in open, violent conflict, whereas in all other types of crisis multi-mandate organisations appear to be more dominant and may generally be better suited to provide services. And both types of organisation, including their ethical approaches, always run the risk of being instrumentalised by other actors.

It is clear that the different types of crisis are not clearly separated in reality. In countries where certain areas or periods are more or less violent, aid is always moving between different objectives and ways of working. It is at the borderlines and overlap between different types of crises that most friction about mandates, finance, cooperation, and ethical approaches occurs.

Alternative global policy options

A logical alternative to intervention by humanitarian organisations is non-intervention.[14] After all, an intervention can make a situation worse, in particular when its instrumentalisation contributes to an escalation in violence, or when insufficient state-building activities are undertaken afterwards. Nevertheless, the "let-them-fight-it-out" or "let-them-figure-it-out" options also have serious negative effects at the national and international levels. In addition to human suffering, the consequences vary from increased drug trade and spread of diseases to terrorism and economic decline.[15]

Fortunately, there are non-humanitarian, non-interventionist policy alternatives that indirectly facilitate humanitarian action, stability, and rebuilding. These alternatives fall into several overlapping categories of international discourse and public policy, discussed below, namely trade, weapons control, economic and financial measures, fighting corruption, public health, and migration policies, as well as peacemaking and state building. Together they mark a shift in attention from the humanitarian crises to the international root causes and interactions of actors from the Global North with those from the Global South.

- A crucial policy alternative would be to *scale down or eliminate subsidies, import restrictions, and other trade barriers* in the United States, Japan, and the European Union in agriculture, commodities, and basic industries such as textiles. Progress in these areas with the World Trade Organization and international trade rounds has been extremely slow. Yet many people in the Global South, including countries in crisis, work in these sectors and their products would be more competitive were it not for these subsidies and barriers. An end to agricultural subsidies on cotton, grain, and dairy products, for example, would provide an income boost for many farmers in the Global South and help to improve or stabilise many weak states by creating conditions under which violence becomes a less viable alternative to make a living.

- A second policy initiative would be to *reduce the availability of weapons*. To a large extent, this means taking action in the rich, industrialised countries that are the main arms exporters. This has already happened with weapons embargoes and, starting at the grassroots, with the International Campaign to Ban Landmines. Other initiatives, for example on small arms, are in the offing. However, structurally, more can be done, but this is difficult as several governments and their military–industrial complex(es) benefit from weapons production and trade.

- A third helpful policy measure would be to *reduce the funds that rebels and corrupt governments obtain through violence*. The World Bank suggested curbing rebel access to commodity markets, as happened with the Kimberley process for certifying conflict diamonds. As a result, the National Union for the Total Independence of Angola (UNITA) and the Revolutionary United Front (RUF) in Sierra Leone lost some of their power, which helped end the civil wars in these countries. The Khmer Rouge took a serious blow when the government of Thailand stepped up scrutiny of the border trade in illegal timber. Such action can be replicated with timber, coltan and other forms of resource extraction in countries in crisis. The independent UN reports on the war economies in Sudan, DRC, Sierra Leone and other countries have been small steps toward ensuring international accountability from warlords and other criminals, as well as their supporters in governments and international enterprises.

- A related alternative policy area to reduce support for violence is to *limit diaspora finance from rich countries to rebel groups*. For example, "Tamil Diaspora organisations raised around $450 million per year during the 1990s, much of it used by the Tamil Tigers to buy arms" (Collier et al. 2003, 144). The Irish Republican Army (IRA), for instance, became more open toward peace overtures when its international resources began to dry up. The importance of limiting finance was also brought home by following the leads to financial support for the Islamic State and al-Qaeda. On the positive side, peace negotiations and international donors can also involve diaspora organisations in business recovery strategies by organising visits home, business forums, and selection of investment and rebuilding opportunities (ibid., 162).

- Another complementary approach would be to *reduce the profits* rebels obtain *from producing and trading drugs*. According to one estimate, opium accounts for one-third of Afghanistan's GNP (Economist 2003, 41) and politically sophisticated drug lords resist government intervention and attempt to influence elections in their favour. These drug lords increasingly cooperate with the Taliban (de Volkskrant 2015). Similar problems occur in Colombia and parts of Myanmar. "Current OECD policy toward … drugs varies, but its main thrust is to encourage the government of developing countries to discourage production. The problem with this production-focused approach is that it makes territory outside the control of a recognised government enormously valuable, and so inadvertently helps to sustain rebellion" (Collier et al. 2003, 144). An alternative would be to penalise illegal consumption of drugs, while simultaneously instituting a government-controlled supply of drugs to registered addicts in order to bring down prices (ibid., 146).

- A sixth policy alternative is *reforming the provision of aid*, in particular its amount and timing. First, donor countries have, with only a few notable exceptions, never achieved the official target of allocating 0.7 per cent of GDP for funding development cooperation. Second, in sudden-onset large emergencies aid tends to be provided at the height of the crisis and then taper off. However, aid can be very productive a few years after the conflict has ended because absorptive capacity and private investment have also increased. The development community, including multi-mandate organisations, does not invest sufficiently in this stage, which reduces the effectiveness of international aid.

- *International debt relief* could be used to foster peace negotiations, in particular when instituted with economic growth and reconciliation policies. Guatemala, for instance, would have been able to establish more rapid democratic progress if it could have reduced debt repayments after the 1996 peace accords. More generally, it would be interesting to link debt relief with building a stronger, more inclusive state. For example, debt relief for Iraq did not deliver sufficient results, as international support failed to address government weaknesses and ethnic and religious divides.

- *Corruption should be fought* harder. In the United States, parts of the war on terror, in particular the highly criticised Patriot Act, expanded "the range of evidence that can be used [in court], which now includes material gathered clandestinely that was previously deemed inadmissible" for prosecuting corrupt foreign dignitaries (Economist 2004, 46–47). This act has also made it easier to deny or revoke visas of corrupt officials and to forfeit property—a type of discretionary and highly individualised sanction with no negative effects for society at large. The handlers of ill-gotten money, in particular financial institutions in the North, should also be scrutinised and, if necessary, punished (ibid.).[16]

- Another policy area considers the fraught issue of *migration and refugee flows* from crisis countries to rich Western ones. Whereas intensive debates continue on the exact effects of brain drain and remittances, offering refuge saves lives and could, over time, help to stabilise countries in crisis by providing resources and expertise from returning migrants and refugees. However, the opportunities for migrants and refugees—and the difference between these two groups is rarely clear-cut—to reach the rich world have dramatically decreased and due to the growing intensity and number of wars and other crises they keep coming in large numbers.

- International policy-makers should also consider the broader *population pressures*. Population pressures in the context of weak states and underdevelopment may contribute to conflict through poverty, unemployment, unsustainable demand on basic services, environmental decline, migration, and sheer desperation. Better health policies, particularly in terms of reproductive health and AIDS, can contribute to longer, healthier, and more productive lives, which helps to stabilise societies.

- The eleventh policy concerns the *root causes* of natural disasters. Climate change and environmental disasters already hit the poorest of the poor hardest, although they are the least responsible for causing them. With some exceptions, such as the prevention of ozone depletion, stemming environmental decline has been disappointing so far, and the number and intensity of natural disasters is increasing. Environmental decline may also be a factor contributing to armed conflict.

- International *diplomacy for making peace* should be reinforced. From Libya to the Fiji Islands, conflicts have nasty contagious effects. It may sound like stating the obvious, but if the Israeli–Palestinian conflict could finally be seriously addressed, this would have tremendous implications for the Islamic world and elsewhere. Preventing and resolving violent conflicts does not just have positive effects within the country itself, but it also helps stabilise neighbouring countries, strengthens economic growth, and removes possible sanctuaries for terrorists.

Any one of these policies on its own will not prevent humanitarian crises, but taken together their cumulative effects can be highly beneficial. These policies have indirect and marginal benefits that, over the long term, can help address crises for large parts of the population. In this respect, they are the logical opposite to the negative effects of economic sanctions, military interventions, and other punitive policies. In short, where sanctions and the use of force disrupt, these policies would reinforce building from within the societies themselves. They either reduce the need for humanitarian interventions or complement attempts to alleviate suffering. Both teleological and consequentialist approaches would become a little easier to carry out.

These policies put the onus of responsibility on the strong Northern states, but also require cooperation between Global North and South. Yet it remains to be seen whether moral concerns and strategic and economic appeals about the negative consequences of conflicts and disasters will offset the special interest groups, societal inertia, and divisions among donor countries to establish these policies.[17] These policies easily run the risk of becoming utopian ideals. They are hard to implement, and will take effect only slowly. Together, they can best be seen as an emancipatory project that requires considerable social struggle over time.

Nevertheless, the upshot of not implementing these types of policies is that crisis regions will only rarely stabilise and development will not take off. Instead, many crises are bound to become chronic, and even intensify, as their root causes are not addressed. The growth in humanitarian needs is currently outstripping the growth in resources for aid. Internal improvements of the humanitarian organisations, of whatever ethic, and reform of the humanitarian system, will not be sufficient to stem human suffering. Without supportive international public policies, humanitarian effectiveness will continue to disappoint.

Conclusions

This chapter began with a critical review of Weiss's Chapter 1. As Weiss convincingly argues, purity of intention does not ensure successful interaction or outcomes. He proposes to find recourse in more evidence-based aid and in shifting to a consequentialist ethic. The first part of this chapter brings out why these solutions are only partial at best. Policies that determine aid flows and practices are rarely based on evidence alone, and different kinds of ethics in a multi-actor environment are likely to become instrumentalised too.

The chapter then proposed two additional angles to the debate on instrumentalisation and cooperation. Firstly, we call attention to how different types of crisis present different parameters of instrumentalisation. Open conflict, refugee crises, fragile contexts, natural hazards, and biological/chemical/nuclear disaster situations pose different types of risks of instrumentalisation. In many instances, a certain level of instrumentalisation may benefit the service delivery of people in need, because it provides incentives for actors to engage positively with aid when they see some of their own objectives realised. There are also many instances where instrumentalisation may be objectionable, yet does little harm in practice. For scholars, we have only an imperfect offering to understand the dynamics of everyday politics of working in a multi-actor environment, and we suggest making the issue of instrumentalisation, be it as politicisation, militarisation, marketisation, or whatever other form, a central research theme. The paradox of instrumentalisation in crisis areas is that it both can facilitate (limited) cooperation with other actors and obstruct humanitarian work. Hence "[t]he remarkable thing about humanitarian organisations is not that other actors are constantly attempting to instrumentalise them by attaching hidden agendas or even taking over their open agendas. Instead, the remarkable thing is how humanitarian organisations manage to elude becoming completely instrumentalised, or even instrumentalise others" (Dijkzeul 2015, 264). This leads to questions as to when, and to what extent, humanitarian organisations allow themselves to be instrumentalised in order to be able to deliver aid. How exactly does such instrumentalisation take place? When is it eluded? When and how do they instrumentalise other actors? These questions beg more empirical research on the ground. The categorisation of different types of crisis provides a first entry point in distinguishing different realities of instrumentalisation. Only if we understand better the differences and overlap among types of crisis can we meaningfully discuss the actual impact of the different roles, ethics, and mandates of the humanitarian organisation involved.

The second angle we propose is to pay attention more systematically to the potential of non-humanitarian policies that help to prevent or mitigate humanitarian crises. Put simply: with more supportive international policies, humanitarian action is either less necessary or it cannot be instrumentalised or abused easily. We distinguished 12 types of (international) policy that can contribute to the prevention and resolution of humanitarian crises. Together they may bring about substantial change in the occurrence of humanitarian crises, but they require considerable international cooperation. While some would dismiss this notion as naive or outside the remit of humanitarians, we suggest that the promotion of these types of policy can be seen as forms of humanitarian diplomacy and hence be considered as highly ethical.

Notes

1 As humanitarian aid is a fungible resource, donor governments can also use it to promote military intervention, to enhance their image, or as a fig leaf for the media and the general public to pretend they are at least doing something to aid victims; warlords and dictators use it to shore up their political legitimacy and authority; and it has become part of a self-perpetuating multi-billion-dollar aid industry with its media marketing and fund-raising (see Chandler, Chapter 2 in this volume). "The history of humanitarianism appears to be full of the unintended consequences which occur when universal desires to 'help the helpless' meet the concrete realities of power inequalities and desperation" (ibid.).

2 As we focus here on the role of evidence in the relationship between military and political decision-making, we will leave aside that some observers argue that the military has a results-based culture directed at outcomes premised on control, which is not the same as evidence-based.

3 See the 2013 Special Issue of *Disasters* on Evidence-based Humanitarian Action, edited by Dennis Dijkzeul, Dorothea Hilhorst, and Peter Walker.

4 These organisations can be Wilsonian organisations, which tend to work closely with (their national) donor governments, or even solidarists that reject the principles in favor of a political cause. Finally, some organisations are simply subcontractors from their donor governments.

5 Although there are associated staffing, public relations, and resource implications.

6 We will provide a few examples. First, take Machiavelli's prince, not exactly a principled actor. But even if *Il Principe*'s use of norms and values is purely instrumental; the associated hypocrisy is only possible as the compliment that vice pays to virtue. Second, classical realists, such as Carr and Morgenthau, were highly sceptical of military interventions and foreign adventures. Their sensitivity to the tragic aspects of political instrumentalisation and unintended consequences of good (and bad) intentions made them call for prudence in international politics. Both examples show political scholars who, basing themselves on their own life's experiences, become extremely sceptical of universalist, linear, reductionist, and generalising scholarly work. David Chandler is right to protest against such universalist, linear, and reductionist approaches. Yet Machiavelli, the classical realists, and Weiss are just a few examples of scholars who have attempted to deal with the complexity of the dynamics of interaction all along.

7 And as indicated in note 1, humanitarian organisations sometimes instrumentalise their own work as part of a multi-billion-dollar industry that perpetuates itself.

8 In terms of a research agenda: debates about aid in crises would benefit from a more realistic acknowledgement of interests, instrumentalisation, and the inevitable unintended outcomes of aid in a multi-actor environment. Only if we understand the networks of various local and international actors, with their open and hidden agendas, and how they try to instrumentalise aid, can we at least attempt to deal more consciously with humanitarian (inter-)action and its unintended consequences. Addressing these epistemological and methodological issues also helps determine what the most promising opportunities for improving humanitarian action are. Even without quick fixes, humanitarian practice and theory can be linked much more closely.

9 This section is based partly on Hilhorst and Pereboom (2015).

10   When organisations interpret their mandate and their areas of activity rigidly, they run a higher risk of limiting flexibility and accountability, and not following up on monitoring and evaluation outcomes.

11   See for example G7+ (2011).

12   Funding for IDPs is more complicated than for refugees. Many donors provide no funding for the internally displaced, as this disaster-affected group is often considered an official responsibility of the host government.

13   MSF became a lead player in the response to the Ebola outbreak.

14   This section is based partly on Dijkzeul (2004).

15   Another policy area short of intervention concerns different types of sanctions, which can be considered a punitive policy. In the past, sanctions have done serious social harm, leading, for example, to a decline in public health and an increase in criminality, and in some cases even to an intensification of humanitarian crises. However, "smart" sanctions that target individuals and corruption (see below) may influence political and commercial elites that are insufficiently accountable and (inadvertently and consciously) cause crises.

16   The recent scandal of HSBC support for tax evasion to Switzerland is just another example.

17   When, in 2005, then UN Secretary General Kofi Annan attempted to link UN reform with proposals in which the Global South and Global North would strike a deal to foster comprehensive human security, including addressing terrorism, nuclear proliferation, and instability, by facilitating more development and (fair) trade, his efforts were thwarted and the ensuing reforms, which included the UN Humanitarian Reform, were minimal. Perceptions of threats between the Global North and South differed too much to foster such international cooperation.

References

Barnett M. (2012) "Book Review: Donini, A. ed. (2012) *The Golden Fleece: Manipulation and Independence of Humanitarian Action*", *International Review of the Red Cross*, 94 (887), 1169–1172.

Collier P. et al. (2003) *Breaking the Conflict Trap: Civil War and Development Policy*, World Bank and Oxford University Press, Washington, DC and Oxford.

DeMars W. (2005) *NGOs and Transnational Networks: Wild Card in World Politics*, Pluto Press, London.

DeMars W.E. and Dijkzeul D. eds (2015) *The NGO Challenge for International Relations Theory*, Global Institutions Series, Routledge, Abingdon.

Dijkzeul D. (2004) "Conclusion: Winning the War and Losing the Peace?", in Dijkzeul D. (ed.) *Between Force and Mercy: Military Action and Humanitarian Aid*, Bochumer Schriften zur Friedenssicherung und zum Humanitären Völkerrecht (50), Berliner Wissenschafts-Verlag, Berlin, 379–412.

Dijkzeul D. and Lynch C. (2006) *Supporting Local Health Care in a Chronic Crisis: Management and Financing Approaches in Eastern Democratic Republic of the Congo*, National Research Council of the National Academies, Roundtable on the Demography of Forced Migration, Committee on Population, Division of Behavioral and Social Sciences and Education and Program on Forced Migration and Health at the Joseph L. Mailman School of Public Health at Columbia University, National Academies Press, Washington, DC.

Dijkzeul D., Hilhorst D. and Walker P. (2013) "Introduction: Evidence-Based Action in Humanitarian Crisis", *Disasters*, special issue on Evidence-based Action in Humanitarian Crises, (3) Supplement 1, 1–19.

Dijkzeul D. (2015) "Heart of Paradox: War, Rape and NGOs in the DR Congo", in DeMars, W.E. and Dijkzeul D. eds, *The NGO Challenge for International Relations Theory*, Global Institutions Series, Routledge, Abingdon, 262–286

Donini A. ed. (2012) *The Golden Fleece: Manipulation and Independence of Humanitarian Action*, Kumarian Press, Sterling, VA.

The Economist (2003) "Afghanistan: Not a Dress Rehearsal", *The Economist*, 16 August, 41.

The Economist (2004) "Corruption in Latin America: Harder Graft", *The Economist*, 10 April, 46–47.

G7+ (2011) "A New Deal for Engagement in Fragile States", 30 November (www.g7plus.org/en/our-journey), accessed 5 November 2015.

Harrel-Bond B.E. (1986) *Imposing Aid: Emergency Assistance to Refugees*, Oxford University Press, Oxford.

Healy S. and Tiller S. (2014) *"Where Is Everyone? Responding to Emergencies in the Most Difficult Places"*, Médecins Sans Frontières, London.

Heyse L. (2006) *Choosing the Lesser Evil: Understanding Decision Making in Humanitarian Aid NGOs*, Aldershot, Ashgate.

Hilhorst D., Christoplos I. and van der Haar G. (2011) "Reconstruction from Below. Magic Bullet or Shooting from the Hip?", *Third World Quarterly*, 31(7), 1107–1124.

Hilhorst D. and Pereboom E. (2014) *Dutch Humanitarian Aid: Now and in the Future. A sector Consultation in Preparation of the Netherlands Humanitarian Summit* (2015), (www.wageningenur.nl/en/Publication-details.htm?publicationId=publication-way-343836353733), accessed 6 June 2015.

Hilhorst D. and Pereboom E. (2015) "Multi-mandate organizations in humanitarian aid", in Sezgin Z. and Dijkzeul D. eds, *The New Humanitarian Actors: Contested Principles, Emerging Practice*, Humanitarian Studies Series, Routledge, Abingdon.

ISDR (2005) *Hyogo Framework for Action 2005–2015: Building the Resilience of Nations and Communities*, UN International Strategy for Disaster Reduction, Geneva (www.unisdr.org/we/inform/publications/1037).

Magone C., Neuman M. and Weissman F. eds (2012) *Humanitarian Negotiations Revealed: The MSF Experience*, Columbia University Press, New York.

Milante G. (2015) "Security and Development", in *SIPRI Yearbook 2015*, Oxford University Press, Oxford.

MSF (2014) "Global bio-disaster response urgently needed in Ebola fight", Sept. 2014 (www.msf.org/article/global-bio-disaster-response-urgently-needed-ebola-fight), accessed 6 June 2015

Prescott G., Doull L., Sondorp E., Bower H. and Mozumder A. (2002) "Hope for the Best, Prepare for the Worst: How Humanitarian Organisations Can Organise to Respond to Weapons of Mass Destruction", Programme for Evidence-based Humanitarian Aid, mimeo (http://reliefweb.int/sites/reliefweb.int/files/resources/FE7C9040B6D35602C1256CAD002F9B00-merlin-hope-jan02.pdf), accessed 6 June 2015.

Sezgin Z. and Dijkzeul D. eds (2016) *The New Humanitarians in International Practice: Emerging Actors and Contested Principles*, Humanitarian Studies Series, Routledge, Abingdon.

Rieff D. (2002) *A Bed for the Night: Humanitarianism in Crisis*, Simon & Schuster, New York.

Slim H. (1997) "Relief Agencies and Moral Standing in War: Principles of Humanity, Neutrality, Impartiality and Solidarity", *Development in Practice*, 7(4), 342–352.

Terry F. (2002) *Condemned to Repeat? The Paradox of Humanitarian Action*, Cornell University Press, Ithaca, NY.

de Volkskrant (2015) "Taliban Verruilen Politiek voor Criminaliteit", *Volkskrant*, 10 February 2015 (www.volkskrant.nl/dossier-afghanistan/taliban-verruilen-politiek-voor-criminaliteit~a3848340/), accessed 6 June 2015.

Weiss T.G. (2013) *Humanitarian Business*, Polity Press, Cambridge.

4 Decoding the software of humanitarian action

Universal or pluriversal?[1]

Antonio Donini

In this chapter I aim to unpack the essence of humanitarianism and humanitarian action—what lies behind it, and how it is evolving. I come from Italy, where we are skilled in a very peculiar science called "dietrologia", or "behindology". So my topic here is the "behindology" of humanitarianism. I will attempt to unscramble the functions that it performs in twenty-first century international relations and the codes that underpin it.

But, first, what is "it"? The concept of humanitarianism is fraught with ambiguities. It connotes several separate but overlapping realities: an ideology, a movement and a profession. Together, they form a political economy. But it is also an establishment, a complex system, a relationship of power. What unites the various facets of humanitarianism is a broad commitment to alleviating the suffering and protecting the lives of civilians caught up in conflict or crisis. Beneath this common goal, however, the ideology, the movement, the profession and the establishment are themselves deeply fractured. Like other "isms"—communism and Catholicism come to mind—humanitarianism propounds lofty aims that serve to hide deep contradictions, conflicting alignments and power plays, manipulations and instrumentalisations, personality cults, struggles over resources and, sometimes, shady financial transactions. It includes Soviet-style card-carrying defenders of orthodoxy, heretics, fellow travellers, revisionists and extremist fringes. It now even has for-profit and military wings.

Because it commands huge resources—some US$22 billion in 2015—and can decide where to use them (or not), organised humanitarianism also constitutes an important form of governance. Not in the sense that there is a single force or source of power that directs its work. Rather than principles, or overarching strategies, what keeps the system (somewhat) together is its network power. "The West does not own and operate humanitarian governance, it maintains a controlling influence over it, much like [it does for] security and economic governance" (Barnett 2013, 386).

As we shall see, an existential malaise is permeating the humanitarian endeavour. Perhaps because it has grown so fast in the past two decades, it may have reached some kind of plateau or structural limit. Like many systems, organised humanitarianism suffers from the classic transition of institutions from a means to an end, to becoming an end in itself. As one observer acutely noted, "The

DOI: 10.4324/9781315658827-6

Weberian struggle between charisma and bureaucracy is alive and well in humanitarian organisational culture today, and the dominance of bureaucracy is felt by many to have a negative effect on the type, tempo, daring and success of operations" (Slim 2015, 16).

Moreover, and to complicate things, there is not one humanitarianism, albeit riven by competing claims and cross-currents, but several. The northern/western humanitarian movement, rooted in various traditions of charity and philanthropy and in the civilising impulses of the Enlightenment, as well as their subsequent manifestations in the expanses of what we now call the Global South, constitutes the dominant, multi-billion-dollar, visible face of humanitarianism. But there are other, lesser traditions as well. Some are ancient and just recently noticed by mainstream humanitarians. Others are emerging and increasingly vocal. Both are challenging the pillars of certitude of the northern humanitarian canon.

I have two starting points: The *first* is about the inherent coloniality of a humanitarian discourse intrinsically linked to the western rhetoric of modernity—a rhetoric of compassion and salvation (yesterday) and development and containment (today)—that has spread from the European centre to the farthest borderlands of the periphery. This western epistemic code still undergirds much of current humanitarianism.

The *second*, and related, focus is on the network power of standards and the isophormism these standards impose. Network power refers to the global dominance of standards that have achieved critical mass in language, technology, trade, law, etc.—as well as in the humanitarian arena (Grewal 2008). The dominance of a particular standard involves a form of power that shapes the functioning of institutions. Because the dominant humanitarian system is "of the North", it is the northern-based agencies that have set the standards and norms that allow it to operate—everything from the codes of conduct and principles to the radio frequencies used by aid agencies, the training provided to security officers, the Sphere standards on the size of tents, and of course clusters, logos and T-shirts. This network power defines the rules of the humanitarian club that new players need to accept if they want to become members. As such, this network power provides the glue that keeps the system somewhat together and allows its disparate parts to communicate with one another. It creates the dominant structures of what has been called the "Empire of Humanity" (Barnett 2011). It creates a self-serving set of dynamics.

My argument is that coloniality and network power combine to shape the humanitarian enterprise and stifle the emergence of potentially more grounded, indigenous or non-westernised approaches. Understanding this combination, and the codes that underpin it, is critical to any discussion on the future of humanitarianism and, in particular, on whether universalism is still a valid project or whether organised humanitarianism will morph into something different or splinter into western and non-western segments and rivulets. And what this means in terms of saving and protecting the lives of survivors of conflict and crisis.

Reveal codes

In the past ten years or so, humanitarianism and humanitarian action have been the sites of scholarly analysis aimed at understanding the functions they perform in North–South relations, world ordering and the promotion of liberal peace (Duffield 2001, Fassin 2010, Donini 2010 amongst others). While much has been uncovered about how political and humanitarian agendas tend to reinforce each other, it is necessary to dig deeper into the nature of humanitarianism by looking at how—as a discourse, an ideology, a set of institutions and professions, and a political economy—it is deeply embedded in a system of knowledge that professes to be universal but is in reality an extension of European and western hubris. This "western code" (Mignolo 2012) is the hidden software of modernity. It is the *patrón de poder*, the matrix of power. It is predicated on the assumption that it is the only game in town and that as the modern (capitalist) system expands, the code replaces all other primitive, non-western and non-modern codes. Hence the inherent coloniality of the code (Mignolo 2012), and, by extension, the inherent coloniality of all aspects of dominant relations—economic, cultural, developmental—between the North and the South, including the humanitarian endeavour. According to Mignolo and other "coloniality thinkers", this western epistemic code still undergirds the processes through which the world is conceptualised, including both liberal and anti-capitalist critiques of the model, and therefore much of current humanitarianism.

But why is this concept important? Isn't this focus on colonialism just a re-hash of the analyses of the Marxist thinkers and other "dependistas" of the 1960s? In part, yes; but with a deeper and interesting twist: the Peruvian sociologist Aníbal Quijano introduced the disturbing concept of "coloniality of power", which he defined as the invisible and constitutive side of "modernity". In an article originally published in 1989 (Quijano 2007), he explicitly linked the coloniality of power in the political and economic spheres with the coloniality of knowledge.

The argument goes like this: coloniality is seen as an exclusively European phenomenon that has spread with modernity. Starting from the Renaissance, it spread around the world through the Reformation, the Enlightenment and the French Revolution, scientific discoveries, and of course the web-like expansion of the capitalist system. In this way, the myth of eurocentrism identifies European particularity with universality *tout court* (Wallerstein 2006). The coexistence of diverse ways of producing and transmitting knowledge is eliminated because now all forms of human knowledge are ordered on an epistemological scale from the traditional to the modern, from barbarism to civilisation, from the community to the individual, from the North to the South, West and East. By way of this strategy of epistemic colonisation, European (and later, western) scientific thought has positioned itself as the only valid form of producing knowledge. The West thus acquires an epistemological hegemony over all the other cultures of the world. Quijano ended the argument with the natural consequence: if knowledge is colonised, the task ahead is to de-colonise knowledge. This epistemic decolonisation could be achieved either by de-linking from the western canon, or by its implosion and the emergence of a "pluriversality" of systems of knowledge. I will return to this thought at the end of the chapter.

Humanitarianism, as an emanation of both western traditions of charity and compassion and the rationality of the Enlightenment, in its current manifestations is of course inherently northern and western. Like its ideological counterparts, for example in the modernisation or development fields, it has sometimes co-opted, sometimes incorporated earlier "non-modern" forms of caring for the suffering of others. And because it is essentially about how we (northern actors) look at the other, the debate about the inherent coloniality of humanitarianism is of crucial importance for the future of the humanitarian enterprise.

In addition to the hidden software—the secret code—that underpins western modernity, and thus the humanitarian discourse, there are the manifest codes of network power. These are easier to unscramble and are linked to globalisation. Globalisation comes as a package; all or nothing, and that "all" embraces "free" market economy, consumerism, scientific positivism and a dismissal of religion unless it supports the greater objective of the free market. Globalisation is also about the expansion of a particular set of values such as democracy and human rights, including individual freedoms that are sometimes seen as at odds with particular traditional or non-western cultures.

The considerable network power of globalisation shapes institutions, values and behaviour to the far ends of the world and reinforces the marginalisation, if not demonisation, of communities or movements that reject the dominant model. Mainstream western humanitarian agencies are increasingly integrated and subjected to such growing isomorphism. Going against the grain butts against power dynamics that push in the opposite direction.

As with other aspects of globalisation, the processes of humanitarian action are guided by a set of standards that are designed by outsiders and imposed through network power (Grewal 2008). 'Network power' refers to the global dominance of standards that have achieved critical mass in language, technology, trade, law and many other areas. The dominance of a successful standard involves a form of power. While these new standards allow for global coordination, they also eclipse local standards, incompatible with dominant ones. Thus many of the choices driving globalisation are only formally free because the network power of a dominant standard makes it the only effectively available option. Networks are the means by which globalisation proceeds. All networks have standards embedded in them. In theory we have the freedom to reject or ignore standards. In practice, David Singh Grewal shows, our choices tend to narrow over time, because "standards have a power that grows in proportion to the size of the network they unite" (Grewal 2008, 27). As such, network power "reflects a new imperialism". In other words, the larger the network, the more difficult it is for an alternative network to survive. In the case of the humanitarian system, the dominant northern network has marginalised earlier or different approaches to saving and protecting lives and now acts as a barrier to entry for local or non-conventional players.

Put slightly differently, the ideology and the practice of humanitarian action operate as one with, and are sometimes functional to, the logic of "Empire", that is, not the imperial reach of one state or even an alliance of states, but a new form of globalised non-territorial power. The dominance of standards, technologies and processes developed in the global North shapes the order in which nation states, global institutions, corporations and even civil society organisations function according to established hierarchical divisions and genealogies (Hardt and Negri 2001, xiv; 2004, xii). From this perspective, humanitarian agencies have to operate within the strictures of the standards. They are functional to the development of "Empire" and as such become the "mendicant orders of Empire" and the "capillary vessels of globalisation". Whether they like it or not, these agencies function as the "powerful pacific weapons of the new world order" (Hardt and Negri 2001, 36), or, in the words of another analyst, as "the laboratories of the new liberal imperium" (Duffield 2007, 135). This was confirmed authoritatively by none other than Secretary of State Colin Powell in his plea to US NGOs to join the US liberal peace agenda in Afghanistan when he elevated the status of NGOs to "the force multipliers" that are part of the US "combat team" (Powell 2001).

In sum, humanitarianism is the product of the expansion of western values and economic power. The capitalist system, building on its colonial past, has displaced all other systems. This power has now become transnational or global; the same network power defines the standards and *modus operandi* of the humanitarian enterprise. If you are a small humanitarian agency in the Global South, you are free not to choose the dominant model, but in practice this is pointless if you aspire to be an important player that attracts contracts and funds. The dominant humanitarian model has reached "critical mass" and the incentives to join it are irresistible. However, the western capitalist model seems to have reached its structural limits, or more precisely, some of its power is leaking eastwards. The question to which we must turn to now is—is there a (relative) decline of the West and a rise of the Rest, and if so, what will happen to the western/northern humanitarian model?

CTRL+ALT+DEL?

Is there a need for a global re-boot of the humanitarian system? Can a western networked system reinvent itself? If it is true that the western epistemic code permeates much of contemporary humanitarianism—whether in the form of a rhetoric of charity, compassion, salvation, universal values or control—can this be changed? This is likely to be a tall order.

Mignolo and other "coloniality" thinkers argue that delinking from the West and the related syndrome of "occidentosis" is possible, and they see glimmers of change arising from localised revolts. They pin their hopes on the likes of Subcomandante Marcos or on radical sovereignty affirmations (Bolivia; the prospects of a South American Union) or the rekindling of non-modern cultures and forms of association. Is something similar likely to happen in the humanitarian domain? For sure, indigenous traditions of compassion are found in all cultures, as various recent studies have demonstrated (Feinstein International Center 2008; Anderson et al. 2012). They sometimes manage to coexist with the dominant system. But the institutions that set the codes for organised compassion remain top-down, sometimes arrogant, sometimes benevolent, but inescapably northern and western in values and structures.

For now

Is a shift from western and network-powered software to open source humanitarianism possible? Is it desirable? Could, as the coloniality thinkers claim for the western code, humanitarianism become more local, building on existing culturally grounded approaches for dealing with crisis? Does technology (so far, western in essence) hold a promise here in liberating localised humanitarianisms, even hand-held humanitarianisms, from the strictures of network power?

One of the peculiar things about humanitarian action is that it is experienced as a transaction without reciprocity. As many have noted (in particular Fassin 2010, 12) it is a dominant discourse that shapes the relationship with the "other" and, in extreme cases, creates its own reality on the ground—as for example when the United Nations High Commissioner for Refugees (UNHCR) "creates" its own forms of sovereignty in refugee camps (Slaughter and Crisp 2009). More fundamentally, perhaps, it is a discourse of inequality that is about bio-politics— what Didier Fassin calls "the politics of life". That compassion entails an asymmetrical relationship is nothing new. The social relationship between the two parties, regardless of the intentions of those concerned, is based on an essentially unequal exchange. Compassion is conceived as a moral sentiment where reciprocity is impossible: "hapless victims" can only receive; they know instinctively that "what is expected of them is the humility of the obliged rather than the claim of the rights holder" (Fassin 2010, 11). As the African proverb says: The hand that gives is always above the hand that receives. Unlike the citizen who, in theory at least, can punish the state through elections, the "victim" has no recourse, no possibility of redress against the governance of humanitarianism.

Some have argued that the humanitarian transaction can become more equal, more culturally sensitive, more grounded (for example, Anderson 2008). And indeed some progress has been made thanks to the adoption of standards of accountability to beneficiaries and increased information on, and access to, mechanisms of redress for those at the receiving end of sub-par humanitarian interventions. And much lip service is given to engagement and participation of those concerned (Brown and Donini 2014). But these measures are tantamount to tinkering with the software, not challenging or replacing it. So far there is no consensus, no clear picture of what a humanitarian paradigm equally acceptable across cultures might look like. Nor, indeed, whether it would be possible or even desirable to pursue such an objective.

Should an open debate where "we" do not determine "their" agenda conclude that some new and more acceptable synthesis is possible, this would go a long way towards re-establishing the *bona fides* of a humanitarian apparatus that is currently seen as blind-sided and compromised. This would imply addressing the question of whether the relationship between the "giver" and the "receiver" is inherently a disempowering one, or whether it could tend towards equality. It would also imply turning on its head the top-down nature of the current enterprise. And what then of our traditional beloved humanitarian principles? Would they still remain valid without their underlying western code? Would they be relegated to the graveyard of good ideas and other "isms"?[2] If we accept that the current humanitarian system is consubstantial with globalisation and "Empire", then what are the implications if "Empire" becomes progressively less western? An idea for a research agenda, perhaps.

Humanitarianism 2.0

The blood-soaked fields of the battle of Solferino are generally seen as the birthplace of modern organised humanitarian action. Humanitarianism 1.0 was the heroic phase articulated around the Dunantist principles of humanity, impartiality and, at times, neutrality, as well as the European traditions of charity and compassion. It was volunteerish and diverse and sometimes unstructured. It was based on the sometimes competing "three Cs": compassion, change and containment (Walker and Maxwell 2009, 21). This arc of diverse and largely unstructured growth lasted until the end of the Cold War, when major quantitative and qualitative change occurred: institutionalisation, professionalisation and proceduralisation on one hand and, because of the important governance functions it performs, instrumentalisation on the other. The different shades of this humanitarian international include Dunantists who strive to maintain fidelity to principle, Wilsonians who tend to align with the values and sometimes the policies of the governments that fund them, faith-based, solidarists, and the like. What characterises these agencies, whether or not they are pressed into the service of liberal peace, is the increasing institutionalisation, standardisation, oligopolisation and normalisation of an enterprise that remains inescapably (for now) northern and western. And the software it runs on is still, essentially, the western code of coloniality.

But will this situation perdure? The big picture, rather puzzling question that we must ask is: Is there only one world or are there various possible worlds? Or, put in another way: is it possible to share a single world where many worlds are possible? Not universal, but pluriversal or polyversal. The manner in which we answer it could have deep implications for the future of organised humanitarianism. The question is important because if there is one world, universal humanitarianism remains a possibility. If it is true that humanitarianism as we know it is linked to the expansion of the modern world—a.k.a. the western capitalist system—now that the West is in retreat, humanitarianism may morph into something less western but nonetheless with a universal discourse and claim to legitimacy. It would continue to be the smiley face of globalisation, whether "Empire" remains western in essence, or not.

However, what if we are heading towards multiple worlds? While globalised capitalism remains a constant, we are already seeing that the Westphalian model (capitalism + democracy) is being challenged by an Eastphalian model based on so much state and not so much democracy.[3] Other "non-phalian" models might be in the offing. If this is the case, then we are likely to see the emergence of a similarly pluriversal humanitarian galaxy. The pretence of the West/North to impose its model of humanitarian governance is likely to ring increasingly hollow when China or India become big international players in disaster relief. They may well promote a different humanitarian discourse. Because of wariness about ideology, this is likely to be state-centred humanitarian aid—without the "ism". And this will challenge our western notions of universality. As Immanuel Wallerstein reminds us, "There is nothing so ethnocentric, so particularistic, as the claim of universalism" (Wallerstein 2006). Or in the words of Quijano (2007, 177): "Nothing is less rational, finally, than the pretension that the specific cosmic vision of a particular *ethnie* should be taken as universal rationality, even if such an *ethnie* is called western Europe." This is tantamount to imposing "provincialism as universalism".

Universality is in the eye of the beholder: the cold metal of the water pump provided by the well-meaning principled humanitarian can feel quite different to the "hapless victim" or to the militant insurgent. Rather than as an expression of compassion or solidarity, it could be seen as redolent of arrogance, alien values or representing a history of colonialism and domination.

Some would argue (read: the coloniality thinkers) that this question cannot be resolved without first addressing the zero-point issue. Colombian philosopher Santiago Castro-Gómez (2005) argues that western knowledge is characterised by what he describes as the "Hubris of Zero Point", a perspective that hides itself and implies that it is not particular. The zero-point view is supposed to be beyond the realm of representation and does not see itself as embodied within a specific culture, space and time. Through it, western knowledge of all kinds deems itself universal, it does not accept that it is fundamentally Eurocentric. Western rationality creates hierarchies and orders reality while remaining outside that which it orders. Thus humanitarianism's claims of universality, because they are essentially embedded in the discourse of coloniality, look very different when seen through the lenses and screens of those who endure or challenge, from different perspectives, this dominant view of the world. And if coloniality is now in retreat and western codes are challenged by other emerging codes, the possibility of plural humanitarianisms cannot be ruled out.

On the other hand, post-modernist thinkers, who see the world ordering web of Empire recreating itself after having incorporated the farthest borderlands and ungoverned spaces, will argue that the dualist centre–periphery model of domination, which was the embodiment of coloniality, is no longer valid (Hardt and Negri, 2001; Duffield 2001). The locus of power is no longer territorial; it has been replaced by the networks and systems of globalisation. From this perspective, there is one world—the world of post-modern capitalism in which relations with the borderlands are governed by liberal peace and military interventionist agendas. Empire is a condition within which all of us are located, all individuals, institutions and states. Empire has no "exteriority" or outside. It has reached the end of the Earth.

It would be a mistake to consider Empire as a uniform totalistic structure that has imposed modernity by replacing pre-existing "non-modern" realities and epistemic codes. In fact, it may be wiser to think of "multiple modernities"

(Eisenstadt 2000), thus recognising that, with the possible exception of the Americas, there have always been "entanglements" between the driving forces of modernity which originated in Renaissance Europe and the rest of the world. As we see today, modernity comes in different hues. All are "entangled" with the original *patrón de poder* and the expansion of the capitalist system, but of course there are variations. Democracy, human rights, the individual versus the collective are valued differently—in Switzerland, India and China—while remaining solidly embedded within the dominant (economic and cultural) model of globalisation.

The implication for humanitarianism, here, is that the possibility of a universal discourse remains. It may be disentangled to some extent from its zero point and evolve by incorporating other traditions but, fundamentally, the nurturing of the principled and universal ethos of organised humanitarianism as we know it could be maintained and have a future. It could take the shape of "multiple humanitarianisms" or it could continue to be driven by the network power of the dominant model, but by and large it would continue on its universal trajectory—buffeted by cross-winds and critical antibodies, but in much the same way as Empire incorporates its critics through dialectical cycles of change and renewal.

So what?

There are a couple of takeaways here. Both for academics and practitioners.

The first is that we need to dig more deeply into the essence of humanitarianism. Here, then, is the research agenda. From an empirical perspective, the challenge is to research whether, where and how humanitarianism—as discourse, ideology, institution, profession and political economy—is likely to (a) remain anchored to its traditional zero point; (b) morph into a post-modern universal set of principles and agendas; or (c) split into post-colonial, more-or-less polyversal strands, and what the implications are for those in need of humanitarian action to secure their survival.

The second is that western/northern aid agencies—and aid workers—need to look at their individual agency and assess how what they do either reinforces or diminishes the hold of the dominant discourse. And become more proficient in measuring the obstacles to a more effective and grounded humanitarian ethos. Agencies and individual aid workers cannot expect to be credible if they fail to recognise, or are in denial about, their functions as conveyor belts for western rationality and force multipliers for interventionist or liberal peace agendas. In places such as Afghanistan and Iraq, there has been much obfuscation about the extent to which "humanitarian" activities were embedded into the military interventions, with deleterious consequences for both the credibility of the humanitarian discourse and the security of aid agency staff (Fast 2014). In many conflict situations, institutionalisation, risk-averseness, anti-terror legislation and insurance considerations all conspire to make the aid effort more remote from the at-risk groups it is supposed to serve. The absence of ground truth corrupts the nature of the humanitarian relationship, which is now mediated through technology rather than empathy. The vast humanitarian galaxy, which prided itself in its proximity to those in need, is now increasingly moving from "face-to-face" to "face-to-screen" (Donini and Maxwell 2014).

These examples show how the institutionalisation and professionalisation of the humanitarian enterprise, and its embedded nature in the processes of promotion of the liberal agenda and containment of what happens in the periphery—what is called instrumentalisation—reinforce the dominant nature of the humanitarian discourse and make it difficult, if not impossible, for grounded approaches to emerge. This is made worse by the cultural insensitivity and sometimes arrogance of personal aid-worker behaviour. The response to the Haiti earthquake showed how language and structure conspired both in undermining the state and in erecting artificial barriers to entry for local groups, who were kept at bay from an overbearing humanitarian behemoth (Schuller 2012). Symbolically, the fact that aid coordination meetings were held in English at the airport, where local agencies had no access, and under US military oversight, says a lot about the dependence of international aid agencies on Empire. Government and local humanitarians who did not conform to the standard were kept out. As one frustrated Haitian aid worker quipped to an international, "the answer to Haiti's problems is not on your computer screens".[4]

Can the fundamental nature of the humanitarian relationship be changed? Will it be swept aside by new forms of providing relief to the most vulnerable? When China, India and middle-income countries from Brazil to Indonesia start playing a more important role in the humanitarian theatre, can the fiction of universality and the reality of the western software that underpins it be maintained? Some would argue that humanitarianism is already on life-support, buffeted by the cross-winds of emerging sovereignty-based discourses in the Global South, especially in Asia.

The first challenge for those who recognise themselves in the values inherent in organised humanitarianism is to determine whether or not it is feasible, intellectually and practically, to devise a more equal and culturally grounded approach to addressing the assistance and protection needs of people *in extremis*, that is, an approach that is based on truly universal values—a sort of "universal universalism"—rather than on the currently dominant western universalism and its codes. Unless this process of reckoning takes place, and takes place soon, humanitarianism as we know it risks becoming increasingly disconnected from the reality of the world of peoples.

Notes

1 I would like to thank Alessandro Monsutti and Jeevan Raj Sharma for thoughtful comments on an earlier version of this chapter.
2 At a meeting organised by the Norwegian Refugee Council on humanitarian principles (Brussels, November 2012), the deputy head of the Organization of Islamic Cooperation (OIC) clearly stated that traditional humanitarian principles were good but "not enough", implying that they had to be brought in line with Islamic precepts.
3 On the concept of Eastphalia see Ginsburg (2011).
4 I am indebted to Martin Barber for this observation.

References

Al-e Ahmad J. (1982) *Plagued by the West (Gharbzadegi)*, Caravan, New York.

Anderson M. (2008) "The Giving–Receiving Relationship: Inherently Unequal?", in *The Humanitarian Response Index 2008*, DARA, Madrid, 97–105,

Anderson M., Brown, D. and Jean, I. (2012) *Time to Listen. Hearing People on the Receiving End of International Aid*, CDA Collaborative Learning Projects, Cambridge, MA.

Barnett M. (2011) *The Empire of Humanity. A History of Humanitarianism*, Cornell University Press, New York.

Barnett M. (2013) "Humanitarian Governance", *Annual Review of Political Science*, 16, 379–398.

Brown D. and Donini, A. (2014) "Rhetoric or Reality? Putting Affected People at the centre of Humanitarian Action", ALNAP Study, Active Learning Network for Accountability and Performance in Humanitarian Action/Overseas Development Institute, London (www.alnap.org/resource/12859), accessed 20 May 2015.

Castro-Gómez S. (2005) *La Hybris del Punto Cero*, Editorial Pontificia Universidad Javeriana, Bogotá.

Donini A. (2010) "The Far Side: The Meta Functions of Humanitarianism in a Globalized World", *Disasters*, 34(S2), S220–S237.

Donini A. ed. (2012) *The Golden Fleece: Manipulation and Independence in Humanitarian Action*, Kumarian Press, Sterling, VA.

Donini A. and Maxwell, D. (2014) "From Face-to-Face to Face-to-Screen: Implications of Remote Management for the Effectiveness and Accountability of Humanitarian Action in Insecure Environments", *International Review of the Red Cross*, 95, 383–413.

Duffield M. (2001) *Global Governance and the New Wars. The Merging of Development and Security*, Zed Books, London and New York.

Duffield M. (2007) *Development, Security and Unending War. Governing the World of Peoples*, Polity Press, Cambridge.

Eisenstadt S. (2000) Multiple Modernities, *Daedalus*, 129, 1–29.

Fassin D. (2010) *La raison humanitaire: une histoire morale du temps present*, Gallimard/Seuil, Paris.

Fast L. (2014) *Aid in Danger. The Perils and Promise of Humanitarianism*, University of Pennsylvania Press, Philadelphia.

Feinstein International Centre (2008) "Humanitarian Agenda 2015: Principles, Power and Perceptions", Final Report: *The State of the Humanitarian Enterprise* (http://fic.tufts.edu/publication-item/humanitarian-agenda-2015-principles-power-and-perceptions/), accessed 20 May 2015.

Ginsburg T. (2011) "Eastphalia and Asian Regionalism", *UC Davis Law Review*, 44(3), 859–877.

Grewal D. (2008) *Network Power: The Social Dynamics of Globalization*, Yale University Press, New Haven, CT.

Hardt M. and Negri, A. (2001) *Empire*, Harvard University Press, Cambridge, MA and London.

Hardt M. and Negri, A. (2004) *Multitude. War and Democracy in the Age of Empire*, Penguin Books, New York.

Mignolo W. (2012) *The Darker Side of western Modernity: Global Futures, Decolonial Options*, Duke University Press, Durham, NC.

Powell C. (2001) "Remarks to the National Foreign Policy Conference for the Leaders of NGOs: Address to US INGOs", Washington, DC, 26 October (http://2001-2009.state.gov/secretary/former/powell/remarks/2001/5762.htm), accessed 20 May 2015.

Quijano A. (2007) "Coloniality and Modernity/Rationality", *Cultural Studies*, 21(2/3), 168–178.

Schuller M. (2012) "Haiti's Bitter Harvest. Humanitarian Aid in the 'Republic of NGOs'", in Donini A. (ed.) *The Golden Fleece: Manipulation and Independence in Humanitarian Action*, Kumarian Press, Sterling, VA.

Slaughter A. and Crisp, J. (2009) *A Surrogate State? The Role of UNHCR in Protracted Refugee Situations*, Research Paper 168, United Nations High Commissioner for Refugees, London (www.unhcr.org/4981cb432.html), accessed 10 May 2015.

Slim H. (2015) *Humanitarian Ethics. A Guide to the Morality of Aid in War and Disaster*, Hurst, London.

Walker P. and Maxwell, D. (2009) *Shaping the Humanitarian World*, Routledge, New York and London.

Wallerstein I. (2006) *European Universalism. The Rhetoric of Power*, New Press, New York.

5 More than morals

Making sense of the rise of humanitarian aid organisations

Kai Koddenbrock

Despite the flurry of publications on humanitarian aid in recent years, one central question has not received enough attention: How come humanitarian aid has been growing constantly in recent years? How can this phenomenon be explained? Many scholars have tackled the question but have predominantly reverted to a change in morals and a new sense of global solidarity, or to some kind of CNN effect, to make sense of this expansion. This chapter suggests instead that the way humanitarian aid organisations shield their operations from public scrutiny plays a big role. Thanks to this separation, NGOs are able to pursue important fund-raising and PR campaigns in the humanitarian marketplace to increase their funding. The reality on the ground of humanitarian aid disappears in the process because it matters little to state donors and is unknown to private donors.

While public debate on humanitarian aid is rather restricted to times of large-scale disasters like the tsunami in 2004, the Haiti earthquake in 2011 or the plight of displaced people in Syria since 2013, the professional and bureaucratic fields of humanitarian aid have expanded massively over the past 20 years. The funds spent on humanitarian aid have risen from about US$6 billion in the 1990s to US$22 billion per year in 2013 (Development Initiatives 2014, 4). Between 2010 and 2012 numbers stagnated because of a contraction of funding during the financial crisis. However, this stagnation was much less pronounced than expected. At the same time, the number of humanitarian field staff at the UN and NGOs is estimated to be 274,000, working for more than 150 NGOs with an annual budget of more than US$10 million a year (United Nations 2013, 11). According to credible estimates, the number of humanitarian workers has doubled since 2000 (Barnett 2011, 3).

In their widely read books *Empire of Humanity* and *Humanitarian Reason*, Michael Barnett and Didier Fassin have brought the study of humanitarian aid and of humanitarian sentiments to the attention of a wider audience in political science, sociology and anthropology. Barnett and Fassin have both worked inside the 'humanitarian system' in the past, Barnett as a UN staff member in the 1990s and Fassin as Vice-president of Médecins sans Frontières (MSF) France in the early 2000s. Socialised in different academic fields – Barnett in International Relations, Fassin in social anthropology – both have combined field research with the attempt to theorise their exposure to the field of humanitarian activity. While

DOI: 10.4324/9781315658827-7

Barnett has ventured into the history of humanitarianism and has provided insights on the workings of UN and NGOs, as is customary in the discipline of IR, Fassin has interrogated humanitarianism in multiple field sites from Caracas to Calais, from Paris to Baghdad. Fassin investigates the humanitarian in unusual policy fields. He has pioneered research on humanitarianism 'at home', producing unusual insights on the role of humanitarian reason in discretionary social policy in rural France, for example. Some of his collaborators have followed in these footsteps (Ticktin 2011).

How do Barnett and Fassin explain the rise in humanitarian aid? In his *Empire of Humanity*, Barnett takes the long view and alludes to shifting 'constellations of the forces of destruction, production and compassion' as a general explanatory ground for the evolution of humanitarian aid (2011, 29). The trio of 'destruction, production and compassion' appeals to the readers' intuition. We agree easily that destruction and the nature of war is a factor in what humanitarian aid wants to do. At the same time, production, wages and poverty determine how many people will be seen as in need of humanitarian aid. Compassion, in turn, is an important factor in shaping the way people relate to problems of destruction and production, and there have been changes in humans' sense of compassion throughout the ages.

Barnett's narrative on the evolution of humanitarian aid, however, relies more on the constant struggle over organisational identity than his proposed trio of forces. Since the 1990s, much of the debate among humanitarian organisations has been about how to deal with needs and rights, the relationship between humanitarianism and human rights (Wilson and Brown 2009), and the differences and similarities between humanitarian aid and development (Koddenbrock 2009). Referring back to his earlier work (Barnett 2009), Barnett essentially explains the shifts in humanitarian aid with these attempts at positioning, which he considers more important than the questions of money or destruction (Barnett 2011, 197). What an organisation will do depends more on its longstanding identity – whether it is more development-oriented, focusing on faith or on the defence of human rights. As a consequence, Barnett falls back on a meso-level of analysis, focusing on organisations rather than forces. The book on humanitarian aid, delving more deeply into the intersection between violence, capitalism and morality, remains to be written.

Didier Fassin's argument is more explicitly moralist. In *Humanitarian Reason* he seeks to explore the 'reconfiguration of what can be called the politics of precarious lives over the past few decades' (2012, 5) and he aims to describe how 'moral sentiments have recently reconfigured politics'. In several illuminating case studies, he shows how the humanitarian logic of discretionary allocation has prevailed over a rights-based claims logic in French social policy, or how inequalities in life-worth are visible when Western MSF staffers were evacuated from Baghdad in 2003 while Iraqi staff members were not. Fassin's arguments are compelling, but they do not suffice to explain why the number and reach of humanitarian organisations has multiplied in recent years.

There are, of course, other attempts at explanation. Mark Duffield, for example, has provided more of a political economy explanation in his *Development, Security and Unending War* (2008). Building on the Malthusian–Marxian concept of surplus populations and Bauman's evocative suggestion of 'wasted lives', he considers the humanitarian system as a system of last resort to assuage open opposition to neoliberalism and continuing inequality in contemporary capitalism. However, Duffield's discussion of capitalism through the Foucauldian/Agambian notion of biopolitics remains cursory. What has changed over the past years, how the NGO form has become so central for the relationship between Western states and their former colonies, is beyond discussion (Shivji 2006).

In this chapter I will build on Barnett's and Fassin's perspectives, but will adopt a more mundane political economy perspective. In this view, the humanitarian system has become a largely self-sustaining professional field, crowded by myriad non-governmental and intergovernmental organisations, which depend on donor funding to operate. The key for their success and growth is to ensure a continuous stream of funding or to increase funding further.

The key characteristic of this field crowded by humanitarian organisations is that it is structured by market logic. As Cooley and Ron showed in their pioneering article, the quest for funding often looks like a 'scramble' (2002), a term alluding to the colonial 'scramble for Africa' in the nineteenth century (Pakenham 1991). Contrary to what humanitarian organisations claim, their decisions on where and how to operate are based not simply on the moral principles of impartiality, neutrality and independence, but on a wealth of other concerns, from funding to visibility and tradition (Krause 2014; Binder, Koddenbrock and Horváth 2013).

At the same time, what humanitarian organisations do on the ground also differs substantially from what they claim. This applies to most organisations' activities, of course. But this divide between claims and reality is much more existential for humanitarian organisations because of the moral high ground they continuously have to occupy to receive private donations and public funding.

In what follows, I will provide insights on the tension between public claims, organisational decision-making, and work on the ground based on results from two research projects: one conducted between 2009 and 2013 in Goma and New York on the practice of humanitarian intervention (Koddenbrock 2015); the other a project for the German Foreign Office on the German humanitarian aid system conducted with colleagues from the Global Public Policy Institute in 2013 (Binder et al. 2013).

Claims and reality in humanitarian aid

Humanitarian aid saves lives. There is no doubt about that. Yet what exactly organisations are doing on the ground and what long-term humanitarian presence does to a country remains often opaque. Humanitarian studies suffer from these two blind spots. More often than not, research on humanitarian aid follows the operating logic of humanitarian organisations, reiterating the importance of humanitarian principles instead of taking a distance. The long-term impact on areas receiving high volumes of humanitarian aid remains in the dark after more than 50 years of humanitarian aid in its current institutional form. Long-term studies of the political economy of humanitarian aid are entirely absent; no organisation to date has been interested in funding this kind of research. Humanitarian organisations choose to remain agnostic about their own long-term impact and find solace in their short-term successes.

Since questions of the long term are not overly relevant either to implementing organisations or to donors who profit from the visibility of their support to the worthy and moral cause of humanitarian aid, an important component of a broader understanding of how humanitarian aid organisations manage to increase their funding and scope of operations lies in the way public claims and operational reality relate. The lack of scrutiny of real operations has helped humanitarian aid to enjoy ever-increasing funding for the past two decades. It has also allowed this multi-billion-dollar enterprise to evolve largely to its own standards. Beneficiary accountability is a buzzword but will never play a substantial role because of the structural inequalities built into the humanitarian system. It will probably never democratise substantially because there are no structural incentives for it. More realistic is increased donor and funder scrutiny. The following analysis is a contribution to this scrutiny.

The reality of humanitarian decision-making

A key source of legitimacy and funding stability lies in the concept and negotiation of beneficiary 'need'.[1] Despite all talk of risk, vulnerability (Darcy and Hofmann 2003) and resilience (Chandler 2012), 'need' continues to be the core rallying call for humanitarian aid. The constant quest of humanitarian actors for more adequate needs assessments serve as important tools of justification and fund-raising towards donors. The UN Inter-Agency Standing Committee's integrated needs assessments and UNHCR's global needs assessments are just two examples. Performing a continued search for the adequate measurement of needs has become ever more important since the humanitarian field has grown and become more publicly visible.

Essentially, need operationalises the principle of impartiality. The existence of objective physical needs[2] makes the practice of impartiality appear possible. It has been repeatedly shown, however, that need is only one among several potentially more decisive factors in humanitarian decision-making (Darcy and Hofmann 2003; Rubenstein 2008; Krause 2014, Binder et al. 2013). This is usually decried as a lack of honesty and calls are made to return to real needs-based delivery. This misses the function of performing the quest for needs measurements. Organisations try to foreground the quest and the invocation of need, not the operational practice to make credible calls for immediate funding.

Donors and organisations alike continuously stress that humanitarian organisations become active 'according to need', 'solely based on need'. This is misleading. As Monika Krause has shown in *The Good Project* (2014), in contemporary humanitarian aid there are myriad triggers of a specific humanitarian operation in a specific place (see also Binder et al. 2013). There are a multitude of factors next to the apparent purity of need, as Krause proved in her interview-based analysis of decision-making among MSF-France and Action contre la Faim (Krause 2014, 22ff).

Krause argues that organisational identity matters, as MSF will cater to medical needs and Save the Children to children's needs. Continuously changing programme priorities from sexual and gender-based violence, to HIV and AIDS, to shelter and education plays a role in shaping who goes where and when to do what. National borders are also decisive as different national standards of living are taken into account to judge the urgency of an emergency. Need is thus not an absolute category but will be weighed against nation-state statistics. These are fraught with methodological difficulties. Organisations also take great care to be present in a perfect number of countries: operations in too many countries create too much overhead, so operations become hard to manage. An insufficient number of operations might, by contrast, create an image of too slim a 'portfolio' (Krause 2014, 28–30). Moreover, donor preferences and media attention matter greatly, along with the possibility of access to the places of identified need. This extends to security conditions and existing infrastructure such as roads. The presence of a military (occupation) force might compromise staff security and may strongly discourages NGOs from going where the need is. Then there is the notion of 'added value', which means that it is more attractive to go to places where there are no other organisations, or where one's set of skills is not yet available. The character of the populations served also plays a role. If it is very spread out, the cost–benefit ratio of an operation will be less positive, because a smaller number of 'beneficiaries' for each aid dollar invested will be reached. This means camps offer ideal environments to reach people quickly. Camps thus tend to be prioritised over remote and sparsely populated areas, although this is not warranted by absolute need figures. Finally, the existence of a strong state and government matters. When they are seen to exist, they are considered responsible for helping its populations in the first place. Needs in failed or weak states will thus be prioritised over needs in the US following hurricane Katrina, for example.

The wealth of these non-principled factors impacting on where needs will be served indicates that, similarly to the principles, need also works as an advocacy tool to secure humanitarian funding. Being more attentive to the operational level, however, reveals that it is even more complicated than that. As seen above, need never shapes humanitarian aid alone. Operationally, humanitarian aid is based on a bundle of bureaucratic considerations and operates within an intricate web of power relations and social structures. The strong focus on the conceptualisation and measurement of needs and principles occupies analysts and policy-makers, and keeps them busy with concepts that operate beyond these self-interested concerns and beyond power structures and governments.

MSF has started to be more explicit about these dependencies on the ground – on its own terms. Former MSF president Bradol now acknowledges, for example, what James Darcy had already indicated in 2003: agencies tend to assess situations in relation to their own programmes (Darcy and Hofmann 2003, 6). Bradol and Jézéquiel reveal that

we are [sometimes, KK] choosing our areas of operation by virtue of their potential for experimentation with new approaches related to early treatment or prevention of malnutrition. … Once again, this is not necessarily a problem, but it is helpful to recognise what really influences our operational decisions. In this case, they are related to a particular view of malnutrition as a global issue: our local operations serve as arguments in a series of negotiations over global food and nutrition policies.

(Bradol and Jézéquiel 2010, 12)

Xavier Crombé was an early advocate for the position MSF adopts publicly today:

It is part of both humanitarian and peacekeeping public relations to make the role of the welcoming state appear smaller than it is. Need and humanitarian principles are all devoid of any engagement with the public authorities or other de-facto authorities. In forums of reflection or in private, humanitarians tend to stress the multiple dependencies they find themselves in. The work of humanitarian NGOs does indeed not take place in a vacuum. We are compelled to negotiate with a certain number of actors, including Western armies, as well as 'rebellious' armed groups, factions, governments or local authorities that are more or less legitimate, in order to have access to the civil populations that we intend to assist. We should therefore acknowledge in a pragmatic way that we are in fact dependent on these interactions to successfully carry out our activities. This is why, rather than talking about independence to describe our position in the relations of force and domination that characterizes our areas of operation, it seems to me more realistic to talk about the ongoing attempt to balance our dependencies.

(Crombé 2006, 5)

MSF has started to challenge the abstract need and humanitarian space approach publicly, but in operational practice is not necessarily taking existing power structures seriously beyond the necessities of negotiation. In Goma, an MSF manager told me how this dependence plays out: it is primarily a nuisance to the capacity of self-directed aid provision.

The manager had been sceptical about the utility of the operations MSF currently pursued in North Kivu. The hospitals and health centres they served were not the ones where need was greatest, according to her. But when they came to the area and had to decide where to engage, they had to negotiate with the provincial ministry of health, which tries to manage NGO and UN service provision as well as they can. The British NGO Merlin, for example, would get the hospitals around Rutshuru; the German Malteser a little health centre on the road towards Rutshuru; MSF a hospital behind Sake, etc.

KK: And the other question, not about the moral duty, but do you think that you have the right to work here?

MSF manager: Yes and no. Yes because we're here to provide the assistance to the local population which would otherwise not have it, and they don't have a voice to ask for it. Then yes, I think, we do have a right to be here.

Again, I think sometimes we get to this blockage where we feel that the right to be here is done through the authorities who, as far as we may know, do not represent whatsoever the people we're actually trying to help. So you're sort of working in two ways: you're trying to make the authorities happy so you can physically have the legal right to stay. But at the same time we're trying to target the population which we think is most vulnerable, and sometimes there is a clash between the two. When we first got here, we had a long debate over where, which health centres we are allowed to support. We felt that we had the right to go out to the most remote health centres, again not necessarily the highest numbers, but maybe the more vulnerable ones. Areas where they have stock ruptures like essential drugs every month. The authorities didn't want that. The authorities wanted us to stay on, like, the main access roads, which is where the numbers are much higher, because for them that was more their priority, you know. The numbers look better at the end of each month. So in the end we kind of had to make a compromise. We did refuse to go to their ones, but we ended up going to ones who had maybe higher patient numbers but are still further away. So yeah, I think we have a right to be here if we actually respond to the needs of the population. But I think often we mistake that right by thinking, well, the authorities have given us the right to be here therefore we can do whatever we like. I think there is a missing link between the authorities and the local population.[3]

In this passage, on one hand a complex negotiation of morality takes place; on the other it shows how MSF calculates and negotiates with the dependencies in which it finds itself. The 'right to work' question during my interview served to gauge interviewees' attitudes towards well known aid criticisms, colonial legacies, or the general moral foundations of their work. This MSF manager argues there are two levels of right: a formal level which is expressed by the authorities giving them work permits and visas, and a material level. At the material level, the legitimacy of the authorities is in doubt because she does not feel the Congolese authorities are representing their people. She deduces from this distinction that organisations are not free to do whatever they like just because they were granted operating permits. They should be striving to do morally sound work all along. MSF thus gains its legitimacy from the material level of right emanating from decent and effective aid provision.

Yet the intricacies of need and their relationship to negotiations with existing power brokers surface clearly here. The MSF manager assumes that their principles require them to go where the most 'vulnerable' are. Vulnerability is a recent variation on the concept of need. In her analysis, MSF's dependence on local political authorities prevents them from doing so. But negotiations lead to a situation both can live with. This is what Crombé has argued for, and that which president Allié turned into the official MSF position in 2011. Obviously, humanitarian aid never happened in a void despite the normative proclamations made. Yet it is obvious from this interview that accepting the role and priorities of actually existing government structures is a hard pill to swallow in operational practice. The progressive tone of recent MSF proclamations meets the reality of host government dependent assistance.

Seen from this angle, it makes intuitive sense that there is not a single external evaluation of MSF operations available publicly. These evaluations might show how hesitant, or even hostile, MSF often is to these negotiations. All publications potentially straddling the disconnect between public claims and operational reality have been undertaken by their own high-level or research staff. The short pieces by former or acting presidents Rony Braumann, Hervé Bradol or Fabrice Weissman, the flagship report on *MSF and Protection – Pending or Closed?* (Soussan 2008), as well as the book-length volumes on *Humanitarian Negotiations Revealed* (Magone et al. 2011) and *In the Eyes of Others* (Abu-Sada 2012), all bear witness to this. Analysts have to rely on these non-independent sources or the annual reports which feature an introduction by the acting president summarising the conceptual debates and challenges taking place throughout the past year and charting the way forward. This fact indicates that acknowledging dependence and the intricacies of decision-making remains part of the public performance at the expense of real scrutiny.

Increased professionalism of humanitarian organisations (see Weiss, Chapter 1 in this volume) thus not only refers to better delivery, financial management or staff selection, but also to effective public relations and reporting in terms of securing legitimacy and thus funds. Protecting the image and integrity of the organisation is one of the most essential concerns of organisations acting in this both moral and economic project market.

NGO decision-making: the German case

Our study on the funding decisions of German federal ministries and their NGO partners offered a similar lesson (Binder et al. 2013). Humanitarian project markets are at least as shaped by market logic as by humanitarian principles. And these markets differ nationally. NGOs originating in the German, French or British humanitarian project market (Stroup 2012) operate differently and are shaped by different factors.

The German humanitarian NGO market is not very big. The country has had more of a focus on development aid since the Second World War. However, between 2005 and 2010, more than 50 German and foreign NGOs have received humanitarian funding from either the Foreign Office (Auswärtiges Amt, AA) or the Federal Ministry of Economic Cooperation and Development (Bundesministerium für Wirtschaftliche Zusammenarbeit und Entwicklung, BMZ) (Channel Research 2011, 88–90). The German NGO market comprises mostly small to medium-sized NGOs with an annual budget of €30 million or less.[4] Only Welthungerhilfe has an annual budget of more than €100 million.

These NGOs emerged from development and civil society initiatives between 1960 and 1980. For this reason, the BMZ has been the key government partner of many German NGOs in terms of financing and normative back-up. As a consequence, most of them pursue a long-term approach to humanitarian assistance. Barely any of the German NGOs can be compared to principled humanitarian organisations such as MSF or the International Committee of the Red Cross. Among German NGOs, creativity in dealing with the principles has always reigned. In our study we identified five factors that shape the German NGOs' distribution decisions:

First, the availability of and nature of funds. German NGOs acquire their humanitarian funds through various channels. Private donations make up 10–30 per cent of the overall budget. AA funding in the past amounted to less than 10 per cent among most German NGOs (Help 2011, 29–31; Malteser 2011, 6; Welthungerhilfe 2011, 36). The BMZ funding, UN and ECHO are a more important funding base for the NGOs. One has to bear in mind that public and private funds are different. Private donations can hardly be used, for instance, to open new offices, because fund-raising campaigns promise that an overwhelming part of donations will reach the recipients. The use of public funds, by contrast, needs to conform to the legal, budgetary and political rules imposed by the funder. NGOs must therefore negotiate constantly over the provenance of their funds, how they are entitled to use them and how they should be spent.

Second, the feasibility of a particular operation. This depends not only on the available funds, but also on the security situation in the area concerned, the availability of staff, knowledge of the area and existing relationships with local partners. For most German NGOs, only operations with a long-term perspective (minimum three years) are attractive. The costs of setting up a new operation are high and the NGOs' mindset is development-oriented. As a consequence, it is much more likely that they will continue or modestly expand existing operations than start new ones.

At a given point in time, an NGO has a particular assistance portfolio. Institutional memory, existing country operations, local partner organisations and relationships with recipients determine this portfolio. Whatever new activity is discussed relates to the existing portfolio. For example, when Malteser considered setting up shop in Banda Aceh, they could not afford it because they already had a security intensive operation going on in Pakistan at the time. When Help e.V. could no longer work inside Iraq, they decided to shift their operations to Syria to assist Iraqi refugees.[5]

Third, media attention also plays a role in NGO decision-making because some mediatised crises generate large private and public donations. Yet our own research did not confirm that the 'CNN-effect' strongly shapes the German NGOs' humanitarian response. The overall stream of operations among German NGOs is more tied to the organisations' history, identity and existing portfolio.

Fourth, needs come in only intermittently. German NGOs do not usually conduct their own needs assessments. They take stock of existing international needs assessments, relate these to their portfolio and choose a country, sector or population group to assist. Within the country, they conduct local investigation missions to decide which specific village or population group will receive support. Need is one, but by no means the most important, decision-making criterion among German NGOs.

Fifth, and finally, added value is a crucial criterion. Added value means operating on the basis of existing know-how, considering the presence of other NGOs in the area or sector concerned and using funds efficiently. If a particular crisis region is already replete with humanitarian actors, there may be little added value in joining their ranks. If the costs for setting up the operation are excessively high, little added value will be created by investing there instead of somewhere else.

MSF's reluctance to play by provincial governments' rules and German NGOs real decision-making show that these NGOs have to be very skilful at convincing donors and funders of their moral purity. That the humanitarian market has grown nearly continuously over the past 20 years indicates that most NGOs have done this job well.

Concluding remarks: towards a political economy of humanitarian aid

Because of the growth of the humanitarian enterprise and the connected flurry of peacebuilding, scholars have started to delve more deeply into the intricacies of aid work (Mosse 2011; Autesserre 2014; Smirl 2015; Koddenbrock 2015). This 'turn to the local' (Chandler 2010; MacGinty and Richmond 2013; Koddenbrock 2013) has generated a more complete understanding of the reality of humanitarian aid. There were already numerous books on the failures of humanitarian aid actors in the conflicts of the 1990s (de Waal 1997; Terry 2002) but so far nobody has invested in longitudinal impact assessments. The growing genre of the humanitarian autobiography (Alexander 2013; Cain, Postlewait and Thomson 2006) is also quite frank about the problems and pitfalls of working in the industry, but more holistic scrutiny continues to be absent.

Despite the recent sophisticated interventions by Barnett and Fassin, for example, two important gaps still exist: What is the long-term effect on areas of heavy humanitarian aid presence like South Sudan, eastern Congo or northern Uganda? And just as importantly: Are there any connections between the rise of humanitarian organisations and shifts in geopolitics and global political economy? (Arrighi 1994; Pettis 2013). Pursuing these questions would greatly enrich the study of contemporary humanitarian aid. In humanitarian studies more narrowly speaking, the concern with public relations, funding and effective delivery has prevented this broader perspective on humanitarian aid from being pursued further. In this chapter, I have focused on the reality of the humanitarian project market. This market thrives on public proclamations and a very different operational reality in terms of both institutional decision-making and aid realities on the ground. The overly clean picture prevailing in public perception explains to some degree why humanitarian aid has been on the rise in recent decades.

Yet humanitarian aid is a practice of constant cooperation and conflict. Its web of dependencies determines the shape of humanitarian aid at a specific time and in a particular place. NGOs such as MSF are reluctant to deal with the priorities of a sitting government if it goes against their philosophy. German NGOs will make aid decisions based on their traditions, the availability of funds by cooperating donors, and calculations of added value. But none of them will acknowledge this too openly. Cooperation and conflict are at the heart of humanitarian aid, but the humanitarian system refuses to say so openly because this kind of transparency would go to the heart of its claim to moral purity.

Notes

1 This passage is adapted from Koddenbrock (2015).
2 Darcy and Hofmann argue that the needs concept originates in development 'basic needs' language and the Maslow pyramid (2003, 16).
3 NGO Goma 7, 16 September 2009.
4 See the annual budgets of Malteser, Help, Care Germany and the German Red Cross, for example.
5 Interviews with Help and Malteser, 1 and 2 May 2013

References

Abu-Sada C. (2012) *In the Eyes of Others. How People in Humanitarian Crises Perceive Humanitarian Aid*, MSF-USA/NYU Center on International Cooperation, New York.
Alexander J. (2013) *Chasing Chaos: My Decade In and Out of Humanitarian Aid*, Broadway Books, New York.
Arrighi G. (1994) *The Long Twentieth Century: Money, Power, and the Origins of Our Times*, Verso, London.
Autesserre S. (2014) *Peaceland: Conflict Resolution and the Everyday Politics of International Intervention*, Cambridge University Press, New York.
Barnett M. (2009) 'Evolution without Progress? Humanitarianism in a World of Hurt', *International Organization*, 63(4), 621–64.
Barnett M. (2011) *Empire of Humanity: A History of Humanitarianism*, Cornell University Press, Ithaca, NY.
Binder A, Koddenbrock K. and Horváth A. (2013) 'Reflections on the Inequity of Humanitarian Assistance: Possible Courses of Action for Germany', discussion paper, Global Public Policy Institute, Berlin (www.gppi.net/fileadmin/user_upload/media/pub/2013/binder-et-al_2013_inequities-humanitarian-assistance.pdf.pdf), accessed 17 June 2015.
Bornstein E. and Redfield P. eds (2010) *Forces of Compassion: Humanitarianism between Ethics and Politics*, School for Advanced Research Press, Santa Fe, NM.
Bradol J.-H. and Jézéquel J.-H. (2010) *Child Undernutrition: Advantages and Limits of a Humanitarian Medical Approach*, MSF CRASH, Paris (www.msf-crash.org/drive/3c82-cahier_nut_va.pdf), accessed 17 June 2015.
Cain K., Postlewait H. and Thomson A. (2006) *Emergency Sex (and Other Desperate Measures)*, Ebury, London.
Chandler D. (2010) *International Statebuilding: The Rise of Post-Liberal Governance*, Routledge, London.
Chandler D. (2012) 'Resilience and Human Security: The Post-Interventionist Paradigm', *Security Dialogue*, 43(3), 213–29.
Channel Research (2011) *Die deutsche humanitäre Hilfe im Ausland*, Channel Research, Berlin.
Cooley A. and Ron J. (2002) 'The NGO Scramble: Organizational Insecurity and the Political Economy of Transnational Action', *International Security*, 27(1), 5–39.
Crombé X. (2006) *Independence and Security*, MSF CRASH, Paris

Darcy J. and Hofmann C.-A. (2003) *According to Need?: Needs Assessment and Decision-Making in the Humanitarian Sector*, HPG Report, Overseas Development Institute, London.

Development Initiatives (2014) *Global Humanitarian Assistance Report*, Development Initiatives, London.

Donini A. (2010) 'The Far Side: The Meta Functions of Humanitarianism in a Globalised World', *Disasters*, 34(2), 220–237.

Duffield M. (2008) *Development, Security and Unending War: Governing the World of Peoples*, reprinted, Polity Press, Cambridge.

Fassin D. (2012) *Humanitarian Reason: A Moral History of the Present*, University of California Press, Berkeley.

Help e.V. (2011) *Annual Report*, Help e.V., Bonn (www.help-ev.de/en/help/help-jahresbericht-2011/), accessed 17 June 2015

Koddenbrock K. (2009) *European Commission and United States Approaches to Linking Relief, Rehabilitation and Development*, Johns Hopkins University Press, Washington, DC.

Koddenbrock K. (2013) *Strategic Essentialism and the Possibilities of Critique in Peacebuilding*, Global Dialogue Series 2, Centre for Global Cooperation Research, Duisburg.

Koddenbrock K. (2015) *The Practice of Humanitarian Intervention: Aid Workers, Agencies and Institutions in the DR Congo*, Routledge, London.

Krause M. (2014) *The Good Project. Humanitarian Relief NGOs and the Fragmentation of Reason*, University of Chicago Press, Chicago and London.

MacGinty R. and Richmond O. (2013) 'The Local Turn in Peacebuilding: A Critical Agenda for Peace', *Third World Quarterly*, 54(3), 763–783.

Magone C., Neumann M. and Weissman F. eds (2011) *Humanitarian Negotiations Revealed: The MSF Experience*, Hurst, London.

Malteser (2011) *Finanzbericht 2011*, Malteser, Köln (www.malteser-international.org//fileadmin/dam/oeffentlich/malteser-international.de/Publikationen/Jahresbericht/Finanzbericht_2011_DE.pdf), accessed 17 June 2015.

Mosse D. (2011) *Adventures in Aidland: The Anthropology of Professionals in International Development*, Berghahn Books, New York.

Pakenham T. (1991) *The Scramble for Africa, 1876–1912*, Random House, New York.

Pettis M. (2013) *The Great Rebalancing: Trade, Conflict, and the Perilous Road Ahead for the World Economy*, Princeton University Press, Princeton, NJ.

Rubenstein J.C. (2008) 'The Distributive Commitments of International NGOs', in Barnett M.N. (ed.), *Humanitarianism in Question: Politics, Power, Ethics*, Cornell University Press, Ithaca, NY, 215–234.

Shivji I. (2006) *The Silences in the NGO Discourse: The Future and Role of NGOs in Africa*, Pambazuka News/Fahamu, Oxford and Cape Town (www.pambazuka.net/en/publications/pz_sr_14.pdf), accessed 27 April 2015.

Smirl L. (2015) *Spaces of Aid: How Cars, Compounds and Hotels Shape Humanitarianism*, Zed Books, London.

Soussan J. (2008) *MSF and Protection: Pending or Closed? Discourses and Practice Surrounding the 'Protection of Civilians'*, MSF CRASH, Paris.

Stroup S. (2012) *Borders among Activists: International NGOs in the United States, Britain, and France*, Cornell University Press, Ithaca, NY.

Terry F. (2002) *Condemned to Repeat? The Paradox of Humanitarian Action*, Cornell University Press, Ithaca, NY.

Ticktin M. (2011) *Casualties of Care: Immigration and the Politics of Humanitarianism in France*, University of California Press, Berkeley.

United Nations (2013) *World Humanitarian Data and Trends*, United Nations, New York de Waal A. (1997) *Famine Crimes: Politics and the Disaster Relief Industry in Africa*, Indiana University Press, Bloomington, IN.

Welthungerhilfe (2011) *Annual Report*, Welthungerhilfe, Bonn (www.welthungerhilfe.de/en/pressrelease-annualreport2011.html), accessed 17 June 2015.

Wilson R. and Brown R.D. (2009) *Humanitarianism and Suffering: The Mobilization of Empathy*, Cambridge University Press, Cambridge, New York.

6   Stronger, faster, better

Three logics of humanitarian futureproofing[1]

Kristin Bergtora Sandvik

Introduction

After a brief slump resulting from the financial crisis, the proliferation of natural disasters and conflict-related emergencies has engendered a strong growth in the humanitarian sector, with expanding budgets, activities and institutional structures (Global Humanitarian Assistance 2014). Despite this growth, there is an increasing operational and financial deficit in the capacity of governments and humanitarian organisations to respond. This has led to calls for changes in the way such crises are understood and managed (OCHA 2014). In this chapter, I offer a tentative account of how the burgeoning humanitarian enterprise is grappling with what is increasingly imagined as a future of permanent emergencies. More specifically, I try to unpack the promise of cooperation as a mode of dealing with this uncertain future.

Humanitarianism has a long history of trying to improve itself incrementally through best practice examples, ever more fine-grained standards, and reforms. As humanitarian actors undertake periodic renewal projects to look and feel better, and to be seen as more credible and more legitimate, talk of the need for a paradigm shift has become an institutionalised feature of contemporary humanitarianism (Binder, Koddenbrock and Horváth 2013; Sandvik 2014a). Presently, the discursive self-flagellation inherent to the DNA of contemporary humanitarianism appears to take a specific direction, concerning itself with the ability of humanitarianism to shift into a modus operandi of *continuous* crisis management. Thus in this chapter I use the emergent concept of *futureproofing* as a prism to ask some questions about cooperation. The concept of futureproofing is loosely borrowed from electronics, communications and industrial design theory. To futureproof is to try to better anticipate the future and develop methods of minimising effects of shocks and stresses of future events. Futureproofing is about increasing resilience: the objective is for a product or system to be of value into the distant future and not be obsolete in the face of technological change.[2] My proposition for this chapter is that, as humanitarians perceive that things get harder – i.e. the response gap continues to increase and the humanitarian space continues to shrink – the focus is on futureproofing the humanitarian system by *becoming* stronger, faster and better.

DOI: 10.4324/9781315658827-8

Reflecting the general drive towards results-based management (Hoffman et al. 2004) and the call for more evidence-based humanitarian action (Dijkzeul and Walker 2013), discussions about possible and desirable humanitarian futures are often focused on forecasting and early warning systems (CDKN 2013; Leopold 2014; Oxfam 2008). This chapter focuses on another thematic aspect of the ambition to futureproof, namely the acknowledgment that humanitarian actors must find *new ways* of cooperating with other actors, cooperate with *new types* of actors (including types of new humanitarian donors, host states, global philanthropy, the private sector, and the volunteer and technical communities), and cooperate *more*.

While private sector involvement has been on the rise over the past 15 years (Binder and Witte 2007), the current optimism regarding the possibility of improving humanitarian action through information technology and a strong focus on innovation (Sandvik et al. 2014) suggests that the parameters of this involvement are changing. While cooperation is rhetorically framed as intrinsic to the future of humanitarian action, I think the quest for cooperation is both filled with ambiguities (with respect to what humanitarians say they want to get out of it, what they really want to get out of it, and what they can get out of it) and riddled with some interesting paradoxes (in terms of how it plays out). As noted above, the focus is heavily on futureproofing the humanitarian enterprise to ensure its continued relevance. Beneficiaries, beneficiary agency and beneficiary accountability occupy surprisingly vague roles in these future-oriented scenarios. In the following, I will try to bring out these ambiguities and paradoxes more clearly by analysing cooperation through the prism of the three logics of humanitarian futureproofing, whereby the sector aims to become *stronger* by reconfiguring the humanitarianism–development nexus, *faster* through private sector cooperation, and *better* through the turn to humanitarian innovation.

The chapter proceeds as follows. The first part identifies a paradox regarding how humanitarians seem to grapple with the relationship between development activities and humanitarian action, contrasted with the metanarrative of shrinking humanitarian space. The suggestion is that if humanitarians think this is the way to go to provide a stronger response, there is a need to articulate further how they will perform the switch from emergency aid to long-term development activities. Otherwise, this switch continues to be a "black box" of humanitarian governance, where the most obvious form of "cooperation" is the crowding out of development actors, projects and rationalities.

The second part identifies some of the conundrums arising from the current emphasis on the private sector as the "magic bullet" for providing a faster and more effective humanitarianism, looking at the particularities of the humanitarian market and the fallacy of shared situational understanding. It is also noted that the private sector is being seen by the humanitarians themselves as an attractive and feasible way of breaking free from the straightjacket of results-based management (RBM). I suggest that this set of conundrums points against any uncomplicated supposition that humanitarian action will "speed up" through more business engagements.

The third part starts from the observation that, while accountability talk has been a staple of humanitarian discourse for the past 20 years, the emergent humanitarian innovation discourse appears to consider accountability and accountability mechanisms overwhelmingly as implicit obstacles to innovation – or as a necessary evil that needs to be complied with at the lowest transaction costs possible. At the same time, the humanitarian innovation discourse is a further manifestation, and realisation, of the push towards beneficiary resilience. Replicating the sensibilities of past renewal efforts, there is an almost uncontested sense of improvement and progress surrounding the humanitarian innovation discourse (Sandvik 2014a). With the rising purchase of the innovation discourse with donors, the UN system, the media and the global public, this disinterest in or even scepticism to accountability mechanisms has potentially significant ramifications. A brief conclusion follows.

Crafting stronger responses: the humanitarian–development nexus revisited

The first logic of humanitarian futureproofing concerns the expansionist impetus of humanitarianism and how it correlates with the emphasis on collaboration. Over time, I have become puzzled by apparent contradictions in how humanitarian actors perceive and discuss the appropriate boundaries for their own activities and professional roles, and the activities and roles of other actors operating in crises and emergencies. These contradictions particularly seem to manifest themselves when humanitarians marshal moral arguments of "non-abandonment". Humanitarians appear to argue at the same time that the sanctity of humanitarian space is a precondition for a strong humanitarian response. To sufficiently strengthen humanitarian response; humanitarians must be able and willing to radically extend their activities well into the terrain of what is usually called "development".

There is significant sector-wide anxiety with respect to the state of humanitarian space. While the technical definitions of this concept vary, a common conception of humanitarian space is the ability of agencies to operate freely and meet humanitarian needs in accordance with the principles of humanitarian action (Collinson and Elhawary 2012). The focus on humanitarian space as "NGO space" (Beauchamp 2008) was popularised through Médecins sans Frontières' Rony Brauman's use of the term *espace humanitaire* to refer to an environment in which humanitarian agencies could operate while remaining independent of external political agendas (Hubert and Brassard-Boudreau 2010). This humanitarian space is also a field of humanitarian governance, meaning the attempt to govern individuals and human collectivities in the name of the preservation of life and the reduction of human suffering (Barnett 2013). Humanitarian governance takes place mainly in what James Ferguson (2006, 40) calls "the humanitarian emergency zone", where a global system of international organisations, donor and troop-contributing nations, and NGOs operate in parallel with as well as across domestic state structures to respond to and administer a permanent condition of crisis (Ferguson 2006, 41).

In particular after 9/11, there has been a persistent concern that humanitarian space is shrinking with serious consequences for protection of civilians and with respect to the security of humanitarian workers. Collinson and Elhawary (2012) observe that, despite the various definitions of humanitarian space in circulation, they seem to coalesce around an understanding of a shrinking humanitarian space, that humanitarian space is under siege (Oosterveld 2012) or in need of safeguarding (Tennant, Doyle and Mazou 2010). This is both a normative claim about the proper role of humanitarian actors, and a set of claims about the nature of threats to the humanitarian space. The shrinking of space is explained by pointing to a perceived "politicisation" of humanitarian aid, which is seen as fundamentally detrimental to principled humanitarian action. From Rwanda to Darfur and Sri Lanka, the perception of a failure of humanitarian action was closely linked to the notion that humanitarian actors were seen as political actors with particular agendas. This development is blamed on donors and stabilisation politics, mission creep among humanitarian actors, or increased outsourcing of aid delivery to commercial security providers (Spearin 2001; Metcalfe, Giffen and Elhawary 2011). A second explanation is that humanitarian space is shrinking due to actors declining adherence to humanitarian principles and International Humanitarian Law, leading to humanitarian access denial and increasing humanitarian worker insecurity (Harmer, Stoddard and Toth 2013; Labonte and Edgerton 2013).

According to critics, the shrinking space narrative builds implicitly on a myth of a "Golden Age" of non-political humanitarianism and unfettered humanitarian access. As observed by Donini (2012), the reality has always been characterised by a gap between the aspiration to a set of ideals and the reality of everyday humanitarian politicking in complex political, military and legal arenas. Empirically, arguments about a loss of humanitarian access also seem to be at odds with the observation that more humanitarians do more things in more places.

However, aside from this, there is something peculiar about the sacralisation of the humanitarian space as a site of action that is undermined, threatened or even destroyed through the presence of other actors. The oddness becomes evident when considering what happens when humanitarians begin to talk about preparedness, early recovery or "protracted crisis". It is my impression that there is a tendency for humanitarian actors to insist that the break between humanitarian action and development is both artificial and detrimental to the long-term effectiveness of the humanitarian response; i.e. that packing up and leaving may, more often than not, entail untenable forms of abandonment.

The parameters of the development–humanitarian nexus have been debated on several previous occasions, debates which have been flavoured by the relevant temporal, spatial and political context (Crisp 2001; World Bank 2014; Sande Lie 2014). Using a deliberately broad brush, I want to suggest that in the present context there is a tension between flagging the untouchability of the humanitarian space and the sentiment that it is the obligation of the humanitarian enterprise to expand the type and timespan of its activities into the domain of development. Moreover, it is not clear how humanitarians will manage this transition in practice.

What is their account of what would actually happen in this process? What are the types of difficulties they foresee and the strategies devised to meet them?

In the humanitarian context, NGOs operate in parallel with, as well as across, domestic state structures to respond to and administer emergencies. In the development context there is a state to contend with. In the context of the expansion of the humanitarian sector in the 1990s, critical attention was given to the extra-democratic accumulation of governance power at the hands of international institutions and its bureaucracies, and the absence of democratic features in the relationship between these organisations and the populations they serve (Ferguson 2006; Reinisch 2001; Vaux 2001; Sandvik 2010). While it is recognised that humanitarian aid must move towards a more "cooperative model", where humanitarians work closely with domestic national and civil society actors, and further down the line towards a consultative model, where humanitarians fill gaps in nationally managed responses, much of the relief effort remains based on a "comprehensive model" of aid, where donors and humanitarian actors intervene to strategically and operationally substitute for the domestic response (Ramalingam and Mitchell 2014). As most recently exemplified by the response to the Haiti earthquake in 2010, this type of intervention is not without costs.

The complicated mandates of humanitarian organisations and competition between them continue to generate coordination problems and massive waste of resources. Humanitarian interventions can undermine local political and bureaucratic structures, citizens' participation and social movements. Humanitarian actors, with their stance of neutrality and their ready access to cash, can unwittingly up-end these local processes and balances of power, for example by gaining support at the expense of local leaders. Intervention can also have perverse effects as slum dwellers in violent contexts scramble for scarce resources, competing with each other for the attention, and cash, of humanitarian actors. As the humanitarian bureaucracy becomes a local actor, it reinforces competition for urban political space, while itself remaining unaccountable to democratic politics (Buscher and Vlassenroot 2010).

Hence, if humanitarian actors are to do more "development work", it seems reasonable that they get better at articulating how they will engage the state, the democratic process, local political actors and agendas for transformative social justice – and that they understand that they will have to engage them in a very different way from how they do it today. There rarely seems to be talk of engaging institutionally with development actors; rather, I get the impression that the prevailing sentiment is that expert knowledge about the populations in question calls for and legitimates that the humanitarian agency extend itself into the development zone. While this type of mission creep is quite precisely mirrored in the eagerness of development organisations and agencies to "become" humanitarian,[3] it creates a different kind of dilemma for humanitarian organisations which emphasise neutrality and impartiality as fundamental to their ability to operate. Supposedly, humanitarians cannot take up a posture of being "neutral and impartial" in the development field and still claim to be accountable actors. Moreover, acting as development actors runs the risk of compromising their claim to neutrality and impartiality as humanitarians, potentially further undermining humanitarian space. As long as there is no articulation of how this "switch" will happen, it remains a black box of humanitarian governance, where humanitarians enter as actors alleviating suffering according to need and exit as political creatures with a social change agenda.[4]

Getting any faster? Conundrums in the embrace of the private sector

The second logic of humanitarian futureproofing is the notion that private–public partnerships in themselves will make humanitarian response *faster* by entrenching market-oriented rationalities, thus enhancing effectiveness. I will try to complicate this narrative by pointing to some conundrums in the vigorous humanitarian embrace of the private sector.

Binder and Witte (2007) noted the emergence of a new form of engagement through partnerships between companies and traditional humanitarian actors, often based on a desire to demonstrate corporate social responsibility (CSR) and to motivate employees. In parallel they observed that the War on Terror had enlarged the scope of traditional work with a role for commercial players to provide relief services. Today, these trends continue as *public–private partnerships* have emerged as a (donor) preferred humanitarian strategy to increase efficiency and accountability (see for example Drummond and Crawford 2014), goals that to some degree seem to merge as efficiency has become an important way of demonstrating accountability. The rationale for a greater inclusion of the private sector in humanitarian action is that partners can contribute to humanitarian solutions with different expertise and resources. Private companies are profit-driven and thus incentivised to comply with the specific deliverables and time frames set out in contracts. Donors are attracted to low overheads and a lesser need for constant engagement and monitoring. Moreover, the private sector owns much of the infrastructure on which information and communication technology is based.[5]

The outsourcing of humanitarian action has been criticised by commentators pointing to the often poor quality resulting from the private actors' lack of understanding of humanitarian action, contextual knowledge and crisis-management skills. Companies are, by their very nature, mainly interested in "brand, employee motivation and doing more business" (van Wassenhove 2014). Intensified private sector engagement thus leads to a marketisation of humanitarian values (Weiss 2013) where "the humanitarian ethos is gradually eroded" (Xaba 2014). Adding to these critiques, in the following I will question notions of efficacy and effectiveness by prodding some of the assumptions underlying the turn to the private sector. I consider how the call for intensified cooperation overlooks persistent tensions inherent in the humanitarian market and in the actors' rationalities. I also identify what seems to be a fairly prevalent sentiment, namely the assumption that such cooperation may serve the double objective of delivering humanitarians from the much-loathed RBM regime, while simultaneously delivering aid more effectively.

The first difficulty is structural: the turn to business cooperation is informed by the notion that the humanitarian market is inherently efficient and effective because it is a regular *market*. However, as noted by Binder and Witte (2007), the humanitarian market may be characterised as a "quasi-market" which exhibits an indirect producer–consumer relationship. In the market for humanitarian relief, the consumer (i.e. the aid recipient) neither purchases nor pays for the delivered service. Aid agencies are the producers, donors the buyers and aid recipients the consumers. As a result, the market is loaded with asymmetries and uncertainties: donors have difficulty determining whether the services they pay for are indeed adequately delivered, while recipients have few means of effectively making complaints or airing grievances. Nielsen and Rodrigues Santos (2013) note the often unanticipated and inappropriate delivery of equipment as well as personnel. In a trenchant critique, Krause (2014) describes this as a market where agencies produce projects for a quasi-market in which institutional donors are the consumers, and populations in need are part of the product being packaged and sold by relief organisations.

Interestingly, the most successful example of humanitarian innovation also represents a concerted effort to remedy the quasi-status of the humanitarian market: over the past decade, the international development community has invested heavily in the so-called financial inclusion agenda, aiming to make poor people less aid-dependent; this is sometimes labelled "resilience through asset creation". The partnership between the World Food Programme and MasterCard uses "digital innovation to help people around the world to break the cycle of hunger and poverty" (MasterCard 2012). For the World Food Programme, this is part of a broader strategy to move away from food aid and to improve food security through cash assets. The underlying rationale is that access to financial services such as credit and savings will "create sizeable welfare benefits" as beneficiaries of aid are drawn further into the market economy as customers. The goal of implementing "cost-effective" electronic payment programmes is to help beneficiaries "save money, improve efficiencies and prevent fraud". The belief is that cash can "go where people cannot", and provide them with choice (Sandvik et al. 2014). However, while these strategies are motivated explicitly by the desire to turn the beneficiary more directly into a customer, the accountability regime constructed around these systems remains directed upwards to donors.

The second assumption to be examined is that of shared motivation and shared values, going beyond disapproving criticisms of "neoliberal governance strategies". I think it is important to recognise that the call for intensified private sector collaboration masks a rather thin shared understanding of both the nature of humanitarian work, and the competence, presence and relevance of the private sector, and that this impinges on how this collaboration plays out. Binder and Witte (2007) observed that past attempts to pursue partnerships with corporate agencies have often been frustrated as agencies are unclear about the intended outcomes for the partnership, or view it as a way of developing a long-term funding arrangement. According to Nielsen (2014), private–humanitarian collaboration is currently characterised by underlying disagreement about what constitutes "meaningful" innovation and how that impinges on responsible innovation, as well as on accountability and CSR more broadly: there is a sense that the humanitarian customer often "does not know what s/he wants". The private sector actor is frustrated about having to take all the risk in the development of products, while humanitarians fret about taking on future risks as they will be the ones to face public condemnation and donor criticism if the product fails to aid beneficiaries in the field. Mays et al. (2012) identify a mismatch between humanitarian and business systems, leading to a clash between entrepreneurial and humanitarian values and the imperative to save lives and alleviate suffering. This resonates with my own observations, as humanitarians complain about being offered inadequate or unfeasible solutions; about being used as stepping stones to access to the greater UN market; or simply about differences in rationality, where the private sector partner frames the transaction commercially by "thinking money" and the humanitarian partner by "activity on the ground".

Finally, the erstwhile push for business management approaches to humanitarian action was the result of a push for greater accountability and a need to professionalise humanitarian work (Binder and Witte 2007; Barnett 2005). Perhaps the most significant import was results-based management, a management strategy "focusing on performance and achievements of outputs, outcome and impact" (OECD/DAC 2002) which provides a framework and tools for not only planning activities but also risk management, performance monitoring and evaluation (Kjellström 2013). Over the course of time, humanitarians have become exasperated and frustrated with the RBM rationale, both because it is sometimes seen to be contrary to principled humanitarian assistance (Binder et al. 2013) and more often since RBM and the results agenda engender a type of bureaucratisation where humanitarians feel that they are "performing monitoring" instead of monitoring performance.[6] While some humanitarians now strive for a shift towards systems accountability (where they will be held to account with respect to their responsibility for maintaining functional and workable supply chains or information-sharing systems, not specifically demarcated deliverables), others see the private sector as the solution to the RBM straightjacket. There seems to have emerged a notion that increased private sector involvement may in fact allow humanitarians to kill two birds with one stone. Much of the allure of partnerships and outsourcing to the private sector seems to be that RBM obligations can be offloaded to these actors, through subcontracting and outsourcing that details deliverables and outcomes. Hence the private sector is both envisioned to be faster at delivering RBM-like outputs – now imagined as a separate objective for humanitarian actors – and quicker to deliver humanitarian response.

A better humanitarianism? Accountability in the humanitarian innovation agenda

The third logic of humanitarian futureproofing is the assumption of progress inherent in the humanitarian turn to innovation. The following discussion focuses on the sphere of innovation centred on "product innovation" and concrete material outcomes, which is most commonly known as *humanitarian technology*. As noted above, there is considerable hopefulness with respect to the potential of this type of technological innovation to make humanitarian action better. This third and final part considers how emergent notions of accountability and beneficiaries' resilience play out in the context of humanitarian innovation discourse.

Whereas the innovation language is a very recent arrival in the humanitarian field, the humanitarian innovation agenda is already becoming an increasingly self-contained field with its own discourse and its own set of experts, institutions and projects.[7] The field is dominated by a few central actors (individuals and institutions), who also produce most of the existing documentation,[8] in addition to the output from the UN systems innovation initiatives.[9] According to community consensus, the humanitarian innovation agenda even has a precisely defined founding moment, 2009, when the ALNAP (Active Learning Network for Accountability and Performance in Humanitarian Action) study on innovations in international humanitarian action was published (ALNAP 2009). Most of the attention has so far been focused on top-down innovation aiming to solve "institutionalised management issues" (Bloom and Betts 2013). However, there is a growing interest in "bottom-up" innovation, with an emphasis on beneficiary cooperation (Bloom and Betts 2014; Couldray and Herson 2014).

At the same time, as a nascent field of practice, humanitarian innovation replicates or mirrors previous and ongoing contestations over knowledge production, resource distribution and governance. This is where I locate a paradox at the interface of how humanitarian innovation deals with accountability and how it perceives the role of beneficiaries. In previous attempts to renew humanitarian action, such as the turn to rights-based approaches or humanitarian reform, accountability was a means to have a better humanitarianism (see Sandvik 2014b). With respect to the humanitarian innovation agenda, however, I argue that the accountability issue is being rendered implicit and invisibilised.

Elsewhere I have noted that the turn to technology and technological innovation has been accompanied by notions of progress and inevitability. Thinking on problems and difficulties is often framed in terms of finding technical solutions, obtaining sufficient funding to move from pilot phases to scale, or placing oneself in a functional regulatory context (for example, achieving access to civil airspace as a precondition for drone deployment; or finding a metal for producing solar-powered cooking stoves that is suitable for the local climate, a metal that is also affordable and possible to import) (Sandvik 2013). In my mind, two issues are particularly important: this is a field permeated by ideas about progress and inevitability. The turn to technological innovation is being seen as *the end of accountability efforts*: it is not something we use to get closer to a better humanitarianism, but something which, once developed and deployed, *is* a better, more accountable humanitarianism (as noted above, a set of assumptions about efficiency is a basic tenet of the market-friendly innovation agenda). This take on accountability seems to reflect the broader approach of the field: so institutionalised that it [accountability] *has now vanished off* the critical radar and become part of the taken-for-granted discursive and institutional framework, something mechanically produced simply by the act of adopting and deploying new technology.

Furthermore, the innovation discourse is focused on empowerment but pays little attention to how power operates. The 2013 report published by the UN Office for the Coordination of Humanitarian Affairs, *Humanitarianism in the Network Age* (OCHA 2013), argues that "everyone agrees that technology has changed how people interact and how power is distributed". While technology has undoubtedly altered human interaction, changes in the distribution of power are far from self-evident (Sandvik et al. 2014) Likewise, I think there should be no inherent assumption that a proliferating humanitarian technology innovation agenda unveils power, redistributes power or empowers. I suggest that the classic problems in humanitarian accountability – to whom is it owed, by whom, how can it be achieved and, most crucially, what would amount to substantially meaningful accountability – remain acutely difficult to answer. These issues also remain *political issues* which cannot be solved only with new technical solutions emphasising functionality and affordability – we cannot innovate ourselves out of the accountability problem, at the same time as the process of technological innovation is not an empty shell waiting to be filled with (humanitarian) meaning. In the following, I want to show how this speaks particularly to the quest for beneficiary participation.

Starting from the work of the Oxford Humanitarian Innovation project and Bloom and Betts (2013) among others, bottom-up user innovation is increasingly presented as the answer to the age-old quest for participation. Bottom-up innovation is also tying in with the strong emphasis put on resilience and resilient beneficiaries currently permeating the entire humanitarian enterprise. This emphasis on self-reliance has some distributive consequences that must be fleshed out. Ramalingam (2013) describes the goal of innovation as about "helping people find innovative ways to help themselves". As noted above in the discussion of the humanitarian "quasi-market", over the past decade the international development community has invested heavily in the so-called financial inclusion agenda, aiming to make poor people less aid-dependent, sometimes labelled "resilience through asset creation". The underlying assumption is that access to financial services such as credit and savings will "create sizeable welfare benefits" as beneficiaries of aid are drawn further into the market economy as customers (for an example see Radcliffe and Voorhies 2012).

In practice, we know that humanitarians arrive late at the theatre – they are not the first responder. Affected individuals, their neighbours and communities are. So there is plenty of resilience. However, there is cause for concern if the engagement with technological innovation, and the notion that humanitarian information is relief, becomes a way of transforming the resilience-agenda further in direction of *making victims more responsible than humanitarian actors for providing humanitarian aid*. A further consequence is that the vocabulary changes meaning; sometimes it becomes wholly unclear who the beneficiary is. In a review of its grant portfolio, the first Humanitarian Innovation Fund annual report describes a project undertaken by Tearfund. Remote management has become a key tenet of humanitarian action: as Tearfund researched remote management strategies, it took care to ensure that "the research and proposed solutions were driven by humanitarian and development actors' involvement in the process, in order to ensure its relevance". This is fine and good. Then the report goes on to talk about "beneficiary accountability practice", and the reader eventually discovers that this refers to humanitarian and development actors (HIF 2013). Moreover, the concomitant talk of the importance of local markets and of "local innovation", "indigenous innovation" or "bottom-up innovation" inevitably begs the question: if bottom-up innovation is about cooperation with local participants, is the private sector perhaps this local participant?

Conclusion

This chapter has examined how the humanitarian enterprise is trying to futureproof itself to meet a future of permanent emergencies through evolving conceptualisations of cooperation as conduits for stronger, faster and better humanitarian responses. I have considered the manner in which each of these logics embodies a particular conceptualisation of cooperation. I have tried to identify paradoxes inherent in the new humanitarian–development nexus, where it appears that humanitarians may see a distinct value (that of a stronger response) in trying to crowd out the development sector and its rationales. I have attempted to unpack the ambiguities of the assumptions of "speed" and efficiency underlying the turn to the private sector and the humanitarian market. Finally, I have questioned notions of progress inherent in the innovation discourse, by pointing to how innovation talk eclipses meaningful notions of accountability. Emerging from this effort to unpack efforts to use cooperation instrumentally to make humanitarian response stronger, faster and better is a lingering unease about where this leaves the beneficiaries, who seem to have all but disappeared from view in this care-for-the-institutional-self model of humanitarian action. According to some commentators, while cooperation is intrinsic to the future of humanitarian action, despite the talk of "more cooperation", the humanitarian system *remains* fundamentally the same. However, that does not mean it has to stay that way.

Going full circle back to the conceptualisation of futureproofing, an important critique is that it may make us feel better in the moment – more comfortable, more secure and more protected – but it is unlikely to be the safe option in the long run; it is an "ongoing task of vigilance that will never [be] completed".[10] At the same time, it is important to be aware that the types of expectations lined up in this form of future-gazing exercise do not just predict, but also shape, desirable futures and organise resources towards them (Te Kulve and Rip 2011). Hence I would argue that the starting as well as end point for effective cooperation – what would make humanitarian action stronger, faster and better in the long run – should be the moral underpinnings of the humanitarian enterprise, namely the imperative to "do no harm"; the humanitarian principles of humanity, impartiality and neutrality (Sandvik et al. 2014); and the commitment to downward, beneficiaries' accountability we can draw out of these.

Notes

1 The chapter builds on my research on protection of civilians and humanitarian technology (Sandvik 2013, 2014a, 2014b; Sandvik and Lohne 2014; Sandvik et al. 2014; Karlsrud et al 2014) and draws on experiential insights from engaging with humanitarian organisations. The chapter is an output from the project AID in CRISIS (2014–16) funded by the Norwegian Research Council.

2 For the most comprehensive overview, see principlesoffutureproofing.com.

3 See for example the case of UN-HABITAT. Mandated to "promote socially and environmentally sustainable towns and cities with the goal of providing adequate shelter for all", UN-HABITAT has been involved in crisis management since the late 1970s. However, only with the endorsement of the Strategic Policy on Human Settlement in Crisis was a normative basis for an emergency response provided. In 2008, the main humanitarian coordinating body, the Inter-Agency Standing Committee, invited UN-HABITAT to join as a full member.

4 Another issue that requires some consideration is the question "where is everybody?" articulated by MSF (2014). Humanitarian operations now aim to address a broader range of situations in a larger number of places. To "stay and deliver" (OCHA 2011) has become the objective, entailing the expansion of international humanitarian system into active conflict zones (Collinson and Elhawary 2012). Increasingly, humanitarian space is fortified humanitarian space, brought on by bunkerisation and remote management. Duffield (2013) has criticised this trend as a spiral towards loss of "ground truth", which will lead to the loss of context and local knowledge. Does the reach towards development work represent a further move towards abandonment?

5 Of course, it is also necessary to be aware of the heterogeneous character of these partnerships within the humanitarian sector. There is a huge variation in the understanding of what constitutes a public–private partnership and what the appropriate label for the work done actually is. In this context, it is necessary to consider that the ability to call one's own work "humanitarian action" is a public relations strategy, a way of carrying out CSR, and a commercial strategy to spearhead access to new markets. Moreover, affected states, donor states, beneficiaries, international organisations and market actors all view the state and the overall organisation, as well as the objective of humanitarian aid, differently. Hence attention must be paid to the ways in which ideology and idiosyncrasies shape the templates upon which such agreements are encouraged and entered into, as well as how they play out in practice. In the following, I want to point to three specific issues.

6 The point is borrowed from Katharina Welle (2014).

7 In humanitarianism, it appears that at present the field is so small (and differentiated from development by the fact that the field of humanitarian studies itself is both emergent and preoccupied by the imperative of emergency thinking) that the work of Bessant and Tidd (2007), focusing on products, processes, positions and paradigms, has become an uncontested and mainstreamed reference point.

8 The Humanitarian Innovation Fund (HIF) was one of the key outcomes of the 2009 ALNAP study. Operational since 2011, HIF awards small and large grants to projects focusing on any humanitarian sector (HIF 2013). The DFID innovation strategy (2012) initiative was an outcome of the 2011 Humanitarian Emergency Response Review (HERR). The Humanitarian Innovation Project (HIP), based at the Refugee Studies Centre at the University of Oxford, began in 2012.

9 See UNICEF at http://unicefinnovation.org; UNHCR at https://www.facebook.com/ UNHCRInnovate and WFP at www.wfp.org/blog/blog/new-wfp-fund-aims-promote-innovation-food-assistance. At the same time, the IFRC World Disasters Report *Focus on Technology and the Future of Humanitarian Action*, and the OCHA report *Humanitarianism in the Network Age* (OCHA 2013), contributed to framing these developments as policy issues. The formal consolidation of the field culminated with

the 2014 Humanitarian Innovation Conference in Oxford, attended by a host of national and international humanitarian actors, the private sector, NGOs and academics. Transformation through technological innovation is also key theme at the 2016 World Humanitarian Summit (WHS) hosted by OCHA in Istanbul.
10 Borrowed from http://icrac.net/2013/10/futureproofing-is-never-complete-ensuring-the-arms-trade-treaty-keeps-pace-with-new-weapons-technology.

References

ALNAP, ed. (2009) *ALNAP 8th Review of Humanitarian Action. Performance, Impact and Innovation*, Active Learning Network for Accountability and Performance in Humanitarian Action, London.

Barnett M. (2005) 'Humanitarianism Transformed', *Perspectives on Politics*, 3(4), 723–40.

Barnett M.N. (2013) "Humanitarian Governance", *Annual Review of Political Science*, 16, 379–398.

Beauchamp S. (2008) *Defining the Humanitarian Space through Public International Law*, On the Edges of Conflict Working Paper, Canadian Red Cross/LIU Institute for Global Issues.

Bessant J. and Tidd J. (2007) *Innovation and Entrepreneurship*, Wiley, Chichester.

Binder A. and Witte J.M. (2007) "Business Engagement in Humanitarian Relief: Key Trends and Policy Implications", study commissioned by the Humanitarian Policy Group, Overseas Development Institute, London.

Binder A., Koddenbrock K. and Horváth A. (2013) *Reflections on the Inequities of Humanitarian Assistance. Possible Courses of Action for Germany*, Discussion Paper, Global Public Policy Institute, Berlin.

Bloom L. and Betts A. (2013) *The Two Worlds of Humanitarian Innovation*, Working Paper Series No. 94, Refugee Studies Centre, Oxford.

Buscher K. and Vlassenroot K. (2010) "Humanitarian Presence and Urban Development: New Opportunities and Contrasts in Goma, DRC", *Disasters*, 34 (suppl. 2), 256–273.

CDKN (2013) *Forecast-based Humanitarian Decisions: Designing Tools and Processes to Link Knowledge with Action* (http://cdkn.org/project/forecast-based-humanitarian-decisions-designing-tools-and-processes-to-link-knowledge-with-action/), accessed 7 April 2015.

Collinson S. and Elhawary S. (2012) *Humanitarian Space: A Review of Trends and Issues*, Research Report 32, Humanitarian Policy Group, Overseas Development Institute, London.

Conneally P. (2013) "What Technologists and Humanitarians Can Achieve Together", in *World Disasters Report, Focus on Technology and the Future of Humanitarian Action*, International Federation of Red Cross and Red Crescent Societies, Geneva, 19.

Couldray M. and Herson M. eds (2014) "Innovation and Refugees", *Forced Migration Review*, Supplement.

Crisp J. (2001) "Mind the Gap! UNHCR, Humanitarian Assistance and the Development Process", *International Migration Review*, 35(1), 168–191.

Dijkzeul D., Hilhorst D. and Walker P. (2013) "Introduction: Evidence-based Action in Humanitarian Crises", *Disasters*, 37 (suppl. 1), S1–S19.

Donini A. ed. (2012) *The Golden Fleece: Manipulation and Independence in Humanitarian Action*, Kumarian Press, Sterling, VA.

Drummond J. and Crawford N. (2014) *Humanitarian Crises, Emergency Preparedness and Response: The Role of Business and the Private Sector*, Humanitarian Policy Group, Overseas Development Institute, London.

Duffield M. (2013) *Disaster Resilience in the Network Age*, DIIS Working Paper No. 23, Danish Institute for International Studies, Copenhagen.

Ferguson J. (2006) *Global Shadows: Africa in the Neoliberal World Order*, Duke University Press, Durham, NC.

Global Humanitarian Assistance (2014) *Global Humanitarian Assistance Report*, Development Initiatives, Bristol.

Harmer A., Stoddard A. and Toth K. (2013) *The New Normal: Coping with the Kidnapping Threat – Aid Worker Security Report*, Humanitarian Outcomes, London.

HIF (2013) *Progress Report 2013*, Humanitarian Innovation Fund, London (www.internews.org/sites/default/files/resources/HIF_ProgressReport_2014-01.pdf).

Hoffman C.-A., Roberts L., Shoham J. and Harvey P. (2004) *Measuring the Impact of Humanitarian Aid. A Review of Current Practice*, Research Report 17, Humanitarian Policy Group, Overseas Development Institute, London.

Hubert D. and Brassard-Boudreau C. (2010) "Shrinking Humanitarian Space? Trends and Prospects on Security and Access", *Journal of Humanitarian Assistance*, 24.

Karlsrud J., Gabrielsen Jumbert M. and Sandvik K.B. (2014) "Ny humanitær teknologi – en kritisk forskningsagenda", *Internasjonal Politikk*, 2, 224–233.

Kjellström M.-L. (2013) "Result-Based Management and Humanitarian Action – Do We Really Want to Go There? A Study on Results Management and Performance Monitoring at Sida's Humanitarian Unit", MA thesis, University of Uppsala.

Krause M. (2014) *The Good Project: Humanitarian Relief NGOs and the Fragmentation of Reason*, University of Chicago Press, Chicago.

Labonte M.T. and Edgerton A.C. (2013) "Towards a Typology of Humanitarian Access Denial", *Third World Quarterly*, 34(1), 39–57.

Leopold G. (2014) "Humanitarian Project Culls Data to Forecast Disasters" (www.datanami.com/2014/06/20/humanitarian-project-culls-data-forecast-disasters/), accessed 7 April 2015.

MasterCard (2012) "MasterCard and the United Nations World Food Programme in Partnership to Deliver 'Digital Food'", Press Release, 13 September 2012 (http://newsroom.mastercard.com/press-releases/mastercard-and-the-united-nations-world-food-programme-in-partnership-to-deliver-digital-food-4/), accessed 2 June 2014.

Mays R., Racadio R. and Gugerty M.K. (2012) "Competing Constraints: The Operational Mismatch between Business Logistics and Humanitarian Effectiveness", Global Humanitarian Technology Conference (GHTC), 2012 IEEE, Seattle, WA, 132–137.

Metcalfe V., Giffen A. and Elhawary S. (2011) *UN Integration and Humanitarian Space: An Independent Study Commissioned by the UN Integration Steering Group*, Humanitarian Policy Group, Overseas Development Institute, London.

MSF (2014) *Where is Everyone? Responding to Emergencies in the Most Difficult Places*, Médecins Sans Frontières, London.

Nielsen B.F. (2014) "Imperatives and Trade-Offs for the Humanitarian Designer: Off-Grid Energy for Humanitarian Relief", *Journal of Sustainable Development*, 7(2), 15–24.

Nielsen B.F. and Rodrigues Santos A.L. (2013) "Key Challenges of Product Development for Humanitarian Markets", Global Humanitarian Technology Conference (GHTC), 2013 IEEE, Seoul.

OCHA (2011) *To Stay and Deliver – Good Practice for Humanitarians in Complex Security Environments*, Office for the Coordination of Humanitarian Affairs, New York.

OCHA (2013) *Humanitarianism in the Network Age*, Office for the Coordination of Humanitarian Affairs, New York.

OCHA (2014) *Saving Lives Today and Tomorrow, Managing the Risk of Humanitarian Crisis*, Policy and Studies Series, Office for the Coordination of Humanitarian Affairs, New York.

OECD/DAC (2002) *OECD/DAC Glossary of Key Terms in Evaluation and Results-Based Management*, Organisation for Economic Co-operation and Development, Paris.

Oosterveld V. (2012) "The Implications for Women of a Shrinking Humanitarian Space", in Perrin B. (ed.), *Modern Warfare. Armed Groups, Private Militaries, Humanitarian Organizations, and the Law*, University of British Columbia Press, Vancouver/Toronto, 246–266.

Oxfam (2008) *Forecasting Humanitarian Needs by 2015: Preliminary Report*, Humanitarian Futures Programme for Oxfam UK, Oxford (www.humanitarianfutures.org/publications/forecasting-humanitarian-needs-by-2015-preliminary-report/) accessed 7 April 2015.

Radcliffe D. and Voorhies R. (2012) "A Digital Pathway to Financial Inclusion", Bill and Melinda Gates Foundation, Seattle, WA (http://ssrn.com/abstract=2186926), accessed 18 September 2014.

Ramalingam B. (2013) "Questioning Innovation", Aid on the Edge blog, (http://aidontheedge.info/2013/01/30/questioning-innovation/), accessed 18 September 2014; no longer available online.

Ramalingam B. and Mitchell J. (2014) "Responding to Changing Needs. Challenges and Opportunities for Humanitarian Action", Montreaux XIII meeting paper, Active Learning Network for Accountability and Performance in Humanitarian Action, London.

Reinisch A. (2001) "Securing the Accountability of International Organizations", *Global Governance*, 7(2), 131–149.

Sande Lie J.H. (2014) "The Humanitarian–Development Nexus: Lessons from Northern Uganda", Humanitarian Studies blog (www.humanitarianstudies.no/2014/05/19/the-humanitarian–development-nexus-lessons-from-northern-uganda/), accessed 7 April 2015.

Sandvik K.B. (2010) "On the Social Life of International Organisations. Framing Accountability in Refugee Resettlement", in Wouters J., Brems E., Smis S. and Schmitt P. (eds), *Accountability for Human Rights Violations of International Organizations*, Intersentia, Cambridge, 287–310.

Sandvik K.B. (2013) "The Risks of Technological Innovation", *World's Disaster Report (2013) Technology and the Future of Humanitarian Action*, International Federation of Red Cross and Red Crescent Societies, Geneva, 135–161.

Sandvik K.B. (2014a) "Teknologi og det humanitære fornyelsesprosjektet" [Technology and the Humanitarian Renewal Project], *Internasjonal Politikk*, 2, 272–281.

Sandvik K.B. (2014b) "Humanitarian Innovation, Humanitarian Renewal", *Forced Migration Review*, Supplement: Innovation and Refugees, 25–27.

Sandvik K.B. and Lohne K. (2014) "The Rise of the Humanitarian Drone: Giving Content to an Emerging Concept", *Millennium Journal of International Studies*, 43(1), 145–164.

Sandvik K.B., Gabrielsen Jumbert M., Karlsrud J. and Kaufmann M. (2014) "Humanitarian Technology: A Critical Research Agenda", *International Review of the Red Cross*, published online 3 December.

Spearin C. (2001) "Private Security Companies and Humanitarians: A Corporate Solution to Securing Humanitarian Spaces?", *International Peacekeeping*, 8(1), 20–43.

Te Kulve H. and Rip A. (2011) "Constructing Productive Engagement: Pre-Engagement Tools for Emerging Technologies", *Science and Engineering Ethics*, 17(4), 699–714.

Tennant V., Doyle B. and Mazou R. (2010) "Safeguarding Humanitarian Space: A Review of Key Challenges for UNHCR", UNHCR Policy Development and Evaluation Service, Geneva.

Vaux T. (2001). *The Selfish Altruist, Relief Work in Famine and War*, Earthscan, London.

Welle K. (2014) "Monitoring Performance or Performing Monitoring? Exploring the Power and Political Dynamics Underlying Monitoring the MDG for Rural Water in Ethiopia", *Canadian Journal of Development Studies/Revue canadienne d'études du développement*, 35(1).

van Wassenhove L.N. (2014) *How Applied Research can Contribute to Improvements in Future Humanitarian Supply Chains*, Contribute Workshop Summary, BI Norwegian Business School, Oslo (www.noreps.no/PageFiles/1156/BI,%20210114,%20slides.pdf).

Weiss T.G. (2013) *Humanitarian Business*, Wiley, Hoboken, NJ.

World Bank (2014) *Humanitarian–Development Nexus: World Bank Group Stepping Up its Support to Crisis and Disaster Risk Management*, World Bank, New York (www.worldbank.org/en/news/feature/2014/12/30/humanitarian-development-nexus-world-bank-group-stepping-up-its-support-to-crisis-and-disaster-risk-management), accessed 7 April 2015.

Xaba T. (2014) "From Public–Private Partnerships to Private–Public Stick 'Em Ups! NGOism, Neoliberalism, and Social Development in Post-apartheid South Africa", *International Social Work*, online 27 January.

Part II

Cooperating in humanitarian action

Changes on the ground

7 Science and charity

Rival Catholic visions for humanitarian practice at the end of empire[1]

Charlotte Walker-Said

> We must cultivate a sense of international responsibility for the child … As confident internationalists … do we dare extend our love to the very ends of the earth and remove the limits of our charity?

With this valiant challenge, Raoul Delgrange, president of the Bureau international catholique de l'enfance (BICE), a Francophone Catholic social organisation, greeted the 1955 BICE International Congress in Venice, praising the work of "1,008 international organizations" that would transform Christian charity in light of a new "global reality … with an emboldened sense of global need" (Delgrange 1957, 24–25). In that same year, Father Thomas Mongo, an African priest who had been named successor to Monsignor Pierre Bonneau, the French bishop of the diocese of Douala in Cameroon, was facing a more local reality: purges and uprisings in the region as part of a violent nationalist insurgency (Atangana 2010, 16–17; Joseph 1977, 316–320; Terretta 2014, 126–133). To reconcile his people and his congregants and to inspire benevolence in the midst of anticolonial political upheaval, Mongo drew up plans to establish a local pilgrimage site and build new churches, and, critically, began preaching more intensively on defining charity as "the love of your neighbour" (L'Effort Camerounais 1958; Tabi 1995, 11).

Analysing humanitarianism during the years of decolonisation reveals a marked divergence between local social patterns and transnational ideology. The Catholic Church at this juncture fostered two humanitarian cultures: a culture of local charity, based on intimate compassion that was inspired by piety and strong social relations; and a cosmopolitical humanitarian culture that emphasised a mass-based emancipatory form of Christian consciousness that sought to widen solidarities and transform possibilities (Cheah and Robbins 1998). This chapter explores how the idiom of charity was envisioned and enacted by African and European agents in the last decade of colonial rule and illuminates the process by which these parallel and competing interpretations of compassionate work gained greater or lesser currency among distinct publics.

During the 1950s, the BICE and the French trust territory of Cameroon were two spheres of intensive contemplation on the subject of charity, where African and European ecclesiastical leaders considered the commitments to which

DOI: 10.4324/9781315658827-10

Christianity and its institutions were bound in the rapidly emerging postcolonial world. In Europe, Vatican representatives and clerical and lay directors of the BICE were actively considering Pope Pius XI's 1927 conceptual formulation of "political charity", in which he called for the Church to move beyond a bounded "social and economic charity" toward "a more vast charity" that could liberate entire societies and fight against "remote and foundational causes" of evil and injustice throughout the world (Pius XI 1926, 1927). During the 1950s, the Church implemented "political charity" as the framework for a new postwar strategy intended to widen its solidarity and stimulate a new sense of responsibility among European Catholics (Coudreau 1960; Dell'Acqua 1957; Fontaine 2012; Pius XI 1927). Another factor influencing the enactment of this mandate was the fact that Vatican and European Catholic leaders perceived the dismantling of empire as the dawn of new international political rivalries and sought to expand international Catholic organisations as a forceful means of countering the influences of Communist, as well as secular and Anglo-Saxon Protestant, values in education, health, social assistance and poor relief (Finkelstein 1955; Ferretti and Bienvenue 2010).

In the political context that emerged in Cameroon after World War II and the 1944 Brazzaville Conference, African Catholic leaders were forced to confront nationalist and Communist ideologies that politicised spiritual life, and responded in part by reinvigorating the role of local charitable action (Foster 2012; Vieira 2005; McKenna 1999). As part of this strategy, Monsignor Thomas Mongo espoused "intimate charity": a human closeness that could cure social ills. Mongo's vision, which African Catholic leaders later extended, was based on a Pauline conception of charity, which linked private religious devotion to neighbourly compassion. Organised through village networks in the interwar period and later through territory-wide Catholic Action—a socio-religious movement originally launched through the French missions, which emphasised collective responsibility for alleviating human suffering—"intimate charity" typified poor relief and social work in Cameroon's villages, towns, and cities (Cador 2009; Etaba 2007, 86–94; Fouellefak Kana-Dongmo 2005, 2006, Mbuzao 2008; Messina et al. 2000, 90–108). "Political charity" and "intimate charity" were not strict terminologies applied to respective European or African conceptualisations of religious work in the years leading up to national independence in Africa, but they do provide a rhetorical baseline from which historians can perceive idealised abstractions and locate evidence of concrete action resulting therefrom.

While scholarship on humanitarianism as part of the legitimation of empire has expanded considerably in recent years, fewer historians have analysed the humanitarian aspirations of the Catholic Church in the transitional years of decolonisation (Mazower 2009; Calhoun 2008; Conklin 2000; Pitts 2006). Some scholars, including Michael Barnett and Gregory Mann, have remarked that the postwar period ushered in a new style of humanitarianism in which nongovernmental and religious organisations engaged seriously with world affairs and transformed the boundaries of empathy (Barnett 2013, 97–158; Mann 2015). Other historians have suggested paying closer attention to Christian solidarities that arose during the late colonial period to better understand the emergence of non-national identities that shaped debates on human rights and questions of sovereignty (Watenpaugh 2010; Chamedes forthcoming). Catholic organisations, sponsored by missionary societies, the Vatican and national churches, had become critical sub-state agents working in Africa throughout the years of intensifying colonialism (Brasseur 1986; Carney 2013; Daughton 2008; Etaba 2007; Foster 2013; White and Daughton 2012). After World War II, Pope Pius XII invited Catholics to "collaborate internationally" in the service of creating a "more active Church in the world" with a greater influence in intergovernmental and nongovernmental organisations, and the BICE took this message particularly to heart (Coudreau 1960). As Mann has revealed, these transnational agents offering aid, social science and activism to Africa soon grew powerful enough to assume functions previously located within the state and local political authority (Mann 2015). This "international-mindedness", as Mark Mazower has termed it, formed part of the expansion of partnerships between government and international institutions that deployed science and ethical universalisms to forge a true international community in which they would be the global governors (Mazower 2009, 66–102). Critically, this globalist sensibility had serious consequences for decidedly civic, communal and fraternal forms of humanitarian relief maturing in Africa, and particularly in French Cameroon.

This chapter's presentation of the rival visions for Catholic humanitarian practice at the end of empire begins with an analysis of the BICE as a critical force in faith-based humanitarian work in the postwar decades. It then presents the longstanding traditions of mutual support among African Catholics in Cameroon, which confronted and eventually lost ground to the BICE's new charitable frameworks. In the long run, the BICE's vision of a supranational Church united through international relief efforts bolstered the European clergy's resistance to decolonising Church institutions in Cameroon, which they believed required "a new phase of evangelisation" (Direction Diocésaine des Oeuvres, Yaoundé, Les Prêtres de l'Archdiocese de Yaoundé s'interrogent. 1959, Archives de la Congrégation du Saint-Esprit, Chevilly Larue, France [henceforth ACSSp] 2J1.7a7). Concerns about Africans' "patriotic preoccupations", "demographic hemorrhage", and the "disruption of village piety" at the end of empire produced a nearly unanimous sense among European Catholics that Africans would very soon become "a people without religion, without spiritual leaders, who are ready to become the prey of communism in the near future" (Pichon 1948, 1949; Évêques du Cameroun 1955). The remaining sections of this chapter reveal how European scepticism of African religious conviction and pious work was constructed in the final years of colonial rule, as well as how it directly resulted in the BICE's paradoxical modernity project to spiritually and morally rehabilitate Africans through a new charitable paradigm based on international coordination rather than fraternal assistance and mutual aid. This ideological development is revealed in part through an analysis of the 1957 International Catholic Conference on African Childhood held in Yaoundé, which was sponsored by the BICE and attended by social scientists, government authorities, ecclesiastical leaders, and representatives of the United Nations

International Children's Fund (UNICEF), the Centre international de l'enfance (CIE) and the World Health Organization (WHO).

This conference was the culmination of over a decade of international Catholic deliberation on the future of both the faith and compassionate work in the world, and sought to build consensus around strategies for rendering religious power more transformative in decolonising regions (BICE 1960a). By examining this conference, as well as the years leading up to its convening in Yaoundé, this chapter presents a sceptical European lay and ecclesiastical Catholic leadership, who, rather than promoting African leadership in the Church in Cameroon, posited that a "universal fatherhood" and an "international brotherhood" in the form of transnational Catholic organisations should direct religious work in the fragile new nation (Rev. Mgr. Marcel Lefebvre, cited in BICE 1960a, 24–25; Dell'Acqua 1957). Building on Mann's study of "nongovernmentality" and the power of international agencies to effectively capture forms of political rationality in Africa during decolonisation, this chapter examines how nongovernmental lay and Catholic ecclesiastical agents devised religious rationales for eroding African sovereignty over the Catholic Church in Cameroon and banished African influence in late twentieth-century Christian humanitarian philosophies.

The BICE and Catholic universality

Founded in 1948 as an organisation devoted to "using Christ's message to justify international humanitarian aid for children", the BICE noted at its inception that the "era of radical change" in which it operated required new commitments that would engender revolutionary progress in support of child welfare (Cardinal Pironio 1988; de Labarthe 1988). The BICE's mission and strategies reflected interwar and postwar European Catholicism's emphasis on recasting its religious identity through the creation of organisations that would operate as the social and cultural axis of human rehabilitation (Droulers 1969; Mayeur 1986). In the years of waning colonial rule, the BICE's leadership, largely comprised of Francophone clergy and laity, called for "worldwide child protection" and the creation of a consortium of "moral training organisations" that would be tasked with translating the Catholic faith into sustained social action "for others" (Finkelstein 1955). These "others" were notably the children of Africa, as well as the "unadapted" and "deficient" children of Europe (L'Enfance dans le Monde 1955; Guindon 1967; Lecavalier 1973).

Scholarly clergymen, high-ranking bishops, and lay technical experts such as Henri Bissonier, chair of psychopathology at the Université catholique de Louvain, Margaret Bédard of the American Catholic Sociological Society, and Abbé Charles-Édouard Bourgeois, a Quebecois priest and medical doctor, among others, managed the BICE throughout the 1950s. Linkages between Catholic universities, research institutes and the Vatican grew stronger in this period, and the BICE developed a press organ to publish collaborative results—the technical journal *L'Enfance dans le monde*—and hosted international congresses in Holland in 1949, Madrid in 1951, Constance in 1953, Venice in 1955, Montreal in 1957, and Lisbon in 1959 as a means of strengthening European Catholic consensus on what constituted a western common culture on child protection (Rollet 2001; BICE 1960b, 10–11). The BICE's work reflected the increasingly transnational dimension of social research, which was informing legislation, societal debate, administrative practices and professionalisation pathways in postwar European nation-states. In this period, a plethora of industries, ministries, foundations and church organisations instilled new scientific norms for social welfare in western countries and structured the knowledge regimes in these domains (Saunier 2008).

Increasingly throughout the 1950s, the BICE was keenly interested not only in organising charitable efforts, but also in producing social scientific knowledge on which benevolent work would be based. Describing itself as "neither a federation of national organs nor a national movement", but rather a "technical bureau", the organisation gained consultative status at UNESCO, the UN Economic and Social Council, and UNICEF (Coudreau 1960, 10). The BICE distinguished itself by pressing for the "heroic support of children" and professed "an at times prophetic devotion to a cause" of identifying children as the most worthy benefactors of the gifts of specialists, researchers, experts and consultants (ICCB 1988a). It fully acknowledged that this emphasis forswore adults, who the BICE deemed "unchangeable", in favour of those "whose souls are more open to the world" (Delgrange 1957, 23). Even more importantly, by upholding the child as a pure innocent and the only incontestable rights-bearer, the organisation could segregate morally deserving from undeserving publics. This remissive formulation of charitable entitlement was used to establish ideologies of a "universal fatherhood", who would be responsible for social and humanitarian work for children, rather than kin and communities.

"Universal fatherhood", as BICE leaders and Monsignor Angelo Dell'Acqua, their strongest advocate in the Vatican, explained, was a means of envisioning Pope Pius XI's call for "political charity" by advocating for a "united human family", with a "sense of responsibility among the men from the farthest regions for men in the poorest" (Dell'Acqua 1957). Père Marie-Dominique Chenu, a BICE affiliate and Catholic theologian, reasoned that "man should not withdraw into inter-individual charity", but rather recognise what can be done "for the common good of the world" (Chenu et al. 1959, 43). This form of charitable boundary crossing was couched as a form of Christian transcendence and moral liberation, rationalised through the determinism of crisis (Finkelstein 1957; Roullet 1961, 73). According to the BICE, Africans had, through lack of social reform and their "natural mutualism", brought about proletarianism and failed to foster a "favourable climate for Christianity" (BICE, 1960a, 31–106). Thus to accomplish truly transformative work on the continent, where polygamy, malnutrition, illiteracy, poverty, women's subjugation and unemployment continued to deprive children of their rights, a more effective form of charity based on Catholic internationalism would be deployed (Ouellet 1957).

Intimate charity

In colonial-era Cameroon, African priests, catechists and nuns were the most common and effective messengers of scripture and doctrine, as well as leaders of pious works, in part because missionary societies suffered from a dearth of foreign workers in every decade in which the Christian churches were present ("Événements, Catéchistes, Pichon", ANC APA 10560/A; Brutsch 1950; Ngongo 1982). In the early 1920s, the Nlong Mission in southern Cameroon succeeded in building a Catholic community of roughly 5,000 Africans through the voluntary work of Ewondo and Bassa catechists who translated scripture, said mass, and heard confessions for their respective ethno-linguistic communities. Nlong catechists organised so much devotional work that they often complained of being overburdened with responsibilities, which included teaching, ministering the sick, visiting the faithful, assisting with religious services, organising construction for churches, chapels and seminaries, and even disciplining sinners (Journal de la Mission de Nlong 1925–1938 ACSSp. 2J2.1a). As much as they organised voluntary networks and recruited aids, they could not keep up with the level of need. After several "interminable" meetings with French missionaries in 1927, the Nlong catechists decided to expand the ranks of Catholic volunteers by starting a Bassa chapter of the Confrérie du Très Saint Sacrement, a pious fraternal organisation that would assist in construction work, and organising Bassa Eucharistic ministry, as well as schedule rotations for village visits and employ catechumens and postulants to make bricks and lead prayer sessions, which would free senior catechists to attend to higher level religious work (Journal de la Mission de Nlong 1925–1938).

By 1946, roughly 500,000 Catholics and catechumens across Cameroon networked through 258 religious associations and 2200 villages with a Catholic affiliation to organise, deliberate, and execute necessary actions for the improvement of social welfare, which included battling illness, unemployment, judicial corruption, spouselessness, polygamy and widow inheritance, among other challenges (Journal de la Mission de Nlong 1925–1938). The most popular Catholic collective in Cameroon was the Confrérie de Sainte Marie (*Ekoan Maria* in Ewondo), a pious confraternal organisation originally launched by the German Pallottine mission that built community through public prayer, social discourse and charitable works (Ekoan Maria, Confrérie de l'adoration réparatrice, Association de Saint Joseph, ACSSp. 2J2.1a; Essono 2013, 214–15; Messina and Slageren 2005, 178–80). Its success launched other pious associations including *Ekoan Anna, Ekoan Agnès, Ekoan Joseph*, the Confrérie de l'Adoration Réparatrice (*Ekpa-Elugu*), the Confrérie du Saint-Sacrement, and others, including the Association of Saint Louis de Gonzague, which recruited young boys to be catechists, teachers, builders and masons in rural congregations (Essono 2013, 130; Criaud 1998, 50–73). The interwar period witnessed the largest expansion of pious collectives and confraternal organisations, which described themselves as "public associations in the service of the Catholic Church for a more human society" (Département de Mbam, ACSSp. 2J1.6.2; Record of September 1931, Vogt, Doumé, ACSSp. 2J1.1a.10; Journal de la mission catholique de Bikop, 1–2 mai 1941, ACSSp. 2J2 1A; Père Eugène Keller (1884–1955), ACSSp. AF 6; Criaud 1998). Collectives such as the Confrérie des cinq plaies de Jésus led dangerous and subversive initiatives in the realm of humanitarian intervention such as rescuing brides from polygamous or forced marriages, uniting spouses without parental consent, and challenging chiefs and judges in tribunals (Cador 2009; Billong 2009, 5; Ekoan Maria, ACSSp. 2J1.7b4).

In 1938, Cameroon's French missionary workers were pulled from rural mission stations by the *mobilisation générale*. In the years that followed, in which Europeans were called to the front, African priests and catechists rose to lead congregations and new spiritual collectives, celebrating all the sacraments and developing charitable consciousness (Cameroun Catholique 1939, ACSSp. 2J1.8b2; Walker-Said 2015, 183–201). Thomas Mongo began his ministry during the war years in south-western Cameroon, a placement which revealed to him the diversity of Christian faith, experience and adversity among Cameroon's diverse ethno-regional societies, and inspired his passion for direct and localised social engagement (Mongo 1960; Ongey 2011; Van Slageren 1972; Notre premier évêque titulaire africain, S. Exec. Mgr. Thomas Mongo, évêque de Douala, 1958 ACSSp. 2J1.9b3). After witnessing the suffering of lepers, he and a group of African Catholic nurses and French volunteers responded by founding the Léproserie de Dibamba and the Léproserie Saint Michel de Nden (Léproserie Saint Michel de Nden, ACSSp. 2J1.7b4). These clinics were not managed solely by priests and missionaries, as Mongo organised the Fraternité des lépreux croyants, a religious confraternity for lepers that assisted in healing and hospice work to strengthen solidarity and promote mutual aid among the afflicted ("Solidarité entre les lépreux", 1959, ACSSp. 2J1.6.2).

Expanding pious brotherhoods and lay and ministerial associations of Catholics whose goals included evangelisation, social support, marriage reform, and poor relief was Mongo's most intensive sphere of Catholic action. He was the leader of the Petits frères et petites sœurs du Père de Foucauld, whose members went on to launch their own movements for children's education and catechism (Mouvements de l'enfance), and was instrumental in leading *Ekoan Maria* in Douala. Mongo also believed that charity was most needed in responding to the challenges of young adults who faced unemployment, poverty and despair, which is what prompted his leadership in the Young Catholic Worker movement (Jeunesse ouvrière chrétienne, JOC), which was launched in Cameroon in 1954 (Cholvy et al. 1991; Pasquier 2005, 2013; Informations catholiques, ACSSp. 2J1.13b1; Action Catholique, 1947–1951, ANC APA 1135/A). The success of African Catholic youth movements in accomplishing change both in outward signs of faith and in social renovation was noted at the 1957 BICE Conference, where French doctors and social workers sought to put the movements' social networks and rural–urban linkages to use to launch new initiatives (BICE 1960a, 98–106).

The Church and the politics of scepticism

Although the 1950s in Cameroon were marked by an increase in pilgrimages, outdoor liturgies and religious festivals attended by nearly one million baptised African Christians (roughly 700,000 Catholics and 300,000 Protestants), the European ecclesiastical hierarchy expressed acute anxiety about the rise of liberalism and the attenuation of spirituality as a result of what one French Social Catholic termed "the regrettable crisis of progress" (Vicaires apostoliques du Cameroun, 1957; Soucadaux and Aujoulat, 1950, 18; Noddings, Réunion des Ordinaries du Cameroun, 1956, ACSSp. 2J1.6.3). Gloomy predictions about Catholicism's future in Cameroon stirred tensions between the indigenous and foreign clergy as well as between Church leaders and African believers. European leaders of the Catholic Church ignited controversy by repudiating the radical anticolonial Union des populations du Cameroun party, which enjoyed considerable support, and by openly doubting whether African Catholics possessed the moral steadfastness and spiritual earnestness required to sustain the Church in times to come (Retif 1954; Brasseur 2005; Gardinier 1963; Joseph 1977; Mbembe 1996).

French pessimism after the war sharply contrasted with optimism and respect regarding African piety in earlier decades (Dubois 1933). For these sceptics, the Douala riots of 1945 were the first indication of moral failure and the decline of Christianity in Cameroon (Aujoulat 1947; Noddings, Témoignage de l'Action catholique d'Outre Mer, 1955, ACSSp. 2J1.7b4). Then, the Union des Populations du Cameroun (UPC)'s openly hostile stance against the Catholic Church and its alliance with the Confédération générale du travail (CGT) further confirmed African moral backsliding. Cameroonian nationalist and leftist newspapers such as Le Patriote kamerunais, La Voix du peuple and Le Crabe noir published vitriolic letters and editorials calling for Marxist revolution, total social and economic upheaval, and the expulsion of all Catholics, which deeply unsettled the European clergy (de Benoist 1986). Catholic press organs responded with harsh denunciations of African labour agitators, calling them dupes and "a mass of malcontents ... who believe those who spread calumnies" (Aujoulat 1947; Évêques du Cameroun 1955).

Criticism and cynicism also marked exchanges between the leadership of the Congregation of the Holy Ghost, or Spiritan Mission, in Cameroon and the Sacred Congregation for the Propagation of the Faith in Rome regarding the appointment of Africans as bishops in the territory (Koren 1982). African priests faced new suspicion of their spiritual fidelity and their capacity to command authority in a volatile postwar Africa, and were overlooked for leadership positions even though the Vatican insisted on diversifying the African episcopate according to the exhortations of Pope Pius XII, who was in favour of a truly global and universal Church fully embedded in local culture (Messina and Slageren 2005, 182; Le sacré de Monseigneur Mongo Thomas, 1956; Lettres de Graffin, Yaoundé, 1952, ACSSp. 2J1.13.b3; Père Henri Neyrand au Cardinal Fumasoni-Biondi, Préfet de la Propagande, Rome, 10 mars 1957, ACSSp. 2J1.9.a3). Even though Pope Leo XIII had been the first to officially accept nationalism as a value compatible with Catholic doctrine in 1891 and by 1951 had Pius XII's encyclical Evangelii Praecones called for complete decolonisation, the European clergy in Cameroon, and particularly Archbishop René Graffin, considered the African clergy in Cameroon too nationalist and repeatedly provided evidence of African priests' and lay ministers' "Marxist sentiments" to strategically retain white authority over Catholic Cameroon (Pius XII 1951; Leo XIII 1891; Levillain 1994, 1370; Bayart 1972; Bouchaud 1958).

Academic scholarship in the 1950s seemed to concur with the European clergy's concerns regarding the state of society in Africa. European social scientists and the French media published ominous accounts of postwar retrogression in Cameroon's growing urban sectors. From studies on rising poverty and declining public health to articles on the falling birth rate and social fragmentation exhibited in divorce courts and orphanages, the worldly priests and missionaries of Cameroon could stay well informed of the deterioration of their pious flocks (Guilbot 1949; Pichon 1948, 1949; Soeur Marie-Andre du Sacré Coeur 1952; Balandier 1950, 1955; Dresch 1946). Reports circulating among the leadership of the Congregation of the Holy Ghost repeated that Africans' faith was "not profound", that the laity was "not transformed", and that their "superficial" attachment to Christ and the sacraments meant that their moral training was incomplete (Direction Diocésaine des Oeuvres, Yaoundé, Les Prêtres de l'Archdiocese de Yaoundé s'interrogent. 1959, ACSSp. 2J1.7a7; Graffin lettres, 1952, ACSSp. 2J1.13.b3). Furthermore, they reasoned, the divorce, adultery, out-of-wedlock births, polygamy, alcoholism, crime and gender inequality present in Cameroonian society was strong evidence of a populace with an intractable "pagan soul" (Direction Diocésaine des Oeuvres, Yaoundé, Les Prêtres de l'Archdiocese de Yaoundé s'interrogent. 1959, ACSSp. 2J1.7a7). Although Christian Europe provided ample illustrations of these very same social ills, African Catholics faced growing suspicion of their capabilities to reform their environment and behaviours, which eventually manifested itself in the Catholic elite's internationally coordinated humanitarian strategies for more vigorous moral improvement.

The 1957 BICE Conference

Given these social and political realities, the context of Cameroon as the site of the 1957 BICE International Catholic Conference on African Childhood is salient. The conference organising committee, including Monsignor Charles-Édouard Bourgeois, the head of the BICE administrative council, Archbishop René Graffin, and a constituency of French Spiritain leaders, chose the territory because of its "international status" and its recent history of political transformation and religious disruption (Dell'Acqua 1960, 14). At the 1949 and 1956 conferences of the French Cameroon missions, which laid much of the groundwork for the 1957 BICE Conference, the clergy equivocated over how effective African Catholic social movements were at fundamentally adapting communities, and whether new systems and institutions were required in coming years to reinforce moral imperatives. Advocates for and against Catholic Action and African Christian youth movements' undertakings did not fall cleanly along racial lines. Bishop Bonneau and Abbé Jean Noddings, a Catholic Action leader from Lille, ardently pressured the Cameroon episcopate and the apostolic delegate for French Africa for more resources to continue their "profound work" (Réunion des Ordinaires du Cameroun à Yaoundé, 1949, 1956, ACSSp. 2J1.6.3). Mongo also emphasised the findings of the French Social Catholic researcher Joseph Wilbois, director of the École d'administration et d'affaires, who had concluded that social action in

Cameroon had led to significant improvements in conditions for women, children and married couples (BICE 1960a, 91–94).

Monsignor Paul Bouque, Bishop of Nkongsamba, as well as Graffin, however, concluded that more had to be done "in order to influence everyday life". What was required was to do more than expand the ranks of African priests, or even create what Graffin termed "secular apostles" to lead lay organisations for charity and outreach. Eliminating "adultery, paganism, gambling, bride price, laziness, non-spousal cohabitation, polygamy" and other deeply sinful habits required the support of new allies. It also demanded that Africans demonstrate more submission to the demands of the Church. At the 1954 conference, Graffin suggested that bishops and parish priests require new demonstrations of allegiance from their congregants, including public pledges to stay true to their faith, renounce polygamy and bride price, and completely refute communism (Séance plénière, Réunion des Ordinaires de missions du Cameroun français, Yaoundé 30 May–4 June, ACSSp. 2J1.6.3). In addition, Catholic social work would be beholden to a new consequentialism that promoted the maximisation of good. In deciding financial allocations, Graffin and his associates agreed to demand "evidence" of medical or social change, pedagogical improvement, psychological transformation, or the elimination of deficiency or delinquency. The Church would combat threats against the faith with verifications of its own progress (La Croix 1957).

At the 1957 BICE Conference, invited scholars such as Paul Verhaegen, a Belgian neurologist and psychologist based in Belgian Congo, discussed new methods of studying the psychology of the African child and the "social evolution" of the African adult (BICE 1960a, 415–17). The results of these technical experiments, argued Verhaegen and his supporters, could be used to measure the impact of Catholic social work in urban centres and rapidly industrialising zones in Africa. Verhaegen's work, as well as that of other European social scientists such as Marcelle Geber, Jenny Aubry and Jacques Lacan, was sponsored by the World Health Organization (WHO) for the purposes of better comprehending the relationships, hierarchies, psychological attachments and standard behaviours of the African family, with particular emphasis on the mother–child relationship, the intellectual and social development of the African child in a rural milieu, and the transitions of African families and children in rapidly burgeoning urban milieus (Berlioz 1955; Vouilloux 1959; Geber 1957, 1973; Verhaegen 1973; Verhaegen and Laroche 1956).

At the conference, European clergymen enthusiastically embraced the scientific discoveries and technical reports produced by psychologists, psychiatrists and biologists about the intellectual capability, biological state and moral nature of African children and the adults who cared for them. Special committees discussed the latest findings on the psychomotor development of the African child, which scientists attributed to the standard of maternal care, the psychological stability of the African mother, or the proletarian status of the African father (Geber 1957). Maternal stress, the "jealousies and rivalries" of the polygamous home, "obstructive" grandparents or other family deficiencies could also have a direct impact on child intelligence, conference reports concluded (Verhaegen 1960). Despite their disparaging assessments of African cultural and family life, BICE Conference attendees also reached a sanguine conclusion: a solution was at hand. Ecclesiastical leaders and organisational directors extrapolated from scientific findings of intelligence scales, personality studies and infant aptitude tests that there was no *genetic* difference between Africans and Europeans, only *social* distinctions, which could be overcome with greater educational and technical investments (Etoga 1956; BICE 1960a, 187–249). Africans were ultimately capable of "intelligence" per the tautology of European tests, and through cultural adaptation they could enjoy the benefits of modernity. Citing the work of psychologist Henri Piéron, Verhaegen and others forwarded the theory of "cultural adaptation corresponding to a change of milieu" that would allow for an "authentic assimilation of [European] culture" (BICE 1960a, 321–40). "Our notion of acculturation", wrote Verhaegen, "presumes nothing about the existence or non-existence of irreducible genetic differences" (Verhaegen and Laroche 1956).

In these results were the scientific substantiations for progressive and technically advanced humanitarian action in Africa. Local charity and compassionate work could indeed be useful, but it was not the deeply transformational liberation from sin and need that rectors such as Graffin sought, and of which Africans were clearly capable. In partnering with social scientists working in Africa, the Catholic Church wished to dovetail charitable missions with medical and scientific investments that would not only improve standards of living, but also instill the moral disciplines of modernity among Africans: nuclear family-building, educational advancement and career placement. Adherence to behavioural codes, rather than spiritual expression, constituted the basis of Christian progress according to the dogmas of emergent partnerships between science and religion.

Consequences for African Catholic social work

The radical transformation of pre-existing charitable forms in Cameroon was most apparent in the process by which international agendas for the reform of health and welfare transitioned away from a longstanding approach of compassionate assistance for all who faced hardship to a new culture of maximising results in the best interest of selected groups (Holborn 1956; ICCB 1988b, 3). The 1957 conference presaged the departure of European support for indigenously managed charity grounded in mutual aid, confraternal organisation, and rural and urban evangelism toward a new methodology for human progress based on scientific humanitarianism, development planning, and international coordination of technical experts for the benefit of "innocent" victims. In 1959, just before the majority of African colonies gained independence, the BICE actively participated in drafting the Declaration of the Rights of the Child, paying particular attention to the denigrating conditions experienced by children in Africa (Aula et al. 2009). The suffering child, then, would not only come under the guardianship of the international order, but his/her condition implied that a revised trusteeship system in Africa should continue as a moral necessity (BICE 1960, 66–70).

With the collaboration of European Catholic leaders in Africa and Europe, the BICE sought to commandeer humanitarian implementation in emerging African nations (Freeman and Veerman 1992, 90–103; Seccaud 2011). Ironies abounded as part of this initiative, as European religious leaders accused Africans of lacking faith and hence of being unfit to lead a religious institution, while they themselves nonetheless used their own scepticism and scientism to legitimise their authority over the Church. Moreover, while decrying the rise of secularism and materialism in Africa, Catholic humanitarian agencies became enamoured of projects that eschewed the phenomenological and the charismatic (the sharing of spiritual gifts) as well as the healing dimensions of community-building and the development of religious solidarities, in favour of projects that glorified the empirical and created new logics that defined economic development as part of the "progress of Christianity" in the postcolonial age (Chenu et al. 1959, 20–44).

Mongo and his compatriots both witnessed and warned against the reconceptualisation of charity into internationally coordinated professional philanthropy. In the last years of French rule in Cameroon, Mongo assumed the lead in the fight to retain control over indigenous Catholic humanitarian strategies that stood apart from the progressive and revisionist humanitarian vision offered by the European high clergy and their colleagues in the BICE as well as in medicine and international governance. Mongo was convinced of Christianity's deep roots in the episteme and ethnopractice of Cameroon's societies and, as a result, believed strongly in the impact of "intimate charity" (Journet 1952, 492–99). In a plenary lecture at the 1957 conference and in a later report, Bishop Mongo emphasised his people's longstanding tradition of charity and social action—what he termed "human centred renovations"—which were not motivated by ideological presuppositions, but rather intimate understandings of social turmoil. For nearly a century, African catechists had organised Christian followers and, in attending to their concerns, shaped perceptions of who was deserving of sympathy, compassion and assistance. For these communities, the child was neither the principal victim, nor the bedrock of futurist imaginings for society and state in Africa. As Mongo informed the 1957 conference attendees, "the child is the *raison d'être* of the household ... but the Universal Church promotes human persons and human societies, molding disciples and developing all whom it touches " (BICE 1960a, 175–78). Mongo portended that misplaced notions of Christian love that excluded African adults "subject to passions and crimes like all other humans" and focused exclusively on economic development in the name of the evolution of the child had an "air of condescension" that would "risk arousing suspicion and turning the hearts" of African Christians away from their agenda (Mongo 1960). Moreover, Bishop Mongo emphasised that a "qualified African laity" had already built a religious and moral infrastructure that made humanitarian gestures "more than an imported product ... or an agent of imperialism" (Mongo 1960). What these local efforts had accomplished was "authentic progress", which was recognised as such by those they affected. Furthermore, by developing the impetus to remedy and assist as part of Christian morality, young African Christians recognised themselves as self-determining individuals as well as sustainers of righteous acts (Ngande and Ngango 1958, 3).

Mongo rejected science's validation of cultural prejudice, arguing that "technical competence is not sufficient" because it lacked a Christian conscience and a sense of responsibility. Moreover, "scientific proof" of the deleterious effects of African patriarchy, tribal structures, family arrangements and the "general state of misery of the black race" assumed that at this moment *"on suppose que nous partons de zéro"* [you are assuming that we are starting from scratch]. This supposition, he stated, would be quite prejudiced and even fatal for the cause of moral formation in Africa. "So no", said Mongo, "thank God, we are not starting from scratch" (BICE 1960a, 179–80). For African priests and lay African Christian leaders, instructions regarding topics such as nutrition, sexuality, communication, hygiene and technical education appeared—in the words of the Congolese philosopher V.Y. Mudimbe—to be particular to one culture, but paradoxically claimed to be fundamental for all humanity (Mudimbe 1973, 35). Pre-dating Bruno Latour's thesis by several years, Mongo perceived European science not as a technical procedure or an objective set of principles, but rather as a culture (Lacan 1966). And by having to interface with scientific "truth", which emphasised alterity and solidified binaries of civil and uncivil realms of human existence, Mongo foresaw the excommunication of Africans from the realm of modern Catholic social action.

Mongo eschewed consequentialist ethics because he believed that utilitarian ambitions often lacked a spiritual foundation. Mongo's deontological ethics sought not to maximise a particular definition of the good, but rather to "civilise and liberate … in a climate of fraternal and non self-interested cooperation" (La Croix 1958). Although to be "civilised" had assumed a politically controversial inflection in the last years of French rule in Cameroon, Mongo determinedly employed the term to assure the Catholic faithful that he meant those with a "conscientious and active faith", which allowed them "to be more profoundly and authentically Cameroonian" (Mongo 1959). Rather than expressing apprehensive admonitions regarding national independence, Mongo associated the forthcoming nation-state of Cameroon as a sacred space of earned autonomy where Christian principles could be enshrined in law, and where colonial extraction and "self-interested philanthropy" would recede to make way for even more local Christian social movements (Mongo 1959; La Croix 1958). Although arguably overly optimistic for the prospects of broad Catholic engagement in politics and society in postcolonial Cameroon, Mongo's November 1959 pastoral letter affirmed that the "competent, lucid, and responsible laity in Cameroon are called to assume total responsibility for the local Church" (Mongo 1959). With this rhetorical volley, Mongo demanded that both African Christians and foreign ecclesiastical leaders recognise the local spirit that animated charity on the ground, which had "a unifying role" and embodied "a concrete programme of action … that oriented responsibility toward the common good" (Mongo 1959).

Conclusion

In a moment when Africans were considering the prospect of liberation from colonial rule, the development of new aid agendas by the international community does not seem surprising. New development paradigms and experts' recommendations inspired European Catholic leaders and prompted their renewed commitments to relief work (Legg 2012). To many African religious leaders in Cameroon, however, new humanitarian agendas seemed utterly divorced from Christ's model of compassion. The indigenous charitable complex, which had served Cameroon for decades, embodied an arguably more "universal" vision of charity than that of the BICE. Decentralised African systems had consistent intentions—to better the lives of local unmarried men, widows, prostitutes, polygamists, lepers, alcoholics, the sick, unemployed youth, young mothers, victims of abuse, and others who suffered (Yonke 1957). Catholic charitable culture and public expressions of piety thrived in interwar as well as postwar Cameroon, even in dynamic experimental moments when discussions of Marxism, radical anticolonialism and nationalism enlivened village meetings and youth group reunions (Mveng 1990, 83; Pichon 1952).

Europeans' preponderant focus not only on technical sophistication, but also on the rights of the African child, seems cynical in that it marginalised the great majority of baptised believers on the continent. However, this cynicism served a useful purpose: justifying foreign ecclesiastical leaders' continued roles as "fathers" in Africa. Child welfare ideologies reoriented international agendas toward strategies rooted in empiricism and metrics that addressed the needs of "innocent" victims, rather than empowering those who had a stake in creating or moderating conditions in which people suffered. In the end, Thomas Mongo and his African colleagues recognised that a spiritually coherent African future based on local, nontechnical charitable and communitarian organising for a diverse public was incompatible with the BICE's formulation of a global, transnational Catholic modernity.

In the decade following World War II, Cameroon was a shared cultural space in which differing concerns over the same problems emerged simultaneously. The records of the 1957 BICE Conference, as well as internal discussions within the Catholic Church and its foreign missions in the decade after World War II, reveal the Janus face of a European clergy confronting modernity, which priests and missionaries defined simultaneously as a new epoch of possibility as well as a cataclysmic turning point. The modern public sphere with its competing ideas about truth and freedom, the market system with its unrelenting pressure to produce and consume, and ideas of citizenship which compelled individuals to become part of the mechanics of the nation-state were all deeply unsettling to the European Catholic clergy, who broadly attributed these phenomena to the unfixed experience of secularism. And yet, while thoroughly criticising prevalent forms of both spiritual and political expression in Africa and claiming a need for the rescue of Christianity's mission on the continent, the European Catholic clergy and its lay partners in humanitarian organising moved toward an analytical approach to charitable assistance unconstrained by religious doctrine. In doing this, they compromised the very basis of their moral authority and sabotaged any legitimacy they claimed as leaders of a universal brotherhood.

Notes

1 This chapter was first published as an article in the journal *French Politics, Culture and Society*. See Charlotte Walker-Said, "Science and Charity: Rival Catholic Visions for Humanitarian Practice at the End of French Rule in Cameroon", *French Politics, Culture and Society*, 33(2), 2015. This research has been funded by grants from the Fulbright IIE, the Social Science Research Council, the Bernadotte E. Schmitt Grant of the American Historical Association and the CUNY Research Foundation. Earlier versions of this chapter were presented at the "Humanitarianism and Changing Cultures of Cooperation" conference organised by Volker M. Heins and Christine Unrau at the Käte Hamburger Kolleg/Centre for Global Cooperation Research, Universität Duisburg-Essen, between 5–7 June 2014.

References

Anya-Noa L. (2003) *Pierre Mebe: Hymne a hospitalite beti*, Abba Ekan/Centre culturel beti, Yaoundé.

Atangana M. (2010) *The End of French Rule in Cameroon*, University Press of America, Lanham, MD.

Aujoulat L.-P. (1947) "Les problèmes sociaux de l'Afrique Noire", *Chronique Sociale de France*, 4(4), 413–423.

Aula A., Tiffreau S., Perrin S., Lavaur A.-L. and Leite A. (2009) *BICE, A Worldwide Network of Organizations at the Service of Children*, Bureau International Catholique de l'Enfance, Paris.

Balandier G. (1950) "Problèmes politiques et économiques au niveau du village Fang", *Bulletin du Institute d'Études Centreafricaines*, 1, 49–64.

Balandier G. (1955) *Sociologie actuelle de l'Afrique noire: Dynamique sociale en Afrique centrale*, Bibliothèque de Sociologie contemporaine, Presses Universitaires de France, Paris.

Barnett M. (2013) *Empire of Humanity: A History of Humanitarianism*, 1st edn, Cornell University Press, Ithaca, NY.

Bayart J.-F. (1972) "Les Rapports entre les églises et l'État du Cameroun de 1958 à 1971", *Revue Française d'Etudes Politiques Africaines*, 80, 79–104.

Bayon G.L. (1986) "Les prêtres du Sacre-Cœur et la naissance de l'Eglise au Cameroun: Kumbo, Foumban, Nkongsamba, Bafoussam", Procure des Missions S.C.J., Yaoundé.

Berlioz L. (1955) "Etude des 'Progressive Matrices' faite sur les Africains de Douala", *Bulletin du Centre d'études et recherches psychotechniques*, 4, 33–44.

Billong S.G.T.K. (2009) "Noces de grâce de la Congrégation des sœurs servantes de Marie de Douala: 70 ans d'existence", Congrégation des sœurs servantes de Marie de Douala, Douala.

Bouchaud R.P. (1958) "Cameroun: Eglise et Communisme", *Spiritain: Missions des Pères du St. Esprit*, 31 (1).

Bowlby J. (1952) *Maternal Care and Mental Health: A Report Prepared on Behalf of the World Health Organization as a Contribution to the United Nations Programme for the Welfare of Homeless Children*, World Health Organization, United Nations, Geneva.

Bowlby J. (1953) *Child Care and the Growth of Love*, Pelican, Harmondsworth.

Brasseur P. (1986) "L'Église Catholique et la Décolonisation en Afrique Noire", in Ageron C.-R. (ed.), *Les Chemins de La Décolonisation de l'Empire Colonial Français, 1936–1956: Colloque Organisé Les 4 et 5 Octobre 1984*, Editions du Centre National de la Recherche Scientifique (CNRS), Paris, 55–68.

Brasseur P. (2005) "La perception du christianisme par les administrateurs français en Afrique noire au lendemain de la Seconde Guerre Mondiale", in Comby J. (ed.), *Diffusion* et *Acculturation du Christianisme (XIXe-XXe S.) Vingt-Cinq Ans de Recherches Missiologiques Par Le CREDIC*, Karthala, Paris, 279–287.

Brutsch J.-R. (1950) "A Glance at Missions in Cameroon", *International Review of Mission*, 39, 302–310.

BICE ed. (1960) *L'enfant dans l'eglise et le monde aujourd'hui*, Bureau International Catholique de l'Enfance/Éditions Fleurus, Paris.

BICE (1960a) *L'Enfant Africain: L'Éducation de l'Enfant africain en fonction de son milieu de base et de son orientation d'avenir*, Études et Documents. Bureau International Catholique de l'Enfance/Éditions Fleurus, Paris.

BICE (1960b) *Dix années de travail catéchétique dans le monde: Au service de la formation religieuse de l'enfance*, Études et documents, Bureau International Catholique de l'Enfance/ Éditions Fleurus, Paris.

Cador G. (2009) *L'héritage de Simon Mpeke: prêtre de Jésus et frère universel*, Desclée de Brouwer, Lethielleux, Paris.

Calhoun C. (2008) "The Imperative to Reduce Suffering: Charity, Progress, and Emergencies in the Field of Humanitarian Action", in Barnett M. and Weiss T.G. (eds), *Humanitarianism in Question: Politics, Power, Ethics*, Cornell University Press, Ithaca, NY, 73–97.

Cardinal Pironio (1988) "Message for the Fortieth Anniversary of the ICCB", *Children Worldwide: International Catholic Child Bureau*, 15(2).

Carney J.J. (2013) *Rwanda Before the Genocide: Catholic Politics and Ethnic Discourse in the Late Colonial Era*, Oxford University Press, Oxford.

Chamedes G. (forthcoming) "Pius XII, Rights Talk and the Dawn of the Religious Cold War", in Pendas D. (ed.), *Religion and Human Rights*, Routledge, New York.

Cheah P. and Robbins B. (1998) *Cosmopolitics: Thinking and Feeling Beyond the Nation*, University of Minnesota Press, St Paul.

Chenu M.-D., de Bovis A. and Rondet H. (1959) *L'Enfant et Son Avenir Professionnel: Esquisse d'une théologie de la création et du travail*, BICE Études et documents, Éditions Fleurus, Paris.

Cholvy G., Comte B. and Féroldi V. (1991) *Jeunesses Chrétiennes au XXe siècle*, Les Éditions ouvrières, Paris.

Conklin A. (2000) *A Mission to Civilize: The Republican Idea of Empire in France and West Africa, 1895–1930*, Stanford University Press, Stanford, CA.

Coudreau P.F. (1960) "Présentation de l'Ouvrage", in *Dix Années de Travail Catéchétique Dans Le Monde Au Service de La Formation Religieuse de l'Enfant*, BICE Études et Documents, Éditions Fleurus, Paris, 9–15.

Criaud J. (1990) *La geste des Spiritains: Histoire de l'Eglise au Cameroun 1916-1990*, Imprimerie Saint-Paul, Yaoundé.

Criaud J. (1998) "Étienne Nkodo: le premier spiritain camerounais", *Mémoire Spiritaine* 8, deuxième semestre, 50–73.

Daughton J.P. (2008) *An Empire Divided: Religion, Republicanism, and the Making of French Colonialism, 1880–1914*, Oxford University Press, Oxford.

De Benoist R.P.J.R. (1986) "L'Hebdomadaire Catholique Dakarois, Afrique Nouvelle, et la Décolonisation de l'A.O.F", in *Les Chemins de La Décolonisation de l'Empire Colonial Français, 1936–1956: Colloque Organisé Les 4 et 5 Octobre 1984*, Editions du Centre National de la Recherche Scientifique (CNRS), Paris, 531–540.

Delgrange R. (1957) "Discours d'ouverture de Monsieur Raoul Delgrange, Président du BICE", in *Frères Universels … l'éducation du Sens International Chez L'enfant, Actes du Ve Congrès du Bureau International Catholique de l'Enfance*, Venise, 2–8 Mai 1955, Éditions Fleurus, Paris, 20–25.

Dell'Acqua M.A. (1957) "Letter to the President of the BICE", in *Frères Universels ... l'éducation du Sens International Chez L'enfant, Actes du Ve Congrès du Bureau International Catholique de l'Enfance*, Venise, 2–8 Mai 1955, Éditions Fleurus, Paris, xiii–xiv.

Dell'Acqua M.A. (1960) "La Conférence internationale d'études du BICE sur l'enfant africain: Yaoundé 2–7 1957", in Bureau International Catholique de l'Enfance (ed.), *L'Enfant Africain: L'Éducation de l'Enfant Africain En Fonction de Son Milieu de Base et de Son Orientation D'avenir*, Études et Documents, Éditions Fleurus, Paris, 11–26.

Dresch J. (1946) "Sur une géographie des investissements de capitaux: L'exemple de l'Afrique noire", *Bulletin de l'Association de Géographes Français*, 59–64.

Droulers P. (1969) *Politique sociale et christianisme: Le Père Desbuquois et l'Action populaire*, Éditions ouvrières, Paris.

Dubois H. (1933) *La pénétration du Christianisme parmi les femmes paiennes*, Missions Catholiques, Lyon.

Dzou A.O. (1994) "Christianisation des Beti du centre Cameroun 1922-1955: essai d'interprétation", Thèse d'université Lyon.

Essono A.K.P. (2013) *L'annonce de l'Evangile au Cameroun: L'oeuvre missionnaire des pallottins de 1890 à 1916 et de 1964 à 2010*, Karthala, Paris.

Etaba R.O. (2007) *Histoire de l'Eglise catholique du Cameroun de Grégoire XVI à Jean-Paul II*, Editions de L'Harmattan, Paris.

Etoga P. (1956) "Il n'y a pas de race supérieure", *Echo Missions 2*, A propos du sacre de Monsegneur Paul Etoga.

Évêques du Cameroun (1955) "Vrai ou fausse indépendence?", Lettres des Évêques du Cameroun, Cameroun Catholique.

Ferretti L. and Bienvenue L. (2010) "Le Bureau international catholique de l'enfance: réseau et tribune pour les spécialistes québécois de l'enfance en difficulté (1947–1977)", *Revue d'Histoire de l'Enfance Irrégulière*, 12, 155–176.

Finkelstein R. (1955) "Save Children", *Child World*, 1, 5–8.

Finkelstein R. (1957) "Préface", in: *Frères Universels ... l'éducation du Sens International Chez L'enfant, Actes du Ve Congrès du Bureau International Catholique de l'Enfance*, Venise, 2–8 Mai 1955, Éditions Fleurus, Paris, v–vi.

Fontaine D. (2012) "Treason or Charity? Christian Missions on Trial and the Decolonization of Algeria", *International Journal of Middle East Studies*, 44, 733–753.

Foster E.A. (2012) "A Mission in Transition: Race, Politics, and the Decolonization of the Catholic Church in Senegal", in White O. and Daughton J.P. (eds), *In God's Empire: French Missionaries and the Modern World*, Oxford University Press, Oxford and New York, 257–277.

Foster E.A. (2013) *Faith in Empire: Religion, Politics, and Colonial Rule in French Senegal, 1880–1940*, Stanford University Press, Stanford, CA.

Fouellefak Kana Dongmo C.C. (2005) "Le christianisme occidental à l'épreuve des valeurs religieuses africaines: le cas du Catholicisme en pays bamiléké au Cameroun (1906–1995)", Thèse de doctorat, Université Lumière Lyon.

Fouellefak Kana Dongmo C.C. (2006) "Acteurs locaux de l'implantation du catholicisme dans le pays Bamiléké au Cameroun", *Chrétiens et Sociétés XVIe–XXIe Siècles*, 13.

Freeman M. and Veerman P. (1992) *The Ideologies of Children's Rights*, Martinus Nijhoff, Dordrecht, the Netherlands.

Fuller E. (1946) "The New Universalism", *World's Children*, 26.

Gardinier D.E. (1963) *Cameroon: United Nations Challenge to French Policy*, Oxford University Press, Oxford.

Geber M. (1957) "The State of Development of Newborn Children in Africa", *The Lancet*, 270, 189–190.

Geber M. (1973) "L'Environnement et le développement des enfants africains", *Enfance*, 26, 145–174.

Goldstein J., Freud A., Solnit A.J. and Burlingham D. (1973) *Beyond the Best Interests of the Child*, Free Press, New York.

Guilbot J. (1949) "Les conditions de vie des indigènes de Douala", *Études Camerounaises*, 27-28, 179–239.

Guindon J. (1967) "La formation des maîtres et éducateurs pour les exceptionnels", *L'Enfant Exceptionnel*, 3, 25–29.

Holborn L.W. (1956) *The International Refugee Organization: A Specialized Agency of the United Nations*, United Nations, New York.

ICCB (1988a) "Serving Children, ICCB's Past, Present, and Future", *Children Worldwide: International Catholic Child Bureau*, 15, 2.

ICCB (1988b) "The Foundation of the ICCB", *Children Worldwide: International Catholic Child Bureau* 15, 3–6.

Joseph R.A. (1977) *Radical Nationalism in Cameroon: Social Origins of the U.P.C. Rebellion*, Oxford University Press, Oxford.

Journet C. (1952) *L'église du Verbe Incarné: La Hiérarchie apostolique*, Desclée de Brouwer, Paris.

Journet C. (2005) *L'Eglise du verbe incarné: Compléments et inédits*, Editions Saint-Augustin, Paris.

Keith C. (2012) *Catholic Vietnam: A Church from Empire to Nation*, University of California Press, Berkeley.

Koren H.J. (1982) *Les Spiritains: trois siècles d'histoire religieuse et missionnaire: histoire de la La Congrégation du Saint-esprit*, Editions Beauchesne, Paris.

de Labarthe O. (1988) *Au Service de l'Enfant: Le BICE hier, aujourd'hui, et demain*, Bureau International Catholique de l'Enfance, Paris.

Laburthe-Tolra P. (1999) *Vers la Lumiere? Ou, le désir d'Ariel: A Propos des Beti du Cameroun: Sociologie de la Conversion*, Karthala, Paris.

Lacan J. (1966) "La science et la vérité", *Cahier Pour l' Analyse*, 1, 7–28.

La Croix (1957) "Yaoundé: Conférence internationale Catholique sur l'Enfant Africain", *La Croix*, 11 January.

La Croix (1958) "Thomas Mongo, a Douala, parle avec La Croix", *La Croix*, 14 May.

L'Effort Camerounais (1958) "Dans son message de Noël évoquant la situation troublée de son diocèse son Exc. Mgr Mongo supplie les siens d'être unis et zélés pour le bien", *L'Effort Camerounais*, 5 January.

L'Enfance dans le Monde (1955) "La formation des éducateurs spécialisés: conception-type d'une école d'éducatrices spécialisées pour l'enfance inadaptée", *L'Enfance dans le Monde*, 3(7), 28–30.

Lecavalier M. (1973) "Techniques d'éducation spécialisée", *Enfant Exceptionnel*, 9, 1–2.

Legg S. (2012) "'The life of individuals as well as of nations': international law and the League of Nations' anti-trafficking governmentalities", *Leiden Journal of International Law*, 25, 647–664.

Leo XIII (1891) Rerum Novarum, Encyclical letter on rights and duties of capital and labor, 15 May.

Levillain P. (1994) *Dictionnaire historique de la Papauté*, Fayard, Paris.

Mann G. (2015) *From Empires to NGOs in the West African Sahel: The Road to Nongovernmentality*, Cambridge University Press, Cambridge.

Mayeur J.-M. (1986) *Catholicisme social et démocratie chrétienne. Principes romains, expériences françaises*, Le Cerf, Paris.

Mazower M. (2009) *No Enchanted Palace: The End of Empire and the Ideological Origins of the United Nations*, Princeton University Press, Princeton.

Mbembe A. (1996) *La Naissance du maquis dans le Sud-Cameroun, 1920–1960: Histoire des usages de la raison en colonie*, Karthala, Paris.

Mbuzao I. (2008) *Actes des Apôtres en Pays Mafa: les débuts de l'Église catholique à Djingliya et à Koza (Diocèse de Maroua-Mokolo, Cameroun)*, Diocèse de Maroua, Cameroun.

McKenna J.C. (1999) *Finding a Social Voice: The Church and Marxism in Africa*, Fordham University Press, New York.

Messina J.P. and Slageren J.V. (2005) *Histoire du christianisme au Cameroun: des origines à nos jours: approche oecuménique*, Karthala, Paris.

Messina J.-P., Mimboé O. and Gantin B. (2000) *Jean Zoa, prêtre, archevêque de Yaoundé: 1922–1998*, Karthala, Paris.

Moeller R. (1993) *Protecting Motherhood: Women and the Politics of Postwar West Germany*, University of California Press, Berkeley.

Mongo S.E.M.T. (1959) "Lettre pastorale de Son Excellence Mgr. Thomas Mongo sur l'Avenir du Pays", *L'Effort Camerounais*, 15 November.

Mongo S.E.M.T. (1960) "L'enfance d'aujourd'hui et l'Eglise de demain en Afrique", in Bureau International Catholique de l'Enfance (ed.), *L'Enfant Africain: L'Éducation de l'Enfant Africain En Fonction de Son Milieu de Base et de Son Orientation D'avenir*, Éditions Fleurus, Paris, 369–378.

Mudimbe V.-Y. (1973) *L'autre face du royaume*, Éditions de l'Âge d'homme, Lausanne.

Mveng E. (1990) *Album du centenaire: 1890–1990: l'Église catholique au Cameroun, 100 ans d'évangélisation*, Conférence Episcopale National du Cameroun, Yaoundé.

Ngande C. and Ngango G. (1958) *Batir la Cité*, Editeur l'Effort Camerounais, Imprimerie Saint-Paul, Yaoundé.

Ngongo L.-P. (1982) *Histoire des forces religieuses au Cameroun*, Karthala, Paris.

Ongey G. (2011) *Douala Archdiocese pays homage to Mgr. Thomas Mongo*, Effort Cameroun.

Ouellet D.H. (1957) "Les Fondements Psychologiques de l'Éducation du Sens International Chez l'Enfant", in *Frères Universels. L'éducation du Sens International Chez L'enfant, Actes du Ve Congrès du Bureau International Catholique de l'Enfance, Venise, 2–8 Mai 1955*, Éditions Fleurus, Paris, 68–87.

Pasquier R. (2005) "Une nouvelle voie missionnaire: l'action catholique spécialisée. L'exemple de la JOC en Afrique noire française", in Comby J. (ed.), *Diffusion et Acculturation du Christianisme (XIXe–XXe S.) Vingt-Cinq Ans de Recherches Missiologiques par le CREDIC*, Karthala, Paris, 419–444.

Pasquier R. (2013) *La jeunesse ouvrière chrétienne en Afrique noire (1930–1950)*, Karthala, Paris.

Pichon F. (1948) "L'effrayant dépeuplement de l'AEF, du Cameroun et d'une manière générale de l'Afrique Noire", *Marchés Coloniaux du Monde*, IV(164), 2347–2348.

Pichon P.F. (1949) "Les causes de la crise de natalité au Cameroun", *Marchés Coloniaux du Monde*, V(176), 567–568.

Pichon P.F. (1952) "Un Vent de Pentecôte", *Pentecôte Sur Monde*.

Pitts J. (2006) *A Turn to Empire: The Rise of Imperial Liberalism in Britain and France*, Princeton University Press, Princeton.

Pius XI (1926) *Rerum Ecclesiae*, Encyclical of Pope Pius XI on Catholic Missions.

Pius XI (1927) *Address to the Italian Catholic University Students' Federation*, FUCI.

Pius XII (1951) *Evangelii Praecones*, Encyclical on Promotion of Catholic Missions, 2 June.

Retif A. (1954) "Le Cameroun sera-t-il chrétien?", *La Croix*, 9 December.

Rollet C. (2001) "La santé et la protection de l'enfant vues à travers les congrès internationaux (1880–1920)", *Annales Démographie Historique*, 1(101), 97–116.

Roullet O. (1961) *Des Enfants on Faim … !* BICE Collection Le Monde et l'Enfant, Éditions Fleurus, Paris.

Saunier P.-Y. (2008) "Les régimes circulatoires du domaine social 1800–1940: projets et ingénierie de la convergence et de la difference", *Genèses*, 2, 4–25.

Seccaud C. (2011) "La conception de l'enfance en droit international: illustration par les enfants travailleurs", *Revue Québécoise de Droit International*, 24(1), 131–170.

Soeur Marie-Andre du Sacré Coeur (1952) *La condition humaine en afrique noire*, Grasset, Paris.

Soucadaux A. and Aujoulat L.-P. (1950) *Cameroun: Les documents de France*, Alépée et Cie, Paris.

Tabi I. (1991) *La Theologie des Rites Beti: essai d'explication religieuse des rites Beti et ses implications socio-culturelles*, Éditions St Paul, Yaoundé.

Tabi I. (1995) *Cameroun Terre Mariale: Les Sanctuaires et Centres de Pélerinage Marial du Cameroun. Manuscrit en l'honneur et Souvenir de l'arrivé de S.S. Jean Paul II au Cameroun*, Sanctuaire Rocher de Marie, Ndonko, Cameroon.

Terretta M. (2014) *Nation of Outlaws, State of Violence: Nationalism, Grassfields Tradition, and State-Building in Cameroon*, Ohio University Press, Athens, OH.

Van Slageren J. (1972) *Les origines de l'eglise évangélique du Cameroun: Missions européennes et christianisme autochtone*, Brill, Leiden.

Verhaegen P. (1960) "Contribution à l'Etude de la psychologie de l'enfant africain", in Bureau International Catholique de l'Enfance (ed.), *L'Enfant Africain: L'Éducation de l'Enfant Africain En Fonction de Son Milieu de Base et de Son Orientation d'Avenir*, Études et Documents, Éditions Fleurus, Paris.

Verhaegen P. (1973) "Psychological Testing in Africa", *Applied Psychology: An International Review*, 22, 85–97.

Verhaegen P. and Laroche J.L. (1956) "Biologie et études sociales", *Eglise Vivante*, 8, 36–44.

Vicaires apostoliques du Cameroun (1957) "Le Catholicisme au Cameroun", *Informations Catholiques Internationales*, 44, 15–25.

Vieira G. (2005) *L'Église Catholique en Guinée à l'épreuve de Sekou Touré (1958–1984)*, Karthala, Paris.

Vouilloux P.D. (1959) "Etude de la psychomotricité d'enfants africains au Cameroun: Test de Gesell et réflexes archaique", *Journal de la Société des Africansites*, 29, 11–18.

Walker-Said C. (2015) "Wealth and Moral Authority: Marriage and Christian Mobilization in Interwar Cameroon", *International Journal of African Historical Studies*, 48(3), 183–201.

Watenpaugh K.D. (2010) "The League of Nations' Rescue of Armenian Genocide Survivors and the Making of Modern Humanitarianism, 1920–1927", *American Historical Review*, 115(5), 1315–1339.

White O. and Daughton J.P. (2012) *In God's Empire: French Missionaries and the Modern World*, Oxford University Press, New York.

Wilbois J. (1947) *Le service social dans les colonies françaises d'Afrique noire*, Bibliothèque de l'Union Missionaire du Clergé, Paris.

Yonke J.-B. (1957) "Alcoolisme – Danger", *Effort Camerounais*, 94 (July).

8 Religion and (non-)cooperation in Tanzanian communication campaigns against female genital cutting

Mathis Danelzik

Introduction: communication campaigns against female genital mutilation as contested humanitarian efforts

Efforts to eradicate "harmful traditional practices" have become a crystallisation point of increasingly intense debates on how to deal with cultural difference globally (McKinnon 2006). They are frequently evoked to discuss most fundamental issues of liberal humanitarianism: universalism and relativism, autonomy and paternalism, certainty and contingency, cultural imperialism and human rights (Nussbaum 2000). While the term "harmful traditional practice" lacks an official definition as well as a complete enumeration of practices, the UN agencies use this notion to describe a phenomenon crucial for the protection of human rights and public health worldwide. "Harmful traditional practices" characteristically are socio-culturally condoned among practising groups, either by a majority or an influential minority, while they are condemned by the international community as human rights violations, health risks, and – often – as violence against women (Winter, Thompson and Jeffreys 2002). Often-mentioned examples are female genital mutilation/cutting, child marriage, sex-selective abortion and female infanticide (OHCHR 1995). In this chapter I will focus on one of these practices, namely female genital cutting (FGC)[1] and the attempts to end the practice. It affects more than 125 million women and girls worldwide, mainly in parts of Africa and Asia, and is considered a grave risk to affected women and girls (UNICEF 2013). From an interventionist perspective, effective communicative efforts are therefore a necessity, especially since "harmful traditional practices" often cannot be effectively prohibited (Antonazzo 2003) and can reasonably be described as one of the biggest causes of human misery (Klasen and Wink 2003, 264).

In order to effect change, the international position needs to be renegotiated in the local context of practising communities. This task is taken on mainly by NGOs via communication campaigns against the practice. Due to the socio-cultural embedding of harmful traditional practices, these campaigns often happen to be paternalistic efforts or at least include paternalistic elements. Within practising communities, communication campaigns regularly are conflict-prone. On the international level and in academic discourse,

DOI: 10.4324/9781315658827-11

postcolonial critiques have called out cultural chauvinism and imperialism woven into those efforts.

Western activists have been accused from within practising groups of being cultural imperialists exploiting their power. At the same time, they are continually urged by African activists to help end the practice. That alone shows that abandonment efforts are part of the "morally complicated creature" (Barnett) mentioned in the Introduction to this volume.

Regarding the efforts to end female genital mutilation/cutting, the nature of cooperation has been in question at least since 1980, when African participants of the Copenhagen World Conference on Women protested Western women's movements' framing of the issue at the time. Since then, the field has seen an intense debate, with a new consensual ideal of cultural sensitivity and indigenous participation emerging for communication campaigns against harmful traditional practices.

In campaign practice, activists as well as pronounced supporters of FGC aim to convince community members of their respective positions. In this process, various concepts are negotiated and made use of to support the respective goals. Religious authority is one of the resources with which various actors strategically engage. This strategic engagement takes place against the backdrop of broader societal discourse on religion as well as specific local contexts. At the same time, the campaigns are communicative spaces in which communities negotiate the meaning of religion and religious authority in general, with implications that may well spill over beyond the campaign context.

In the following, I will give an account of the strategies used to make religious authority into a resource for the goals of FGC abandonment. I hope to offer insights about the nature of those campaigns, especially in regard to socio-cultural change and power. The tensions and difficulties coming with the implementation of the culturally sensitive, indigenous and participatory ideal in campaign practice are highly relevant for the reflection on humanitarian efforts and the challenges of (non-)cooperation they face.

My findings are based on field research conducted during an overall period of eleven months, investigating the campaigns of four initiatives in Tanzania. Three of the campaigns are enacted by sub-groups of the Inter-African Committee on Traditional Practices Affecting Women and Children (IAC), operating in different regions of the country, namely Dodoma-IAC (DIAC), Tanga-IAC (TIAC) and Mara-IAC (MIAC). For all of them, the abandonment of FGC is the prime goal. The fourth group, IMARA (Kiswahili for "strength" or "endurance"), is independent from IAC and has a slightly different focus as it concentrates mainly on HIV/AIDS in its work, but touches on the issue of FGC in the context of their programmes to make male foreskin amputation safe. A crucial criterion for selecting these groups was that all four groups were founded and also almost exclusively represented by Tanzanians, therefore fulfilling the international dominant ideal of "indigenous" activists who work "from within" and holding up the ideal of "cultural sensitivity" as standard of their campaigns. The preferred research method was ethnographic in nature, with participatory observation and ethnographic interviews conducted in English or Kiswahili.

Campaigns against FGC as challenges of cooperation

Campaigns against FGC and their critics

Campaigns against FGC have a long history. The first campaigns can be traced back to precolonial times: attempts to end the practice are documented at least in nineteenth-century Sudan, which was then under Egyptian rule (Abusharaf 2000, 164; El Bashir 2006, 142).

A new dynamic emerged during European colonial rule, when the practice was used as a proof of Western superiority and the campaigns – becoming more prevalent – became part of the crude mixture of racist ideology, veiled exploitation and humanitarian motives referred to as the "civilising mission" of European powers. In general, the result of these attempts was "a backlash against further Western infringement on African cultural beliefs and practices" (Masterson and Swanson 2000, 10), at times elevating FGC to an important symbol of defiance against colonial rule (Robertson 2002, 62; Thomas 2003, 25). This is especially true for Kenya, but does not hold for Tanzania (Winterbottom, Koomen and Burford 2009, 51). However, in Tanzania, as in other African countries, FGC became a controversial issue in postcolonial times: in the context of nation-building processes, FGC was included in the distinctions drawn by the independent Tanzanian government between modern socialist Tanzanian subjects and supposedly problematic backward groups representing a savage past.

One central aspect of the political agenda of the Tanzanian state after independence was the "development of backward populations". With this agenda the postcolonial state repeated strategies of justification of colonial rule (Hodgson 1999, 225; Schneider 2006a, 109). While reports on groups such as the Maasai as lacking hygiene could be found in the press, the state launched campaigns against traditional forms of dress, forcing Maasai to cut their hair and wear trousers (Rekdal 1999, 107). These campaigns were then presented as undertaken "for their own good" and with their consent (Schneider 2006b, 111–122). In this context, the state of Tanzania also took issue with "harmful traditional practices", which were seen as a proof of backwardness and barbarity (Winterbottom et al. 2009, 54, 63). By pegging the Maasai, the Gogo, the Kuria and others as traditional, primitive and backward, and as fundamentally different, Tanzanian elites and media "othered" them in order to construct the "modern" identity of the independent Tanzanian state and its subjects, which in turn fostered the essentialising of tradition and the solidification of the view that FGC was an integral part of their identity on the side of at least a part of the stigmatised populations. In such a traditionalist construction of identity, abandonment of FGC – like any other perceived deviation from tradition – can easily be constructed as a loss, a destruction of culture and an alienation from one's cultural core.

Internationally, the issue received attention from within the Western feminist movement in the 1970s, which took up the cause as an especially egregious form of violence against women. Two of the authors who dominated the debate on FGC in Western feminism at the time were Fran Hosken and Mary Daly. For example, Fran Hosken stated:

> Though violence against women in all kinds of vicious ways goes on all over the world there is one difference: for African men to subject their own small daughters to FGM in order to sell them for a good bride-price shows such total lack of human compassion and vicious greed that it is hard to comprehend.
>
> (Hosken 1993, 16)

Also, Mary Daly (1978) called the practice as a "sadistic crime", focused on men as perpetrators and described the women as "mentally castrated" victims of brainwashing.

Soon after, African women protested against the way Western feminists portrayed the issue. They identified racist and neo-colonial attitudes in it and criticised campaigns as arrogant and imposing. For example, at the 1980 international conference in Denmark sponsored by the United Nations for the International Decade for Women, African women accused political activists such as Fran Hosken of inappropriate cultural interference. What was especially troubling for many Western feminists at the time was that those African women raising dissent were themselves activists for women's rights, the majority of them being against the practice (Walley 2002, 33). However, they questioned the assumed notion of feminist sisterhood as grounds for international cooperation on the topic, and overall.

Since then there has been a continuous debate on the limits and the ethics of Western action on the practice, which has made its ambiguities and dilemmas visible. As already pointed out by Ellen Gruenbaum in the early 1980s (Gruenbaum 1982, 6), the issue of externally induced change has not only an ethical dimension, but also a strategic one, if resistance to change efforts inhibits their effectiveness by alienating potential allies in both international and local contexts, as well as making themselves vulnerable against push-back in the name of protecting "authentic" culture (Nnaemeka 2005, 37; Obiora 2005, 194). The connection between this debate and the quality of campaigns against FGC is summed up as follows by Leslye Obiora:

> Through the years in Africa, outside interventionists, whether colonialist or missionary (and now feminist), continue to presume that it is their duty as the "advanced" to elevate and enlighten the "backward". It is characteristic of these interventionists to pay scant attention to crucial issues including the wishes and opinions of the supposed beneficiaries of their benevolence, the overall implications of intervention, and the possibility of more "benign" intervention. Not surprisingly, their campaigns, often couched in terms of virtual monopoly on good judgment, are perceived as unduly ethnocentric and presumptuous. Such campaigns conform to patterns and habits that have historically provoked righteous indignation and engendered cultural resistance to Western "missionary" exploits.
>
> (Obiora 1997, 329)

In this context, perceived legitimacy becomes one of the central resources for campaigns against FGC, and the need to find other ways of global cooperation became apparent for most actors. From this situation, a new model for campaigns has emerged that to this day has reached a virtually universal consensus among both activists and donors. It is supposed to solve the cooperation issues in the international arena and proposes a cooperative mode of conduct for campaign practice.

The ideal of cultural sensitivity – key to cooperation?

This new ideal of campaigns emerged in the 1990s: cultural sensitivity. Its aim is to solve the moral dilemma, to bridge the differences in the feminist camp and, not least, to find a more effective way to fight "harmful practices". This ideal comprises three fundamental aspects: a) respecting local cultural concepts, moral values and social structures; b) working with participatory and dialogical methods, approaching people eye-to-eye; and c) putting African activists at the centre of the campaigns in order to work "from within" and removing Western activists from the ground work, limiting their role to securing funding of campaigns and lobbying international organisations and policy processes. The more Western intervention became suspect, the more African commitment and expertise appeared as key to reach both legitimacy and efficiency of campaigns:

> In organizing for change, effectiveness is better guaranteed if the change has been diligently earmarked as necessary and is supported by the people at the grassroots level. The value of change that is meant to improve their lot must be judged largely from their own point of view. They are more familiar with the dynamics of and conditions for meaningful change than outside experts. As such, they are best suited to engineer and spearhead a program for change.
>
> (Obiora 2005, 195)

One important milestone in the establishment of cultural sensitivity as a norm was the "Culture Initiative" by the United Nations Population Fund (UNFPA). Its aims were defined as follows:

> [It] attempts to explore the contribution of culturally sensitive approaches and partnerships with local power structures and institutions to the effective implementation of rights-based population and development programmes. The review demonstrates that development entry points and constraints that derive from social and cultural systems and structures cannot be overlooked or underestimated.
>
> (UNFPA 2004a, 1)

Also, UNFPA emphasised that campaigns should be led by local persons and activists whenever possible (UNFPA 2004a, 33; 2006, 41–44) and induce change "from within" (UNFPA 2004b). Another crucial concept in this context is "ownership": projects and campaigns should be "owned by the community" (UNFPA 2007, 56). Apart from UNFPA, many other crucial organisations, such as UNICEF, UNIFEM and WHO, have published guidelines for culturally sensitive campaigns and/or programming.

By now, there is virtually unanimous consent in the donor community and in academia about the desirability of cultural sensitivity. The wide success may also be based on the ambiguity of its rationale, i.e. its oscillation between ethical and strategic considerations, which offers reasons to adhere to it for both postcolonial critics and abandonment activists.

The emergence of this ideal certainly constitutes an example of changing cultures of cooperation, both between Western and African activists and with regard to the relationship between African activists and their target groups. Surprisingly, however, there is little scrutiny concerning either the actual practice of campaigns adhering to this ideal, or its premises. While postcolonially inspired authors should be partly credited for the new sensibilities embedded in "cultural sensitivity", they continue to focus on the rather comfortable task to pick apart remaining racist and culturally chauvinistic currents within discourse (e.g. Nnaemeka 2005). Meanwhile the difficult, but arguably much needed, critical engagement with the ideal of "cultural sensitivity" remains undeveloped.

While "cultural sensitivity" has effectively bridged the divides on the international level, its practical effects on the campaign level have yet to be examined in many respects. Against this background, the next section concentrates on one aspect of campaigns, namely the cooperation and non-cooperation with religious authorities in the aforementioned Tanzanian campaigns against FGC. This analysis sets out to illuminate the dilemma "cultural sensitivity" poses in the face of regularly occurring dissent on fundamentals between activists and their target groups. It shows the conflicts occurring in the triangle of a) respecting local cultural concepts, values and social structures; b) having a procedural ideal such as employing participatory and dialogical methods; and c) wanting to execute the most effective abandonment effort possible.

"Cultural sensitivity" – while commendable, and a considerable improvement – proves insufficient to solve these dilemmas and to orient decision-making on both strategic and ethical issues regarding campaign challenges as well as issues of cooperation, because those issues go way beyond the impetus "cultural sensitivity" offers.

Religious authority as strategic challenge and opportunity

One of the big challenges campaigns face is the occurrence of fundamental dissent: is pain traumatising and therefore to be avoided, or a character-transforming experience that helps children to develop into adults? Should one think in terms of honour or dignity? Is the biomedical model pre-eminent or inapplicable with certain supernatural phenomena such as ancestors' curses? Who has the authority to interpret negative events and to determine whether they are connected to the withering of traditions? These deep – indeed paradigmatic – forms of dissent do not necessarily surface, but they are a defining challenge for many campaigns, as a whole body of anthropological literature on the meanings attached to harmful practices in communities proves. When paradigmatic dissent occurs, activists struggle to be persuasive. Too fundamentally different are the respective basic assumptions. This leaves activists searching for tools and resources to make their stance against the practice matter in the minds of their target groups. Among others, it is in this function where religion plays a big role. Religion can be a powerful force for change or stability of the practice. Even though one might prefer a painful rite of passage, or see the practice as an important part of cultural identity, one might be prepared to give it up if it is against the will of one's God. As is true for all norms, religiously grounded norms, too, are negotiated by believers with other norms and sometimes ignored in practice. Nevertheless, religious authority is important, because religiously grounded norms are universal in the sense that they demand compliance in all aspects of life and with the entitlement to override conflicting norms stemming from other sources. Collaboration with religious authorities is also regarded an essential component of "cultural sensitivity" (Nnaemeka 2005, 42). UNFPA emphasises the importance of relying on existing social hierarchies in order to win the confidence of the target group (UNFPA 2004a, 36; 2007, 46f).

In the following, I will analyse the role Christianity, Islam and so-called "traditional religions" play in campaigns against FGC as sources of religious authority. As a background information, the following should be noted: while most girls and women cut in the world are Muslim, only a fraction of Muslims worldwide practise FGC. Members of other religious groups practise FGC as well, in some countries to a greater degree than Muslim populations in the same country. This is the case for Tanzania, where Christians are more likely to practise FGC than Muslims (UNICEF 2013, 73).

Not everybody who practises FGC and happens to be a member of a particular religion does so for religious reasons. Others abstain from practising because they see it as going against their religion. The empirical relationship is not straightforward. In Tanzania, FGC always has been a multicultural issue. Not more than 20 per cent of Tanzanian females were affected and the practice is present in only around 20 ethnicities out of 120. Most practitioners are Christians and most Tanzanian Muslims do not practice mutilation.

Winning clerics as allies

For campaigns, the gain in winning over clerics of any religion or denomination that has influence in their target groups is obvious. First of all, the aforementioned entitlement to override other norms makes religious arguments backed by respective authorities a potentially powerful tool. Secondly, campaigns sometimes find themselves struggling to find inroads into new communities and to overcome initial mistrust or disinterest. Clerics offer avenues to enter communities, including the opportunity to gather information and find potential new multipliers.

As any other type of access, community access through a specific congregation runs the risk of tying the campaigns to existing cleavages within target communities. Notwithstanding, there is also an opportunity quickly to reach a critical mass within a community, depending on its size and structure. It therefore does not come as a surprise that all of the NGOs that were analysed recurred to religious arguments, albeit in different frequency and importance for the campaign. While all of the NGOs that were analysed reached out to Christian and Muslim clerics, the incorporation of Christian religious authority is more intense.

TIAC's campaign is the one where Christian clerics figure most prominently. None of the Tanzanian activists interviewed knew of any Christian churches or clergy who support FGC. However, at the beginning of the campaigns, not all clerics were willing to talk about the practice. One reason for this earlier restraint seems to be the risk for clerics to alienate their congregation in the context of competition between religions and denominations over members. This risk already had become apparent during colonial times. Various Christian missions, including those in Tanzania, made negative experiences when trying to broach the issue among their faithful (Groop 2006, 109–115). Cases have been reported in different countries, best documented for Kenya (Thomas 2003, 29). What is more, clerics are themselves exposed to social pressure in practising communities, as was reported by interview partners. In 2004, one TIAC activist, who is at the same time a Lutheran lay preacher, had the experience that members abandoned his parish because he had begun to problematise FGC. In the meantime, however, all of the members who were lost temporarily have returned. These examples show that clerics maintain their authority only under certain conditions. In order to do so, they must avoid departing too strikingly from the positions of their members. Therefore activists have to put effort into mobilising religious authorities, even if they share activists' views on the practice.

By now, however, activists largely succeed in integrating Christian clergy into their campaigns. Many Christian communities raise the issue of FGC and integrate it into their development and humanitarian projects. Roof organisations such as the Christian Social Services Commission or the Christian Council of Tanzania also publicly condemn FGC (Tanzanian Coalition against FGM 2008).

The increasing success in mobilising Christian clergy to speak out on the issue exemplifies a crucial trait of both the challenge and the opportunity to end harmful practices: as soon as change begins to occur, some of the mechanisms stabilising the practice increasingly lose power or even turn, and begin to accelerate change. In this case, the stronger the public condemnation of the practice, the easier it is for religious organisations to be outspoken in opposition to it, thereby reinvigorating the impulse for change. It also means, however, that in the initial figuration, change depends on a simultaneous, multi-tiered change of cultural concepts, social structures and incentives to be able to stem the aligning factors keeping the practice in place. This is why the abandonment of harmful cultural practices is among the most difficult challenges of behavioural change, and why different practices and efforts share specific requirements, patterns and characteristics (Mackie and LeJeune 2009).

Essentialising Islam

Among the Western public, FGC is often associated with Islam and sometimes described as an Islamic practice. In the context of professional analysis and activism against FGC, however, it is common to criticise this tendency and to emphasise that Islam does not prescribe the practice (Obermeyer 1999, 88; WHO et al. 2008, 6). Others claim that Islam forbids FGC or, since the practice is older than Islam, that it has no relationship to it. This position is not only most widespread among activists, it can also be regarded as common sense in the academic discourse (Davis 2001, 530–533). Tanzanian Muslim authorities generally abhor the practice and nowadays are willing to speak out against it. However, the relationship between Islam and FGC is more complicated than both positions suggest.

In the following, I will focus on how international discourse as well as local activists essentialise Muslim religious authority and theology to be able to utilise it for the abandonment of FGC. This essentialisation has two main elements. The first component consists in never engaging with a complicated theological debate on the legitimacy of FGC, which has been going on within Islam. Thereby, an important contextualisation of the role of religious authority for FGC abandonment or continuation is glossed over: while only a fraction of Muslims in the world is not abhorred by the practice, the theological discussion on FGC is not unanimous by any means and includes a considerable support for FGC. The second component consists of putting forth an authoritarian relationship between Muslim clergymen and members of their religious communities, which might strengthen the impact of Muslim authorities speaking out against the practice, but which also needs to be seen in the context of greater societal issues, especially regarding women's rights.

The theological controversy within Islam regarding FGC revolves mainly around the authenticity and interpretation of five Hadiths, or reports on statements and stories from the life of the prophet Mohammed (cf. Asmani and Abdi 2008, 15). In recent years, the anti-FGC movement has won ground with several anti-FGC Fatwas issued by various actors, something Abu-Sahlieh calls a "complete new trend in Islamic society" (Aldeeb Abu-Sahlieh 1999, 140). Some of these Fatwas are a direct result of activists nudging religious authorities on the issue, others are results of evolving views without any strategic intervention. For example, an ongoing debate on the issue at one of the intellectual centres of Sunni Islam, the Al-Azhar University, had resulted in a number of contradicting Fatwas in the past 50 years (Aldeeb Abu-Sahlieh 2006, 59), but over time has shifted against FGC (cf. Abdel Hadi 2006, 110). Another milestone in this development is the "Banjul Declaration" of 1998, the result of a convention of Christian and Muslim African clerics initiated by the Pan-African umbrella organisation of IAC. The document states that neither Christianity nor Islam can be deployed in order to justify FGC and expresses concern in view of "incorrect interpretations and misuse of Islamic teachings" (Favali 2001, 67f). In 2009, a Fatwa on FGC was issued by Yusuf Al-Qaradawi, arguably one of the most influential Sunni clerics worldwide (Gräf and Skovgaard-Petersen 2009, 1). This Fatwa argues that the sources of Islamic law neither condemn nor call for FGC, but that it should be stopped in light of knowledge concerning the psychic and physical damage it entails and for the fact that it is an alteration of God's creation (Al-Qaradawi 2009). However, the very same Fatwa makes reference to a different work by Al-Qaradawi in which he seems to recommend partial amputation of the clitoris (Aldeeb Abu-Sahlieh 1999, 154). The same position can be gathered from his statement published on the website islamonline.net (Galal 2009, 160–161), where users were able to ask for religious counselling.[2]

However, successes for the anti-FGC movement are pitted against contradicting theological opinions on the issue. Analyses of the different theological stances within Islam have been given little attention, as they complicate the argument that there is no religious ground for the practice in any religion, which is often referred to in campaigns. In their study for USAID, Ibrahim Lethome Asmani and Maryam Sheikh Abdi conclude that the majority within each of the four main Sunni schools of jurisprudence recommends or endorses at least certain forms of FGC, with the Shafi'i school even viewing it as obligatory (Asmani and Abdi 2008, 13).[3] As Hamid Al-Bashir puts it:

> Most scholarly statements about FGM say merely that it is a teaching of the third order – that is, the practice is Islamic, but not as binding an obligation for believers as first- and second-order Sunna. However, the three orders of Sunna lie along a continuum and, by implication, the most pious people observe third-order commands.
>
> (El Bashir 2006, 156)

Kecia Ali sums up her analysis by saying that it would be wrong to assert that FGC is unambiguously rejected by Islamic theology and jurisprudence:

> FGC, however, is not merely a customary practice incorrectly understood as having religious authority despite its lack of sanction in authoritative scholarly sources. Rather, female circumcision of some type is either recommended or required by the dominant classical view of all Sunni schools of Islamic jurisprudence [...]. A number of modern jurists have suggested the question is open to re-examination. [...] Thus, a blanket denial [...] that "Islam" permits FGC is patently false and obscures the very real status of some type of circumcision for women as an accepted practice according to traditional jurisprudence, even if the majority of Muslims reject FGC as abhorrent and do not practice it.
>
> (Ali 2006, 102)

Arguably, there are various reasons why the prevailing opinion on theological stances on FGC in Islam omits pro-FGC stances. Local anti-FGC activists have no interest in undermining their message of FGC going against the religions of their target groups, especially when it would mean to bring up the existence of pro-FGC stances against local religious authorities, who also essentialise Islam as being unequivocally against FGC. In international discourse, hinting at the complicated nature of theological debate in Sunni Islam would run the risk of entangling the information with anti-Islam sentiments and discourses. This, in turn, could lead to a dynamic resembling the experience during European colonisation, when FGC became an anti-colonial symbol.

Finally, the need to present Islamic theological thought on FGC as unequivocally rejecting the practice is intensified by the second form in which Islam is essentialised in anti-FGC discourse and action: efforts to turn religion into a force for abandonment of FGC are usually based on an opinion-leader model, in which religious authorities act as multipliers with access to larger networks, through which anti-FGC messages will be spread by the weight the opinion carries with it. The supposed multiplier effect, however, varies with the nature of the relationship between those authorities and the common believer. It therefore does not come as a surprise that anti-FGC discourses and campaigns put forth an authoritarian concept of the relationship between religious authorities – be that a local Imam, Christian lay preacher, or another type of leader of any rank – and common believers.

This, however, as well as any categorical statement that Islam forbids or allows FGC, misrepresents one of the most interesting features of Islam: its ambivalent relation to religious authority. A Fatwa, which is an expertise issued by someone educated in religious law (a Mufti), only has persuasive authority and competes in virtually any issue with other, contradicting Fatwas. It is the duty of the pious Muslim to pick those Fatwas that he or she regards as capturing the will of God. As put by Abou El Fadl:

> A fatwa may be authoritative for some Muslims but not others. The decision to accept or reject a fatwa is entirely up to each individual Muslim. One group of Muslims may defer to one jurist and abide by his fatwa because they respect his learning and judgment, while another group may completely ignore it because, for whatever reason, they do not believe his fatwa to be correct. A Muslim's decision to accept or reject a fatwa, however, is not supposed to be based on whim or mood; every Muslim is expected to reflect upon and ponder each fatwa and abide by it only if he or she believes that it truly and accurately represents the will of God. Although each fatwa reflects the opinion of a learned person about what God desires or wills, it is up to the recipients of the fatwa not to follow it blindly or unthinkingly. According to Islamic law, practising Muslims must exert a degree of due diligence in researching the qualifications of the jurist issuing the fatwa, and also the evidentiary basis for the jurist's opinion, before deciding to follow or reject any particular fatwa.
>
> (Abou El Fadl 2005, 29)

Compared to centralised and totalised authority models present in many other religions, this is an amazingly liberal feature. Because of this feature, Kecia Ali, a feminist author on Islam and body practices, argues that the question whether a practice is Islamic or not, is beside the point (Ali 2006, 98). It cannot be finally answered, because there is no central authority to resolve the question.

Liberal Muslim scholars acknowledge that many Muslims in the world experience a tension between their individual responsibility to judge right and wrong and social pressure to submit to a more authoritarian model, in which they need to align themselves with rules set by leaders or communities. At the same time, progressive Muslim scholars still pin their hopes for change exactly on the opportunity for a concept of religious authority that stresses the personal responsibility to choose positions among competing forms of expertise individually.

When NGOs make use of religious leaders as multipliers, they are inclined to at least implicitly adhere to an authoritarian relation between religious leaders and common believers, because it may make the best use of the potentially overriding effect of religious norms in comparison to competing ones. In my research, this became apparent especially in two of the campaigns. In one interview, an activist stressed that campaigns benefited from the "godly authority" of both Christian and Muslim clergy:

> religious leaders, whether it is a Moslem or a Christian […]: when they speak, it is not only human, it is divine, something having the origin from God. So it is God himself speaking through the mouth of this religious leader. So they are very, they trust religious leaders [because] of that. […] They are there to represent God.

In the case of FGC, this treatment of authority helps to put an end to it, because Tanzanian Muslim leaders reject the practice. However, from a wider perspective of women's rights, such an authoritarian model might have detrimental effects as well.

In Tanzania, Sufism competes with an influx of Wahhabi and Salafi fundamentalist versions of Islam from the Arabian peninsula since the 1970s. The latter movement is called Ansar Sunna, might have had ties to Al-Qaida at one point, opposes a secular state and has a literal understanding of the Quran. Ansar Sunna jeopardises the general autonomy of women by presenting the female body as a moral problem, proposing rigid notions of purity and restricting women's movements and dress choices. It is precisely here that the movement has appeared to be attractive for other – mainly male – Tanzanian Muslims (Becker 2008, 267–272).

In the context of human rights and women's rights discourse, authoritarian relationships between religious leaders and believers are generally seen as the root cause of many problems. This is also true for the essentialisation of Islam as having one pure core, as opposed to a multi-vocal discourse through which individuals humbly attempt to pick those counsels that best approximate God's will. Instead, the understanding of religion that is usually fostered in this context is one that makes dissent among authorities visible, strengthens individual autonomy, and fosters the awareness that all attempts to determine the "will of God" will remain preliminary and possibly erroneous. Along these lines, Muslim feminists from Egypt, for example, reclaim the right to legal interpretations for every believer, whether male or female (Badran 2009, 178). This runs counter to the strategy of relying on religious authority in fighting FGC. As put by Aldeeb Abu-Sahlieh (1997, 58) "With common people, we have to find a way to help them escape the authority of religious leaders and texts."

To conclude this example, the Tanzanian activists' and the Anti-FGC movement's choice of making use of an authoritarian model turns out to be a double-edged sword: while religious authority and leadership can be deployed as a means to fight FGC, the message – "always obey religious authority!" – will likely run counter to broader initiatives for women's empowerment and women's rights. On the other hand, putting forth a model stressing individual choice in a pluralistic religious discourse may result in more attention for the existing theological debate on FGC within Sunni Islam, as well as proponents of FGC bringing their positive view of the practice in accordance with their religious convictions.

Marginalising "traditional religion"

Apart from Islam and Christianity, other religions play an important role in campaigns against FGC, too. These religions are often referred to as "traditional African religions" (Deegan 2009, 29). This term is as problematic as is the term "harmful traditional practices" (Danelzik 2014) and therefore will be used in quotation marks here.[4] Presumptions and stereotypes prevail in descriptions of "traditional religions" (Magesa 2009, 46–52), eclipsing considerable diversity among religions labelled as traditional.

In Tanzania, the percentage of believers of "traditional religions" among the target groups of the campaigns cannot be determined. Adherents to "traditional religions" seem to be completely absent in some target groups, whereas in others they play a central role or even represent the majority. Syncretistic faiths are widespread in Tanzania, too (Lodhi and Westerlund 1999, 100; Becker 2007, 22, 24). It is therefore difficult to determine which faiths correspond to which self-identifications given by interviewees (Magesa 2009, 52). Furthermore, a homogenising way of talking, for example of the religion "of the Maasai", obscures regional and local differences in religious convictions and practices.

In Tanzania, adherents to some religious groups see FGC as a practice devoid of religious meaning, while other target groups see it as a supernaturally destined duty. In the conversations I had, various circumcisers declared they were following their vocation or the call of ancestors as revealed to them in dreams or through certain experiences, such as a miraculous finding of medicinal herbs or knives used for cutting. These assertions suggest that the continuation of FGC is at least partly argued for in supernatural terms and as required by the ancestors (Gachiri 2000, 91–93). They also report punishments inflicted by the ancestors on former circumcisers who stopped practising after campaigns' activities. For example, some ex-circumcisers said they were suffering weight loss, headache or back pain as a consequence of "laying down the knives". Some of these declarations may be part of a strategy of senior women to negotiate compensations for stopping to cut. In any case, these practitioners emphasise the transcendent nature of the obligation to practise FGC.

When activists are confronted with assertions of this kind, they often cannot effectively challenge them, for example, deny that pain in the back is due to the punishment of an ancestor. Their encounter with "traditional" religion and its authorities is fraught with other difficulties, too. Often, these religious leaders draw their prestige from acting as custodians of customary practice, of which FGC often is seen as an integral part. Those leaders are therefore likely to disagree with the campaign goals. Since there is no more prestigious leader to turn or holy book to point to, and activists certainly cannot claim superior knowledge about the various beliefs than the respective religious leaders, proponents who incorporate supernatural elements in their understanding of FGC pose a considerable challenge for activists. They struggle to find appealing arguments and connect with the opposing world view. In other words, activists are confronted with an incommensurable position on FGC, when "traditional religions" favour FGC.

A part of the activists I researched took to a strategy which is fundamentally different from the one applied in relation to Islamic and Christian leaders. While they chose a respectful demeanour towards the mostly elderly followers of "traditional religion", which appears to be in line with the ideal of "cultural sensitivity", they used their access to public schools to convert the children and grandchildren of those followers. These activists ultimately hope for the extinction of incommensurable beliefs. As one activist put it:

> But if the community [...] knows this is illegal, this is bad, this is evil, at the end of the day [...] people will just fly away [from traditional religious authority]. I would have concentrated in teaching and educating the grassroots, the youngsters. [The authority] will just die with his set of beliefs. Dogmas which he thought will never change.

This can be understood as a long-term strategy of coping with incommensurable views on the practice. Rather than arguing with the incommensurable socio-cultural formation of "traditional religion", they choose to undermine it by attempting to direct potential followers away from such belief systems. Talking to adolescents, some of the activists asserted that "traditional religion" equals "worship of the devil", thereby subsuming other religions under a Christian model, in which the existence of witchcraft does not need to be denied, but is declared evil. Audiences are thereby pointed towards Christianity, and to a lesser degree Islam, as effective protection. Interestingly, the Christian activists I observed tackling "traditional religion" as a problem never explicitly included Islam in their criticism, and were careful not to be understood as evangelising Muslims to become Christians. Therefore their arguments were focused against what was seen as the superstition of "traditional religion", rather than indicating which religion one should adopt instead.

Asked about why their message to follow their respective religious orders was restricted to Christians and Muslims, excluding adherents of "traditional religion", some activists actively made a distinction between the proper (abrahamic) religions (*dini*) and superstition (*ushirikina*) and used the term pagan (*wapagani*) for the followers of the latter:

> **Question**: You say to Christians "You have to live how Christianity tells you to and Christianity says: Don't circumcise." You say to Muslims: "You must live the way Islam tells you to and Islam says: Don't circumcise." And then there are the others, the wapagani and there, the priests say: "It is our tradition, we must circumcise, otherwise our gods, our ancestors will be angry." And there you don't say: "You must live the way your authorities prescribe" but you say "You must not live that way."

Answer: First of all, the people who – as opposed to all others – are not told "act the way you are told", they don't have Religion [*dini*], they have not yet had education and had not understood and did not know about the drawbacks which circumcision can have. We tell them: "Keep the good customs and stop those which can affect the health of people."

The difference in how activists approach different believers is clear. Activists are inclined to treat "traditional religion" as a problem, in cases where incommensurable support for FGC flows out of it. The condescension towards "traditional religion" contained in that strategy is prevalent in Tanzanian society, and therefore more likely to be adopted by activists, as is the more cautious demeanour when it comes to the relation between Christians and Muslims.

Conclusion: conceptualising practices of cooperation/regarding communication campaigns as socio-cultural phenomena

Religious authority is a resource for both the continuation and the end of a controversial practice that is utilised mainly through essentialising, not only by activists, but by proponents of FGC as well. Those strategies, as well as the campaigns as a whole, are shaped by the societal context in which they take place, and are themselves complex and ambivalent factors in how Tanzanian society shapes its relation with religious leadership.

Rather than a mere call to abstain from a practice, anti-FGC campaigns and humanitarian action in general are to be seen as socio-cultural phenomena, which are part of a fundamental struggle over hegemony of competing social, moral and cultural orders. Within the campaigns, alternative concepts of community, family, dignity, sexuality, and many more are articulated and fought over. Such campaigns are therefore unavoidably controversial, but not to the same degree to all parts of their target groups. Activists find allies and adversaries among their target communities, with whom they engage in various, often power-laden forms. The idea that indigenous activists would somehow absolve us from ethical issues around paternalistic action, which is embedded in the ideal of cultural sensitivity, does not stand. It is indeed a very Western view to think that sharing citizenship would make resentment disappear in communities approached by campaigns and dissolve issues of controversial paternalistic influence and cultural interventionism. At the same time, attempts to frame campaigns against female genital cutting as an illegitimate outsiders' intervention fail as well. They, too, are a result of a specific essentialisation that portrays indigenous activists as Westernised sell-outs pitted against an authentic traditional core identity.

The ideal of cultural sensitivity and participation is supposed to address fundamental challenges of cooperation in humanitarianism on the global and the local level. How to arrange global cooperation, especially in a postcolonial context? How to include the people who are supposed to benefit from the humanitarian action in local campaigns? How to absolve abandonment efforts from problematic elements criticised by postcolonial thinkers?

Strategies of essentialising and marginalising seem to be at odds with the ethical ideal of cultural sensitivity. At least in the campaigns I researched, those strategies are employed (by some of the activists) because their preference to stop female genital mutilation is stronger than the procedural ideals of conducting the campaign in a culturally sensitive way. The ideal of cultural sensitivity has been successful in bridging fault lines between interventionists and postcolonial critics in international discourse, but it covers up crucial issues rather than solving them. Even though the tension between the procedural ideals of the anti-FGC movement and their goal should be obvious, little attention has been paid to how limited the contribution of the ideal of cultural sensitivity is when it comes to dealing with this tension. As the examples given demonstrate, we need to become much savvier on the specific ethical questions emerging in such campaigns. Rather than looking for answers in epistemology and dissolving points of dissent into the abstraction of universalism versus relativism, there is a need for an applied ethics of campaigns against "harmful traditional practices" (Galeotti 2007).

As the marginalisation of "indigenous" religion demonstrates, local campaigns crucially deviate from international humanitarian consensus in some respects. It is unclear how these political differences between the NGOs conducting the campaigns and their humanitarian and feminist Western donors should be resolved in a postcolonial context, in which African NGOs are supposed to be the main actors, while the actual power relations still are based on the funding donors can procure. Who should have the say in determining what values and ideologies to promote? Which strategies are legitimate? Is this itself a question of cultural sensitivity? What are the cultures of cooperation, both between donors and activists on the ground, and between activists and their target groups? Clearly, they are complicated and power-laden. Campaigns against "harmful traditional practices" by African activists certainly are neither transmission belts for internationally dominant positions, nor mere translators that connect different cultural logics. Rather, in the pursuit to end a multiply stabilised, highly harmful practice and in the face of much adversity, they engage actors pursuing their own socio-cultural ideals, which can be controversial both locally and internationally.

Notes

1 UN organisations define the practice as follows: "The term 'female genital mutilation' (also called 'female genital cutting' and 'female genital mutilation/cutting') refers to all procedures involving partial or total removal of the external female genitalia or other injury to the female genital organs for non-medical reasons" (WHO et al. 2008, 1). The terminology for the practice is a controversial issue because of the inherent evaluation contained in the choice of the term: the term "female genital mutilation" (FGM) expresses a conscious condemnation of the practice as a severe human rights violation (WHO et al. 2008, 22). It has become more widely accepted than the formerly used term "female circumcision", which is rejected by many adversaries of the practice since it suggests an equivalence of the practice with the removal of the foreskin of men (Baum 2004, 1081). A third group of authors use terms that attempt to abstain from framing the practice either way; those authors do not want to be part in the battle over defining power that is prevalent within the discourse (Bishop 2004, 481). Among them, the term

"female genital cutting" is currently used most frequently (e.g. Hernlund and Shell-Duncan 2007). UNICEF and UNFPA use the term "female genital mutilation/cutting" (FGM/C) in order to express their attitude of condemning the practice while avoiding discriminating against affected persons (UNICEF 2005, 2). I share the concern expressed by UNICEF and UNFPA and I regard the most common forms of the practice (type Ib-III, i.e. clitoridectomy, excision and infibulation; WHO et al. 2008, 24) as mutilation. However, as the present definition of genital mutilation suffers from inconsistencies (Danelzik 2014) I will use the term "female genital cutting" and the acronym FGC henceforth.

2 The advice section is no longer accessible.

3 Interestingly, the spread of the Shafi'i school shows some correspondence with the diffusion of the practice of FGC. This school of thought is especially widespread in East Africa, the Southern part of the Arabic peninsula and South East Asia, where the practice seems to have spread concomitantly with Islamisation (Ali 2006, 100; Coulson 1964, 101). Far from being an African phenomenon, there is considerable prevalence in a dozen Asian countries, with circumstantial evidence in more. The data on FGC in Asia is still not as developed as for African countries. An overview of studies can be found at www.stopfgmmideast.org/background/research.

4 Some authors therefore prefer the term "indigenous religion", which also has problematic connotations: it runs the risk of presenting Islam and Christianity as imperialistic, inauthentic influences from without as opposed to authentic, "native" alternatives. Both concepts are misleading.

References

Abdel Hadi A. (2006) "A Community of Women Empowered: The Story of Deir El Barsha", in Abusharaf R.M. (ed.), *Female Circumcision*, University of Pennsylvania Press, Philadelphia, 104–124.

Abou El Fadl K. (2005) *The Great Theft. Wrestling Islam from the Extremists*, Harper Collins, New York.

Abusharaf R.M. (2000) "Revisiting Feminist Discourses on Infibulation: Responses from Sudanese Feminists", in Shell-Duncan B. and Hernlund Y.(eds), *Female "Circumcision" in Africa*, Lynne Rienner, Boulder, CO, 151–166.

Al-Qaradawi Y. (2009) [untitled] (www.target-human-rights.com/HP-08_fatwa/index.php?p=fatwaQaradawi), accessed 20 June 2015.

Aldeeb Abu-Sahlieh S.A. (1997) "Jehovah, His Cousin Allah, and Sexual Mutilations", in Denniston G.C. and Milos M.F. (eds), *Sexual Mutilations*, Plenum Press, New York, 41–62.

Aldeeb Abu-Sahlieh S.A. (1999) "Muslims' Genitalia in the Hands of the Clergy", in Denniston G.C., Hodges F.M. and Milos M.F. (eds), *Male and Female Circumcision. Medical, Legal, and Ethical Considerations in Pediatric Practice*, Kluwer Academic/Plenum Publishers, New York, 131–171.

Aldeeb Abu-Sahlieh S.A. (2006) "Male and Female Circumcision: The Myth of the Difference", in Abusharaf R.M. (ed.), *Female Circumcision*, University of Pennsylvania Press, Philadelphia. 47–72.

Ali K. (2006) *Sexual Ethics and Islam. Feminist Reflections on Qur'an, Hadith, and Jurisprudence*, Oneworld, Oxford.

Antonazzo M. (2003) "Problems with Criminalizing Female Genital Cutting", *Peace Review*, 15(4), 471–478.

Asmani I.L. and Abdi M.S. (2008) *De-Linking Female Genital Mutilation/Cutting from Islam*, Frontiers Program/USAID, Washington, DC.

Badran M. (2009) *Feminism in Islam. Secular and Religious Convergences*, Oneworld, Oxford.

Baum B. (2004) "Feminist Politics of Recognition", *Signs*, 29(4), 1073–1102.

Becker F. (2007) "The Virus and the Scriptures: Muslims and AIDS in Tanzania", *Journal of Religion in Africa*, 37(1), 16–40.

Becker F. (2008) *Becoming Muslim in Mainland Tanzania, 1890–2000*, Oxford University Press, Oxford.

Bishop J.P. (2004) "Modern Liberalism, Female Circumcision, and the Rationality of Traditions", *Journal of Medicine and Philosophy*, 29(4), 473–497.

Coulson, N.J. (1964) *A History of Islamic Law*, Edinburgh University Press, Edinburgh.

Daly M. (1978) *Gyn/Ecology: The Metaethics of Radical Feminism*, Beacon Press, Boston.

Danelzik M. (2014) "Racialized body modifications – framing genital mutilation, cosmetic surgery and gender assignment surgery", *Networking Knowledge*, 7(3), 21–39.

Davis D.S. (2001) "Male and Female Genital Alteration: A Collision Course with the Law?", *Health Matrix*, 11(2), 487–570.

Deegan H. (2009) *Africa Today. Culture, Economics, Religion, Security*, Routledge, London.

El Bashir H. (2006) "The Sudanese National Committee on the Eradication of Harmful Traditional Practices and the Campaign Against Female Genital Mutilation", in Abusharaf R.M. (ed.), *Female Circumcision*, University of Pennsylvania Press, Philadelphia, 142–170.

Favali L. (2001) "What is Missing? (Female Genital Surgeries – Infibulation, Excision, Clitoridectomy – in Eritrea)", *Global Jurist Frontiers*, 1(2), 1–99.

Gachiri E.W. (2000) *Female Circumcision. With Reference to the Agikuyu of Kenya*, Paulines Publication Africa, Nairobi.

Galal E. (2009) "Yūsuf al-Qaradāwi and the New Islamic TV", in Gräf B. and Skovgaard-Petersen J. (eds), *Global Mufti*, Columbia University Press, New York, 149–180.

Galeotti A.E. (2007) "Relativism, Universalism, and Applied Ethics: The Case of Female Circumcision", *Constellations*, 14(1), 91–111.

Gräf B. and Skovgaard-Petersen J. (2009) "Introduction", in Gräf B. and Skovgaard-Petersen J. (eds), *Global Mufti*, Columbia University Press, New York, 1–15.

Groop K. (2006) *With the Gospel to Maasailand. Lutheran Mission Work among the Arusha and Maasai in Northern Tanzania 1904–1973*, Åbo Akademie University Printing House, Åbo.

Gruenbaum E. (1982) "The Movement Against Clitoridectomy and Infibulation in Sudan: Public Health Policy and the Women's Movement", *Medical Anthropology Newsletter*, 13(2), 4–12.

Hernlund Y. and Shell-Duncan B. eds (2007) *Transcultural Bodies. Female Genital Cutting in Global Context*, Rutgers University Press, New Brunswick.

Hodgson D.L. (1999) "Images and Interventions: The Problems of Pastoralist Development", in Anderson D. and Broch-Due V. (eds), *The Poor Are Not Us*, James Currey, Oxford, 221–239.

Hosken F.P. (1993) *The Hosken Report*, Women's International Network News, Lexington.

Klasen S. and Wink C. (2003) "'Missing Women': Revisiting the Debate", *Feminist Economics*, 9(2/3), 263–299.

Korieh C. (2005) "'Other' Bodies: Western Feminism, Race, and Representation in Female Circumcision Discourse", in Nnaemeka O. (ed.), *Female Circumcision and the Politics of Knowledge*, Praeger, Westport, 111–132.

Lodhi A. and Westerlund D. (1999) "Tanzania", in Westerlund D. and Svanberg I. (eds), *Islam Outside the Arab World*, Curzon, Surrey, 97–110.

Mackie G. and LeJeune J. (2009) *Social Dynamics of Abandonment of Harmful Practices. A New Look at the Theory*, Special Series on Social Norms and Harmful Practices, Innocenti Working Paper No. 2009-06, Innocenti Research Centre, Florence.

Magesa L. (2009) *African Religion in the Dialogue Debate. From Intolerance to Coexistence*, Lit Verlag, Berlin.

Masterson J.M. and Swanson J.H. (2000) *Female Genital Cutting: Breaking the Silence, Enabling Change*, International Center for Research on Women, Washington, DC.

McKinnon C. (2006) *Toleration. A Critical Introduction*, Routledge, London.

Nnaemeka O. (2005) "African Women, Colonial Discourses, and Imperialist Interventions: Female Circumcisions as Impetus", in Nnaemeka O. (ed.), *Female Circumcision and the Politics of Knowledge*, Praeger, Westport, 27–45.

Nussbaum M.C. (2000) *Women and Human Development: The Capabilities Approach*, Cambridge University Press, Cambridge.

Obermeyer C.M. (1999) "Female Genital Surgeries: The Known, the Unknown, and the Unknowable", *Medical Anthropology Quarterly*, 13(1), 79–106.

Obiora L.A. (1997) "Bridges and Barricades: Rethinking Polemics and Intransigence in the Campaign against Female Circumcision", *Case Western Reserve Law Review*, 47(2), 275–378.

Obiora L.A. (2005) "The Anti-Female Circumcision Campaign Deficit", in Nnaemeka O. (ed.), *Female Circumcision and the Politics of Knowledge*, Praeger, Westport, 183–208.

OHCHR (1995) *Harmful Traditional Practices Affecting the Health of Women and Children*, Fact Sheet No. 23, Office of the High Commissioner for Human Rights, Geneva.

Rekdal O.B. (1999) "The invention by Tradition. Creativity and Change among the Iraqw of Northern Tanzania", PhD thesis, University of Bergen.

Robertson C.C. (2002) "Getting Beyond the Ew! Factor. Rethinking U.S. Approaches to African Female Genital Cutting", in James S.M. and Robertson C.C. (eds), *Genital Cutting and Transnational Sisterhood*, University of Illinois Press, Urbana, 54–86.

Schneider L. (2006a) "Colonial Legacies and Postcolonial Authoritarianism in Tanzania: Connects and Disconnects", *African Studies Review*, 49(1), 93–118.

Schneider L. (2006b) "The Maasai's New Clothes: A Developmentalist Modernity and Its Exclusions", *Africa Today*, 53(1), 101–129.

Tanzanian Coalition against FGM (2008) *Report on the Commemoration of Zero Tolerance to FGM Day Held in Dodoma from 5th and 6th February 2008*, Tanzanian Coalition against FGM, Dodoma.

Thomas L.M. (2003) *Politics of the Womb. Women, Reproduction, and the State in Kenya*, University of California Press, Berkeley.

UNFPA (2004a) *Culture Matters. Working with Faith-based Organizations: Case studies from Country Programmes*, United Nations Population Fund, New York.

UNFPA (2004b) *Guide to Working from Within. 24 Tips for Culturally Sensitive Programming*, United Nations Population Fund, New York.

UNFPA (2006) *Ending Violence against Women. Programming for Prevention, Protection and Care*, United Nations Population Fund, New York.

UNFPA (2007) *Programming to Address Violence against Women. 10 Case Studies*, United Nations Population Fund, New York.

UNICEF (2005) *Changing a Harmful Social Convention: Female Genital Mutilation/Cutting*, United Nations International Children's Emergency Fund, Florence.

UNICEF (2013) *Female Genital Mutilation/Cutting: A Statistical Overview and Exploration of the Dynamics of Change*, United Nations International Children's Emergency Fund, New York.

Walley C.J. (2002) "Searching for 'Voices'. Feminism, Anthropology, and the Global Debate over Female Genital Operations", in James S.M. and Robertson C.C. (eds), *Genital Cutting and Transnational Sisterhood*, University of Illinois Press, Urbana, 17–53.

WHO, OHCHR, UNAIDS, UNDP, UNECA, UNESCO, UNFPA, UNHCR, UNICEF and UNIFEM (2008) *Eliminating Female Genital Mutilation. An Interagency Statement*, Geneva.

Winter B., Thompson D. and Jeffreys S. (2002) "The UN Approach to Harmful Traditional Practices", *International Feminist Journal of Politics*, 4(1), 72–94.

Winterbottom A., Koomen J. and Burford G. (2009) "Female Genital Cutting: Cultural Rights of Defiance in Northern Tanzania", *African Studies Review*, 52(1), 47–71.

9 Islamic charities from the Arab world in Africa

Intercultural encounters of humanitarianism and morality

Mayke Kaag

Introduction

As has also been shown in the first part of this volume, the global humanitarian landscape has increasingly diversified over the past three decades, with an increasing role for NGOs of various backgrounds (Macrae et al. 2002). While this diversity has been acknowledged and explored, and the challenges of cooperation and coordination have long been debated in academic and policy circles, the possibly particular role of Islamic NGOs in humanitarianism is only recently developing as a field of investigation. While these organisations have already been present on the ground[1] and offering relief in different settings since the end of the 1970s, they have been operating under the radar of most Western observers, and it is only after 9/11 that they became a focus of attention as allegations were raised that a number of them were involved in funding terrorism and supporting Al Qaeda. More recently, they have also received more positive coverage as a result of an increased interest in faith-based organisations (FBOs) as providers of relief and actors in development. From this perspective, it is assumed that Islamic NGOs are more efficient than others in giving support and providing relief to Muslim populations because of their shared belief with the target group (Benthall 2008; De Cordier 2010).

In this chapter, I look more in detail at Islamic NGOs acting as transnational humanitarian[2] actors and discuss the prospects and challenges for cooperation between them and others in the field of relief and development. I have chosen to use the term 'humanitarian' in a rather broad sense, including not only emergency relief but also activities that are more broadly directed towards improving the life of people, as the Islamic charities studied here do not normally consider 'humanitarianism' and 'development' to be separate categories, as will be explained later. In my discussion, I focus particularly on transnational Islamic NGOs from the Gulf region and their work in Africa.[3] Specific attention is paid to these charities' interactions with other humanitarian actors, such as Western (Christian and secular) NGOs. These encounters can be labelled intercultural both in terms of cultural/religious background and in terms of working approaches. In addition, there is the intercultural encounter with African target groups: even in cases where Islam may seem to form a common denominator at first sight, different

DOI: 10.4324/9781315658827-12

views of Islam may mean intercultural navigating, competition and sometimes clashes between charities and African target groups, which may also have repercussions in the wider society. Finally, the chapter underlines that intercultural encounters are also interpersonal encounters, the study of which is indispensable to obtain an in-depth understanding of the humanitarian process on the ground, where culture is negotiated and shaped in interaction, and where people may behave in more pragmatic ways than could be predicted when looking only at their ideological stances and cultural backgrounds.

Transnational Islamic NGOs in Africa

Care for the poor and support of the needy is important in Islam and has always been part of local and national arrangements (Krafess 2005). The establishment of international Islamic organisations for providing relief elsewhere in the world is a fairly recent phenomenon that at the same time can be positioned within the broader emergence of international organisations in the twentieth century and the global Islamic revival from the early twentieth century onwards that helped Islam to (re)emerge as an important identity marker in all spheres of life (Petersen 2014). The establishment of the first transnational Islamic NGOs in the late 1970s and early 1980s was more specifically triggered by the war in Afghanistan and financially made possible by the oil boom in the Arab countries (Ghandour 2002).

These NGOs increasingly extended their work to other parts of Asia and into Africa. The International Islamic Relief Organization (IIRO or IIROSA), one of the first Saudi transnational NGOs (created in 1978 by the Saudi government), started its work in Africa in the early 1980s. Also, the Kuwaiti organisation African Muslims Agency (AMA) was among the transnational Islamic NGOs starting to work in Africa in the 1980s. This first wave of arrivals of Gulf-based Islamic charities occurred during a period of serious droughts in the Sahel, the effects of which in terms of human sufferings, publicised by the mass media, led to extensive humanitarian efforts worldwide. Islamic charities also started to offer humanitarian relief in the affected areas.

A second wave of Gulf charities arriving in Africa can be discerned from the mid-1990s onwards. Saudi Arabia had seen an upsurge of NGOs that were relatively independent from the Saudi state, but often still administered by members of the Saudi elite, and they were looking for an outlet for their funds. This meant that the group of Islamic NGOs in Africa became increasingly diversified, and alongside GONGOs[4] there appeared a group of relatively private charities in the late 1990s, such as the Al-Makka Al-Mukkarama Foundation, Al-Haramain, and others.[5]

The establishment of transnational Islamic charities did not remain restricted to the Arab World. Over the years Muslim communities had settled in the West and they started to establish transnational Islamic relief organisations in the 1980s. Among them were Islamic Relief and Muslim Aid in the UK, founded by Egyptian and Bangladeshi migrants, respectively. Petersen (2014) describes how these charities, particularly after 9/11, changed their approach and started to provide a less Islamic and more secularised form of aid. Islamic Relief and Muslim Aid are nowadays part of the mainstream Western humanitarian and development system, and function very much like Oxfam International or secularised Christian NGOs such as Care. They receive a lot of funding from Western development and funding agencies such as DFID and USAID, which over the past few years have tried to develop collaborative relationships with 'moderate' Islamic organisations (Petersen 2014; Thaut, Stein and Barnett 2010). However, not all transnational Islamic charities based in the West have followed that same path of increased secularisation. Al-Muntada Al-Islami, for instance, founded by Saudi students in Great Britain, has remained very similar to the Islamic charities operating from the Gulf and thus outside the mainstream (read: global, Western-dominated) aid architecture. In the rest of this chapter I will focus on this latter category of transnational Islamic charities from the Gulf and their homologues.

Islamic NGOs from the Gulf working in Africa normally aim to influence both people's material and moral well being. In combining material aid with proselytisation, they embed their work in religiously inspired ideas on transnational solidarity and the importance of enhancing the *umma*, the global community of the faithful.

Concerning material aid, the activities of Islamic charities from the Gulf in Africa include emergency relief, care for orphans, medical care and the construction of wells, mosques and schools. The care for orphans is a core activity of most NGOs, be it by financing orphanages or by sponsoring orphans who stay with their families through a kind of foster parents plan. The care for orphans is rooted in Islam: the Prophet was himself an orphan and many hadiths refer to the value of taking care of them (see also Benthall and Bellion-Jourdan 2003; Petersen 2011).

Aid to refugees is often given by way of the distribution of parcels of food and other necessities in refugee camps that may be under the supervision of the UNHCR or other large donors. Concerning health care, several NGOs run small clinics. A popular activity is the organisation of medical caravans (AMA, Al-Muntada Al-Islami). A team of medical doctors and nurses travels through the country, organises consultations for the population, and executes simple operations. These caravans generally have a strong publicity effect.

In the field of education, Islamic NGOs have constructed schools (both for formal education and Qur'anic schools) and assure their functioning. They also finance the salaries of teachers in existing schools. All organisations consider the teaching of, and in, Arabic very important. For them, Arabic stands for a way of living that is inspired by Islam and Arab culture, whose values in their view have been marginalised in many African countries that inherited a Francophone or Anglophone public school system from their former coloniser, and where private schools used to be Christian missionary schools. Arabisation, teaching of Islam and the Arabic language are thus seen as an antidote to the effects of Western colonialism and contemporary influences from 'the West' (see Hunwick 1997). Increasingly, Islamic charities have also started to focus on skills training, such as sewing classes for widows and unmarried girls – the idea being that this will offer them the opportunity to gain some income by decent means so that they do not need to enter into prostitution.

Organisations such as AMA focus primarily on education, while others, like the IIRO, have a more diversified portfolio. Some invest predominantly in the construction of large centres that integrate a mosque, a school, an orphanage, a centre for professional education and a women's centre, while others have more dispersed and smaller projects.

As Islamic NGOs, and not merely as NGOs run by Muslims, the organisations studied also have a missionary (da'wa) function. They are ultimately concerned with the advancement of Islam, either by deepening people's understanding of Islamic principles and improving Muslims' religious practices (re-Islamisation) or by conversion of non-Muslims (Islamisation). This missionary aspect comes most explicitly to the fore in their activities in the field of religious education and the promotion of Islam (sponsoring Qur'anic teachers, distributing learning materials) but in fact underlies all their other activities as well.

Islamic NGOs from the Gulf states generally disseminate what is often called a Salafi form of Islam. Salafism is a modernist current that claims to follow the 'pious predecessors' (Arabic, salaf), the first generation of Muslims, whose practice of Islam it considers to be the purest form (Ghandour 2002). Salafis seek an Islamic revival through the elimination of what they consider to be foreign innovations (bid'a). The many Sufi orders prominent in Africa are targeted in an attempt to 're-educate' African Muslims about Islam and purify Islam of allegedly un-Islamic practices (see Rosander 1997). Gulf charities also work in areas that have no longstanding Islamic traditions and often in zones that are considered as fringe regions between Muslim Africa and regions in which animist and, more recently, Christian traditions can be found, such as southern Chad, southern Sudan and the Casamance region in Senegal. Here their activities are geared less towards re-education and more towards conversion.

The Islamic character is manifest not only in these NGOs' activities, but also in their funding. A large part of the latter is constituted by zakat (obligatory alms giving) and sadaqa (voluntary alms giving), coming from donors in the Gulf. In Saudi Arabia, zakat is collected by the government as a tax; in most other countries, Muslims may pay their zakat at their own discretion. The Quran gives eight categories of people for whose support zakat should be used. These are the poor, the needy, those who have responsibility over them (zakat collectors and administrators), recent converts or those about to convert, slaves in order to be freed, debtors, travellers and warriors (Benthall and Bellion-Jourdan 2003, 10). Quranic texts and hadiths[6] often exhort Muslims to practise certain forms of charity, while also indicating the recompense one gets from it, such as the erasing of sins and peace in the Hereafter. In the case of care for orphans, for instance, a number of verses in the Quran promise the highest rewards for those who look after them (Krafess 2005). This embeddedness in Islamic prescriptions and recommendations thus has a clear influence on the agendas of the NGOs under study: in the case of zakat, the destination of the funds is given, while in other cases, donors often want their donations to be used for specific uses. The transnational Islamic solidarity as substantiated by the work of the Islamic charities thus requires a specific accountability towards the donors so as to ensure that the charity is beneficial (in material terms) to the target group but equally (in terms of blessing) to the donor.

How strong the humanitarian aspects and the religious aspects are depends on the organisation but also on the audience and the context. To a Western researcher such as the author of this chapter, the charities may tend to stress their humanitarian aspect[7] whereas to their donors in Saudi Arabia they may stress their Muslim character and missionary function. This is, for instance, also visible in the difference between the English version and the Arab version of several organisations' websites. It probably holds true, too, for the different forums in which they participate: several organisations, such as the IIRO, the World Assembly of Muslim Youth (WAMY) and AMA, participate both in humanitarian forums such as the NGO forum of the UN and UNICEF, and in Islamic forums such as the World Muslim League.

At a more practical level, there is generally not much collaboration between the Gulf charities as most of them are in fact quite solitary, and consultation and coordination with others is minimal. In their study of Saudi Arabia's humanitarian assistance, Al-Yahya and Fustier (2011) conclude that this is a problem for the Saudi humanitarian aid structure at large.

Gulf charities and other humanitarian and development actors: encounters between different humanitarian systems and visions

As can be deduced from the foregoing, in a way these organisations' objectives and approaches are rather different from those of so-called mainstream Western humanitarian and development organisations. Where most Western NGOs, for instance, would put an accent on capacity development, a great deal of the activities of these Arab charities could be labelled 'charity': a well is constructed, and where Western organisations would then establish a well committee in order to manage the well sustainably, for these charities the well is it, and their involvement would often stop at that point.

This is very much related to the ideas of development underlying the programmes of these transnational Islamic NGOs. As has been argued, these are rooted in and justified by Islam, or, as put eloquently by Petersen (2012, 140), 'the provision of aid is explained and legitimated with reference to Muslim traditions and concepts such as zakat, sadaqa and the hadiths, rather than the Millennium Development Goals, the Universal Human Rights Declaration or the Human Development Index'. This means that, on one hand, their material interventions are very much individual-oriented: compassion informed by religion leads the work of these organisations to be directed towards lessening the suffering of the individual, such as the orphan and the poor, and not so much towards the material advancement of *communities*, as in the mainstream Western understanding of 'development'. On the other hand, a more community-oriented understanding of development is indeed very present in these organisations' perceptions and approaches, but in this case does not concern material aspects so much as it does the enhancement and enlargement of the *umma*, the global Muslim community – often interpreted in both a spiritual and a geographical sense.

The importance of religious aspects often translates into an accent on moral education and moral disciplining, for instance concerning the right behaviour and dress for women, the importance of praying five times a day, abstaining from alcohol, etc. It should, however, be emphasised that Western interventions that claim to be neutral, are also often equally morally loaded (Baaz 2005; Bornstein 2003; Ferguson 1990). This may not concern moral education in a religious sense, but still there are very value-loaded messages implied concerning family and gender roles, societal ideals, the accent on individual identities instead of on social identities, etc.

Western and Arab NGOs meet each other in the field and the aforementioned differences do not facilitate rapprochement, let alone collaboration, between them. They hold a lot of prejudices and preconceived ideas about one another. My fieldwork experience is that most of the time they remain each in their own corner. In mainstream development fora at country and provincial levels, Islamic organisations from the Gulf are most often not invited. In that sense, they are still a blind spot for many Western development organisations, including large multilateral organisations such as the UNDP. At the local level, sometimes modest collaboration takes place, for instance in a schooling workshop in southern Chad where a Catholic organisation invited AMA to participate. In Somalia, Oxfam International has worked with WAMY (Clarke 2010, referring to both organisations' publications in 2004). In her study on Qatar Charity in Niger, Dugger (2011) mentions that there was a rather prudent rapprochement between this organisation and the Oxfam GB country office in Niamey, although up to that moment it had not yet led to concrete collaboration. The British organisation Life for African Mothers collaborates with Al-Muntada Al-Islami facilitating midwifery training courses in Ghana.[8] Most of the time the initiative comes from a Catholic organisation, as interfaith dialogue appears to be actively stimulated in the Catholic church. Protestant organisations are much less inclined to collaborate with other faith organisations, and also the Arab charities themselves may speak about it and have an interfaith dialogue discourse, but rarely take the initiative.

At this point, it should be emphasised that it is not useful merely to analyse different humanitarian systems and visions in abstract terms. The way in which the encounter between different humanitarian systems ultimately takes shape is very much determined by the local context. Thus, where staff in their head offices in the UK, the Netherlands, Saudi Arabia or Qatar may easily talk about intercultural and interreligious dialogue in eloquent terms, this may mean something completely different in the field. This may well be illustrated by the Protestant mission in Chad, which is sponsored by ICCO,[9] a Dutch secular NGO from a Protestant background, but that nevertheless produced a booklet stating in a rather belligerent way: 'We will not rest until 100 per cent of the Chadian population has become Christian.' The reality in Chad is that charities have to work in a national context in which religion is very much politicised and where antagonistic relationships have existed between the Christian south and the Muslim north for a long time. After Independence, southerners came to rule the country as the south had been more developed by the French during the colonial era. After years of civil war, the Muslims took power in the 1980s and since then, Islam has become very much associated to power. Southern Chad has been animist and Christian, but increasingly also Muslims have migrated to the south (for instance, cattle holders fleeing the droughts in the north, and also Muslim administrators replacing Christian administrators). In this context of being a transition area between Christian and Islamic spheres of influence, (transnational) Christian and Islamic organisations are competing fiercely for clients. This partly takes the form of a battle for visibility in space, Islamic NGOs erecting small mosques in villages all over southern Chad, the Catholic Church investing in a particularly large Church in the provincial capital. There is little direct confrontation between the Christian and Islamic organisations, but the people at the grassroots who are the target groups of the NGOs' activities feel the tension all the more, as is shown by the following case.

In a small village in the south of Chad, I met a former priest who had recently converted to Islam. He had always and every Sunday collected money for the Church but never had he experienced that the Church did something for him and his community. He told me impassionedly how he found the light when he read a small booklet entitled 'The Way to Islam' given to him by people who had come to the village to preach. And he went to the mosque in another village near to the main road and said that he wanted to convert. But there they said that he had to think it over first and they sent him away. After five days he returned to say that he was decided and then they warmly welcomed him. And a few days later, ten other men with their families followed his example. At this point a nun from the diocese came to the village and told them that it was the devil who had brought them to Islam and that they should not listen to him. They in turn answered that they had not converted for money or anything like that, and when she saw that she could not convince them, she left. The former priest said bitterly that now, everywhere in the diocese, it is taught that he is the embodiment of the devil. I saw that this was very painful for him. What I found very painful is that he had sent a letter to the Islamic NGO intervening in the area and that was directly or indirectly involved in his conversion, to ask for a mosque, and that he never received an answer. It seemed to me that he was treated in much the same way by both institutions (Kaag 2007).

What we observe here is a kind of political battle between Christian and Islamic organisations, expressed in moral terms. Categories among the local population, such as local elites, may play upon these dynamics to their profit. A local chief, for instance, managed to get a community centre funded by an Islamic NGO, an asset that significantly added to his prestige. The poorest and the least educated, who already suffer the most, appear as the real victims of this competition. People in southern Chad indicated that they felt that it leads to cleavages in villages and families. A high official at the Department of Religious Affairs of the Ministry of the Interior in Ndjamena that is charged with overseeing all religious activities of international actors in the country stated that these may come to the aid of people with the best intentions and are often also helpful in a material sense, but nevertheless often cause harm from a social perspective.[10] In the next section, I will take a closer look at this encounter between Gulf charities and their African target group, with a particular focus on cultural and religious aspects.

Islamic charities and their African target groups: encounters between different strands of Islam

For several years the idea has been gaining ground that Islamic relief and development organisations would be more apt to work in Muslim contexts because of their perceived cultural proximity to their target groups, which would make them more effective. However, the fact that the organisations and their target groups share the same religion does not mean that they share the same culture, among other things because the strands of Islam, as well as its cultural expressions, may differ.

As indicated above, transnational Islamic NGOs from the Gulf often act very much on their own. There is also little collaboration with local NGOs. Gulf charities generally prefer to deal directly with their target groups without involving intermediary organisations, as there is little trust beyond their own organisation and (personal) network. Interestingly, in Chad, the local staff of Al Muntada Al-Islami created a local organisation, 'L'Association des amis de la société' (Association of the Friends of Society), when the transnational NGO had to leave the country in 2008.[11] This association now appears to have begun to serve as a local intermediary for relief from the Gulf. The Qatari Cheikh Thani bin Abdullah Foundation, for instance, in 2014 financed the organisation for the distribution of food and non-food items as part of a relief convoy to Sudanese refugees in east Chad for the amount of US$2,026,022.[12]

As also underlined by De Cordier (2010), whether there is some truth in the idea of cultural proximity between Islamic charities and their target groups – again – depends very much on the local context. In Chad, for instance, there has been a process of arabisation, defined here as an increased cultural orientation towards the Arab world expressed in the adoption of elements of transnational Arab elite culture (e.g. language, styles of clothing, social and cultural values) as a reference. There is a cultural proximity there, even despite the fact that many Muslims in Chad are sufi.[13]

In Senegal the large majority of Muslims is also sufi, but here the sufi orders are far more prominent as identity markers than in Chad. Most Muslims belong to one of the main Sufi orders in the country, the Tidjaniyya, the Khadriyya and the Muridiyya. This adherence is characterised by close and personal bonds between the believers and their *marabout* (religious leader). In particular the Mourides express their religious fervour and their attachment to their *marabout* in very strong terms and in very visible ways. The Muridiyya is particular in as far as it is 'home-grown' and was founded by Cheikh Ahmadou Bamba at the end of the nineteenth century. The city of Touba in central Senegal is its religious centre. Not only among the Mourides, but in Senegal in general, there is a strong sense of pride at being a Senegalese Muslim, a sense of self respect. It means that Senegalese normally will not easily accept others telling them how to practise their religion. Muslims with a *salafi* orientation, however, would consider sufi forms of belief and practice *bid'a* (unlawful innovation), requiring religious re-education to be eliminated. From the foregoing, it is clear that there is little cultural proximity between most Senegalese Muslims and the Arab charities. There is a reformist minority in Senegal to whom their message appeals, however. The Saudi organisation WAMY, for instance collaborates with the Senegalese reformist student organisation Union de la Jeunesse Musulmane du Sénégal (UJMS). In general, in discourse both Gulf charities and Senegalese Muslims underline belonging to the *umma* uniting all Muslims, but in practice there is a lot of difference in how Islam is lived and expressed. In addition, there is a sense of racism that is strongly felt by many African Muslims.

It should be noted that the possibility of a cultural disconnection with their target groups in Africa is not limited to these Islamic charities from the Gulf, as it may also pertain to Islamic NGOs that have adopted a 'mainstream' secular approach, such as Islamic Relief (Petersen 2014) – the local population may, for instance, not understand that the organisation sees religion as something private and personal and is not inclined to finance mosques and the like. Indeed, these kinds of tensions are not particular to Islamic relief organisations but may also be familiar to international Christian organisations in their relation to their target groups. Taking a still broader perspective, the existence of a gap between helpers and beneficiaries holds true for many relief and development interventions in general, where staff belonging to a certain elite culture have to relate to less well-off segments of a population (De Cordier 2010). What I want to argue here is that in general, one should not attach too much importance to religion as a common denominator in encounters between humanitarian organisations and their target groups and assume that it facilitates humanitarian action, as this may be true only up to a certain point. Beyond this, it could even become counterproductive, as it raises expectations of shared visions and does not help to acknowledge differences and possible sources of conflicts.

Humanitarian action as interpersonal encounters

In the foregoing I have argued that it is important to look at the differences in approaches and visions of the different humanitarian systems to which Arab charities and Western NGOs belong, but also at the hidden and not-so-obvious similarities, such as the fact that interventions of both categories are loaded with moral messages, and that meaningful cultural gaps may exist between them and their target groups. Indeed, the study of Islamic charities may provide a mirror in which to look critically at 'mainstream', Western, often taken-for-granted practices in the field of humanitarianism.

I have also underlined that the way in which these systems take shape in intercultural encounters between organisations in the field and between Arab charities and their target groups is very much determined by the national and local context, including political dynamics, cultural aspects and prevalent forms of Islam.[14]

However, in the end, humanitarian encounters are also interpersonal encounters. In this respect, it should be emphasised that the Arab directors of these Islamic charities are all experienced expats. The country director of AMA in Chad, for instance, is a Moroccan who previously worked in Burkina Faso, and the country director of al-Makka al-Mukarrama was a Saudi who served in Bosnia – all have a lot of knowledge of various (African) contexts and are able to adapt and be flexible accordingly, for instance in relation to local norms of gender seclusion or women's dress. They may thus be more pragmatic than could be predicted from merely looking at their ideological and religious background. From their side, African sufi religious leaders often also take a pragmatic stance. In Senegal, for instance, WAMY organised a medical caravan in Touba at the request of the general Caliph of the Mouride sufi order. The WAMY country director proudly declared that he was also in touch with the Caliph of the Tidjaniyya in Tivouane,[15] although it had not yet yielded any concrete projects.[16]

In the West, Arab NGO staff are often viewed in a very negative light and accused of trying to force a strict or even radical form of Islam upon Africans as part of a geopolitical agenda. However, already in view of the fact that they choose to live in the capital of a poor sub-Saharan country instead of in luxury in Doha or Jeddah, these people should be considered as equally idealistic as Western aid workers. This recognition could create a beginning of appreciation for one another.

People may overcome prejudices through their experiences, and change cultures through their actions and reactions. Partly as a result of this dynamic, the humanitarian field is ever-changing, as is also underlined by Petersen (2012). For the Islamic NGOs, in particular, it is important to remark that they are increasingly staffed by a new generation who are interested in learning more about organisational management and the like, which they consider to be more advanced in Western (Christian and secular) organisations. This may result in a process of professionalisation, as many Western NGOs have seen in the 1990s, forced by a changing aid culture that has increasingly laid more emphasis on accountability and transparency. Such a professional rapprochement might contribute to increased possibilities of coordination and even collaboration between Islamic charities and other humanitarian actors, at least in practical terms.

Conclusion: challenges of cooperation

In this chapter I have tried to illuminate that the work of Islamic charities from the Gulf in Africa includes moral and political encounters with other providers of aid and moral and cultural encounters with local target groups, which are shaped by global, national and local contexts.

Concerning the interaction between transnational Islamic charities and their non-Islamic counterparts, on one hand, it poses a challenge for both parties that, at the global scale, everything related to Islam appears so politically loaded. Islamic charities seem to need to justify themselves and their approaches all the time, which makes it difficult to have an open dialogue. Islamic NGOs are very much on the defence, and because of this attitude Western observers may think that the former may indeed have things to hide. Suspicion on both sides is further reinforced by the fact that humanitarian action and counterterrorism programmes have become increasingly interlinked (Pantuliano et al. 2011), which makes it an ever bigger challenge to overcome prejudice on both sides.

On the other hand, there is also an opposite development of increased interest in FBOs/faith-based approaches, in which various Western development and humanitarian actors have started to see Islamic charities as possible partners, while there is also a growing interest among Western development and relief organisations in Islamic principles of charity and in Islamic finance. Initiatives for exchange and collaboration appear, however, to be still rather incidental and confined to specific cases. This changing appreciation means that there are increased opportunities for Islamic charities from the Gulf to link up with non-Islamic relief and development organisations, but to make it happen, they too should take a proactive stance.

In the end, of course, it is all about lessening the needs of those who suffer. And it is here that the core problems of collaboration between Islamic charities from the Gulf and Western humanitarian actors may be identified. The definition of suffering, and hence also the solution, differs. However, research on Islamic NGOs is also useful in that it provides a mirror to critically assess Western – so-called mainstream (that is, considered by Western observers as such) – humanitarian and development interventions. It allows us to see that many Western development interventions are also morally loaded and come with their own messages about what is important and valuable in life. That recognition could lead to more appreciation and common ground for exchange and appreciation. It also suggests that probably collaboration is possible only in partial fields, for instance in distributing goods in a refugee camp. But collaboration and coordination in this, and even appreciation of each other's efforts and idealism, would mean a big step forward in humanitarianism.

Notes

1 There are actually an estimated 400 international Muslim charities globally (Petersen 2014). Transnational Islamic charities are to be found in many African countries and cover most of the continent (Salih 2003), although as a result of the 'War on Terror' a number of Islamic charities from the Gulf region have been forced to close down (Kaag 2007; Belew 2014).
2 In this chapter, I will use the term 'humanitarian' in a rather broad sense, so not focusing on emergency relief only, but also on activities that are more broadly directed towards improving the lives of people.
3 Empirical data for this research have been gathered during fieldwork in Chad (2004, 2012, 2014) and in Senegal (2009, 2011).
4 Government operated non governmental organisation, such as IIRO.
5 See Montagu (2010) for a useful discussion of the Saudi domestic voluntary sector and its evolution over time.
6 A collection of traditions containing sayings of the prophet Muhammad which, with accounts of his daily practice (the Sunna), constitute the major source of guidance for Muslims apart from the Quran.
7 Thus they did not tell me much about their *da'wa* activities and I only got information on this while in the field.
8 www.lifeforafricanmothers.org

9 ICCO started as Interkerkelijke Coordinatie Commissie Ontwikkelingssamenwerking (Interchurch Coordination Commission for Development Co-operation), but now uses the acronym as its full name. See www.icco.nl.
10 Interview, October 2014.
11 For more on this case, see Kaag (2014).
12 UNOCHA Financial Tracking Service 6 February 2015, Other humanitarian funding to Chad 2014, http://fts.unocha.org (table ref: R4).
13 Sufism is a broad current in Islamic belief and practice, in which Muslims seek to find divine truth and knowledge through direct personal experience of God. In this sense, sufism could be seen as in contrast with more scripture-oriented currents in Islam.
14 Elsewhere (Kaag 2012) I have also elaborated on other aspects such as the specific needs existing on the ground, and the way 'development' and 'humanitarian assistance' are organised locally.
15 Tivouane is a city in Senegal that serves as the religious capital of the Sy branch of the Tidjaniyya.
16 Interview, spring 2011.

References

Al-Yahya K. and Fustier N. (2011) *Saudi Arabia as a Humanitarian Donor: High Potential, Little Institutionalization*, GPPi Research paper no. 14, Global Public Policy Institute, Berlin.
Baaz M.E. (2005) *The Paternalism of Partnership. A Postcolonial Reading of Identity in Development Aid*, Zed Books, London and New York.
Belew W. (2014) 'The Impact of US Laws, Regulations, and Policies on Gulf Charities', in Lacey R. and Benthall J. (eds), *Gulf Charities and Islamic Philanthropy in the 'Age of Terror' and Beyond*, Gerlach Press, Berlin.
Benthall J. (2008) 'Islamic Charities in Southern Mali', in *Islam et sociétés au sud du Sahara*, 1, new series, Les Indes savantes, Paris.
Benthall J.and Bellion-Jourdan J. (2003) *The Charitable Crescent: Politics of Aid in the Muslim World*, I.B. Tauris, London.
Bornstein E. (2003) *The Spirit of Development. Protestant NGOs, Morality, and Economics in Zimbabwe*, Routledge, New York and London.
Clarke G. (2010) 'Trans-faith Humanitarian Partnerships: The case of Muslim Aid and the United Methodist Committee on Relief', *European Journal of Development Research*, 22(4), 510–528.
De Cordier B. (2010) 'On the Thin Line Between good Intentions and Creating Tensions: A View on Gender Programmes in Muslim Contexts and the (Potential) Position of Islamic Aid Organisations', *European Journal of Development Research*, 22, 234–251.
Dugger C. (2011) *Qatar Charity in Niger: Biopolitics of an International Islamic NGO*, Working Papers Series no. 73, Refugee Studies Centre, University of Oxford, Oxford.
Ferguson J. (1990) *The Anti-Politics Machine. 'Development', Depoliticization and Bureaucratic Power in Lesotho*, Cambridge University Press, Cambridge.
Ghandour A.-R. (2002) *Jihad Humanitaire. Enquête sur les ONG Islamiques*, Flammarion, Paris.
Hunwick J. (1997) 'Sub-Saharan Africa and the Wider World of Islam: Historical and Contemporary Perspectives', in D. Westerlund and E.E. Rosander (eds), *African Islam and Islam in Africa. Encounters between Sufis and Islamists*, Hurst and Co, London, 28–54.
Kaag M. (2007) 'Aid, *Umma* and Politics: Transnational Islamic NGOs in Chad', in R. Otayek and B. Soares (eds), *Muslim Politics in Africa*, Palgrave Macmillan, New York, 85–102.

Kaag M. (2012) 'Comparing Connectivities: Transnational Islamic NGOs in Chad and Senegal', in M. and De Bruijn R. van Dijk (eds), *The Social Life of Connectivity in Africa*, Palgrave Macmillan, New York, 183–201.

Kaag M. (2014) 'Gulf Charities in Africa', in R. Lacey and J. Benthall (eds), *Gulf Charities and Islamic Philanthropy in the 'Age of Terror' and Beyond*, Gerlach Press, Berlin, 79–94.

Krafess J. (2005) 'The Influence of the Muslim Religion in Humanitarian Aid', *International Review of the Red Cross*, 87(858), 327–342.

Macrae J. et al. (2002) *Uncertain Power: The Changing Role of Official Donors in Humanitarian Action*, HPG Report 12, Overseas Development Institute, London.

Montagu C. (2010) 'Civil Society and the Voluntary Sector in Saudi Arabia', *Middle East Journal*, 64(1), 67–83.

Pantuliano S., Mackintosh K., Elhawary S. with Metcalfe V. (2011) *Counter-Terrorism and Humanitarian Action. Tensions, Impact and Ways Forward*, Policy Brief 43, Humanitarian Policy Group, Overseas Development Institute, London.

Petersen M.J. (2011) 'For Humanity or for the Umma? Ideologies of aid in Four Transnational Muslim NGOs', PhD thesis, University of Copenhagen.

Petersen M.J. (2012) 'Islamizing Aid: Transnational Muslim NGOs after 9.11', *Voluntas*, 23(1), 126–155.

Petersen M.J. (2014) 'Sacralized of Secularized Aid? Positioning Gulf-based Muslim Charities', in R. Lacey and J. Benthall (eds), *Gulf Charities and Islamic Philanthropy in the 'Age of Terror' and Beyond*, Gerlach Press, Berlin, 25–51.

Rosander E.E. (1997) 'Introduction: The Islamization of "Tradition" and "Modernity"', in D. Westerlund and E.E. Rosander (eds), *African Islam and Islam in Africa. Encounters between Sufis and Islamists*, Hurst and Co, London, 1–27.

Salih M.A. (2003) 'Islamic NGOs in Africa: The Promise and Peril of Islamic Voluntarism', in A. de Waal (ed.), *The Islamic Project and its Enemies: Jihad, Civil Society and Humanitarianism in North-East Africa*, Hurst, London, 141–181.

Thaut L., Stein J.G. and Barnett M. (2010) 'In Defense of Virtue: Credibility, Legitimacy Dilemmas, and the Case of Islamic Relief', in P.A. Gourevitch, D.A. Lake and J.G. Stein (eds), *The Credibility of Transnational NGOs. When Virtue is not Enough*, Cambridge University Press, Cambridge, 137–164.

10 The changing role of China in international humanitarian cooperation

Challenges and opportunities

Hanna Bianca Krebs

Introduction

The economic and political rise of China has gone hand-in-hand with the country's expanding role in the international humanitarian sphere. China's growing integration into the multilateral humanitarian architecture has dovetailed with increasing contributions following major disasters, including the Indian Ocean tsunami in 2004, the Kashmir earthquake in 2005 and Cyclone Nargis in 2008. With a contribution of $87 million in humanitarian assistance, China was the largest humanitarian donor among the BRIC countries (Brazil, Russia, India, China) in 2011. Although China's economic power is yet to reflect the volume of its international humanitarian assistance, the country has become an indispensable partner which the international community cannot afford to exclude. As the then-UN Emergency Relief Coordinator Valerie Amos stated after her October 2014 visit to Beijing, China is key to shaping future of global humanitarian action (UN News Centre 2014).

At the same time, there is a widely held view that China does not always behave as a responsible power should, or play a role proportionate to its economic heft. Analysis of China's humanitarian activities often emphasises a divide between the country and 'the West', and is often critical of China's perceived failure to adhere to established norms and practices within the humanitarian field. China is often depicted as inherently different from Western countries in its approach: disagreements over China's aid to 'rogue states', its state-led and infrastructure-based approaches, or the doctrine of the 'Responsibility to Protect' (R2P) all serve as examples. However, in a future where the international community and China can cooperate fully on humanitarian issues, a few essential understandings will need to be adjusted.

At the most fundamental level, there is a need to understand not only *how* China approaches humanitarian action, but also *why* it has taken a different path, as the country's unique humanitarian history has moulded China's cultural 'humanitarian' ideals, distinct from the 'West', which will continue to shape China's aid policy. Moreover, future humanitarian cooperation with China will require a departure from the prevalent sentiment of the 'China threat' to overcome mutually obstructive misconceptions, especially since many of China's actions

DOI: 10.4324/9781315658827-13

today resemble those of 'traditional' donor countries. Developments such as China's increasing willingness to channel humanitarian aid through multilateral mechanisms, or the country's expanding role in peacekeeping, offer a widening window of opportunity for collaboration. Given that China's engagement in global humanitarian action is likely to increase, efforts from both China and the international community will be needed to integrate the country further into the existing aid structure, and to make necessary adjustments for a more collaborative humanitarian community.

This chapter first offers a brief review of China's concept of humanitarianism in a historical perspective. It then assesses the development of China's humanitarian action in the post-Cold War era with the aim of shedding some light on the points of convergence and divergence between the country and the international community. Finally, it discusses the implications of China's approach to humanitarian action with respect to the 'traditional' donor countries in the present and the future.

'Humanitarianism' in Chinese history

Humanitarianism in ancient China

Humanitarianism (*rendao zhuyi* 人道主义) as a concept and practice is deeply ingrained in China's history. The fundamental values underpinning the idea of humanitarianism – concern for others or kindness – are reflected in a plethora of literature in the Chinese classics of Confucius written more than two millennia ago. In the *Five Classics* of the traditional Confucian canon written before 300 BC, the most central of the fundamental attributes defining the ideal of humanity (*rendao* 人道)[1] is the concept of *ren* (仁). *Ren* lies at the core of Confucian thought and appears more than any other word in the *Analects* of Confucius (Hua 1995, 115). It can be translated as benevolence, humaneness, kindness, philanthropy and mutual love between two humans – as evidenced in the character itself, which fuses the characters 'human' (人) and 'two' (二). The notions of Confucian *ren*, coupled with Buddhist sentiments of charity (*shan* 善), permeated traditional Chinese philanthropy for centuries, which was exercised first as a privilege of the elite, and later by broader sections of Chinese society (Smith 2009).

Of equal importance for ancient Chinese humanitarian action was the Confucian notion of a harmonious world order guaranteed by the dual ideal of responsibility and state legitimacy. On an individual level, every member of society had a clearly defined responsibility according to his or her status, as well as an obligation to be obedient to their social superiors. Accordingly, the emperor, who stood at the top of this social hierarchy, assumed the role of a moral agent (Hirono 2013). He was the ultimate benefactor responsible for safeguarding the wellbeing of his citizens by benevolent governance, particularly in times of misfortune. The Confucian concept of imperial responsibility was reinforced by the ancient belief in a cosmic link between natural disasters and human conduct which long pre-dated Confucianism. The Chinese term for natural disasters, *tianzai* (天灾),

literally means 'heavenly disaster', and conveys the traditional interpretation of natural calamities as a form of divine retribution: Heaven's punishment for immoral human behaviour, its extent and severity depending on the social importance of the miscreant (Elvin 1998; Lewis 1990). Since the emperor's conduct was of pre-eminent importance, his responsibility was to prevent misfortunes from occurring in the first place through moral conduct, and if they did occur, to take swift and appropriate measures to restore normality.

The ruler's ability to alleviate suffering effectively translated into his legitimacy to rule, understood as the 'Mandate of Heaven' (*tianming* 天命). As popular dissent against a government could and often did result in the end of a dynasty – for the 'Mandate of Heaven' was employed to justify not only the right to rule, but also the 'right to rebel' – the emperor constantly sought the moral approval of his people by fulfilling his responsibilities to the best of his ability (Lei and Tong 2014). Illustrative of the link between an emperor's disaster management capabilities and his political legitimacy is the story of China's legendary first ruler, Yu the Great (c. 2200–2100 BC), who became emperor by successfully regulating flooding through sophisticated hydraulic systems for flood control (Hirono 2013, 207) and by means of granaries and water-conservation projects (Shapiro 2001). State disaster response has held such traditional importance for the imperial agenda that early literature on the policies, practices and institutions of disaster and famine relief can be dated back to as early as the Southern Song Dynasty (1127–1279) (Chen 2012, 131).

China's humanitarianism in the twentieth century

Although this age-old concern with state responsibility and legitimacy still held currency, China found itself in a phase of intensive self-scrutiny and soul-searching at the turn of the twentieth century when Western ideas infiltrated Chinese debates. China's interactions with the West were by no means new: missionary schools had been offering free food, housing and medical care since the late sixteenth century; by the mid-1800s both missionary and unaffiliated doctors were building hospitals with money given by Western philanthropists or raised by subscription from local Chinese (Spence 1990, 204-7). However, the use of Western notions in domestic discourses increased dramatically after Imperial China suffered humiliating defeats at the hands of foreign powers. The Opium Wars against Great Britain in the mid-nineteenth century and Japan's victory in the First Sino-Japanese War in 1895 resulted in unequal treaties and territorial concessions. Weakened by maladministration and external threats, the imperial government had also proved unable to respond adequately to a devastating famine in the north of the country in 1877–78 which left 13 million people dead (Yeophantong 2014, 8). There was a growing belief that, rather than Chinese traditional values, Western technology and modernisation were the answers to China's perceived weaknesses.

These ideas found their fullest expression following the founding of the Republic of China in 1912. Starting as a student movement against the new government's weak response to the Treaty of Versailles, which ceded Shandong province to

Japan, what has been commonly known as the May Fourth Movement gave rise to a new, iconoclastic Chinese intelligentsia. Humanitarianism was now presented as something 'Western'; something progressive and integral to the salvation of their country from backwardness and doom. This 'Western' definition of humanitarianism bore various interpretations: at times it was closely associated with the idea of democracy and equality, while left-wing understandings of it related it to Bolshevism (Krebs 2014a, 7–8). The number of joint Chinese–Western relief organisations, such as the China International Famine Relief Commission (CIFRC), increased in parallel with this increase of Western ideas in discourses.

When Mao Zedong came to power in 1949, the country was purged of these Western influences and the concept of humanitarianism was redefined as a 'Marxist humanitarianism', a form of humanitarianism based on the Marxist doctrine of class struggle aimed at 'safeguarding the dignity and rights of the working class' (Marx and Engels 2011, 97) As such, Marxist humanitarianism was understood as being 'essentially different from bourgeois humanitarianism', which was labelled as a 'tool used by the bourgeoisie to cover up capitalism's merciless exploitation and oppression, to cover up class contradictions, and to deceive the proletariat' (Wen 1960, 101). More radically, the traditional belief in a cosmic link between human (mis-)conduct and natural disasters was completely reversed: disasters were no longer feared as divine punishment for humankind, but were regarded as something that could be overcome or transformed with the passion for revolution. This conviction led to the use of the slogan 'Man Must Conquer Nature' (*Ren Ding Sheng Tian* 人定胜天) during a mass mobilisation campaign known as the Great Leap Forward (Dikötter 2010, 174), and found institutional expression with the abolition of the Central Committee on Disaster Relief in 1958, which had been established eight years earlier to coordinate the government's disaster management work (Chen 2012, 134).

Religious institutions such as temples, shrines and monasteries were closed (Becker 1996, 51), missionaries expelled or incarcerated and their medical and educational institutions taken over by the state (Westad 2012, 326; Varg 1977, 305–6). All of this meant that when the Great Leap Forward produced a widespread famine between 1958 and 1961, traditional coping mechanisms such as private charity, state assistance and mutual help failed. The same was also true when the devastating Tangshan earthquake struck in 1976: the government rejected international assistance altogether, including from bodies such as the United Nations and the International Committee of the Red Cross (ICRC), and prevented foreign journalists from entering the disaster area, instead recommending that the victims lead thrifty lives and resume production as soon as possible (Chen 2012, 134–35). Rather than the traditional responsibility to protect citizens after disasters, the new understanding of 'humanitarianism' under Mao meant the responsibility to improve their living standards by means of an egalitarian community at home, and to support proletarian revolutions abroad, with China as the guardian of the Third World against the capitalist West (Krebs 2014a, 14).

Since international legitimacy derived from China's support to 'help the proletariat of the world revolt' (Chan 2013, 61), China became highly active in aid-giving in this period, while accepting little to no outside assistance when it was struck by disasters itself. After an initial focus on Asia (North Korea, Vietnam, Cambodia, Nepal), Chinese economic assistance turned to the Middle East and, especially, Africa (Cooper 1976, 117). Infrastructure aid to Africa included the construction of a 1,900 km rail line between Tanzania and Zambia until the Chinese aid-giving policy declined in the 1970s (Bartke 1989, 10, 13). Although all but shut down domestically, the Chinese Red Cross Society saw its most lively phase internationally, sponsoring efforts to repatriate Japanese citizens stranded in China in the early 1950s and offering disaster relief support to some 140 countries in Africa, Asia, Latin America and Eastern Europe (Reeves 2014, 226). Under Mao, it was first and foremost the wish to become both the guardian of the Third World – founded on its support for national liberation movements; and the true leader of the Communist bloc – based on its revolutionary zeal, which shaped China's aid policy.

China's post-Cold War humanitarian engagement

The reform era under Mao's successor Deng Xiaoping allowed for a gradual economic liberalisation of China. Humanitarianism (*rendao zhuyi* 人道主义) re-emerged in intellectual discourse in the early 1980s after leading Party members encouraged the Party leadership to redefine Marxism–Leninism in a kinder and gentler form (Davies 2007, 120–21; see also Hua 1995; Goldman 1994). This re-evaluation of humanitarianism was part of a wider questioning of Marxism–Leninism in the wake of the Cultural Revolution.

A ten-year social experiment conducted between 1966 and 1977 under Mao, the Cultural Revolution had caused massive civil unrest; tens of thousands of people were killed; and millions of 'intellectuals' and 'bourgeois' were forced into manual labour. The upheaval destroyed a large amount of the political credibility the Party had accumulated, and plunged it into a legitimacy crisis (Harding 1987). Many scholars, drawing on their own disillusionment during the Cultural Revolution, came to challenge what they saw as an ossified interpretation of Marxism in the atmosphere of gradual liberalisation. In parallel, in a 'renaissance of Confucianism' (Holbig and Gilley 2010, 21), influential scholars reassessed traditional Confucian values (Goldman 1994, 77). Regarded as a repressive ideology throughout the Mao period, many discourses now stressed the ancient Confucian emphasis on harmony and responsibility. Some referred to the values Confucianism shared with Western humanitarianism; one news article emphasised that, although European humanitarianism originated during the Renaissance, 'the same world view was already expressed in the humanitarian doctrines of Confucius almost 2000 years before the Renaissance, and it became later the fine tradition of Confucianism' (*ibid*). With these new interpretations, the Chinese understanding of humanitarianism began to lose some of the historical burden of its Western capitalist connotations (Hirono 2013, 208).

This return to the Confucian orthodoxy had initially emanated from society rather than the government; by the mid-1980s, however, the Party was also turning towards these old teachings in a bid to reinforce the legitimacy of its rule. The violent crackdown on protesters in Tiananmen Square in 1989 added special urgency to the restoration of state legitimacy, and the complexity and flexibility of Confucianism made it easy to incorporate into both Maoism and more liberal interpretations (Moody 2011). Those elements of Confucianism most suited to supporting the status quo – social order, stability, harmony, acceptance of hierarchy and the knowing of place – were translated into a 'tailor-made socialist Confucianism' (Holbig and Gilley 2010, 22), and references to Confucian-sounding ideas began to permeate official discourses during the presidency of Hu Jintao between 2002 and 2012. The ancient Confucian link between popular support and the state's ability to respond to crises also regained its old centrality: following the end of Mao's regime, the term 'parental officials' (*fu-mu guan* 父母官) – an expression tracing back to the Han dynasty (206 BC–220 AD) – resurfaced, confirming the renewed validity of China's traditional notion of state humanitarianism underpinned by the age-old paternalistic state–society relationship (Tong 2011, 151 n16).

Internationally, China has since visibly shifted from an isolationist to a more pragmatic stance, and has become increasingly involved on the international humanitarian stage. This is to a large part motivated by the import of technical know-how which accompanies international humanitarian cooperation. More decisively, however, it is the Chinese government's desire to be seen as a responsible global power which has driven the country to become progressively enmeshed in the international community. The country joined the World Trade Organization (WTO) in 2001, and gradually increased its contributions to the World Food Programme (WFP) throughout the past decade. It provided food aid during the famine in North Korea in the 1990s (Kim 2010, 113), and offered significant funds following the Indian Ocean tsunami in 2004, the Kashmir earthquake in 2005 and Cyclone Nargis in 2008. China's response during the tsunami was unprecedented in both size and in form, as for the first time the country channelled humanitarian donations through multilateral mechanisms, mainly UN agencies (Binder and Conrad 2009, 9–10).

Reflecting this increased willingness to cooperate internationally, China also ceased to reject foreign aid as a source of shame (Chan 2013, 57). Japan launched its Overseas Development Assistance programme in China in 1980, the same year the country acceded to the World Bank and the International Monetary Fund, and during the 1980s China was one of the world's largest recipients of World Bank loans (Mitchell and McGiffert 2007, 17). Long-standing suspicions of foreign aid agencies also eased remarkably: where once the ICRC was dismissed as a lackey of Western imperialism, in 2013 China welcomed its president on a visit to Beijing (Reeves 2014, 226–27). Even more tellingly, when a major earthquake devastated large parts of Sichuan Province in Western China in 2008, the government's response gained widespread praise for its efficiency and for granting almost unlimited access to affected areas to both foreign and domestic aid workers. Although the timing of the disaster almost certainly fed into this unparalleled level of openness – China, amidst preparation for the Olympic Games in Beijing in

August 2008, was acutely aware of the need to improve its image as a responsible great power (Hirono 2013, 214) – the Wenchuan experience nonetheless serves as an illustrative contrast to the government's (non-)handling of the Tangshan earthquake in earlier times.

Lastly, China has been increasingly active in UN peacekeeping missions. The fact that China is the largest contributor to UN peacekeeping operations among the five permanent members of the Security Council, with 2,222 troops, UN experts and police on the ground by January 2015, also speaks for the country's growing reputational concern and sense of international responsibility (United Nations 2015). During the Darfur conflict in 2003, China's willingness to use its economic and diplomatic leverage over the Sudanese government has also helped secure its consent to intervention, ultimately resulting in the deployment of a hybrid UN–African Union force. Aspiring to project the image of a responsible great power, China has gradually departed from ideology and adapted a more pragmatic, realist stance towards humanitarian crises.

Points of divergence: China and 'the West'

While the post-Cold War era in particular has witnessed growing convergence between China and the international community pertaining to global norms and practices, disagreements with Western countries can surface in discourses around humanitarian action, with various implications for international cooperation.

Firstly, China is often decried for an approach in foreign aid that is too closely linked to its pursuit of natural resources. For instance, a great part of Chinese aid to Latin America – the region which received the most aid from China between 2001 and 2011 – was in natural resources programmes (Wang, Warner and Wolf 2013, xiv–xv). In Africa, which comes second in terms of aid received from China, assistance in natural resource programmes and infrastructure markedly replaced the previously more prevalent forms of aid programmes such as debt cancellation and humanitarian aid following the China–Africa summits in 2003 and 2006 (ibid.). In addition to its economic relations with the Syrian government, China's aid to 'rogue states' such as Sudan and Zimbabwe has been criticised in the West not only as driven by economic motives (Nakano and Prantl 2011, 12), but also as sustaining autocratic regimes or compromising progress on human rights (Hirono and Suzuki 2014, 447).

Chinese aid-giving is at times also denounced for being overly politicised. For instance, the 'aid competition' between China and Taiwan looms large on China's aid formulation: its economic assistance to Dominica in 2005 and Costa Rica in 2007 closely followed each country's diplomatic recognition of the People's Republic of China in lieu of Taiwan (Wang et al. 2013, 28), and China reacted sharply by stalling a peacekeeping operation or vetoing peacekeeping-related proposals when countries such as Haiti, Guatemala and Macedonia had displayed friendly gestures towards Taiwan (Gill and Reilly 2000, 57 n27).[2] That geopolitical deliberations shape China's aid preference is arguably nowhere more conspicuous than in the ASEAN region, where China's relations with the individual states are extremely divergent. Cambodia, for example, has of late become one of China's closest diplomatic allies, and consequently received such great amounts of Chinese aid (Sato et al. 2011) that it has given rise to considerable concerns about aid dependence (Ciorciari 2013; Ear 2012). The Philippines, by contrast, has less friendly ties with China due to territorial disputes in the South China Sea, and the relationship was on a further downward trend when the former was struck by the devastating Typhoon Haiyan in 2013. China's disproportionately low initial pledge of US$100,000 in aid to the Philippines was so visibly related to the two countries' diplomatic tensions that it reaped not only international but also domestic criticism.[3]

Additionally, disagreements between China and the 'traditional' donor countries may also surface in the more practical aspects of aid-giving. China is often criticised for its preference for bilateral, government-to-government aid provision, which tends to bypass a wider range of civil society actors. Another difference is that the military plays a prominent role in Chinese domestic relief: the People's Liberation Army (PLA) has responded to a series of natural disasters, such as the floods in the late 1990s or the 2008 snow and ice storm (Mulvenon 2010, 5). The Wenchuan earthquake became one of the largest mobilisations of the PLA with a total of 146,000 troops deployed (Zhang 2014, 79), followed by a swift deployment of personnel in response to the Yushu earthquake in 2010. More recently, the PLA has assigned about 300 service personnel on multiple medical missions to fight the Ebola virus in West Africa, building observation and treatment centres in Sierra Leone and Liberia (Eurasia Review 2015). Therefore neither the ICRC principle of independence distancing legitimate humanitarian actors from government entities and state armed forces, nor the Oslo Guidelines on the use of military as the last resort to meet humanitarian needs, necessarily applies for China.

Furthermore, Chinese aid often garners appreciation which is disproportionate to its actual size as it is offered without the domestic conditions that other bilateral and multilateral donors frequently place on assistance, such as democratic reform, the liberalisation of markets and environmental protection (Chanboreth and Hach 2008). China's conditions on aid are often international rather than domestic, for example requiring aid recipients to support the 'one-China' principle regarding Taiwan and China's agenda in the United Nations (Lum, Morrison and Vaughn 2008, 8). This 'no-(domestic-)strings-attached' approach has been criticised for failing to promote democracy, sustainable development and environmental conservation, and equally for making it more difficult for Western donors and UN agencies to link annual aid packages to political reforms (Ciorciari 2013, 17; Marks 2000, 94). For instance, Angola has found China 'a more supportive and less critical partner' than the International Monetary Fund (IMF), and Iran reportedly looks to China for ways to enliven the economy without losing political power (quoted in Chan, Lee and Chan 2008, 13). Similarly, '[w]hen Cambodia falls under pressure from international bodies to reform its human rights abuses, corruption, oppression of its people, or misuse of power, it turns to China for financial support' (Ear 2012, 29–30), as was the case when China delivered $600 million in aid when Western and UN donor agencies pressed Cambodia to uphold its promise to draft and enact an anti-corruption law in 2006 (Ciorciari 2013, 18).

Yet arguably the most conspicuous point of contention between China and the West is the concept of humanitarian intervention enshrined in the doctrine of the 'Responsibility to Protect' (R2P). The painful experience of foreign interventions in the preceding century led the country to develop strong concepts of state sovereignty and non-interference in domestic affairs. These were woven into its political fabric and enshrined in Mao Zedong's 'Five Principles of Peaceful Coexistence', which formed the cornerstone of Chinese foreign policy. Therefore, while China has endorsed the basic tenets of R2P – first at the 2005 World Summit, and then in Security Council Resolution 1674 – and has largely supported UN Resolutions under Chapter VII authorising the use of force, for historical, cultural and political reasons the country is likely to remain cautious about humanitarian interventions and the use of force without the consent of the country concerned (Teitt 2008). Resistance to democracy at home and its own human rights practices, China's multi-ethnic character and the existence within it of separatist movements all make the country particularly sensitive to questions of sovereignty.

Illustrative of China's strong sentiments about intervention was its veto against referring the Syrian crisis to the International Criminal Court in May 2014 – its fourth veto relating to Syria. This has attracted considerable attention since China had used its veto power only six times in its entire history; however, this stance springs from an earlier experience of an intervention in 2011. True to its usual form in the UN Security Council, China had abstained from voting for UN Resolution 1973 to authorise the use of force in the conflict in Libya. In this case, however, China's (and Russia)'s abstention translated into effective endorsement of the R2P principle, thus implicitly allowing for a breach of China's non-intervention principle. Although UN-authorised, China retrospectively found this controversial intervention to have exceeded the R2P mandate to protect civilians, since it ultimately went as far as evoking a regime change. The Libyan precedent serves to explain China's renewed assertiveness and reversion to its traditional commitment to non-interference, evident in its attitude towards the Syrian crisis.

Given the scope of the Syrian unrest, China's vetoes have been strongly condemned by Western governments as being uncooperative and too insistent upon the principles of sovereignty and non-intervention. China, in turn, has consistently employed strong language in discourses on humanitarian intervention, with Chinese representatives stating in 2001 that 'the conceptualisation of humanitarian intervention is a total fallacy' (ICISS 2001, 392). At other times it was expressed that 'the new interventionism of the so-called "human rights over sovereignty" constituted "hegemonism in essence"' (quoted in Kent 2013, 144); or something that could lead to a new era of 'gunboat diplomacy' (United Nations 1999). However, despite these differences, even with regard to humanitarian intervention, the recent years have witnessed a remarkable shift from ideology to pragmatism (Davis 2011). The fact that China has not rejected the concept of R2P outright but has attempted to render R2P compatible with its own foreign policy norms (Nakano and Prantl 2011, 209) indicates that the country is oscillating between adhering to the principles of sovereignty and non-interference, and avoiding the image of inaction in the face of mass atrocities.

Implications for international humanitarian cooperation

As discussed in the previous section, differences between China and the wider international community undeniably exist in both the practical and conceptual aspects of humanitarian cooperation, which have come to the fore in a number of instances. These disagreements are compounded by sentiments of the 'China threat', which has emerged in the early 1990s amid concerns of the country's rising economic power, military capabilities and nationalism and – to varying degrees – persists to this day.

Importantly from the international perspective, recent Chinese initiatives that appear to offer an 'Asian', if not 'Chinese' alternative to existing instruments are a source of concern for many policy-makers. Apart from regional security fora such as the Shanghai Cooperation Organisation (SCO) and the Xiangshan Forum, the country has taken important strides towards the creation of Chinese-led development institutions. The New Development Bank, a multilateral development bank to be headquartered in Shanghai and operated by the BRICS states (Brazil, Russia, India, China, South Africa), appears to offer a clear alternative to the Western-dominated World Bank and IMF, as does the Asian Infrastructure Investment Bank (AIIB), whose signing ceremony was held in October 2014. The 'One Belt and One Road' policy, also known as the 'New Silk Road' initiative, is aimed at complementing the AIIB in supporting infrastructure investments across Asia. Taken together, these initiatives are often regarded as pragmatic steps China is taking towards establishing a 'new world order' with far greater Chinese political and economic influence than exists in current mechanisms; one which many fear could fail to meet international environmental, social and governance standards.

Misgivings also exist around the perception that China is challenging international norms with conceptual alternatives. China has shown support for Brazil's alternative formula for R2P, 'Responsibility while Protecting' (RwP), which aims to establish basic criteria to assure minimum use of force in interventions (Pu 2012, 342). Following domestic discussions around the RwP concept, the vice president of a think tank reporting to the Chinese Foreign Ministry proposed the concept of 'Responsible Protection' (RP: *fu zeren de baohu* 负责任的保护), which he describes as China's endeavour to build 'a just and reasonable new international political order' (Ruan 2012). Among others, RP calls for an international accountability mechanism, but in essence it seeks to implement even stricter regulations on interventionism which would inevitably delay, if not entirely inhibit, the practice of humanitarian intervention.

Although the jury is still out on whether or not these fears are justified, what is clear is that China is aspiring to secure a place worthy of a global power within the international system. While among the international community there exists a view that China should *adopt* 'Western' values, such as democracy, solidarity, human rights and the rule of law, China deems that the same must be *adapted* in China: to 'sinify' the prevailing international system with some of its own distinctive values. It is imperative to recognise that Chinese humanitarian policy is set to continue growing, and it will do so the 'Chinese way'; which will mean that rather than enforcing existing norms upon China, efforts must be made to identify ways through which to accommodate certain Chinese characteristics in the current aid structure (Krebs 2014b). In a future where the international community and China can fully cooperate on humanitarian issues, a few fundamental understandings will need to be adjusted so as to overcome mutually obstructive misconceptions.

At the most essential level, a higher degree of openness would be required to accept cultural differences regarding the notion of humanitarianism. For instance, based on the ancient Chinese legacy of the 'Mandate of Heaven', it is important to know that China's notion of humanitarianism has for millennia been shaped by the ideals of responsibility and state legitimacy (Krebs 2014a). In this understanding, social welfare has always been a key virtue in the execution of government power, which constitutes 'the most enduring facets of China's philanthropic habitus' (Reeves 2014, 215) Although, in China, it is not the individual but the state which is considered the moral agent, meaning that strengthening the state would effectively strengthen society (Hirono 2013), the Confucian emphasis on unity of society and state also effectively blurs the lines between civilian and government or military actors, so that the PLA's image as the 'people's army' legitimises the armed forces as agents of humanitarian relief (Teitt 2014, 4; He 2001). Given China's own history of humanitarianism, it is not the Western humanitarian principles of humanity, neutrality, impartiality and independence that motivate China to humanitarian action: China believes in strong government action and top-down state building, focuses on sovereignty over humanitarian intervention, and emphasises economic development over democratisation.

Secondly, for a more inclusive and truly global community, it is imperative for 'traditional' donors not to let the sentiment of the 'China threat' dominate their attitude towards China. Excessive condemnation of ulterior motives driving China's aid policy runs counter to a constructive relationship, particularly in instances when the accuser is not entirely free from fault: for example, despite outcry over China's aid for 'rogue states', Western governments, too, have provided support for regimes with questionable human rights records, as evinced by British and American backing for the Mubarak regime in Egypt, or the British government's close relations with the Gaddafi regime in Libya until 2011. Since foreign policy calculations figure in aid calculations in Washington, London and Brussels just as much as they do in Beijing, it becomes clear that, despite frequent claims that China is somehow 'different' from the West, when it comes to national self-interest its behaviour is perhaps not so different after all (Hirono and Suzuki 2014, 445). Rather than pressuring other countries to conform to established norms, the question should point towards how these can be adjusted to be truly universal.

On a more pragmatic level, China today remains outside the informal and formal governance structures shaping contemporary humanitarian action, and continued efforts both from the West and China will be required to effectuate better integration. It is not a member of the Organisation for Economic Cooperation and Development (OECD) Development Assistance Committee (DAC) or of the United Nations Office for the Coordination of Humanitarian Affairs' (OCHA)

Donor Support Group (ODSG); nor is it part of the Good Humanitarian Donorship initiative (Teitt 2014).

One key obstacle to humanitarian cooperation with China will remain the question of R2P, as without more radical domestic political reforms it is unlikely that China will fundamentally change its stance regarding humanitarian intervention, particularly without host country consent. Despite its role in the Darfur crisis, the country's approach to R2P shows inconsistencies, as evidenced by its opposition to any intervention in Myanmar in the aftermath of Cyclone Nargis in 2008, or its strong position regarding the Syria crisis. With regard to intervention, China appears to find itself between a 'pluralist push' emphasising the protection of civilians as the primary responsibility of their respective governments, and a 'solidarist pull' which conveys the image of a responsible power willing to socialise in the emerging normative context of R2P (Cupac 2014). A further challenge is China's lingering sentiment of responsibility as the guardian of the Third World, which makes the country cautious not to appear to be 'taking sides' with the powerful, and at the same time runs counter to its wish to be seen as a prestigious global power. For a number of factors, therefore, China will continue to review calls for international intervention on a case-by-case basis (Bates and Huang 2009, 35).

However, China's increasing engagement with international structures, including the channelling of humanitarian aid through multilateral mechanisms, indicates a strong normative change in aid policy and practice. As testified in China's preparedness to use its leverage over Sudan in 2003, the country can exert immense influence on global humanitarian governance. Its growing wish to be seen as a responsible power has also resulted in a policy shift in the 1990s from condemning peacekeeping activities to participating in them: China has become more flexible in dealing with the question of sovereignty, and more supportive in non-traditional peacekeeping (Hirono and Lanteigne 2011, 243), with the highest number of peacekeepers deployed among the P5 (Permanent Members of the UN Security Council). China's realist stance also finds expression in its efforts to diffuse the fear around the 'China threat' by means of the pragmatic policies of 'peaceful rising' (*heping jueqi* 和平崛起) and 'harmonious world' (*hexie shehui* 和谐社会) under President Hu Jintao (Hsu and Chao 2008, 5). In terms of recent international humanitarian engagement, China's response to the Ebola crisis in West Africa marked the extension of Chinese humanitarian aid to countries facing a public health emergency for the first time (Taylor 2015); and China committed over $20 million worth of in-kind assistance to Nepal weeks after the country was struck by an earthquake in April 2015 (FTS 2015). Taken together, these developments offer a widening window of opportunity for collaboration, especially as China's engagement in global humanitarian action is likely to increase.

Humanitarian cooperation with China should be made a priority area; there exist a variety of tools that both China and the international community could employ to strengthen their commitment to engage. Firstly, efforts should be made to facilitate greater interaction, and to increase, regularise and sustain close strategic dialogue and coordination at the highest policy-making level. These could include official exchanges, familiarisation visits and joint training activities through a formal, bilateral working-level mechanism between Western governments and China, or through increased consultation with the Chinese Mission to the UN (Bates and Huang 2009, 33). Secondly, international players should identify and propose areas where China could play a more active part in policy planning, coordination and leadership roles at UN humanitarian agencies, and encourage the country to increase its financial contributions and logistical support to relevant mechanisms to allow for more predictable funding than has hitherto been the case. Finally, the international community should capitalise on the growing Chinese engagement in peacekeeping, as this presents a solid future basis upon which to strengthen other aspects of joint humanitarian action. Increased openness and transparency in the PLA could be encouraged by means of a joint peacekeeping research centre in order to institutionalise mid- to low-level military exchange to allow for a more collaborative relationship. Knowledge transfer could also be increased by inviting China to participate in or observe more peacekeeping exercises and simulations, including those conducted by NATO or with other European and US allies (Bates and Huang 2009, 35).

Conclusion

China's humanitarian aid is marked by significant fluctuation. Peaking in 2005, when the country provided relief to Asian countries affected by the Indian Ocean tsunami, its foreign aid dramatically declined again the following year, with another spike in 2011. Yet China's increasingly assertive foreign policy agenda strongly suggests an expansion in the country's international humanitarian role in the future, as erratic and unpredictable though its course may be. For the international community, increased Chinese engagement would be significant not only in terms of monetary contributions and political leverage, but also with regard to human and material resources. For China, stronger international cooperation presents several strategic benefits: First and foremost, it provides an opportunity to reshape the country's international profile and increase its influence in the UN, and to import valuable technical know-how to improve its domestic humanitarian structures. The considerable overlap of interests between China and Western countries in closer humanitarian engagement offers a promising basis for a joint response to ever-rising humanitarian demands.

At the same time, while optimism is integral for future cooperation with China, it will be equally important for Western countries to manage expectations. Not surprisingly for a country as large, diverse and complex as China, cultural and historical factors will continue to shape its actions, and the ensuing disagreements and obstacles are sure to challenge humanitarian cooperation – particularly with regard to the concept of R2P. Therefore, while deepening China's integration in existing mechanisms is essential, the current international aid system would need to consider adjustments conducive to more inclusive humanitarian efforts not in competition, but in collaboration with China, as there can be no global aid system without China.

Notes

1 'Four Principles Underlying the Dress of Mourning', 3 (*Sang Fu Si Zhi*), Book of Rites (*Li Jing*).
2 It should be stated, however, that although Haiti established diplomatic relations with the Republic of China, the People's Republic ultimately decided not to use its veto power.
3 While criticism of this modest pledge was the most vocal among Western media, disapproval was also expressed by the *Global Times,* a Chinese newspaper usually known for its nationalist editorial lines.

References

Austin G. (2013) 'China's Power: Searching for Stable Domestic Foundations', in Austin G. and Zhang Y. (eds), *Power and Responsibility in Chinese Foreign Policy*, ANU e-Press, 69–104.
Bartke W. (1989) *The Economic Aid of the PR China to Developing and Socialist Countries*, K.G. Saur, Munich, London, New York, Paris.
Bates G. and C. Huang (2009) *China's Expanding Role in Peacekeeping. Prospects and Policy Implications*, Policy Paper no. 25, Stockholm International Peace Research Institute, Stockholm.
Becker J. (1996) *Hungry Ghosts: China's Secret Famine*, John Murray, London.
Binder A. and Conrad B. (2009) *China's Potential Role in Humanitarian Assistance*, Humanitarian Policy Paper Series, Global Public Policy Institute, Berlin (www.isn.ethz.ch/Digital-Library/Publications/Detail/?ots591=0c54e3b3-1e9c-be1e-2c24-a6a8c7060233&lng=en&id=136264), accessed 10 June 2015.
Chan G. (2013) 'Power and Responsibility in China's International Relations', in Austin G. and Zhang Y. (eds), *Power and Responsibility in Chinese Foreign Policy*, ANU e-Press, 48–68.
Chan L., Lee P. and Chan G. (2008) 'Rethinking Global Governance: A China Model in the Making?', *Contemporary Politics*, 14(1), 3–19.
Chanboreth E. and Hach S. (2008) *Aid Effectiveness in Cambodia*, Working Paper 7, Wolfensohn Center for Development, Brookings Institution, Washington, DC.
Chen G. (2012) 'China's Management of Natural Disasters: Organizations and Norms', in Chung J.H. (ed.), *China's Crisis Management*, Routledge, London, 130–148.
Ciorciari J. (2013) *China and Cambodia: Patron and Client?*, IPC Working Paper Series Number 121, Gerald R. Ford School of Public Policy, University of Michigan.
Cooper J. (1976) *China's Foreign Aid: An Instrument of Peking's Foreign Policy*, Lexington Books, Lanham, MD, Toronto, London.
Cupac J. (2014) 'Emerging International Norms and State Behavior: Chinese Foreign Policy between "Pluralist Pull" and "Solidarist Push"', *CEU Political Science Journal*, 9(1/2), 39–61.
Davies G. (2007) *The Language of Chinese Critical Inquiry*, Harvard University Press, Cambridge, MA, London.
Davis J. (2011) 'From Ideology to Pragmatism: China's Position on Humanitarian Intervention in the Post-Cold War Era', *Vanderbilt Journal of Transnational Law*, 44(2), 217–283.
Dikötter F. (2010) *Mao's Great Famine: The History of China's Most Devastating Catastrophe, 1958–62*, Bloomsbury, London.
Deng Z. and Guo S. (2011) *Reviving Legitimacy: Lessons for and from China*, Lexington Books, Lanham, MD.
Ear S. (2012) *Aid Dependence in Cambodia: How Foreign Assistance Undermines Democracy*, Columbia University Press, New York.
Elvin M. (1998) 'Who Was Responsible for the Weather? Moral Meteorology in Late Imperial China', in Low M. (ed.), *Beyond Joseph Needham: Science, Technology, and Medicine in East and Southeast Asia*, University of Chicago Press, Chicago, 213–237.

Eurasia Review (2015) *China: Defence Diplomacy Analysis*, 22 February.

FTS (2015) Financial Tracking Service: NEPAL – Earthquake – April 2015 (https://fts.unocha.org/pageloader.aspx?page=emerg-emergencyDetails&appealID=1100), accessed 28 May 2015.

Gill B. and Reilly J. (2000) 'Sovereignty, Intervention and Peacekeeping: The View from Beijing', *Survival* 42(3), 41–59.

Goldman M. (1994) *Sowing the Seeds of Democracy in China: Political Reform in the Deng Xiaoping Era*, Harvard University Press, Cambridge, MA, London.

Harding H. (1987) *China's Second Revolution: Reform after Mao*, Brookings Institution, Washington, DC.

He X. (2001) 'The Chinese Humanitarian Heritage and the Dissemination of and Education in International Humanitarian Law in the Chinese People's Liberation Army', *International Review of the Red Cross* 83(841), 141–154.

Hirono M. (2013) 'The Three Legacies of Humanitarianism in China', *Disasters* 37 (supplement 2), 202–220.

Hirono M. and Lanteigne M. (2011) 'Introduction: China and UN Peacekeeping', *International Peacekeeping*, 18(3), 243–256.

Hirono M. and Suzuki S. (2014) 'Why Do We Need "Myth-Busting" in the Study of Sino-African Relations?', *Journal of Contemporary China*, 23(87), 443–461.

Holbig H. and Gilley B. (2010) *In Search of Legitimacy in Post-Revolutionary China: Bringing Ideology and Governance Back In*, GIGA Research Programme: Legitimacy and Efficiency of Political Systems no. 127, GIGA German Institute of Global and Area Studies/Leibniz-Institut für Globale und Regionale Studien, Hamburg.

Hsu C. and Chao C. (2008) *China's Humanitarian Diplomacy Concepts and Practices: A Theoretical Analysis on Harmonious World*, paper presented at the Second Global International Studies Conference, Ljubljana, 23–26 July 2008.

Hua S. (1995) *Scientism and Humanism: Two Cultures in post-Mao China, 1978–1989*, State University of New York Press, Albany, NY.

ICISS (2001) *The Responsibility to Protect: Research, Bibliography, Background*, International Commission on Intervention and State Sovereignty/International Development Research Centre, Ottawa.

Kent A. (2013) 'China's participation in International Organisations', in Austin, G. and Zhang Y. (eds), *Power and Responsibility in Chinese Foreign Policy*, ANU e-Press, Canberra, 132–166.

Kim S.C. (2010) 'North Korea's Relationship with China: From Alignment to Active Independence', in Dürkop C., Lam P.E. and Ganesan N. (eds), *East Asia's Relations with a Rising China*, Konrad Adenauer Stiftung Korea and Japan Office, Seoul, 102–143.

Krebs H. (2014a) *Responsibility, Legitimacy, Morality: Chinese Humanitarianism in Historical Perspective*, HPG Working Paper, Humanitarian Policy Group, Overseas Development Institute, London.

Krebs H. (2014b) *The 'Chinese Way'? The Evolution of Chinese Humanitarianism*, HPG Policy Brief, Overseas Development Institute, London.

Lei S. and Tong Y. (2014) *Social Protest in Contemporary China, 2003–2010: Transitional Pains and Regime Legitimacy*, Routledge, London.

Lewis M. (1990) *Sanctioned Violence in Early China*, State University of New York Press, Albany, NY.

Lum S., W. Morrison and B. Vaughn (2008) *China's 'Soft Power' in Southeast Asia*, CRS Report for Congress, Congressional Research Service, Washington, DC.

Marks P. (2000) 'China's Cambodia Strategy', *Parameters*, 30, 92–108.

Marx K. and Engels F. (2011) *The Communist Manifesto*, Penguin, London.

Mitchell D. and McGiffert C. (2007) 'Expanding the "Strategic Periphery": A History of China's Interaction with the Developing World', in Eisenman J., Heginbotham E. and Mitchell D. (eds), *China and the Developing World. Beijing's Strategy for the Twenty-first Century*, M.E. Sharpe, Armonk, NY, 3–28.

Moody P.R. (2011) 'Confucianism as a Legitimizing Ideology', in Deng Z. and Guo S. (eds), *Reviving Legitimacy*, Rowman & Littlefield, Lanham, MD, 111–130.

Mulvenon J. (2010) 'Party-Military Coordination of the Yushu Earthquake Response', *China Leadership Monitor*, 28 June (www.hoover.org/sites/default/files/uploads/documents/CLM33JM.pdf), accessed 28 April 2015.

Nakano R. and Prantl J. (2011) *Global Norm Diffusion in East Asia: How China and Japan Implement the Responsibility to Protect*, NTS Working Paper Series no. 5, Centre for Non-Traditional Security Studies, Singapore.

Pu X. (2012) 'Socialisation as a Two-way Process: Emerging Powers and the Diffusion of International Norms', *Chinese Journal of International Politics*, 5, 341–347.

Reeves C. (2014) 'The Red Cross Society of China: Past, Present, and Future', in Ryan J., Chen L. and Saich T. (eds), *Philanthropy for Health in China*, Indiana University Press, Bloomington, IN, 214–233.

Roberts M. (2004) *Making English Morals: Voluntary Association and Moral Reform in England, 1787–1886*, Cambridge University Press, Cambridge.

Ruan Z. (2012) 'Responsible Protection: Building a Safer World', *China International Studies*, 34, June 2012.

Sato J., Shiga H., Kobayashi T. and Kondoh H. (2011) '"Emerging Donors" from a Recipient Perspective: An Institutional Analysis of Foreign Aid in Cambodia', *World Development*, 39(12), 2091–2104.

Shapiro J. (2001) *Mao's War against Nature: Politics and Environment in Revolutionary China*, Cambridge, Cambridge University Press.

Smith J. (2009) *The Art of Doing Good. Charity in Late Ming China*, University of California Press, Berkeley, CA, London.

Spence J. (1990) *The Search for Modern China*, Norton, New York.

Taylor I (2015) 'China's Response to the Ebola Virus Disease in West Africa', *Round Table: The Commonwealth Journal of International Affairs*, 104(1), 41–54.

Teitt S. (2008) *China and the Responsibility to Protect*, Asia-Pacific Centre for the Responsibility to Protect, Brisbane.

Teitt S. (2014) 'China and the International Humanitarian Order', *R2P Ideas in Brief*, 4(8).

Tong, Y. (2011) 'Morality, Benevolence, and Responsibility: Regime Legitimacy in China from Past to Present', *Journal of Chinese Political Science*, 16(2), 141–159.

United Nations (1999) *Official Records of the 54th General Assembly 8th Plenary meeting* (www.un.org/ga/54/pv54e.htm), accessed 5 November 2015.

United Nations (2015) *Contributors to the United Nations Peacekeeping Operations. Monthly Summary of Contributions January 2015* (www.un.org/en/peacekeeping/contributors/2015/jan15_1.pdf), accessed 9 June 2015.

UN News Centre (2014) 'China "Key" to Shaping Future of Global Humanitarian Action – Top UN Relief Official', 1 November 2014 (www.un.org/apps/news/story.asp?NewsID=49229#.VXg5UlI3Tx4), accessed 10 June 2015.

Varg P.A. (1977) *Missionaries, Chinese, and Diplomats: The American Protestant Missionary Movement in China, 1890–1952*, Octagon Books, New York.

Wang X., Warner E. and Wolf C. (2013) *China's Foreign Aid and Government-Sponsored Investment Activities*, RAND Corporation, Santa Monica, CA (www.rand.org/pubs/research_reports/RR118), accessed 9 June 2015.

Wen Y.B. (1960) 'The Authors of the Marxist Classics on Bourgeois Humanitarianism', translations of an article of Wen Yi Bao [Literary Gazette]' in Joint Publications Research Service (eds), *Marxist-Leninist Doctrines and Humanitarianism*, US Joint Publications Service, Washington, DC, 1–275.

Westad O.A. (2012) *Restless Empire: China and the World since 1750*, Bodley Head, London.

Yeophantong P. (2014) *Understanding Humanitarian Action in East and Southeast Asia: A Historical Perspective*, HPG Working Paper, Humanitarian Policy Group, Overseas Development Institute, London.

Zhang J. (2014) 'The Military and Disaster Relief in China: Trends, Drivers and Implications', in Sakai M., Jurriëns E., Zhang J. and Thornton A. (eds), *Disaster Relief in the Asia Pacific. Agency and Resilience*, Routledge, Abingdon, 69–85.

11 Between marketisation and altruism

Humanitarian assistance, NGOs and private military and security companies[1]

Jutta Joachim and Andrea Schneiker

Introduction

While the International Committee of the Red Cross (ICRC), the United Nations (UN) and non-governmental organisations (NGOs) have traditionally been viewed as the classical humanitarian actors occupying the formal international and Western humanitarian 'system' (Harvey et al. 2010, 13; Slim 2006, 18–21; Bernard 2011, 891), new actors have entered the scene in recent years. In addition to companies such as Walmart (Hopgood 2008) and state militaries (Wheeler and Harmer 2006), private military and security companies (PMSCs) have, as we have shown elsewhere (Joachim and Schneiker 2012, 2014), gained 'a solid foothold in the humanitarian space and in post-conflict settings' (Rosén 2008, 80). These companies offer (security) services for other humanitarian actors or deliver humanitarian assistance directly (Joachim and Schneiker 2012). Humanitarian actors, especially international NGOs, the UN and the ICRC, are reported to have hired PMSCs to, for example, protect their facilities and staff in dangerous environments such as Sierra Leone, Congo, Afghanistan, Darfur or Somalia (Pingeot 2012; Singer 2004; Stoddard, Harmer and DiDomenico 2008), while PMSCs such as ArmorGroup (now part of G4S), RONCO and DynCorp carried out de-mining operations for the US and UK government (Spearin 2008, 369). The influx of new actors is reflective of changes in the humanitarian sector more generally, including professionalisation, commercialisation and marketisation, and has sparked a discussion in both the scholarly community as well as that of practitioners about the meaning of humanitarian assistance. According to Barnett and Weiss, it is even indicative of the fact that humanitarianism is undergoing an 'identity crisis' (Barnett and Weiss 2008, 2011).

It is against this backdrop that we examine the interaction between PMSCs and humanitarian NGOs in this chapter. When NGOs and PMSCs work in the same areas, they might cooperate in what Abrahamsen and Williams (2009) refer to as 'global security assemblages' and define as 'settings where a range of different global and local, public and private security agents and normativities interact, cooperate and compete to produce new institutions, practices, and forms of security governance' (ibid., 3). As a representative of the ICRC already explained in 2004:

DOI: 10.4324/9781315658827-14

Meanwhile these companies are an important actor that one needs to come to terms with. If you are a humanitarian organisation assisting victims in a conflict zone, you should be in contact with all the actors, especially ones that are armed. We of the ICRC want people to know who we are, why we are here and how we work.

(Voillat 2004; see also Ruffa 2013)

While hardly ever admitted openly, cooperation between humanitarian NGOs and PMSCs has become a reality, and for many NGOs a necessity, to protect the lives of aid workers (Anders 2013, 282). Nevertheless, and as recent scholarship indicates, relationships between NGOs and PMSCs 'are marred by mutual suspicion and difficulties' (ibid., 281) and cooperation proves challenging because of 'often-incompatible aims, philosophies and cultures' (Egnell 2013, 240). For example, given the relationships that companies frequently maintain with state security, police or military services, associating with them may by extension 'compromise the appearance of neutrality, and therefore jeopardise security' of the NGOs (Stoddard et al. 2008, 23). Abrahamsen and Williams speak of frequently voiced fears that PMSCs themselves might become a source of insecurity and that poorly paid guards may collude with criminals and conspire against clients (Abrahamsen and Williams 2005, 4). Furthermore, NGOs are also troubled by the non-transparency of the PMSC industry and their economic motives, which these organisations conceive of as incompatible with their own principled beliefs (Stoddard et al. 2008, 23). PMSCs, by comparison, are often less concerned about their interactions with humanitarian NGOs, not only because they are seen as means to increase the number of contracts and therefore profits, but because they also are considered to boost companies' reputations (see Joachim and Schneiker 2012).

Contrary to most existing publications that study the interaction *per se*, or are concerned with the potentially negative implications (Anders 2013; Cockayne 2006; Stoddard et al. 2008), we are interested in the self-representation of these actors and the self-understandings or various identities that find expression through them. For this purpose, we have analysed the webpages of selected humanitarian NGOs and PMSCs as well as the journal of the international association of PMSCs, the International Stability Operations Association (ISOA). What we find supports, on one hand, existing studies that observe a marketisation trend in the humanitarian field (e.g. Cooley and Ron 2002). Yet it also adds to this literature, on the other hand, because we show that this process of marketisation is not limited to actions, as commonly assumed, that is, humanitarian NGOs adopting practices otherwise common for commercial companies and firms providing humanitarian assistance. Instead, it extends much further. NGOs and companies are not only becoming alike in what they are doing, but also resemble each other in how they view themselves by drawing on sources of authority generally and respectively claimed by others. At the same time as PMSCs increasingly present themselves as 'New Humanitarian Agent[s]', as a representative of the company ArmorGroup (now part of G4S) was quoted in

2001 (James Fennell, cited in Vaux et al. 2001, 13, n12); and claim, as Triple Canopy, to 'strive to enhance the lives of people in the places where we serve' (Triple Canopy 2012), humanitarian NGOs are using language of commercial actors when emphasising their expertise, efficiency and excellence.

The observed isomorphism among PMSCs and humanitarian NGOs with respect to their identities has implications for research on global governance. First, it suggests that the withering of boundaries between, for example, public and private actors, but also between private actors, is not only due to different actors performing increasingly similar tasks, but also is the result of intersubjective processes and is taking place at a potentially more fundamental identity level. Second, the findings also call into question the assumption that private and public actors bring with them, and contribute to, governance processes such as multistakeholder dialogues or private partnerships because of their different resources, interests and identities. The assimilation of PMSCs and humanitarian NGOs points instead to an alternative explanation for their participation and growing cooperation: the fact that the actors involved can identify with each other.

The chapter is structured as follows: before elaborating on our theoretical framework, we discuss our sample and methods. We then turn to our analysis, documenting the assimilation between PMSCs and NGOs in the context of ongoing changes in the humanitarian field, and concluding with a summary of our findings.

Sample and methods

This chapter is based on an analysis of the webpages of fifteen PMSCs[2] and humanitarian NGOs.[3] PMSCs are defined here as transnational companies selling military and police-related services, including protection of persons, compounds or equipment, training, surveillance or risk assessments. In the literature on PMSCs it is quite common to categorise companies according to the services they offer, distinguishing, for example, between offensive or defensive companies (e.g. Abrahamsen and Williams 2007; Percy 2009), or based on their proximity to the battlefield (Singer 2001/02, 2003). Apart from the fact that many PMSCs do not easily fit such taxonomies because they offer a broad range of services (e.g. as a consequence of mergers), we find that these categories do not matter in our case. The companies in the chosen sample refer to themselves as humanitarian actors regardless of the kinds of services they offer. Turning to humanitarian NGOs, we selected the bigger and leading organisations in the field (Harvey et al. 2010; Taylor et al. 2012) based on the assumption that they are more likely than smaller ones to adopt a corporate mindset for their work.

We conducted a discourse analysis of NGO and PMSC webpages and the ISOA journal, examining text as well as photos and symbols. Even if the 'the construction of a Web site is only a partial indicator of what a group values and how it operates' (Pudrovska and Marx Ferree 2004, 118), the internet presentation of PMSCs and humanitarian NGOs is nevertheless an important source of information for our study, for reasons that Pudrovska and Ferree aptly formulate:

188 J. Joachim and A. Schneiker

analysis of Web sites provides a new and useful form of data about an organisation's identity and priorities, because, unlike media representations of the group, it is self-directed and, unlike many structural features of the organisation, it is relatively resource-neutral. Thus, a Web site provides an open space for self-representation to the rest of the world.

(ibid., 118; see also Warkentin 2001, 36–37)

Identity, PMSCs and humanitarian NGOs

In the International Relations discipline, where this chapter is situated, the concept of identity has acquired its status as an analytical category only recently with the so-called 'constructivist turn' and the burgeoning of research informed by post-structuralist, feminist and constructivist approaches. As constituting and socially constructed factors, identities can be defined as 'sets of meanings that an actor attributes to itself while taking the perspective of others' (Wendt 1994, 385). Rather than a singular identity, actors' preferences and aims are most often influenced by multiple identities which intersect, co-exist or are in conflict with each other. This also applies to PMSCs (Carmola 2010) and humanitarian NGOs (Renouf 2011). According to Carmola (2010), PMSCs 'combine the worlds of the military, business world, and the humanitarian NGOs in unfamiliar ways' (Carmola 2010, 28), while Renouf (2011) finds humanitarian NGOs to be caught between an identity based on principles of neutrality, independence and impartiality, and one that is outright political. Identities help actors to orient and position themselves in the international system and its structure. They offer criteria based upon which it becomes possible to determine one's belonging to a group (in-group), but also to set oneself apart from other groups (out-group) (Wendt 1994, 385). According to Fearon and Laitin, identities specify

(1) rules of membership that decide who is and is not a member of the category; and (2) content, that is, sets of characteristics [...] thought to be typical of members of the category, or behaviors expected or obliged of members in certain situations.

(Fearon and Laitin 2000, 848)

In the literature on PMSCs, greater attention has been dedicated more recently to the self-representation and the identities of companies (e.g. Joachim and Schneiker 2012; Kruck and Spencer 2013), for both empirical as well as theoretical reasons. With respect to the former and responding in part to scandals involving staff of PMSCs and subsequent negative press, companies spend great efforts 'to [not] be perceived by the voting public as immoral, unpatriotic mercenaries' (Dunigan 2011, 17). The turn to identity in PMSC studies is, however, also a result of frustration with common categorisations of PMSCs based on services because they ignore the influence of ideational factors and the discursive power of companies (Joachim and Schneiker 2012, 2). Yet, as Doris Fuchs observes with respect to companies more generally, these play an important role in an increasingly competitive industry where companies not only survive and thrive by selling goods or services, but also 'by actively participating in public debates on the definition of political problems and solutions, as well as offensively and defensively shaping their image as economic, political, and societal actors' (Fuchs 2005, 772). PMSCs actively construct their identities and how they are perceived (Olsson 2007). At one point, they may present themselves as a 'force multiplier', helping governments, or rather their militaries, to achieve their political and military aims more effectively; at another as a customer-friendly company just like a bank or insurance company; and then again as humanitarian, able to make the world a better one, and sometimes as all three (Carmola 2010, 28). Taking the identity-producing role of PMSCs into account not only offers a more comprehensive understanding, but also acknowledges that the respective companies are political rather than apolitical, as has commonly been assumed.

Humanitarian NGOs like PMSCs, position and define their identities in relation to others, be they other NGOs, the recipients of their assistance, international governmental organisations (IGOs), governments and their militaries, commercial companies, and more recently, as we will show, PMSCs. They do so by debating and pronouncing 'who they are and what practices are reflective of their identity' and by making claims about 'who they believe they are not and the practices that they deem illegitimate' (Barnett and Weiss 2008, 5). While these identity-constructing practices have been readily acknowledged in the literature on humanitarian NGOs, scholars for the most part have assumed that the respective organisations reassert and define their identity by emphasising how they are different from others (ibid., 5; Vaughn 2009). In the following section, however, we present evidence that suggests the contrary. Rather than setting themselves apart from other humanitarian actors, and in this case PMSCs, NGOs align themselves and construct their identity with reference to commercial companies.

A Humanitarian–managerial identity? The alignment of humanitarian NGOs and PMSCs

Studying the web presentations of both PMSCs and humanitarian NGOs, we observe isomorphism among both types of actor. While PMSCs present themselves increasingly as humanitarian actors, NGOs exhibit characteristics generally associated with the corporate/managerial sector.

Of Do-gooders, saviours of the world and humanitarian service providers

Private military and security companies construct their humanitarian identity in a material and an ideational sense. At the same time as they provide humanitarian goods and services, they present themselves as actors concerned about the well-being of people and as ameliorating the suffering of those in need. When compared with humanitarian NGOs, the discourse of PMSCs is nearly identical (Gómez del Prado nd, 2).

The company Arkel, for example, '[d]elivers food to those who've been hit by disaster and have no means for sustenance, provides meals as part of life support in places where food service is remote or non-existent [...]' (Arkel 2014). These are services we would rather typically expect of humanitarian NGOs such as *Oxfam International*, which 'help[s] people caught up in natural disasters and conflict [and ...] typically provide[s] clean water, food and sanitation in disaster zones' (Oxfam 2014b); or CARE International, which 'ensure[s] that people have enough to eat, a roof over their head, clean water and adequate hygiene supplies' (CARE International 2014b).

Alignment with humanitarian NGOs is not limited to claims about services, but also extends to the values that PMSCs claim motivate their actions. The PMSC L-3 MPRI, for example, asserts its aim 'to make the world a better place tomorrow' (L-3 MPRI 2012), while 'KBR and its employees are striving to make the world around them a better place' (KBR 2012). Statements such as these are nearly identical with those of the International Rescue Committee, which claims '[that it] restores safety, dignity and hope to millions who are uprooted and struggling to endure. The IRC leads the way from harm to home' (International Rescue Committee 2013); or the humanitarian NGO ADRA, according to which 'ADRA improves the lives of people around the world' (ADRA 2014). The assertions of PMSCs are also similar to those of CARE International, which 'strive[s] to serve individuals and families in the poorest communities in the world' based on a vision 'to seek a world of hope, tolerance and social justice, where poverty has been overcome and people live in dignity and security' (CARE International 2014c).

Photos and symbols that we found on the webpages of PMSCs resemble those used by humanitarian NGOs. The pages and ads of companies such as DynCorp, L3-MPRI (now Engility), Triple Canopy and Blackwater (now Academi) show photos of sad and needy-looking children, just as we are used to seeing them on the webpages of humanitarian NGOs (DynCorp 2012; L-3 MPRI 2012; Triple Canopy 2014; Blackwater 2006). Nevertheless, these photos also have another dimension to them. PMSCs appear to borrow from the legitimacy of, or at least link themselves more directly to, traditional and accepted humanitarian actors. The web presentation of Triple Canopy speaks to this point. Showing sad-looking children waving out of a tent, one immediately thinks of the UN and its refugee camps rather than a PMSC. That it is the tent of such a company becomes apparent only upon a closer look, where one can find the name of the company Triple Canopy on one side of the tent in faded writing.

Finally, evidence for isomorphism can also be found with respect to logos or even company names. In the case of the latter, it is often impossible for an outsider to determine whether the respective actor is a PMSC or a humanitarian NGO. For example, Pax Mondial or SOS International would lead us to expect that these are non-profit humanitarian organisations. Yet, instead, they are the names of two PMSCs with SOS International also carrying out top-secret missions for the US government and others (Brinkmann, Hollenstein and Kempman 2013, 9).

Marketisation of humanitarian NGOs? Humanitarian managers with expertise and flexibility

At the same time as we find PMSCs taking on a humanitarian identity, humanitarian NGOs are appropriating language typical of the corporate sector. Rather than moral reasoning for their assistance, we found the NGOs in our sample almost exclusively emphasise their entrepreneurial and managerial qualities, including their expertise, flexibility and versatility.

All of the NGOs we studied stress their vast expertise of having worked with victims of conflict or natural disasters and use statistical figures to support their claims. CARE International, for example, claims to have worked in 87 countries in 2013 and to have reached out to 97 million people (CARE International 2014a); while ActionAid International asserts to have worked with 15 million people in 45 countries (ActionAid International 2014); and ADRA stresses that it is active in more than 120 countries (ADRA 2014). While numbers can be taken to be an indicator for the knowledge and experience that the organisations possess about how to respond and assist in crisis, they are also indicative of the competition to which NGOs are increasingly subject due to the growth in this sector. Vying with others for both funding and projects, humanitarian NGOs need to not only prove themselves, but also increasingly set themselves apart from their contenders. The language they use in this respect is strikingly similar to that of PMSCs.

Just as PMSCs refer to themselves as 'seasoned contractor[s]' (KBR 2012), so do the NGOs in our sample conceive of themselves in that manner and, like PMSCs, they praise the qualifications of their personnel. MercyCorps, a humanitarian NGO, for example, refers to its staff as 'seasoned emergency responders' (MercyCorps 2014); and the International Rescue Committee prides itself for its 'Emergency Response Team' comprised of '17 specialists' 'with expertise in key areas necessary to assess critical survival needs and mount an effective response to sudden or protracted emergencies' (International Rescue Committee 2014). We found nearly identical language on the webpages of the following PMSCs: KBR, which refers to itself as 'a seasoned contractor, with experience in providing solutions for both natural and manmade emergencies' (KBR 2012); and Pax Mondial, which stresses that it has '[a] breadth of expertise' (Pax Mondial 2014). Rather than focusing on people in need, as we would expect of humanitarian NGOs, the organisations we studied engage in a self-referential discourse similar to PMSCs and speak almost only of their capabilities.

Like the PMSC KBR, which claims that 'services [are] tailored to meet [our clients] needs, schedules and budgets is our main priority' (KBR 2012), CARE International stresses its flexibility and versatility, asserting that 'each emergency response is tailored to the needs of each situation' (CARE International 2014b). Both humanitarian NGOs as well as PMSCs maintain that they are ready anytime to go anywhere to assist those who suffer. The NGO International Rescue Committee, for example, states that it is '[a]lways [p]repared' (International Rescue Committee 2014) and 'delivers rapid, lifesaving aid' when 'catastrophe strikes' (International Rescue Committee 2014), while on the webpage of Oxfam International one can read '[w]hen disaster strikes we're there' (Oxfam 2014a). Similar claims can be found on PMSC pages, including that of Pax Mondial, which prides itself that its 'multi-faceted capacities allow us to take a quick and seamless approach […]. In the immediate aftermath of a disaster, for instance, Pax can quickly provide shelter and medical care for victims of the catastrophe' (Pax Mondial 2014). Similarly to the company KBR, which 'has been first on the scene in the wake of many disasters, providing critical support when it was needed most' (KBR 2012) and ready 'to react to any challenge anywhere, at anytime, providing aid and advice to those dealing with extreme difficulty' (ibid.), the Norwegian Refugee Council, an NGO, in reference to the flood in Pakistan, stresses its exceptionalism by priding itself to be 'the first international humanitarian organisation to plan for relief activities in the aftermath of the current floods in Balochistan' (NRC 2012). The International Rescue Committee claims to have been at the 'frontlines of many of the worst crises in recent times' (International Rescue Committee 2014) and to 'always [be] on standby', 'to deploy to a crisis within 72 hours' (ibid.). And the NGO MercyCorps claims that '[it] saves and improves lives in the world's toughest places' (MercyCorps 2014).

What to make of the alignment of humanitarian NGOs and PMSCs?

In this section, we will offer some initial propositions as to why these processes might take place by turning to the literature on humanitarian assistance which has increasingly paid attention to the changing conditions both within the field and among humanitarian actors. Of the three trends – politicisation, marketisation and militarisation – that are frequently mentioned, the latter two might provide clues as to why NGOs increasingly exhibit a managerial face.

Marketisation is often attributed to both the influx of (new) actors in the humanitarian field and the rising competition for funds and projects. The literature on isomorphism considers these conditions to be a fertile ground for alignment processes. Wanting their organisations to survive, the respective actors will emulate the more successful in the field or adapt to what their environments ask of them; in the case of NGOs, most likely their donors (Frumkin and Galaskiewicz 2004). Scholars such as Donini et al. (2008, 4) and others (e.g. Smillie and Minear 2004, 8) have pointed out that, since the end of the Cold War, humanitarian assistance has become a 'multi-billion dollar enterprise' (Donini et al. 2008, 4; cf. also Smillie and Minear 2004, 8) accounting for US$17.9 billion in 2012 (Buston and Smith 2013, 4). Although exact figures regarding the number of humanitarian aid workers are hard to come by (Walker and Russ 2010, 11–12), experts in the field estimate their number to have increased by 77 per cent between 1997 and 2005 (Stoddard et al. 2006, 1) amounting to 200,000 (Collinson and Elhawary 2012, 10) with most of them working for NGOs (Taylor et al. 2012, 26). Recent estimates suggest that NGOs account for approximately a quarter of the international humanitarian assistance provided between 2007 and 2011 (Buston and Smith 2013, 61), while Taylor et al. deem the number of organisations currently to be approximately 4,000 (Taylor et al. 2012, 9). In addition to the rising numbers of NGOs, Smillie and Minear (2004, 183–202) also consider the influx of new private actors and what Duffield (1997) refers to as the 'privatisation of aid' for the intensification of competition among humanitarian NGOs in particular, and marketisation more generally (see also Fowler 2005).

Rather than deciding where to put their efforts and who to assist based on needs, NGOs, according to Gordenker and Weiss, behave like 'vendors of goods and services' (Gordenker and Weiss 1997, 444) in the 'aid marketplace' (Smillie and Minear 2004, 8; Collinson and Elhawary 2012, 21), making choices about their engagement based on whether a crisis lends itself for campaign purposes and translates into more donations (Cooley and Ron 2002). Apart from having to vie with others for funding and projects, NGOs increasingly need to report to their donors how they spent the money and with what effect. Their accountability and answers might determine their livelihood, that is, whether they will receive continued funding or are tasked with another project, but also may be a reason why NGOs look more alike and increasingly resemble businesses. As Frumkin and Galaskiewicz note, 'through regulation, accrediting, oversight, and funding relations, public sector organisations have been described as forces pushing nonprofits and business firms toward greater levels of homogeneity' (Frumkin and Galaskiewicz 2004, 284).

Next to commercialisation, the changes in the political context of humanitarian NGOs and toward what some have referred to as 'heightened militarisation' could be argued to be a source of the observed isomorphism. Contrary to the Cold War period, aid organisations today increasingly provide help in the midst of violent conflicts (Donini et al. 2008, 4; Collinson and Elhawary 2012, 5). Often as part of multi-dimensional missions in response to so-called 'complex emergencies' (Buston and Smith 2013, 79; Schloms 2003), NGOs work closely with state military actors and/or PMSCs either for purposes of their own protection or for the delivery of services.

Because of these types of interactions, NGOs might alter their views or undergo changes in their self-understanding. This is what constructivist approaches, but also neo-institutionalism, would suggest. While proponents of the former presuppose that identities and interests are shaped intersubjectively and through processes involving persuasion, neo-institutionalists work from the assumption that institutions are organisational fields and information networks which fuel standardisation and professionalisation through the exchange of information and ideas (DiMaggio and Powell 1991[1983]). Hence the adoption of a managerial face appears as a plausible response to the described changes in the humanitarian field. However, rather than being encouraged by competition alone, the assimilation of humanitarian NGOs and PMSCs might be encouraged through the interactions of individuals from the respective sectors in 'global security assemblages' (Abrahamsen and Williams 2009). Focusing on diamond mining in Sierra Leone and oil extraction in Nigeria, Abrahamsen and Williams show how through such assemblages important concepts such as that of security are 'shaped and influenced by new normative orders beyond the nation-state and by the growing power of private actors who interact with the state to such a degree that it is often difficult to determine where the public ends and the private begins' (ibid., 6). Similar transformative processes are conceivable with respect to humanitarianism and the interactions between humanitarian NGOs and PMSCs that are part of assemblages.

Commercialisation and militarisation are only two of potentially more trends which might precipitate the alignment we observe among PMSCs and humanitarian NGOs. While the propositions formulated above require further research, involving interviews with humanitarian actors, scholars have started to reflect on the implications the blurring of boundaries between the involved actors might have, and to which we will briefly turn in the concluding section.

Conclusion

In this chapter we show that marketisation affects not only what humanitarian NGOs do, but also how they view themselves. In addition to moral values, the organisations in our sample increasingly and sometimes exclusively portray their work in a manner we would expect of commercial and profit-oriented enterprises. Rather than emphasising that their staff provide assistance in an empathetic and respectful manner (Barnett and Snyder 2008, 143; Fearon 2008, 51; Van Brabant 2010, 9), or that they will try to prevent or eliminate human suffering, as we would expect of humanitarian NGOs, we find such statements on the internet pages of PMSCs, while the NGOs themselves much more frequently and sometimes even exclusively draw attention to their effectiveness, efficiency and flexibility, attributes we associate with commercial enterprises.

While organisational theory provides a fruitful ground for helping to explain the observed isomorphism, from a neoliberal governmentality perspective the assimilation of humanitarian actors is indicative of a blurring of the private–private divide, that is, between companies on one hand and civil society organisations on the other. Unlike the boundaries between public and private actors, the withering of those between private ones has received little attention, which is surprising in light of the potentially severe implications when humanitarian NGOs 'substitute a logic – and an ethic – of consequence for an ethic of obligation' (Gross Stein 2008, 134). According to Gross Stein, such a logic 'would argue that humanitarians should only give assistance when it is effective, irrespective of whether it is needed' (ibid., 134). This rather disconcerting conclusion needs to be considered in light of the potentially negative effects of the cooperation between humanitarian NGOs and PMSCs, including not only commercialisation of humanitarian assistance, but also its professed militarisation in light of the armed protection that many companies provide or the relationships they maintain with state military actors. Nevertheless, and in contrast to most of the existing works which are concerned with the problems and challenges that interactions of humanitarian NGOs and PMSCs might entail, we point to a source other than 'insecurity' that might explain their cooperation and one that is even more worrisome: the alignment of their identities.

Notes

1 We would like to thank Henriette Lange and Stefanie Schmidt for their invaluable research assistance, and the participants of the workshop 'Humanitarianism and Changing Cultures of Cooperation' (Essen, 5–7 June, 2014) for their helpful comments.
2 Arkel, Blackwater, DynCorp, KBR, L3-MPRI, Pax Mondial, SOS International, Triple Canopy.
3 Action Aid, ADRA, Care International, International Rescue Committee, Mercy Corps, Norwegian Refugee Council, Oxfam.

References

Abrahamsen R. and Williams M.C. (2005) *The Globalisation of Private Security: Country Report Kenya*, Economic and Social Research Council of the UK, Swindon.
Abrahamsen R. and Williams M.C. (2007) 'Securing the City: Private Security Companies and Non-state Authority in Global Governance', *International Relations*, 21(2), 237–253.
Abrahamsen R. and Williams M.C. (2009) 'Security Beyond the State: Global Security Assemblages in International Politics', *International Political Sociology*, 3(1), 1–17.
ActionAid International (2014) *Who We Are* (www.actionaid.org/who-we-are), accessed 11 August 2014.
ADRA (2014) *An Overview of Our Work* (www.adra.org/site/PageNavigator/work), accessed 15 August 2014; URL no longer available online.
Anders B. (2013) 'Tree-Huggers and Baby-Killers: The Relationship between NGOs and PMSCs and its Impact on Coordinating Actors in Complex Operations', *Small Wars & Insurgencies*, 24(2), 278–294.
Arkel (2014) *About Us* (www.arkel.com/about-us), accessed 4 March 2014; URL no longer available online.
Barnett, M. (2009) 'Evolution without Progress? Humanitarianism in a World of Hurt', *International Organization*, 63(4), 621–663.
Barnett M. and Snyder J. (2008) 'The Grand Strategies of Humanitarianism', in M. Barnett and T.G. Weiss (eds), *Humanitarianism in Question: Politics, Power, Ethic*, Cornell University Press, Ithaca, NY, 143–171.
Barnett M. and Weiss T.G. (2008) 'Humanitarianism: A Brief History of the Present', in M. Barnett and T.G. Weiss (eds), *Humanitarianism in Question: Politics, Power, Ethics*, Cornell University Press, Ithaca NY, 1–48.
Barnett M. and Weiss T.G. (2011) *Humanitarianism Contested: Where Angels Fear to Tread*, Routledge, London and New York.
Bernard V. (2011) 'The Future of Humanitarian Action: Editorial', *International Review of the Red Cross*, 93(884), 891–897.
Berndtsson J. and Stern M. (2011) 'Private Security and the Public–Private Divide: Contested Lines of Distinction and Modes of Governance in the Stockholm–Arlanda Security Assemblage', *International Political Sociology*, 5(4), 408–425.
Blackwater (2006) Advert, *Journal of International Peace Operations*, 2(2), 2.
Brinkmann B., Hollenstein O. and Kempman A. (2013) 'Das Millionengeschäft für die Zulieferer. Sie arbeiten wie Spione: Private Firmen helfen US-Diensten', *Süddeutsche Zeitung*, 16 November, 9.
Buston O. and Smith K. (2013) *Global Humanitarian Assistance Report 2013*, Global Humanitarian Assistance, Bristol.
CARE International (2014a) *Home* (www.care-international.org), accessed 11 August 2014.
CARE International (2014b) *Emergency Response* (www.care-international.org/what-we-do/emergency-response.aspx), accessed 11 August 2014.

CARE International (2014c) *Core Values* (www.care-international.org/about-us/core-values. aspx), accessed 16 January 2015.

Carmola K. (2010) *Private Security Contractors in the Age of New Wars: Risk, Law and Ethics*, Routledge, London and New York.

Cockayne J. (2006) 'Commercial Security in Humanitarian and Post-Conflict Settings: An Exploratory Study', *International Peace Academy* (www.ipinst.org/2006/03/commercial-security-in-humanitarian-and-post-conflict-settings-an-exploratory-study), accessed 6 July 2013.

Collinson S. and Elhawary S. (2012) *Humanitarian Space: A Review of Trends and Issue*, Humanitarian Policy Group, Overseas Development Institute, London.

Cooley A. and Ron J. (2002) 'The NGO Scramble: Organizational Insecurity and the Political Economy of Transnational Action', *International Security*, 27(1), 5–39.

DiMaggio P.J. and Powell W.W. (1991[1983]) *The New Institutionalism in Organizational Analysis*, University of Chicago Press, Chicago, IL.

Donini A., Fast L., Hansen G., Harris S., Minear L., Mowjee T. and Wilder A. (2008) *Humanitarian Agenda 2015: Final Report. The State of the Humanitarian Enterprise*, Boston: Feinstein International Center, Tufts University (https://nautinst.org/objects_store/ humanitarian_agenda_2015_-_final_report_2008_.pdf), accessed 1 May 2014.

Duffield M. (1997) 'NGO Relief in War Zones: Towards an Analysis of the New Aid Paradigm', *Third World Quarterly*, 18(3), 527–542.

Dunigan M. (2011) *Victory for Hire*, Stanford University Press, Stanford, CA.

DynCorp (2012) *Supporting Stability and Human Progress Across the Globe* (www.dyn-intl. com/media/277/development_brochure.pdf), accessed 11 April 2012; URL no longer available online.

Egnell R. (2013) 'Civil–Military Coordination for Operational Effectiveness: Towards a Measured Approach', *Small Wars & Insurgencies*, 24(2), 237–256.

Fearon J.D. (2008): 'The Rise of Emergency Aid', in M. Barnett and T.G. Weiss (eds), *Humanitarianism in Question: Politics, Power, Ethics*, Cornell University Press, Ithaca, NY, 49–72.

Fearon J.D. and Laitin D.D. (2000) 'Violence and the Social Construction of Ethnic Identity', *International Organization*, 54(4), 845–877.

Fowler A. (2005) *Aid Architecture: Reflections on NGDO Futures and the Emergence of Counter-Terrorism*, INTRAC Occasional Papers 45, International NGO Training and Research Centre, Oxford.

Frumkin P. and Galaskiewicz J. (2004) 'Institutional Isomorphism and Public Sector Organizations', *Journal of Public Administration Research and Theory*, 14(3), 283–307.

Fuchs D. (2005) 'Commanding Heights? The Strength and Fragility of Business Power in Global Politics', *Millennium*, 33(3), 771–801.

Gómez del Prado J.L. (nd) *Private Military and Security Companies and Challenges to the UN Working Group on the Use of Mercenaries* (http://havenscenter.org/privatemilitaryconference 2008), accessed 30 June 2013.

Gordenker L. and Weiss T.G. (1997) 'Devolving Responsibilities: A Framework for Analysing NGOs and Services', *Third World Quarterly*, 18(3), 443–455.

Gross Stein J. (2008) 'Humanitarian Organizations. Accountable – Why, to Whom, for What, and How?', in M. Barnett and T.G. Weiss (eds), *Humanitarianism in Question: Politics, Power, Ethics*, Cornell University Press, Ithaca, NY, 124–142.

Harvey P., Stoddard A., Harmer A., Taylor G. with DiDomenico V. and Brander L. (2010) *The State of the Humanitarian System. Assessing Performance and Progress. A Pilot Study*, Active Learning Network for Accountability and Performance (ALNAP), London (www.odi.org.uk/sites/odi.org.uk/files/odi-assets/publications-opinion-files/5825.pdf), accessed 12 May 2014.

Hopgood S. (2008) 'Saying "No" to Wal-Mart? Money and Morality in Professional Humanitarianism', in M. Barnett and T.G. Weiss (eds), *Humanitarianism in Question: Politics, Power, Ethics*, Cornell University Press, Ithaca, NY, 98–123.

International Rescue Committee (2013) *Who We Are* (www.rescue.org/about), accessed 5 April 2013.

International Rescue Committee (2014) *Emergency Response Relief* (www.rescue.org/our-work/emergency-response), accessed 11 August 2014.

Joachim J. and Schneiker A. (2012) 'New Humanitarians? Frame Appropriation through Private Military and Security Companies', *Millennium: Journal of Internationals Studies*, 40(2), 365–388.

Joachim J. and Schneiker A. (2014) 'All for One and One in All: PMSCs as Soldiers, Business Managers and Humanitarians', *Cambridge Review of International Affairs*, 27(2), 246–267.

KBR (2012) *Main* (www.kbr.com), accessed 13 April 2012.

Kruck A. and Spencer A. (2013) 'Contested Stories of Commercial Security: Self- and Media Narratives of Private Military and Security Companies', *Critical Studies on Security*, 1(3), 326–346.

L-3 MPRI (2012) *Home* (www.mpri.com/web/), accessed 15 April 2012; URL no longer available online.

MercyCorps (2014) *Our Team* (www.mercycorps.org/about-us/our-team), accessed 6 June 2014.

NRC (2012) *Pakistan. Emergency Assistance to Flood Affected* (www.nrc.no/?did=9144961), accessed 17 August 2014.

Olsson C. (2007) 'The Politics of the Apolitical: Private Military Companies, Humanitarians and the Quest for (Anti-)Politics in Post-Intervention Environments', *Journal of International Relations and Development*, 10(4), 332–361.

Oxfam (2014a) *Emergency Response* (www.oxfam.org/en/emergencies), accessed 15 August 2014.

Oxfam (2014b) *How we Fight Poverty* (www.oxfam.org/en/explore/how-oxfam-fights-poverty), accessed 15 August 2014.

Pax Mondial (2014) *Stabilization & Development* (www.paxmondial.com/services/stabilization-development), accessed 1 June 2014.

Percy S. (2009) 'Private Security Companies and Civil Wars', *Civil Wars*, 11, 57–74.

Pingeot L. (2012) *Dangerous Partnership. Private Military & Security Companies and the UN*, Global Policy Forum/Rosa Luxemburg Foundation, New York, Berlin.

Pudrovska T. and Marx Ferree M. (2004) 'Global Activism in "Virtual Space": The European Women's Lobby in the Network of Transnational Women's NGOs on the Web', *Social Politics*, 11(1), 117–143.

Renouf J. (2011) 'Understanding How the Identity of International Aid Agencies and their Approaches to Security are Mutually Shaped', PhD thesis, Department of International Relations, London School of Economics (http://etheses.lse.ac.uk/171/1/Renouf_Understanding_How_the_Identity_of_International_Aid_Agencies_and_Their_Approaches_to_Security_Are_Mutually_Shaped.pdf), accessed 24 August 2012.

Rieff D. (2002) *A Bed for the Night*, Simon & Shuster, New York.

Rosén F. (2008) 'Commercial Security: Conditions of Growth', *Security Dialogue*, 39, 77–97.

Ruffa C. (2013) 'Introduction: Coordinating Actors in Complex Operations', *Small Wars & Insurgencies*, 24(2), 206–210.

Schloms M. (2003) 'Humanitarian NGOs in Peace Processes', *International Peacekeeping*, 10(1), 40–55.

Singer P.W. (2001/02) 'Corporate Warriors: The Rise of the Privatized Military Industry and its Ramifications for International Security', *International Security*, 26(3), 186–220.

Singer P.W. (2003) *Corporate Warriors. The Rise of the Privatized Military Industry*, Cornell University Press, Ithaca, NY.

Singer P.W (2004) *Should Humanitarians Use Private Military Services?* (www.brookings.edu/~/media/research/files/articles/2004/6/summer per cent20defenseindustry per cent20singer/singer20040628.pdf), accessed 17 February 2015.

Slim H. (2006) *Global Welfare: A Realistic Expectation for the International Humanitarian System?*, ALNAP Review of Humanitarian Action: Evaluation Utilisation, Active Learning Network for Accountability and Performance, Overseas Development Institute, London, 9–34.

Smillie I. and Minear L. (2004) *The Charity of Nations. Humanitarian Action in a Calculating World*, Kumarian Press, Bloomfield, CT.

Spearin C. (2008) 'Private, Armed and Humanitarian? States, NGOs, International Private Security Companies and Shifting Humanitarianism', *Security Dialogue*, 39(4), 363–382.

Stoddard A., Harmer A. and Haver K. (2006) *Providing Aid in Insecure Environments: Trends in Policy and Operations*, HPG Report 23, Overseas Development Institute, London.

Stoddard A., Harmer A. and DiDomenico V. (2008) *The Use of Private Security Providers and Services in Humanitarian Operations*, HPG Report 27, Overseas Development Institute, London.

Taylor G., Stoddard A., Harmer A., Haver K., Harvey P., Barber, K. Schreter L. and Wilhelm C. (2012) *The State of the Humanitarian System*, Active Learning Network for Accountability and Performance, Overseas Development Institute, London.

Triple Canopy (2012): 'Home' (www.triplecanopy.com), accessed 31 August 2012.

Triple Canopy (2014) 'Corporate Social Responsibility' (www.triplecanopy.com/about-us/csr/), accessed 3 September 2014.

Van Brabant K. (2010) *Managing Aid Agency Security in an Evolving World: The Larger Challenge*, European Interagency Security Forum, London.

Vaughn J. (2009) 'The Unlikely Securitizer: Humanitarian Organizations and the Securitization of Indistinctiveness', *Security Dialogue*, 40(3), 263–285.

Vaux T., Seiple C., Nakano G. and Van Brabant K. (2001) *Humanitarian Action and Private Security Companies: Opening the Debate*, International Alert, London.

Voillat C. (2004) 'Wir müssen jetzt handeln' (www.dw-world.de/dw/article/0,2144,1369593,00.html), accessed 17 October 2008.

Walker P. and Russ C. (2010) *Professionalizing the Humanitarian Sector. A Scoping Study* (http://fic.tufts.edu/assets/Professionalising_the_humanitarian_sector.pdf), accessed 14 August 2014.

Warkentin C. (2001) *Reshaping World Politics: NGOs, the Internet, and Global Civil Society*, Rowman & Littlefield, Lanham, MD.

Wendt A. (1994) 'Collective Identity Formation and the International State', *American Political Science Review*, 88(2), 384–396.

Wheeler V. and Harmer A. (2006) *Resetting the Rules of Engagement. Trends and Issues in Military–Humanitarian Relations*, HPG Report 21, Overseas Development Institute, London.

12 The impact of the Security Council on the efficacy of the International Criminal Court and the Responsibility to Protect[1]

Aidan Hehir and Anthony F. Lang Jr

Introduction

In the mythology of the old west, the sheriff made judgments and executed punishments. His image in popular culture (or, more accurately, American political culture) was of a lone hero standing up to criminals without the backing of a fully defined legal order. But there are two central problems with the sheriff. First, while his role is legally authorised, the sheriff's selection of which criminals to pursue and what punishment to inflict is purely discretionary. As a result, law enforcement reflects his personal and professional interests. Second, he conflates in one person the three different functions of law in a political order: legislation, judgment and enforcement. While he might have the legal 'right' in one sense – or might see himself as being morally right – to act, in so doing he will increase his own power at the expense of other agents in the community.

International relations has long had self-appointed guardians of law and order – most obviously (and literally) in the case of the George W. Bush-era US – which, impatient with the procedural delays that come with formal legal methods, sees itself standing sheriff-like before the onslaught of evil (Gray 2004). When emergency situations arise – either terrorists or war criminals – someone ostensibly needs to act to stop them. A sheriff differs from a vigilante, though, in that the former is an official authorised by the state while the latter is an individual acting purely in his or her own interests. The vigilante may be acting in accordance with a shared normative sensibility about who deserves punishment, but that is not an officially sanctioned role. The sheriff, however, is officially sanctioned and may act in conformity with shared normative and legal principles. At the same time, the sheriff consolidates his power with each enforcement action and remains outside of any institutional check or judicial review in his decision on how to, or what to, enforce when it comes to transgressions of the law (Wheeler 2001). Thus a sheriff's actions may be formally legal but they remain disconnected from justice and, as a result, potentially illegitimate.[2]

Our contention in this article is that humanitarian intervention and the punishment of human rights violators in the current international order is being framed in such a way that it consolidates the position of sheriffs rather than strengthening judges (a metaphor for a stronger legal order). We focus on the Responsibility to Protect (R2P) and the International Criminal Court (ICC) as evidence of the framework being consolidated that enables the selective and arbitrary use both of military force and punitive censure rather than strengthening the formal procedures of a normative legal order. We argue that the efficacy of both R2P and the ICC remains compromised by the powers vested in the UN Security Council (UNSC) and point to examples from the Arab Spring to illustrate these claims. We argue that, so long as the international legal order remains unchanged, we cannot expect R2P or the ICC to operate in a manner consistent with normatively sound principles of legal theory.

This chapter suggests the contours of a reformed international legal order that might better function to protect populations and individuals without creating the problem of the sheriff. It does so not by abandoning law enforcement and punishment, but rather by more clearly articulating how they must be connected to a legal and political order in which law making and law enforcement are clearly defined. Our approach advocates a more explicit constitutional order, one in which the powers and practices of law making are separated from law enforcement and which includes a more purposeful law making, or legislative, function within which norms such as R2P can be translated into rules or even laws. In so doing, we circumvent the idea that making R2P a legal obligation is too difficult, for it both incorporates existing legal principles and also can be made a more robust legal instrument if it arises from a clearly defined law-making structure.

In the first section, we briefly review the powers of the UNSC as an institution with 'primary responsibility for the maintenance of international peace and security'. We then turn to the nature of law enforcement and punishment in international relations, with a special focus on the use of force. The next section looks at the manner in which the powers of the UNSC contrive to inhibit the consistent application of both R2P and the ICC. After exploring these theoretical points, we turn to instances arising from the Arab Uprisings as evidence of this selectivity and punitive elements of the international response. We conclude with general suggestions on the contours of the reforms we feel are required.

The Security Council

The unrivalled power of the UNSC derives from the privileged position given to the five permanent members. Their position reflects their power at the founding of the organisation, power levels that continue to be constituted by their military and economic might in the current international order (perhaps more so for some of the five than others) (Bosco 2009).

As noted in our introduction, the UNSC has substantially increased its authority in the international order. This increased authority is seen by some as a positive development, but we see its increasing authority as more problematic. To understand why this is the case, it is useful to briefly review the legal powers of the UNSC according to the UN Charter. The powers and functions of the UNSC are laid out in Article 24 of the UN Charter which confers on the UNSC 'primary responsibility for the maintenance of international peace and security'. It then goes on to note that more specific powers are enumerated in Chapters VI, VII, VIII and XII of the Charter. But all these powers relate back to this primary responsibility, one that is conferred on the UNSC by the member states of the UN.

The word 'primary' suggests that while the UNSC may have most of the responsibility for peace and security, it is not the only organ even within the UN system to have this responsibility. Both the General Assembly and the International Court of Justice (ICJ) also have responsibilities in this area, and, as noted by Anne Peters, 'the different organs must observe the institutional balance and pay each other mutual due respect'(Peters 2012, 767).

In addition, within the international or global constitutional order, the UNSC might seem to be an 'executive' body in accordance with the traditional division of powers in a legal system; yet there is nothing in the Charter that labels the UNSC an executive. If considered in a constitutional sense, the Charter is clear that the UNSC must report to the General Assembly, a seemingly innocuous provision but one that has, in fact, important constitutional implications. The provision that the UNSC issue regular reports to the General Assembly was inserted by the smaller states which wished to ensure that the Council understood its role as 'a trustee of the membership (or of the international community) institutionalised in the General Assembly, which must render its "accounts" to the trust givers' (Peters 2012, 777). This suggests that the UNSC was designed to be constrained in some broad sense by its institutional relationship to the General Assembly. Further, while the UNSC is not formally subject to judicial review by the ICJ or any other organ, the 2008 Kadi decision by the European Court of Justice points to the importance of judicial review in order to ensure the UNSC adheres to its responsibilities.[3] There are, of course, numerous legal and political complexities of this case, but it provides one instance of how the UNSC was somehow subject to review by a judicial body.

The Charter alone does not determine the role of the UNSC; as with any 'living' constitution, the international political and legal order is shaped by the practices of those who compose it. In the case of the UNSC, its practices have evolved as a result of various political realities, primarily the Cold War. Since the end of the Cold War, the UNSC has become active across a range of issues and conflicts. This activity can be interpreted in numerous ways; for some it represents the achievement of the UNSC's responsibilities in the international order, while for others it constitutes a form of global 'mission creep' in which the UNSC has increased its powers to the detriment of other agents (Fraser and Popovski 2014). The authority of the UNSC also relates to the power and legitimacy of those states that compose it, particularly the Permanent Members of the United Nations Security Council (P5). For some theorists, the UNSC's authority relies on the fact that it is controlled by these powers, which they claim have a kind of *de facto* authority for governing the international order.[4] Others argue that the P5's powers actually undermine the authority of the UNSC by delegitimising its mandate and practice, a position often linked to calls for reform of the UNSC (Imber 2006).

202 A. Hehir and A.F. Lang Jr

The emergence of new institutions in the international order can both challenge and reinforce the authority of institutions such as the UNSC. For instance, the ICC now shares the responsibility for creating peace and security in the international political and legal order. The ICC's legitimacy does not rely on the UNSC as the war crimes tribunals in the former Yugoslavia and Rwanda did, as they were created by UNSC resolutions. Instead, the ICC arose from a treaty giving it a firm foundation in the international legal order. But there are links between the two institutions which derive in part from their responsibility for maintaining international peace and security. Articles 13 and 16 of the Rome Statute create the link between the two: Article 13 allows the UNSC to refer cases to the ICC, while Article 16 allows the UNSC to defer the pursuit of a case or situation in order to allow other mechanisms of peace-making to be pursued. The two institutions have seen a range of interactions, some of which we describe below.

Embedded selectivity: R2P and the ICC

The international legal and political order is constituted by rules which arise from both formal processes (e.g. treaties) and informal understandings (e.g. diplomatic practice). In order for the system to function, however, these rules need enforcement. Importantly, the enforcement of the law and the punishment of those who violate it is not simply about those individual instances; over time, practices of enforcement and punishment shape the wider legal and political order. It is our contention that while the international legal and political order does indeed reveal moments of law enforcement and punishment, the present conflation of institutional responsibilities, which is actually further enabled by the discourse of R2P, is consolidating an unjust political and legal order. The argument we make here, therefore, is directed toward how a revised international legal and political order might both ensure the protection of individuals and also create a more just political and legal order.

Debates have long raged on whether international law is actually law. The crux of these debates for the purposes of this chapter is not really the question whether international law exists, but rather whether it works. There are myriad international laws on a vast array of subjects; indeed, such is its scope, life as we know it would be impossible without international law. Yet international law is judged primarily on its efficacy in two particular areas: the use of force and the protection of human rights. While the routine adherence to the majority of international laws goes unremarked, the occasional and 'spectacular' violations of international law in these areas generate outrage. The 2003 invasion of Iraq and the murderous campaign waged since 2011 by President Assad, for example, naturally lead people to wonder 'where is international law?'.

The existence of a body mandated to enforce law – by both judging that a law has been violated and determining the nature of the requisite punishment for this infraction – is essential for any legal system. Of profound importance for the functioning of this body, and indeed the legal system over which it presides, is its legitimacy, which is dependent upon its perceived impartiality and record of practice (Falk, Juergensmeyer and Popovski 2012).

At present the international body serving this function is the UNSC; as we discuss later this is fundamentally problematic because the UNSC does not constitute an impartial judicial body. Though mandated to act on behalf of the international community of states, the UNSC is very obviously a body of states with particular national interests which have often inhibited the enforcement of the very international laws the body is charged with enforcing.

If the enforcement of law – domestic or international – is evidently a function of political interest, then this has grave consequences not just for the legal system, but for order amongst the subjects of this system. Arbitrary and politicised law enforcement breeds contempt for the legal system amongst its subjects, who are naturally inclined to determine that their safety and survival is dependent on their own initiative rather than the higher authority to which they are formally bound. By opting out of the legal system – formally or not – states may certainly have more formal freedom, but in practice this freedom will be repeatedly violated by other free-riders, thus precipitating a world order that is 'chaotic and incomprehensible' (Koskenniemi 2006, 69). Therefore, as Hans Kelsen noted, the manner in which law is enforced is 'the essential stage in any legal procedure' and of paramount importance to the health and efficacy of the legal regime, especially at the international level:

> As long as it is not possible to remove from the interested states the prerogative to answer the question of law and transfer it once and for all to an impartial authority, namely, an international court, any further progress on the way to the pacification of the world is absolutely excluded
>
> (Kelsen 1972, 13).

While Kelsen – and indeed many others – reflected on the manner in which international law was enforced in a number of key areas, our focus here is on the enforcement of international law with respect to human rights.

In the contemporary era, R2P and the ICC have become the two most prominent institutions of international human rights enforcement. R2P seeks to prevent and, more controversially, halt human rights violations, while the ICC is orientated towards punishing those who violate human rights. Therefore, while R2P and the ICC deal with different legal areas – with the former oriented towards emergency response and the latter retrospective punishment – both share a number of commonalities. Most obviously both deal with egregious human rights violations: R2P's remit is the 'four crimes' outlined in Paragraph 138 of the 2005 World Summit Outcome Document, namely genocide, war crimes, ethnic cleansing and crimes against humanity; while the ICC is mandated to try those accused of genocide, crimes against humanity and war crimes.[5] Secondly, both relate to 'law enforcement': R2P is analogous to the emergency response provisions within domestic legal systems – such as most obviously the role of the police; while the ICC clearly parallels the role played by domestic courts. This is not to suggest, of course, that the international legal order is comparable with any existing domestic legal order; rather the point is that a normative legal order – domestic or international – would comprise both an emergency response component and a judicial punishment process as part of the means by which the laws are enforced. Finally, the efficacy of both is essentially dependent upon the same body; the UNSC. As we discuss below, the manner in which R2P and the ICC are operationalised depends upon the acquiescence of the UNSC, and more specifically the P5.

Law enforcement, punishment and R2P

In 2005 two paragraphs of the World Summit *Outcome Document* made reference to R2P; in essence, they stated that individual states had certain responsibilities towards their own citizens and also that the international community had a concomitant responsibility to act if the host state was unable or unwilling to abide by this responsibility. While this commitment was certainly laudable, it is hardly new (Bassiouni 2009; Peters 2009, 513; Stahn 2007, 99; Reinhold 2010, 55). Each of the 'four crimes' was illegal long before 2005; indeed, there is no shortage of international laws proscribing human rights abuses (Landman 2005, 14). Likewise, that the international community had the right to intervene in the domestic affairs of states to prevent and/or halt these crimes was also established – and indeed actualised – before 2005 (Chesterman 2011, 1; Hehir 2013, 137). Of course, as is well known the enforcement of international human rights law has been erratic; indeed it was this inconsistency that the International Commission on Intervention and State Sovereignty (ICISS) explicitly sought to address.

This inconsistency stems from the institutional structure of the UN and specifically the power – particularly the veto – wielded by the P5. The only viable legal basis for external intervention in the domestic affairs of a state – without the state's consent – is Chapter VII of the Charter, which is dependent on the assent of the UNSC. Unsurprisingly, then, the enforcement of international law – specifically the use of force for the protection of human rights – is prey to the political exigencies of the P5. The powers vested in the P5 were consciously designed so as to reflect the realities of power in international politics and orient the organisation towards the maintenance of order rather than the pursuit of justice (Berdal 2003, 7; Bosco 2009, 10–38; Bourantonis 2007, 6; White 2004, 645; Mertus 2009, 98; Simpson 2004, 68). R2P has not altered in any way the institutional arrangements for enforcing international law or the remit of the P5, nor has it created an alternative source of authority to the UNSC, and therefore law enforcement remains dependent on the political will and national interests of the P5.

The absence of legal reform is not seen, however, as problematic by many of R2P's advocates, who argue that R2P is 'revolutionary' because it creates a framework for ostensibly irresistible moral advocacy (Feinstein 2007; Scheffer 2009, 95). R2P has become, in essence, a means by which normative pressure is consolidated and political will mobilised so as to change the decision-making calculus of the P5 (International Coalition for RtoP 2015; Bellamy 2009, 119; Evans 2008, 223).

Legal reform is rejected by many as utopian; the ostensibly more realistic strategy is to craft arguments that will convince states to abide by their previous commitments to respect human rights (Evans 2008, 137).

Thus at present the existing mechanisms by which R2P is enforced remain a matter of political will which is by definition transitory and context-specific. While a case can be made that democratic states are somewhat receptive to moral advocacy – though this is far from assured, as the 2003 invasion of Iraq and the non-intervention in Darfur attest (Hehir 2008, 76-96) – the willingness of China and Russia to accede to humanitarian appeals is surely negligible. As these states become increasingly more powerful, the efficacy of moral advocacy will arguably diminish (Hehir and Murray 2012, 387).

R2P's endorsement of the present system echoes, therefore, the powers vested in the sheriff, as noted in the introduction, where the legal authority to act is not accompanied by any duty; the UNSC *may* take action but it is under no obligation to do so and thus the P5 merely have a 'discretionary entitlement' (Berman 2011, 161). Thus, somewhat perversely, the centrality of UNSC authorisation in the application of R2P has in fact further consolidated the P5's primacy, despite its powers actually constituting one of the original catalysts for the ICISS's proposal.

Punitive practices play a role in the law enforcement process, but they also play a central role in creating political order. One can see this in the traditional liberal conception of a constitutional order in which the three parts of the political system – legislator, executive and judiciary – create rules and then enforce them. In this model, the legislative body makes the law, the judge determines if an individual had violated the law leading to the imposition of a sentence, and the executive carries out that sentence. Within that model, it might seem as if the legislator alone creates the order through the creation of rules that define it. But the related judicial role of finding parties guilty and determining their sentence is also part of the creation of a just political order.[6] The judgment of a judicial body regarding both how to interpret the law and the sanction applied when the law is violated plays a crucial role in the political order that emerges.

A slightly different way to see this traditional constitutional division of labour can be found in an early essay by John Rawls, where he argued that there are two types of rules: those that justify a practice as a whole, and those that justify a particular application of that practice. He uses this distinction to make the case that punishment can be justified in both utilitarian and retributive ways. The practice of punishment as a means of enforcing justice in a society – that is, as an institution – is utilitarian. But the particular application of punishment in specific cases – the action of punishment – is best understood as retributive. One way to see this distinction is through the different roles played by a legislator and a judge. The legislator constitutes the political through law making, with a focus on the good for the society as a whole. The judge, while seeing his or her role as ensuring that justice is done to this individual, also plays a role in constructing that larger order, although this might not be obvious at first. In so doing, both look to the political community, albeit, as Rawls notes, one toward its future and one towards its past (Rawls 1969, 108). Punishment, as oriented toward violations taking place in the past, constructs the future of the political society.[7]

If law enforcement includes both acts of protecting those whose rights are being violated in situations of conflict and the punishment of those doing the violating, a properly constituted legal order would be one in which these functions are undertaken by different institutions. In an ideal world, the UNSC should be engaged in duty-oriented practices that entail the protection dimension: halting violations taking place and enabling the capture or arrest of those engaged in those violations. But in order to protect the rights of the accused and, more importantly perhaps, to protect the wider international legal order, a different institution should be tasked with trying and sentencing – i.e. punishing – those who are found guilty of such violations. The roles of these two institutions should be somehow connected. But the current connection between the institutions allows the UNSC to play an active role in the punitive process by giving it the ability to make choices about where the ICC should be active, and it gives the UNSC the ability to halt a prosecution that the ICC prosecutor or a state party wishes to pursue. The reason for the ability of the UNSC to play a role in the prosecutor's decisions seems to rely on the assumption that only by co-opting the powerful would the ICC be able to function. The reason for the deferral role is to allow a peace process to be pursued without the interference of judicial activities. Yet the decision to give the UNSC the power of deferral was a highly contested one at the Rome Conference. According to William Schabbas, the debate became in part about the powers of the P5 and their ability to control what should have been a completely independent judicial institution (Schabbas 2001, 65–66). At this moment of creating the Court, many could already see the potential for the UNSC to politicise its activities. The deferral role has some political logic; there may indeed be times when the blind pursuit of justice will interfere with the possibility of political solutions. The active prosecutorial role, however, seems less well grounded in long-term political logic and seems designed only to appease the powerful states in order to allow the ICC to function.

The emergence of R2P, however, has given the UNSC even more power to combine these roles than the ICC statutes allow. As we will make clear below, because its normative agenda does not include any limits on the UNSC, and because the interventions that might be undertaken under the guise of R2P can quickly conflate protection and punishment – as was clearly the case with respect to Libya – the current formulation of the principle will (potentially) give even more power to the UNSC to override the institutional responsibilities of the ICC.

R2P has rarely been defended as a punitive mode of intervention by any of its proponents. Yet it is our contention that, in order to ensure that states uphold their responsibilities to their own citizens, punitive measures are sometimes necessary. Moreover, the few times that R2P has been invoked by the Security Council or individual states in justifying a military action, a discourse of punishment *has* appeared. While interventions are not generally described as punitive – indeed, it is rare that punishment as a formal legal or even political concept is employed in international affairs – a number of international political practices linked to R2P have strong punitive dimensions, the most obvious one being economic sanctions (Onuf 1974). Military intervention, even when labelled humanitarian, can also be punitive. Especially when interventions are undertaken in response to harms inflicted on a population and when the intended outcome is 'bringing perpetrators to justice' and/or 'regime change' rather than simply providing humanitarian aid, interventions look and sound more like punitive measures than purely humanitarian ones.[8]

The ICC, like any judicial body, has its own selectivity issues; cases will be pursued only when prosecutors, state parties or the UNSC agree. But by giving the UNSC a role in deciding which cases to pursue, the power of the UNSC is further increased. R2P alone, of course, does not create this problem, for the P5 have their own reasons for seeking to increase their power in the international legal and political order. What we are arguing here is that R2P further increases the power of the UNSC by giving it the ability to punish in situations of conflict, a responsibility that is best left with the ICC, where it can better conform to liberal norms of a fair trial.

In what follows, we demonstrate how – through a focus on cases drawn from the Arab Uprisings – the use (and non-use) of R2P has contributed to a political and legal order that increases the power of the UNSC to the detriment of the wider international legal and political order.

Arab Spring

The UNSC's response to the crisis in Libya was unusually swift, and characterised, at least initially, by unprecedented collective unity. While some criticised the intervention for a variety of reasons (Kuperman 2013; McKinney 2012; Walzer 2011), the focus here is not on the merits of the intervention itself but on the means by which it was sanctioned, and the broader context.

If China and/or Russia had chosen to veto Resolution 1973 the intervention would not have occurred; evidence suggests President Obama in particular considered UNSC approval to be a *sine qua non*. What then explains the Chinese and Russian abstentions? The most plausible explanation relates to the position adopted by the African Union (AU) and especially the Arab League; neither China nor Russia wished to block an initiative which these regional organisations supported. This was reflected in the Chinese statement; 'We also attach great importance to the position of African countries and the AU. In view of this ... China abstained' (UNSC 2011, 5). Russia also explained its abstention was an expression of support for the Arab League's call for action (ibid. 8). Indeed, according to Gareth Evans the Arab League's support 'was absolutely crucial in ensuring that there was both a majority on the Council and no exercise of the veto by Russia or China' (Evans 2011) while another scholar stated that without its support, 'China and Russia would have certainly vetoed Resolution 1973' (Bellamy 2011, 263). It is also clear that the US's position was greatly influenced by the AU's but most particularly the Arab League's stance (Clinton 2011).

The position of the Arab League – and the members of the Gulf Cooperation Council (GCC) in particular – on the Arab Uprisings has been far from consistent (Colombo 2013), and the reasoning behind their support for military action against Libya points towards obviously geopolitical motives (Bellamy and Williams 2011, 825, 842). This inconsistency was most evident in Bahrain. While the Arab League's statement on 12 March championed the right of the Libyan people 'to fulfil their demands and build their own future and institutions in a democratic framework' (League of Arab States 2012, 2), just two days later, acting through the GCC, Saudi Arabia and Qatar sent troops into Bahrain to help the embattled monarchy crush protesters calling for democratic change. A 'campaign of retribution' followed as the foreign troops, primarily from Saudi Arabia, enabled the government to escalate its draconian crack-down (International Crisis Group 2011, 4). Despite this, Western states, the US in particular, criticised the violence 'relatively mildly' and supported the Crown Prince's promises to reform. The Bahrain Centre for Human Rights claimed that the desultory international response emboldened the Khalifa Monarchy; 'the authorities in Bahrain, due to the lack of international consequences, have no incentive to stop the human rights violations' (Bahrain Centre for Human Rights 2012).

The selectivity has been more obvious, however, with respect to the situation in Syria. To date it is estimated that over 191,000 people have died while over 11 million people – more than half of Syria's total population – have been displaced either internally or abroad (Cumming-Bruce 2014). There is no doubt it is overly simplistic to argue that the lack of military intervention in Syria[9] constitutes definitive evidence that the intervention in Libya was thus motivated by oil, geopolitics, etc. The situations are clearly different and the dynamics of Syria's relationship with key regional and international actors arguably militates against the kind of action taken against Libya. The charge of selectivity regarding Syria, however, should not focus only on Western states; while the US, UK and France have been denounced by many for failing to act robustly, the position of Russia, and to a lesser extent China, evidences a far more obviously inconsistent approach to abiding by R2P. Russia and China have four times vetoed resolutions on Syria yet in each case the draft resolutions sought only to impose modest economic and political sanctions against Assad's regime and certainly did not suggest intervention. Indeed, beyond just blocking international attempts to censure Syria, Russia has continued to supply the regime with offensive weaponry (Harding 2013).

This episode has troubling implications for R2P. Despite the various effusive declarations that it is a 'revolutionary' concept, R2P has obviously not inhibited Russia from engaging in a very public display of cynical geopolitics and neither has it forestalled division at the UNSC. As the situation continued to deteriorate throughout 2012, on 3 August the General Assembly took the unusual step of condemning the UNSC in a non-binding resolution (UN General Assembly 2012). In early August 2012, Kofi Annan stepped down as United Nations/League of Arab States Joint Special Envoy for the Syrian Crisis, decrying the 'finger-pointing and name-calling in the Security Council' which had impeded his efforts (UN News Centre 2012). The UNSC's response to the crisis was neither timely nor decisive, and this arguably cost innumerable lives; in her final speech to the UNSC as UN High Commissioner for Human Rights, Navi Pillay stated, 'greater responsiveness by this council would have saved hundreds of thousands of lives' (Pillay 2014). The manner in which the UNSC dealt with Syria certainly deflated the optimism which followed the 2011 intervention in Libya; as Evans noted, 'the shame and horror of Syria' has led to 'a real sense of disappointment' (Evans 2014).

Whether in the form of the Arab League's intervention in Bahrain, the West's shameful silence over this intervention, or Russia's policy of protecting Syria at the UNSC, the international response to the Arab Uprisings has alleviated the suffering of certain groups while ignoring the plight of others. Perversely, the power and international standing of NATO, the Arab League and Russia have arguably grown as a result of their various actions during the crises; each have at certain points shaped the 'international' response to the dominant concern of the day. Where actors have had their designs thwarted – as surely even the US and Russia at various times have – this has been a result of old-fashioned power politics rather than the influence of R2P. Thus, like the sheriff, the P5 consolidate their power with each enforcement action whilst remaining outside of a judicial review process. Like the sheriff, the P5's actions may be legal but they are of dubious legitimacy.

As we noted above, not only is the problem of UNSC its selectivity, but there is also a strong punitive dimension to the way in which R2P has been invoked in the context of UNSC action. Indeed, it is not simply that the UNSC makes R2P more punitive, but that R2P itself, as it is currently constituted, includes a punitive dimension. This means that invocations of the norm around debates about intervention soon become debates about punishing wrongdoers. In the case of the international community's response to the Arab Uprisings, we see this in both the intervention that did take place (Libya) and the one in which it did not (Syria). A year after the intervention in Libya, Benjamin Freidman wrote:

> One [reason to intervene] was to show other dictators that the international community would not tolerate the violent suppression of dissenters. That reverse domino theory has obviously failed. If Qaddafi's fate taught neighbouring leaders like Bashar al-Assad anything, it is to brutally nip opposition movements in the bud before they coalesce, attract foreign arms and air support, and kill you—or, if you're lucky, ship you off to the Hague.
>
> (Friedman 2012)

It seems evident that the intervention in Libya included both deterrent and retributive dimensions. Unlike others, though, this intervention targeted primarily the leadership, not just Qaddafi but members of his family.

UNSC Resolution 1973 was largely punitive; its operational clauses included five elements: 1) a deferral of the situation in Libya to the International Criminal Court (ICC); 2) an arms embargo; 3) a travel ban for those within the regime; 4) the freezing of assets of those in the regime; and 5) the creation of a sanctions committee to monitor compliance with the resolution. Of these five, only one, the arms embargo, was not explicitly punitive. The others all targeted the regime and the leadership of Libya. The intervention was hailed by supporters for both stopping atrocities and deferring future ones: 'Fulfilling the responsibility to protect involves identifying the scenarios whereby civilians may be the victims of mass atrocities, *adopting strategies to deter perpetrators from committing future crimes*, and crucially, employing protective strategies to halt current attacks' (International Coalition on R2P and Global Centre for the Responsibility to Protect 2011). A subsequent statement from the same organisation, again calling for intervention, implied more clearly a punitive logic: 'Behind the firm voice of the Arab League and its support for more forceful action lies the conviction that the Libyan regime *should face the consequences for its brutal actions*' (Global Centre for the Responsibility to Protect 2011).

Resolution 1973 set out the important operational clause of allowing 'all means necessary' for three objectives: 1) protect civilians; 2) create a no-fly zone; and 3) enforce the arms embargo. But, as became clear soon after military operations began, the mission of protecting civilians means not simply stopping harms against them but hurting those who are doing the harming; in other words, inflicting harm for violating a rule, the definition of punishment noted above. In a press conference on 8 April 2011, the deputy commander of the mission hinted at the punitive logic underlying the means of protecting civilians:

> On Wednesday, we engaged forces in central Libya including an air defence facility near Surt under our mission to protect civilians and civilian population areas. The pressure of NATO aircraft and the accuracy of our strikes continue to pressure those who would bring harm to innocent civilians.
>
> (Lungescu and Harding 2011)

On 27 June 2011, the ICC issued arrest warrants for three individuals charged with crimes against humanity: Muammar Gaddafi, Saif al-Islam Gaddafi and Abdullah al-Sanussi (ICC 2011). The indictment – designed to support the rebels against the Gaddafi regime (Aljazeera 2011) – relied primarily on events that took place in February 2011 surrounding the use of military force against protestors. When the ICC's arrest warrants were issued, NATO's spokesperson stated:

> The arrest warrants are yet another signal from the international community to the Qadhafi regime. Your place is on trial; not in power, in Tripoli. It is not for NATO to enforce that warrant. That is for the appropriate authorities … we have made clear from the start that there is no purely military solution. It's the combination of our continued military pressure and a reinforced political pressure that will bring about the transition to democracy that the Libyan people demand and deserve.
>
> (NATO 2011)

Note the spokesperson affirms that the arrest warrants are part of the same strategy as the military campaign, yet makes it clear that the military campaign is not about arresting individuals. The idea that the intervention and the ICC could work in parallel had been part of the larger intervention; as US Secretary of Defence, Robert Gates stated at a press conference in Cairo, 'the international community has a number of "hammers in its toolbox", one of which is the ICC' (US Department of Defense 2011).

On 20 October 2011 Qaddafi was killed by rebel soldiers. Only two days later, the NATO Secretary General announced the 'liberation of Libya'. While NATO had insisted on keeping itself separate from the ICC indictment and tried to keep its focus on protection of civilians rather than punishment, the fact that the intervention ended almost as soon as Qaddafi was killed suggests that his death – or punishment of sorts – fulfilled their mission. The wider discourse of the intervention and the fact that the intervention ended after the death of Qaddafi points to the overarching punitive nature of the intervention, especially when coupled with ICC indictment. While the case against Qaddafi's son and al-Sanussi continues, the punitive element of the intervention itself seems clear here.

While there has not been an intervention against Assad's forces in Syria, the arguments being made in support of intervention parallel the punitive logic of the Libyan intervention. The US government's initial response to Assad's use of chemical weapons called for accountability in language stronger than most diplomatic statements; Secretary of State John Kerry argued in his press conference of 26 August 2013 that 'there is accountability for the use of chemical weapons so that it never happens again … President Obama believes there must be accountability for those who would use the world's most heinous weapons against the world's most vulnerable people' (Kerry 2013). While accountability is not necessarily the same as punishment, the primary means of holding agents accountable in a political system is by punishing those who violate the rules. Further, in the case of Syria, it would appear that the threat of punishment may have prompted the regime to respond, as it soon decided to turn over its chemical weapons materials to the international community.

In response to the call for a punitive intervention in Syria, some international legal scholars have emphasised the illegality of punishment or the related ideas of reprisals and countermeasures in the current international legal order. One analyst, echoing the analysis here, though taking a directly opposed position, argued that punitive intervention violates the primary legal structure concerning the use of force, the UN Charter (Moore 2013).

A different account, also from an international legal position, argues that the current international legal order does not allow for the idea of state crime and so it cannot support the idea of punitive intervention (Stahn 2013). Both these accounts suggest that non-lethal modes of intervention would be preferred to punitive intervention. In the case of Syria, though, it is difficult to see what this would mean. As suggested by the fact that the regime dropped its chemical weapons programme in part because of the pressures placed on it by the Obama administration, perhaps one can conclude that the deterrent threat of punishment accomplished some good.

In addition to the deterrent nature of a possible punitive intervention, there are also suggestions for a retributive one. In August 2011 the UN Human Rights Council established an Independent International Commission of Inquiry on the Syrian Arab Republic with a mandate to 'identify those responsible with a view of ensuring that perpetrators of violations, including those that may constitute crimes against humanity, are held accountable' (Independent International Commission of Inquiry on the Syrian Arab Republic 2014). Navi Pillay, stated in December 2013 that the Commission's findings made it clear that the regime would be held accountable and that she believed members should be tried before the ICC (BBC News 2013). In January 2013, Switzerland proposed that the UNSC should refer the case of Syria to the ICC in a letter signed by both the United Kingdom and France. Philippe Sands argued that the proposal to try members of the regime before the ICC is a 'justified gamble' (Sands 2013). Though not interventions, these developments suggest that a wider discourse of retributive punishment surrounds and informs the international response to Syria.

Reform

Both R2P and the ICC emerged during a period when there were widespread calls for reform of the UN; NATO's unilateral intervention in Kosovo in 1999, coupled with the fallout from the Rwandan genocide, had created a consensus, albeit heterogeneous, in favour of reform, particularly of the UNSC. Yet the ICISS did not substantively address the very issue that arguably impelled its formation, namely the question of authority (Focarelli 2008, 191; Stahn 2007, 99).[10] Thus arguably the most concerted effort in the modern era aimed at reforming the manner in which the international community responds to intra-state crises culminated in literally no alteration to the existing discredited legal and political system. Likewise, while the ICC was initially lauded as major step forward for international law and the punishment of human rights violators, the court's functioning and capacity continue to be impeded by the constitutional competencies afforded to the UNSC.

Not reforming the UNSC has a number of negative consequences. First, as the reaction of the 'international community' to a particular crisis remains in essence dependent on the disposition of the UNSC, the key factor in determining how violations of human rights are addressed and/or punished remains the political will of the P5. Thus perpetrators of systematic human rights abuses can shield themselves from external censure if they have cultivated an alliance with one of the veto-wielding P5. Despite the emergence of R2P and the ICC, therefore, certain oppressive regimes have continued to focus on cultivating an alliance with a member of the P5 rather than change their illegal behaviour. In any system where legal censure is not guaranteed – either because of the judiciary's ineffectiveness, its lack of coercive capacity or its susceptibility to corruption and/ or the influence of power – potential law breakers are naturally less wary of breaking the law (Hurrell 2005).

Another adverse consequence is that the UNSC and the ICC continue to stand accused of impotence and/or hypocrisy. Various commentators have derided the UNSC and the ICC for their failure to act against Assad in Syria (Freedland 2014). Their capacity to act, however, has been hamstrung by their respective constitutional competencies which inhibit their capacity for independent action; as discussed earlier, the UN High Commissioner for Human Rights published a report in late 2013 suggesting that the Assad regime's tactics amounted to war crimes which could come under the purview of the ICC. Yet the next stage – enforcement/punishment – was stalled because it was a matter for the P5 to determine how to respond (BBC News 2013). Additionally, when either organisation *has* acted, they have been criticised for engaging in hypocritical *realpolitik*, and being handmaidens to power. While the UN and the ICC are both imperfect institutions, erosion of support for these primary bastions of international law, multilateralism and universal jurisprudence undoubtedly constitutes a setback for those who support the evolution of a world order which places a primary emphasis on the protection of individual human rights.

We consider the *status quo* untenable and reform essential. The problem is certainly not the absence of laws proscribing human rights violations – there are few areas *not* covered by international law (Hakimi 2010, 343-344; Landman 2005, 14) – nor is there a problem with respect to either the principle of international censure or a lack of an international judicial body. The primary problem, as outlined in earlier sections, is the process by which human rights laws are upheld and violators punished (Bassiouni 2009, 37). The problem can thus be located primarily at the point of enforcement; thus the requisite reform need not require a complete transformation of the present legal order. The starting point would be to build on the provisions related to R2P in the 2005 World Summit Outcome Document and the vast corpus of human rights law, and consolidate these into a legally binding treaty which reiterates the proscription against various forms of human rights abuses and, crucially, outlines both the point at which these abuses are to be considered so severe as to warrant external involvement of some kind – though not necessarily military intervention – and the manner in which this decision would be taken, by whom, and through which legal processes. These processes would, we feel, necessitate the establishment of an independent and accountable judicial body with the power to determine both that a violation of the law has occurred and the nature of the resultant punishment. The nature of the punishment would, of course, potentially vary – as is the case with respects to judicial decisions domestically – and allow for judicial decisions which reflect the reality that in certain contexts particular types of punitive action – most obviously military intervention – would potentially do more harm than good. Through the imposition of alternative measures – including sanctions, suspension of UN membership, travel bans and ICC referrals – violators would incur punishment of some form. Additionally, and crucially, the very availability of these punitive sanctions would serve as a deterrent.

This judicial body could also, we contend, come into being without necessitating the dissolution of the UNSC; conceivably it could be triggered into action in situations where the UNSC is demonstrably deadlocked despite consensus in the General Assembly in favour of punitive action, as was very obviously the case with respect to Syria. The new body would therefore challenge the UNSC's 'unconditional exclusive legitimacy' rather than its legitimacy *per se* (Buchanan and Keohane 2011, 41). A further consideration would be the establishment of a military force within the UN at the disposal of the new body mandated to undertake coercive action should states be unwilling to deploy their troops. Such a force would be used only in very rare cases; there would need to be an atrocity of a grave magnitude, no alternative diplomatic means, deadlock at the UNSC and the unavailability of member state forces. The number of cases where this could happen would, we feel, be very small. Nonetheless, such a force – which has long been suggested – would potentially redress the unedifying spectacle of inertia in the face of egregious human suffering and its very existence would act as a deterrent in itself.

The goal avowed here can of course be criticised, not unreasonably, as utopian. That said, we offer the following rejoinders; first, the primary aim here is to demonstrate that the existing system – even post-R2P and the ICC – remains fundamentally corrupted by the constitutional competencies of the UNSC, specifically the P5. Achieving agreement around this claim would constitute progress as it would hopefully impel those concerned about human rights to desist from engaging with strategies which, we feel, are doomed to fail, and instead work on determining how the reforms we advance in general terms might be implemented in practice. Additionally, the temper of the international community is demonstrably in favour of reform; the UNSC is widely acknowledged as lacking legitimacy in terms of its membership and competencies as reflected in the statements from the General Assembly, the UN Secretary-General and the general trend amount commentators and academics. Our call for reform is not therefore an aberration, but rather is reflective of many voices in the international community. The international system is, famously, very different from the domestic legal system and thus the institutional configuration and theoretical foundations – normative and real – of domestic legal orders naturally do not equate with that which exists internationally; yet to assert this as a counter to those, like us, who advocate legal reform is somewhat paradoxical, as it suggests that the normative systemic configuration cannot be achieved because it does not presently exist. We are certainly not alone in suggesting alternative means of improving the international response to intra-state crises and the commission of mass atrocities; as Susan Meyer argued, 'without major changes in the UN, R2P will go the way of the Genocide Convention' (Meyer 2009, 56).[11]

Conclusion

R2P as understood by some of its defenders and as framed in some UNSC resolutions conflates the punitive and law enforcement functions. When the UNSC engages in actions that conflate law enforcement, protection and punishment, it might contribute to a peaceful resolution in a particular case, but in the longer term such actions reconstitute the legal and political order in such a way that the UNSC's powers grow unchecked. So, while we agree that there must be some role for the UNSC in the maintenance of international peace and security, we also believe that this role must be part of a better defined legal and political order with a strengthened judicial structure, organised around both the ICC and the ICJ.

Many hold that R2P has increased the chances that the UNSC will act and that this constitutes progress when compared with bygone eras when – ostensibly – there was consistently no response (Weiss 2011, 5; Badescu 2010). It is our contention, however, that R2P entrenches the very structural problems that have contrived to produce the poor record advocates of R2P sought to redress. At present R2P facilitates a world order in which certain agents – specifically the P5 – can selectively increase their own power and still fail to uphold the protection of individuals. This deleterious selectivity was readily apparent during the UNSC's response to the Arab Uprisings, particularly with respect to the situations in Libya, Bahrain and Syria.

A fundamental principle underpinning any legal order is the removal of selectivity from law enforcement, and to that end the constitutional separation of the judiciary from the executive, lest we have the sheriff-like scenario whereby the three different functions of law in a political order – legislation, judgment and enforcement – are conflated in one agent. At present – even post R2P – the international legal system comprises just such a constitutional conflation; the UNSC thus operates as a 'political core in a legal regime' (White 2004, 645, 666). So long as this remains the case, the enforcement of international law will be compromised. While R2P and the ICC certainly constitute progressive developments, there remains what Anne Peters terms a 'missing link', which is precisely the gap between law and enforcement (Peters 2009, 535).

We readily acknowledge that the proposals we advance are not necessarily going to be adopted in the near future. But we do see these as an improvement on the current calls for strengthening R2P, which fail to take into account this longer-term political and legal critique. We find the idea that we must submit to the *status quo* because reform is unrealistic (Bellamy 2014, 11) unconvincing; that the international and domestic are very different legal orders is axiomatic; that they should – and will always – be so is fatalistic and, in essence, unhelpful. There have been myriad proposals advanced which advocate reform of the international legal system (Centre for UN Reform Education 2014) – and of the powers of the UNSC in particular – all of which essentially cohere with Hans Kelsen's conception of the current system as 'primitive' and but a 'stage in an evolutionary process' (Kelsen 1945, 338). Our contribution has been not to provide a detailed proposal, but rather to argue, on the basis of the fate of R2P and the ICC during the Arab Uprisings, that those concerned with human rights protection must accept that any proposals that seek to redress the appalling record of international responses to intra-state crises will fail if they do not aim to reform the current legal system.

Notes

1 This chapter was first published as an article in the journal *Criminal Law Forum*, see Hehir A. and Lang A. (2015) "The Impact of the Security Council on the Efficacy of the International Criminal Court and the Responsibility to Protect", *Criminal Law Forum*, 26(1), 153–179. It is reprinted with permission of Springer Science+Business Media.
2 We acknowledge, of course, that in some contexts sheriffs undertook their duties in conformity with the rule of law, such as seeking warrants for arrest and ensuring they did not expand their institutional power. The physical location of the sheriff, cut off from any other legal institutions, meant that in almost all cases his actions would result

in his power being increased in relation to those he governed. Further, we recognise that the term sheriff derives from older sources in English law where it had a different institutional relationship to the orders of law.

3 There are numerous discussions of the Kadi Case in law and politics. A good introduction to some of the key issues can be found in Wessel (2008).

4 See, for instance, D. Lake, *Hierarchy in International Relations*, who argues that the US has legitimate international authority because of its provision of public goods in the international system. G.J. Ikenberry makes a related point, arguing that the US has played a key role in advancing a liberal world order and so should be considered authoritative in some broad sense at the global level.

5 The ICC is also tasked with prosecuting violations of the law of aggression, but this remains a controversial crime. The ICC has sought to give more precision to the definition of the crime of aggression in its 2010 Review Conference, but it is unlikely that individuals will be brought before the Court for this crime in the near future. Moreover, because of its contested status, it tends not to be seen as part of the international legal framework in which human rights and international criminal law intersect. Hence it is largely outside the concerns of our analysis here.

6 These roles are simplified here, of course. The judicial body plays a central role in interpreting rules through its appellate function, in the US Supreme Court, or as a court of first instance, as in the German Constitutional Court. When it comes to sentencing, moreover, the roles of different institutions might vary across different contexts; for instance, sentencing from guidelines might come from the legislator or perhaps from the executive. For a description of the relationship between sentencing and punishment, see Easton and Piper (2005).

7 An alternative conception of how punishment creates political and even social order can be found in Michel Foucault's account of how punishment became discipline. Foucault's assessment, while powerful and insightful, is less relevant for our purposes here, as we wish to propose alternative legal and political structures through which international punitive measures might be more just, something that Foucault would find more problematic; see Foucault (1977).

8 For a definition of, and empirical evidence for, the existence of punitive intervention, see Lang (2008).

9 In September 2014 the US led a bombing campaign against Islamic State (IS) militants in Iraq and Syria; while thus technically there has been a military intervention in Syria, this was undertaken in response to the threat posed by IS rather than in response to the humanitarian crisis in Syria.

10 For an alternative perspective see Glanville (2012).

11 See also Buchanan and Keohane (2011); Hurrell (2005, 30); Pattison (2010).

References

Aljazeera (2011) 'ICC Issues Gaddafi Arrest Warrant', al-Jezeera OnLine, 28 June (www.aljazeera.com/news/africa/2011/06/20116278148166670.html), accessed 1 August 2013.

Badescu C.G. (2010) *Humanitarian Intervention and the Responsibility to Protect*, Routledge, London.

Bahrain Centre for Human Rights (2012) *No Peace No Progress* (www.bahrainrights.org), accessed 25 August 2014.

Bassiouni C. (2009) 'Advancing the Responsibility to Protect Through International Criminal Justice', in Cooper R.H. and Kohler J.V. (eds), *Responsibility to Protect: The Global Moral Compact for the 21st Century*, Palgrave Macmillan, Basingstoke.

BBC News (2013) *UN Implicates Bashar al-Assad in Syria War Crimes*, BBC Online (www.bbc.co.uk/news/world-middle-east-25189834), accessed 7 February 2014.

Bellamy A. (2009) *Responsibility to Protect: The Global Effort to End Mass Atrocities*, Polity, London.

—— (2011) 'Libya and the Responsibility to Protect: The Exception and the Norm', *Ethics and International Affairs*, 25(3), 263–269

—— (2014) *The Responsibility to Protect: A Defence*, Oxford University Press, Oxford.

Bellamy A. and Williams P. (2011) 'The New Politics of Protection? Cote d'Ivoire, Libya and the Responsibility to Protect', *International Affairs*, 87(4), 825–850.

Berdal M. (2003) 'The UN Security Council: Ineffective but Indispensable', *Survival*, 45(2), 7–30.

Berman F. (2011) 'Moral Versus Legal Legitimacy', in Reed C. and Ryall D. (eds), *The Price of Peace*, Cambridge University Press, Cambridge.

Bosco D. (2009) *Five to Rule Them All: The United Nations Security Council and the Making of the Modern World*, Oxford University Press, Oxford.

Bourantonis D. (2007) *The History and Politics of Security Council Reform*, Routledge, London.

Buchanan A. and Keohane R. (2011) 'Precommitment Regimes for Intervention: Supplementing the Security Council', *Ethics and International Affairs*, 25(1), 41–63.

Centre for UN Reform Education (2014) 'Security Council Reform: Current Session of the General Assembly' (www.centerforunreform.org/?q=node/23), accessed 12 March 2014.

Chesterman S. (2011) '"Leading from Behind": The Responsibility to Protect, the Obama Doctrine, and Humanitarian Intervention after Libya', *Ethics and International Affairs*, 25(3), 279–285.

Clinton H. (2011) 'There's 'No Way' United States Will Take Unilateral Action in Libya', CBS News, 16 March (www.cbsnews.com/8301-503544_162-20043991-503544.html), accessed 2 September 2012.

Colombo S. (2013) 'The GCC Countries and the Arab Spring', in Davies J. (ed.), *The Arab Spring and Arab Thaw*, Ashgate, Surrey.

Cumming-Bruce N. (2014) 'Death Toll in Syria Estimated at 191,000', *The New York Times*, 22 August (www.nytimes.com/2014/08/23/world/middleeast/un-raises-estimate-of-dead-in-syrian-conflict-to-191000.html?_r=0), accessed 25 August 2014.

Easton S. and Piper C. (2005) *Sentencing and Punishment: The Quest for Justice*, Oxford University Press, Oxford.

Evans G. (2008) *The Responsibility to Protect: Ending Mass Atrocity Crimes Once and For All*, Brookings Institution Press, Washington, DC.

—— (2011) 'The RtoP Balance Sheet After Libya', 2 September (www.gevans.org/speeches/speech448%20interview%20RtoP.html), accessed 28 November 2011.

—— (2014) 'After Syria: The Future of the Responsibility to Protect', S.T. Lee Lecture, Institute for Advanced Study, Princeton, 12 March (www.gevans.org/speeches/speech545.html), accessed 2 June 2014

Falk R., Juergensmeyer M. and Popovski V. eds (2012) *Legality and Legitimacy in Global Affairs*, Oxford University Press, Oxford.

Feinstein L. (2007) 'Beyond Words: Building Will and Capacity to Prevent More Darfurs', *The Washington Post*, 26 January.

Focarelli C. (2008) 'The Responsibility to Protect Doctrine and Humanitarian Intervention: Too Many Ambiguities for a Working Doctrine', *Journal of Conflict and Security Law*, 13(2), 191–213.

Foucault M. (1977) *Discipline and Punish: The Birth of the Prison*, trans. by A. Sheridan, Vintage Books, New York.

Fraser T. and Popovski V. eds (2014) *The Security Council as Global Legislator*, Routledge, London.

Freedland J. (2014) 'Why it's a Good Time to be a Dictator Like Kim Jong-un', *The Guardian*, 18 February (www.theguardian.com/commentisfree/2014/feb/18/north-korea-good-time-to-be-dictator), accessed 14 March 2014.

Friedman B.H. (2012) 'Intervention in Libya and Syria isn't Humanitarian or Liberal', *The National Interest*, 5 April (http://nationalinterest.org/blog/the-skeptics/intervention-libya-syria-isn%E2%80%99t-humanitarian-or-liberal-6739), accessed 1 August 2013.

Glanville L. (2012) 'The Responsibility to Protect Beyond Borders', *Human Rights Law Review*, 12(1), 1–32.

Global Centre for the Responsibility to Protect (2011) 'Libya: Time for Decision', 11 March (www.responsibilitytoprotect.org/index.php/crises/190-crisis-in-libya/3323-global-centre-for-the-responsibility-to-protect-libya-time-for-decision), accessed 24 January 2014.

Gray C.S. (2004) *The Sheriff: America's Defense of the New World Order*, University Press of Kentucky, Lexington, KY.

Hakimi M. (2010) 'State Bystander Responsibility', *European Journal of International Law*, 21(2), 341–385.

Harding L. (2013) 'Syria's New Anti-aircraft Missiles Will Be Game-changing, Say Defence Analysts', *The Guardian*, 30 May (www.guardian.co.uk/world/2013/may/30/syria-anti-aircraft-missile-system), accessed 24 January 2014.

Hehir A. (2008) *Humanitarian Intervention After Kosovo*, Palgrave Macmillan, Basingstoke.

— (2013) 'Libya and The Responsibility to Protect: Resolution 1973 as Consistent with the Security Council's Record of Inconsistency', *International Security*, 38, 137–159.

Hehir A. and Murray R.W. (2012) 'Intervention in the Emerging Multipolar System: Why R2P will Miss the Unipolar Moment', *Journal of Intervention and Statebuilding*, 6(4), 387–406.

Hurrell A. (2005) 'Legitimacy and the Use of Force: Can the Circle be Squared?', in Armstrong D., Farrell T. and Maiguashca B. (eds), *Force and Legitimacy in World Politics*, Cambridge University Press, Cambridge.

ICC (2011) 'The Prosecutor vs Saif al-Islam Gaddafi and Abdullah Senussi', Document number ICC01/11-01/11 (www.icc-cpi.int/en_menus/icc/situations%20and%20cases/situations/icc0111/related%20cases/icc01110111/Pages/icc01110111.aspx), accessed 1 August 2013.

Ikenberry G. (2006) *Liberal Order and Imperial Ambition: Essays on American Power and International Order*, Polity Press, London.

Imber M. (2006) *UN Security Council Reform: 'From Here to Eternity'?*, Foreign Policy Centre, London.

Independent International Commission of Inquiry on the Syrian Arab Republic (2014) 'About the Commission', UN Human Rights Council (www.ohchr.org/EN/HRBodies/HRC/IICISyria/Pages/AboutCoI.aspx), accessed 7 February 2014.

International Coalition for RtoP (2015) 'Founding Purposes of the Coalition', (www.responsibilitytoprotect.org/index.php/about-coalition/founding-purposes), accessed 13 July 2015.

International Coalition on RtoP and the Global Centre for the Responsibility to Protect (2011) 'Open Letter to the UNSC', 4 March (www.responsibilitytoprotect.org/index.php/crises/190-crisis-in-libya/3239-international-coalition-for-rtop-and-global-centre-for-rtop-send-open-letter-to-the-security-council-on-the-situation-in-libya), accessed 24 January 2014.

International Crisis Group (2011) 'Popular Protests in the Middle East and North Africa: Bahrain's Rocky Road to Reform', *Middle East/North Africa Report* 111, 28 July.

Kelsen H. (1945) *General Theory of Law and State*, Harvard University Press, Cambridge, MA.

—— (1972) *Peace Through Law*, Harvard University Press, Cambridge, MA.

Kerry J. (2013) Press Conference, 26 August (http://politicalticker.blogs.cnn.com/2013/08/26/full-remarks-kerrys-pointed-remarks-on-syria/), accessed 31 August 2013.

Koskenniemi M. (2006) 'What is International Law For?', in Evans M. (ed.), *International Law*, Oxford University Press, Oxford.

Kuperman A. (2013) 'NATO's Intervention in Libya: A Humanitarian Success?', in Hehir A. and Murray R.W. (eds), *Libya, The Responsibility to Protect and the Future of Humanitarian Intervention*, Palgrave Macmillan, Basingstoke.

Lake D. (2009) *Hierarchy in International Relations*, Cornell University Press, Ithaca, NY.

Lang A.F. Jr (2008) *Punishment, Justice and International Relations: Ethics and Order after the Cold War*, Routledge, London.

Landman T. (2005) *Studying Human Rights*, Routledge, London.

League of Arab States (2012) *The Outcome of the Council of the League of Arab States Meeting at the Ministerial Level in its Extraordinary Session on the Implications of the Current Events in Libya and the Arab Position*, Cairo, 12 March (http://responsibilitytoprotect.org/Arab%20League%20Ministerial%20level%20statement%2012%20march%202011%20-%20english.pdf), accessed 25 September 2014.

Lungescu O. and Harding Rear Admiral R. (2011) 'Press Briefing on Events Concerning Libya', 8 April (www.nato.int/cps/en/natolive/opinions_72150.htm), accessed 24 January 2014.

McKinney C. (2012) *The Illegal War on Libya*, Clarity, Atlanta, GA.

Mertus J. (2009) *The United Nations and Human Rights*, Routledge, London.

Meyer S. (2009) 'In Our Interest: The Responsibility to Protect', in Cooper R.H. and Kohler J.V. (eds), *Responsibility to Protect: The Global Moral Compact for the 21st Century*, Palgrave Macmillan, Basingstoke.

Moore J. (2013) 'Punitive Military Strikes in Syria Risk Inhumane Intervention', OUP Blog, 2 September (http://blog.oup.com/2013/09/syria-us-military-strikes-international-law-pil), accessed 7 February 2014.

NATO (2011) 'Press briefing on Libya', 28 June (www.nato.int/cps/en/natolive/opinions_75808.htm), accessed 24 January 2014.

Onuf N. (1974) *Reprisals: Rituals, Rules, Rationales*, Centre for International Studies, Princeton, NJ.

Pattison J. (2010) *Humanitarian Intervention and the Responsibility to Protect*, Oxford University Press, Oxford.

Peters A. (2009) 'Humanity as the A and Ω of Sovereignty', *European Journal of International Law*, 20(3), 513–544.

—— (2012) 'Article 24', in Simma B. et al. (eds), *The Charter of the United Nations: A Commentary*, 3rd edn, vol. I, Oxford University Press, Oxford.

Pillay N. (2014) 'UN Human Rights Chief Criticises UN Over Global Conflicts', *The Guardian*, 22 August (www.theguardian.com/world/2014/aug/22/un-human-rights-chief-criticises-security-council-over-global-conflicts), accessed 25 August 2014.

Rawls J. (1969) 'Two Concepts of Rules', in Acton H.B. (ed.), *The Philosophy of Punishment: Collected Papers*, Macmillan, London.

Reinhold T. (2010) 'The Responsibility to Protect: Much Ado About Nothing?', *Review of International Studies*, 36(S1), 55–78.

Sands P. (2013) 'Referring Syria to the International Criminal Court is a "Justified Gamble"', *The Guardian*, 16 January (www.theguardian.com/commentisfree/2013/jan/16/syria-international-criminal-court-justified-gamble), accessed 7 February 2013.

Schabbas W. (2001) *An Introduction to the International Criminal Court*, Cambridge University Press, Cambridge.

Scheffer D. (2009) 'Atrocity Crimes: Framing the Responsibility to Protect', in Cooper R.H. and Kohler J.V. (eds), *Responsibility to Protect: The Global Moral Compact for the 21st Century*, Palgrave Macmillan, Basingstoke, 77–89.

Simpson (2004) *Great Powers and Outlaw States*, Cambridge University Press, Cambridge.

Stahn C. (2007) 'Responsibility to Protect: Political Rhetoric or Emerging Legal Norm?', *American Journal of International Law*, 101(1), 99–120.

—— (2013) 'Syria and the Semantics of Intervention, Aggression and Punishment', EJIL Talk, 19 September (www.ejiltalk.org/syria-and-the-semantics-of-intervention-aggression-and-punishment/), accessed 4 February 2014.

UN General Assembly (2012) 124th Plenary Meeting, 3 August (www.un.org/en/ga/search/view_doc.asp?symbol=A/66/PV.124), accessed 14 March 2014.

UN News Centre (2012) 'Kofi Annan Resigns as UN–Arab League' Joint Special Envoy for Syrian Crisis, 2 August (www.un.org/apps/news/story.asp?NewsID=42609#.VBAkIvldWSo), accessed 25 August 2014.

UNSC (2011) Security Council 6498th Meeting, S/PV.6498, 17 March, United Nations Security Council.

US Department of Defense (2011) News Transcript, Department of Defense, 23 March 2011, Cairo,Egypt (http://archive.defense.gov/Transcripts/Transcript.aspx?TranscriptID=4795), accessed 24 January 2014.

Walzer M. (2011) 'The Case Against Our Attack on Libya', *The New Republic* 20 March.

Weiss T. (2011) 'R2P Alive and Well After Libya', *Ethics and International Affairs*, 25(3), 287–292.

Wessel R. (2008) 'The Kadi Case: Towards a More Substantive Hierarchy in International Law', *International Organization Law Review*, 5(2), 323–327.

Wheeler N. (2001) 'Reflections on the Legality and Legitimacy of NATO's Intervention in Kosovo', in Booth K. (ed.), *The Kosovo Tragedy: The Human Rights Dimension*, Frank Cass Publishers, New York, 146–163.

White N. (2004) 'The Will and Authority of the Security Council After Iraq', *Leiden Journal of International Law*, 17(4), 645–672.

Index

End of chapter notes are denoted by a letter n between page number and note number.

Médecins Sans Frontières (MSF) 6, 7, 24, 29, 60, 63, 64; decision-making 88–91; principles 3–4, 57
media attention 92
medical caravans 157
medical interventions 44–5
Melching, Molly 49–50
memory, institutional 30
MercyCorps 32, 191, 192
Mignolo, Walter 74, 76
migration 66
militarisation of humanitarianism 5, 19–20, 60, 193–4
military: evidence-based culture 28–9, 33, 55–6; private military and security companies 185–94; role in Chinese domestic relief 175, 178
military interventions *see* humanitarian interventions
Millennium Development Goals 22
Minear, Larry 29, 32, 192, 193
misfortune and injustice 3, 13n2
missionary function, Islamic NGOs 158
modernity, western 73, 74–5
Mongo, Thomas 115, 116, 121, 123–4, 126–7, 128
moral education 160
moral scepticism 7–8
MSF *see* Médecins Sans Frontières (MSF)
Mubarak regime 178
Mudimbe, V.Y. 127
Muhammadiyah 7
multilateral aid 21
multi-mandate organisations 57, 59, 60–1, 62, 63, 64, 69n4
Muslim Aid 7, 156–7
Muslim feminists 146
Myanmar 5, 66, 179

National Union for the Total Independence of Angola (UNITA) 65
NATO 209, 210–11, 212
natural disasters 17, 62–3, 67, 169–70, 171, 175
natural resources, and Chinese aid programmes 174
Nazi Germany 3
needs assessments 87, 92
Negri, Antonio 76
neo-institutionalism 193
neoliberal governmentality 194
Nepal earthquake (2015) 179
networking and communications 30
network power 72, 73, 75–6

neutrality principle 2–3, 4, 18, 23, 31, 33, 78, 101
New Development Bank 177
'New Silk Road' initiative 177
'new wars' 20–1, 41
NGOs *see* non-governmental organisations (NGOs)
Nicholson, George 48
Nielsen, Brita Fladvad 103–4
Niger 160
Nigeria 193–4
Nigeria–Biafra War 24
Nlong Mission, Cameroon 120
Noddings, Jean 123
non-governmental organisations (NGOs) 1, 18, 21; budgets of 24–5, 84, 91, 192; decision-making 87–93, 193; founding of 24; German 91–3; growth of 84–94; Islamic 155–65; long-term impacts 86–7; numbers of 25, 192–3; and private military and security companies 185–94
non-interference principle 176
non-intervention 64
non-state actors: marketisation of humanitarianism 26–7; reducing funding to 65–6
norms and interests 58
North, Douglass 48
North Kivu 89–91
North Korea 173
Norwegian Refugee Council 192
nuclear disasters 63–4

Obama, Barack 207, 211
Obiora, Leslye 138, 139
OCHA *see* United Nations Office for the Coordination of Humanitarian Affairs (OCHA)
OECD *see* Organisation for Economic Co-operation and Development (OECD)
Ogata, Sadako 23, 59
'One Belt and One Road' policy 177
'organic' versus 'political' understandings of humanitarian interventions 44–50
organisational theory 194
Organisation for Economic Co-operation and Development (OECD) 21, 25, 178
orphans, Islamic care for 157, 158
Oslo Guidelines 175
Ottawa land mine treaty 4
Overseas Development Institute 31
Oxfam 24, 31, 32, 160, 190, 192
Oxford English Dictionary 17

For Product Safety Concerns and Information please contact our EU
representative GPSR@taylorandfrancis.com
Taylor & Francis Verlag GmbH, Kaufingerstraße 24, 80331 München, Germany